Writing God and the Self

Distinguished Dissertations in Christian Theology

Series Foreword

We are living in a vibrant season for academic Christian theology. After a hiatus of some decades, a real flowering of excellent systematic and moral theology has emerged. This situation calls for a series that showcases the contributions of newcomers to this ongoing and lively conversation. The journal *Word & World: Theology for Christian Ministry* and the academic society Christian Theological Research Fellowship (CTRF) are happy to cosponsor this series together with our publisher Pickwick Publications (an imprint of Wipf and Stock Publishers). Both the CTRF and *Word & World* are interested in excellence in academics but also in scholarship oriented toward Christ and the Church. The volumes in this series are distinguished for their combination of academic excellence with sensitivity to the primary context of Christian learning. We are happy to present the work of these young scholars to the wider world and are grateful to Luther Seminary for the support that helped make it possible.

Alan G. Padgett
Professor of Systematic Theology
Luther Seminary

Beth Felker Jones
Assistant Professor of Theology
Wheaton College

www.ctrf.info
www.luthersem.edu/word&world

Writing God and the Self
Samuel Beckett and C. S. Lewis

SHARON JEBB

☙PICKWICK *Publications* • Eugene, Oregon

WRITING GOD AND THE SELF
Samuel Beckett and C. S. Lewis

Distinguished Dissertations in Christian Theology 5

Copyright © 2011 Sharon Jebb. All rights reserved. Except for brief quotations in critical publications or reviews, no part of this book may be reproduced in any manner without prior written permission from the publisher. Write: Permissions, Wipf and Stock Publishers, 199 W. 8th Ave., Suite 3, Eugene, OR 97401.

"neither" from *The Complete Short Prose Samuel Beckett 1929–1989*, copyright © 1976 by Samuel Beckett, copyright © 1995 by the Estate of Samuel Beckett. Used by permission of Grove/Atlantic, Inc. Faber and Faber Ltd & Grove/ Atlantic, Inc.

Lines from "De Profundis," "Tu ne Quaesiersis," and "As the Ruin Falls," POEMS by C. S. Lewis copyright © C. S. Lewis Pte. Ltd. Extracts reprinted by permission.

Pickwick Publications
An Imprint of Wipf and Stock Publishers
199 W. 8th Ave., Suite 3
Eugene, OR 97401

www.wipfandstock.com

ISBN 13: 978-1-60899-738-1

Cataloging-in-Publication data:

Jebb, Sharon.

    Writing God and the self : Samuel Beckett and C. S. Lewis / Sharon Jebb.

    x + 282 p. ; 23 cm. Includes bibliographical references and index.

    Distinguished Dissertations in Christian Theology 5

    ISBN 13: 978-1-60899-738-1

    1. Theology in literature. 2. Beckett, Samuel, 1906–1989—Religion. 3. Lewis, C. S. (Clive Staples), 1898–1963. I. Title. II. Series.

PN49 .J40 2011

Manufactured in the U.S.A.

For George

"Perhaps the loss of a sense of belonging through a publicly defined order needs to be compensated by a stronger, more inner sense of linkage. Perhaps this is what a great deal of modern poetry has been trying to articulate; and perhaps we need few things more today than such articulation."

—Charles Taylor, *Malaise of Modernity*, 91

Contents

Acknowledgments ix
Introduction 1

CHAPTER 1
I'll Sprout a Head at Last, All My Very Own 21
Beckett—Self and Psychology

CHAPTER 2
God, Fomenter of Calm 58
Beckett—Theology

CHAPTER 3
The Soul's Leap Out 87
Beckett—Mysticism

CHAPTER 4
A Warped and Masked Reality 124
Lewis—Psychology

CHAPTER 5
I: A Sacred Name 162
Lewis—Theology and Self

CHAPTER 6
Men and Gods Flow In and Out and Mingle 208
Lewis—Mystical Theology

Conclusion 259
Bibliography 265
Index 277

Acknowledgments

C. S. Lewis expressed some views on friendship with which I would not feel entirely comfortable. And yet even here, his writing is evocative. Friends, he said, are those who are beside us, absorbed in the same common interest; they are seldom those who are face to face with us. And so here I wish to take his image, which is such a profoundly rich image for this book, and adjust it slightly by thanking those friends who have been side by side, engaging with me in the subject, and those who have been face to face as it were, maintaining engagement with me while I have been so preoccupied in the project.

It is a project that was conceived and nurtured whilst completing my Masters degree at Regent College, Vancouver. I particularly want to thank Dr. James Houston, for conveying by word and deed, not just the concept of the "double knowledge" but the "holy carelessness" that comes from such a knowledge. Equally, without Dr. Maxine Hancock, I may never have embarked on this project. Her wisdom and encouragement are a constant source of inspiration to me. Two others specifically encouraged me with regards to this project; Dr. Loren Wilkinson and Dr. Thena Ayres, and I gratefully thank them both.

At St Andrews University, the community guided and sustained me. There, as at Regent, I felt in my secret heart "humbled before the rest," wondering what I was doing there, "lucky beyond desert to be in such company," as Lewis put it in *The Four Loves*. I am particularly grateful to Professor Trevor Hart, for his judicious "eye," sane encouragement, tolerant supervision and ongoing wisdom. I also want to thank Dr. Ruth Etchells, Michael Partridge, Prof. Alan Torrance, and Prof. Philip Winn for giving their time on differing occasions. Discussions with contemporaries included various doctoral research companions, not least my two wonderful housemates—Louise Lawrence and Poul Guttesen—and Kirstin Jeffrey Johnson, Jane Rowlands, Julie Canlis, Stephanie Smith, Chelle Stearns, Gisela Kreglinger, and Vijay Pillai. With these people it felt as if "something beyond the world, open(ed) itself to our minds as we talked" (*The Four Loves*). So too—often overlapping with the former—Colin Bovaird, Lynda Kinloch, Jill Keays, Ian Barnett, Mary Oakes, Joan Pries, Oliver House, Sonia Wilson, Simon and Liz Lockett, Joy and Mike Nicholson all helped in many and various ways, be it library research or accommodation while I researched, in St. Andrews, Edinburgh, Belfast, Vancouver and Oxford. Prof. John Gillespie and Michael Partridge were gracious and interested examiners.

And finally, my utmost thanks goes to those who supported me most throughout the years of study—at every level—be it financially, emotionally, or in the small but endless day-to-day practicalities. To my parents, who have been unstintingly and unselfishly supportive of me throughout my education, and to George, my husband, who has been graciously and patiently present both face to face and side by side throughout the work for the dissertation, I am grateful beyond words. It is their involvement in my life which has shown me in practice what this thesis has taught me in theory; namely just how little we do things in our own strength. "We're all limbs and part of one Whole. Hence, of each other. Men, and gods, flow in and out and mingle."

Introduction

> "Now we see but a poor reflection; then we shall see face to face. Now I know in part, then I shall know fully, even as I am fully known."
>
> 1 Corinthians 13:12

Know Thyself?: The Question of the Self

THIS BOOK AROSE OUT of an observation that much recent fiction in English demonstrates signs of obsession with a search for a somewhat elusive "self." This is not a new observation. As Louis Sass points out, the self is a preoccupation that has been the theme of the last several centuries of Western culture, and one that occasionally appears to recede, only to reappear in another guise:

> It is true that, in the more avant-garde fields of the human studies (in literary theory and French psychoanalysis, for example), this modern turn to the "self" has been superceded by theoretical strategies that aim to destroy the claims of this secular god. But even in these quarters—the realms of "postmodernism" and "poststructuralism"—selfhood remains a central obsession: for, as we shall see, many who claim to disbelieve in the self seem to take an inordinate delight in dancing around its burning image.[1]

In a similar way, I noted that those fictional texts that spoke most obsessively about the "self" were those that found the concept of God either nebulous or incredible. Again, there have been many who have commented on the way in which the self has become this "secular god," usurping the role of religion.[2] But what struck me most in my reading of fiction was not the mere fact of a shift in focus, but the profound sense of desperation that accompanies this apotheosis of the self. Could it be that we have lost an understanding that is central to our well-being? Have we,

---

1. Sass, "Self and Its Vicissitudes," 17.
2. See, for example, Rieff, *Triumph of the Therapeutic*.

as it were, lost the baby with the bathwater? Is it not possible to have an adequate sense of self without a sense of God? Or, more specifically, is a sense of oneself as a particular person coterminous with a particular sense of God? More specifically still, does the sense of the self look very different from the elusive self when expressed by a writer who does believe in God, specifically the Christian God?

There are many who would argue that a Christian writer's view of the self is likely to be fairly unhealthy, even diminished. Surely the presence of God, or the assumption that he exists, necessarily diminishes the self or the self's ability to flourish? Worse still, does Christianity not call for the negating of the self? One who voices such criticisms is Daphne Hampson. Let us hear her thoughts then, in order to spread the backdrop to our explorations in different models of the self. As a self-proclaimed post-Christian feminist Hampson rejects any proposal that would appear to diminish the individual's autonomy; an autonomy that she feels is clearly threatened by positing God as a necessary correlate to selfhood. The fully mature person is autonomous; literally, one rules oneself.[3]

> To be "autonomous" is to let one's own law rule one: literally in Greek to be autonomous (self-law). The word etymologically, does not mean independence. It need not imply conceiving of oneself as an isolated atom in competition with others. Indeed that it has come to hold such connotations may tell us much about the male psyche within patriarchy; as though the only way to be oneself, to take responsibility for oneself, were to set oneself over against others.[4]

For Hampson, to be properly autonomous is for persons to be "centred in themselves and open to one another."[5] Centered and open. The traditional concept of God (and Hampson is speaking specifically of the God of the Christian tradition, as she understands it) is not only irrelevant, but is set in opposition to the self. Christians hold that God is in some way "other," and that he (or his conception), is some kind of ultimate authority, to whom reference must be made.[6] "It follows that if God is an other and is God, the relationship to God must ultimately, by definition, be heteronomous."[7] Heteronomy lies at the heart of Christianity:

---

3. Hampson, *Swallowing a Fishbone*, 1.
4. Ibid., 1.
5. Ibid., 2.
6. Ibid., 9.
7. Ibid., 9.

> But Christianity, through the fact that it is a religion of revelation, conceives of a God who in some way is other than and set over against humankind. God is not simply to be known through the beauty of the world or within human relations. True . . . there have been other conceptions of God present within the western tradition. Nevertheless, Christianity cannot evade some notion of God as "Other"; and the biblical tradition, not least, is profoundly anthropomorphic and heteronomous.[8]

For Hampson then, Christianity carries connotations of a God who is predominantly transcendent and *heteros* or other. As a consequence, humans necessarily conceive themselves in a di-polar construal of reality in relation to God; where God is strong, they are weak; where God is good, they are sinful. In relation to this kind of God, she believes that humans can only be diminished. Women in particular have been damaged by this perception; to submit to it is a woman's undoing.[9] This is the position of a child, not an adult. Maturity lies in being centered in oneself and open to another.[10] To be an adult is to come into one's own. The perception of love as a giving up of the self, which is so deeply embedded in Christianity, is not useful to women—indeed it has been a damaging theme. Love is better seen as an exchange between two parties (*philia*) rather than the self-giving in which *agape* consists. What is required is not *kenosis* but empowerment.[11] "We need a much more radical shift, and a different shift, than that which *kenosis* represents, still presupposing as it does a world of privilege and its divestment."[12] So too, the language of "ecstasy" (standing outside oneself) and "flow" is surely connected to a male understanding of the Trinitarian relationship and may be tied in with men's experience of their sexuality; whereas women tend to speak of mutuality and reciprocity.[13] Rather than a Trinitarian emphasis, feminists tend to perceive a monotheistic or unitary conception of that which surrounds another (but is not pantheism).[14] In short, anything that suggests heteronomy—that the other comes first—Hampson believes to be dangerous; it is time for humans to focus on their own self-actualization.

8. Ibid., 150–51.
9. Ibid., 3.
10. Ibid., 2.
11. Hampson, *After Christianity*, 142–45.
12. Ibid., 145.
13. Ibid., 160–68.
14. Ibid., 165.

Humans need to come into their own, to take control.[15] They must extricate themselves from Christianity, and put themselves at the center of the picture.[16] And then, through their knowing of themselves, they can come to a perception of God.[17] It is this that will enable one to gain one's true self.[18] Self-knowing then would seem to be the priority; although God is still necessary to facilitate the development of this "true self." At the same time, in this self-actualization people are also realizing God in the world. In this sense, the God whom she envisages is entirely immanent and "a dimension of all that is." The God in whom Hampson believes is one with all there is, always and everywhere present, bigger than the self but not other than it.[19] It is a form of immanentalism. At one point she says that God is the dimension through which we come to be most fully ourselves.[20] If there is any paradox to the way in which humans must put themselves first, and the fact that it is God who enables them to become fully themselves, she does not explain it. Her approach does not tend towards the paradoxical but towards the rational.[21]

This can be seen, for example, in her views on a Trinitarian Godhead. God is emphatically *not* a person—although many may find that a sense of presence leads one to speak as if he were a "person."[22] But that is precisely the kind of thinking which she wishes to undermine. She wishes to dispense with an anthropomorphically conceived God, or a God who has specifically human characteristics; one who relates to humans, for this can only require accountability. Equally, Jesus may have been deeply aware of God but no more than other humans; he is not divine, therefore cannot be an aspect of the Trinity. The particularity of Jesus as Son of God, is not possible, because God does not stand in a peculiar relationship to any individual person. "For me Christianity has become not credible because I cannot believe that one human being, and one alone, could have a second and divine nature (particularity); or that there could be one and only

---

15. Hampson, *Swallowing a Fishbone*, 16 and 151.
16. Ibid., 16.
17. Hampson, *Theology and Feminism*, 171–73.
18. Hampson, *Swallowing a Fishbone*, 152.
19. Ibid., 10–11.
20. Hampson, *After Christianity*, 10.
21. This seems to correspond closely to the point at which she has most problems with Luther's understanding of the relation between God and the self. How can God be conceptualised as foundational to the self and yet also as "an other" with whom the self interrelates? Hampson, *Christian Contradictions*.
22. Ibid., 171.

one, example of resurrection."[23] In this respect, she says, "I do not believe in uniqueness."[24] The "scandal of particularity" is one that she rejects as untenable. The resurrection raises questions of theodicy; if God can break into the natural order in this way, why has any suffering occurred?[25] Prayer does have efficacy, however, because despite this, Hampson's God is not powerless. Healing, for example, remains within her belief structure, but faith in the God of Christian revelation is too much of a leap; "it would be a rash person who would wager such faith."[26]

For Hampson, the idea of the Trinity does embody relationality but given the maleness of the imagery (Father and Son), she finds it an unhelpful symbol for feminists who seek genuine reciprocity.[27] We must find new models for relationality, ones that are altogether more helpful:

> We must be clear, however, that the Utopian society which feminists envisage, in which people are able to relate as whole persons, does not represent a going back beyond the Enlightenment paradigm but a progression beyond it.[28]

The Enlightenment has given humans a chance to come into their own. No longer are they tied to a religion that states that humanity is taken into God, and consequently results in God as the focus of attention rather than humanity.[29] Instead, the Enlightenment paradigm of human equality has put humans at the center, although the self that the Enlightenment advocated was a "self-contained and essentially aggressive" monad which existed essentially in competition with others.[30] This is not the idea of the self that Hampson would wish to propose. Rather she advocates a relational self, in-tune with "all that is." This presence, this new way of conceiving of God needs to be articulated in new ways, and that is a task that still lies ahead, as does further articulation of this relational self.[31]

Daphne Hampson's arguments are specifically tied to feminist thinking, but the selections that she makes with regard to belief in God are not unusual. For Hampson is by no means the first to propose such a

---

23. Hampson, *Swallowing a Fishbone*, 113.
24. Hampson, *Theology and Feminism*, 8.
25. Ibid., 8–11.
26. Hampson, *After Christianity*, 12.
27. Hampson, *Theology and Feminism*, 154.
28. Hampson, *After Christianity*, 12.
29. Hampson, *Theology and Feminism*, 154.
30. Hampson, *After Christianity*, 7.
31. Hampson, *Theology and Feminism*, 173.

self, just as she is not alone in opting for a God who is "a dimension of all that is" rather than a Trinitarian sovereign "Other." Nor is she alone in advocating, "Know then thyself, presume not God to scan/the proper study of Mankind is Man." Alexander Pope may have written those words during the Enlightenment, but it has been a recurring emphasis throughout history, not least in the Delphic adage of the Greek philosophers, *Gnothi seauton*, or "Know Thyself." But Hampson is a clear exponent of a particularly contemporary emphasis, wherein the stress lies not upon "we cannot know," but on the idea that the time has come when we must rule ourselves. For her, God is not a necessary element in the search for self-understanding. If anything, he would be a hindrance.

Given this lightly sketched "model"—a self, centered upon itself, yet in relation to others and in relation to a God who is a dimension of all that is—a number of questions spring to mind. If the self is best "cultivated" under these conditions, has it been seen to flourish in the years since God was "overthrown" and such a model was first proposed? (Hampson says that we need to move beyond the assertiveness and competitiveness of the Enlightenment self—but is her model so very different from the Enlightenment models—such as Schleiermacher's—which she desires to move beyond?) Equally, we would want to be sure that we fully understood the Christian model of the self that we are rejecting, for it has been articulated by illustrious thinkers throughout a sixteen hundred year history. Let us turn next to this concept, in order to understand what model Hampson is seeking to replace.

Prior to the end of the sixteenth century the Christian tradition had stressed the necessity of knowledge of God for self-knowledge. It is, as James Houston puts it, a "double knowledge"; knowledge of God and knowledge of self cannot be separated.[32] To put it more forcibly, humans cannot know themselves without also knowing God. To try to know oneself on one's own throws everything, as it were, out of balance. Bernard of Clairvaux expressed it in this way:

> As for me, as long as I look at myself, I see only one subject after another for bitter regret. But if I look up and lift up my eyes towards the help of the Divine Compassion, the joyful sight of God tempers at once the bitter revelation of myself . . . Thus the knowledge of thyself will be a step to the knowledge of God: He will become visible in His image, which is renewed in thee; whilst thou, beholding with confidence as in a glass the glory of the Lord,

---

32. Houston, "Double Knowledge," 308–26.

art changed into the same image from glory to glory, even as by the Spirit of the Lord (1 Cor iii.18).[33]

For Bernard, to remove God from our vision leaves bitterness (*contra* Hampson, for whom the inclusion of God imposes weakness and sinfulness upon humans). Equally, God's very "visibility" decreases as one's vision becomes more and more "short-sighted" and self-focused, whereas the shift to focus upon the compassionate God leads to a "happy vision" that tempers our distorted sight. Bernard was not alone in his judgment of the necessity of the double knowledge. It is present, in various ways, in the thought of Augustine, Luther, Calvin and Teresa of Avila, amongst others. Regardless of the nuances that arise from their contexts and experiences, each perceives a profound connectedness of God and the self, a strong sense that the self *cannot* be known outside the context of God. Augustine believed that it is the love of God which gives rise to selfhood; the God who had created him—and sustained him—knew him better than he knew himself. "What I do know of myself I know because You shed your light on me; and what I do not know of myself I shall not know until 'my darkness shall become as noonday' in the vision of Your face."[34] Denys Turner says that for Augustine, recognition of God entailed a recognition of himself. More specifically, "the truth Augustine discovered was that to discover his own inwardness was the same thing as to discover God and that to discover God was to discover his own inwardness—either discovery was the discovery of his true selfhood."[35] Yet even for Augustine—sometimes perceived as a prophet of inwardness—an *interior homine*—God was Other.[36] As he wrote in the *Confessions,* "You are always there above me, and as I rise up towards you in my mind, I shall go beyond even this force which is in me, this force which we call memory . . . I must pass beyond memory . . ."[37] Rowan Williams underlines the fact by citing from *Enarrationes in Psalmos*; "I have become aware that my God is some reality above the soul. I reflected on these things, and poured out my soul above myself that I might touch him . . ."[38] Final delight is to be found *super me*, beyond oneself, not in oneself. The integral connectedness of God and the self did not lead Augustine towards any blurring of the boundaries between God

33. Bernard of Clairvaux, *Cantica Cantorum*, 237.
34. Augustine *Confessions* 10.5.
35. Turner, *Darkness of God*, 69–70.
36. See, for example, C. Taylor, *Sources of the Self*.
37. Augustine *Confessions* 10.18. For Augustine, memory was the mind in its entirety.
38. Williams, *Wound of Knowledge*, 77–80. Williams attributes this quotation to *Enarrationes in Psalmos*, 41, 8.

and humans. The Plotinian idea that divinity is within and identical to the soul he clearly rejected.[39] For Augustine, God is radically Other, and yet, paradoxically, utterly integral to the self.

John Calvin appears to have had a very similar emphasis. His *Institutes* open with the statement, "Nearly the whole of sacred doctrine consists in these two parts: knowledge of God and of ourselves." But it sounds even clearer in the French version of the *Institutes*, published one year later, which opened with, "In knowing God, each of us also knows himself."[40] Here the two "knowledges" are much more closely connected, merging almost into one single "knowing." For Calvin the foundation of knowledge comes from God. In Book 1 chapter 1 he explains, "No man can survey himself without forthwith turning his thoughts towards the God in whom he lives and moves; because it is perfectly obvious, that the endowments which we possess cannot possibly be from ourselves; nay, that our very being is nothing else than subsistence in God alone."[41] It follows that one cannot think about oneself without also thinking of God on whom one is completely dependent; every good thing possessed by a human being flows from God. Equally, for Calvin, "it is evident that man never attains to a true self-knowledge until he have previously contemplated the face of God, and come down after such contemplation to look into himself." This is necessary to prevent complacency or arrogance. The two knowledges are tied together by a "mutual tie." Karl Barth comments that Calvin views "the whole (*summa*) of doctrine from this double angle . . . Here is the synthesis in which more or less clearly all the theses and antitheses of his theology unfold in their dialectic of opposition and relationship, and to which, when rightly understood, they all seek to point."[42]

Those who wrote of this double knowledge were quite emphatic about the connection between the two; Teresa of Avila calls it a matter of utmost importance. In *Interior Castle* she states: "in my opinion we shall never completely know ourselves if we don't strive to know God."[43] True self-knowledge, she says, requires humility; but the grace of God gives boldness. And like Bernard, she believes that the attempt to understand the self without God, results only in self-obsession. As Teresa puts it, "If we are always fixed on our earthly misery, the stream will never flow free from the mud of fears, faintheartedness, and cowardice. I would be look-

39. See Cary, *Augustine's Invention of the Inner Self*.
40. See Houston, "Double Knowledge."
41. Calvin, *Institutes for Christian Religion*, ch. 1, section 2.
42. Barth, *Theology of John Calvin*, 162.
43. Teresa of Avila, *Interior Castle*, 43.

ing to see if I am watched or not."[44] The knowledge of God gives freedom from fear and cowardice and concern for the opinions of others; people are ennobled and without bitterness. This sounds remarkably like an ideal towards which Daphne Hampson would wish to strive, but which she would want to approach antithetically, for she would baulk at the very Otherness which these people emphasize in their concept of God. They all stress the fact that God is both immanent and transcendent. For Teresa, as for Augustine and Calvin, God is other than the self and the self must turn from itself and towards God.

And so we come to the nature of this book. Is it possible to find a means of testing the assumption that there is a "mutual tie" between the knowledge of God and the knowledge of self? As the issue originally become apparent to me through literary works, then it seems appropriate to return to the literary works in order to explore further. Could it be that the examination of these models in literature would enable us to give "flesh" to them? By examining two prominent twentieth century authors who were particularly concerned with these issues, might it be possible to gain a sense of the outworking of the two different emphases? It seems like one way of putting flesh on the theory. Further, by engaging not simply with their written texts but with their lives as texts, I think that that we can test the claim implicit in Hampson's work. My aim is to let their "texts" unfold gradually, teasing out the implications of their attitudes towards the self and God. The writers themselves shall set the agenda. By putting them in dialogue with their influences, it should be possible to understand more profoundly the ideas and concepts that they embraced. Using insights gleaned from theology and psychology, it may be possible to overcome, even partially, the dichotomization of these disciplines which has happened, for it makes immense sense that, alongside the loss of the double knowledge, the study of God and humanity would have been forced asunder into the very disparate disciplines which are practiced today.

Saints and Scholars: Why Samuel Beckett and C. S. Lewis?

A strange juxtaposition of similarities and contrasts in the lives and works of Samuel Beckett and C. S. Lewis makes them altogether more suitable dialogue partners than may be evident to the superficial glance. Despite the ultimate near antithesis of their literary form and theological underpinnings, their initial literary forays show them to have been much more

44. Ibid., 43–44.

similar than might be expected from their mature works. In fact, in their late teens and early twenties Beckett and Lewis showed a remarkable likeness to each other in many ways. Both were born in Ireland to Church of Ireland parents within a decade of each other. Both were exceptionally widely read in the fields of philosophy and literature and in a wide range of languages—although Lewis was more classically oriented and Beckett more attuned to modern European thought. Both aspired towards poetic achievements and sought publication; both were interested in the new psychology of Freud and Jung; both were conflicted in their attitude towards parents and homeland; and both equally fascinated by the observation of their own mental processes. Both were extremely sensitive to suffering, and struggled to reconcile it with the idea of a good God. Equally pertinent to this project, both were tenacious in their grappling with issues related to the knowledge of self. Of the many recent writers who touch on "self" related ideas, these two writers were amongst the most loquacious on the subject.

To speak of the similarities between them is not to ignore the differences. Despite these early shared traits, the two men took increasingly different paths, so that the similarities become less and less visible, leading to very different bodies of work. Neither received encouragement nor critical acclaim for their poetic endeavors—the genre in which both men would have preferred to write—and each turned to other genres. Lewis stayed within academia; Beckett did not. More significantly, Lewis felt that he was taken hold of by the God of Christianity; Beckett spent his life in a highly ambivalent posture towards the same God. Beckett exhibits a desperate search for a sense of the self, whereas Lewis articulated an emphatic belief in the connectedness of God and self. The concomitant decisions, attitudes and beliefs were to be highly significant in both men's lives and work—as the texts upon which we shall focus demonstrate. In Beckett's case the most suitable text is actually a trilogy, *Three Novels*, wherein the narrators become increasingly overcome by a heightened subjectivity.[45] For Lewis, the chosen text is *Till We Have Faces*, a later work in his oeuvre, which stands in sharp delineation from Beckett's trilogy for a host of reasons, but certainly in substantial part because of Lewis's almost antithetical ideas on the self. In addition to these texts, I shall cite from various "secondary" texts by both authors where related issues of God and the self are addressed. Although all of the primary texts (in English) were published between 1955 and 1958, the secondary texts come from a wider spread of

---

45. The translation I have used is entitled *Three Novels*. Other editions may use the title *Trilogy*.

dates, the reasons for which I shall delineate as I look at each writer specifically and prepare the way for my "readings" of each author.

Beckett

The question of the self is a constant in Beckett's oeuvre, a body of work that oscillates endlessly around certain themes. No critic has suggested that there is any substantial change to Beckett's stance on the self in *Three Novels* (*Molloy*, *Malone Dies*, and *The Unnamable*). David Pattie has pointed out, "Certainly, Beckett's concerns do remain remarkably consistent from the beginning of his writing life to its end; but the form and style through which those concerns were expressed were subject to change, making the idea that Beckett's path is entirely marked out in his early critical work difficult to sustain."[46] It is Beckett's concerns, rather than his form and style, which are the focus here; his concern with the self and with God, although evident throughout his work, are perhaps most clearly voiced in his earlier work. Of Beckett's explicit theorizing—and there is relatively little to be found in the Beckett canon—I shall make use of *Proust*, first published in 1931, twenty-four years before *Molloy*. This disquisition, purportedly on the work of Marcel Proust, is therefore a very early piece and must be used with care. Whilst bearing this in mind, I believe that it can be seen that Beckett's comments on this topic in *Proust* are particularly pertinent, and prefigure, to a remarkable degree, his concerns as they would be played out in fictive form, twenty-four years later. For the same reason, I shall occasionally refer to *Dream of Fair to Middling Women*, Beckett's first novel, written immediately after *Proust*, although not published until 1993.

Any reading of Beckett requires a certain understanding of tone. Those critics who would wish to see Beckett as playful and ironic are reading him, I believe, against the grain. Although his humor *is* often ironic and playful, I suggest that his view is essentially tragic, not comic. Moreover, many critics approach Beckett's work as if there is a "key" to understanding his work—that there is a riddle to be solved. Much ink has been spilt upon attempts to elucidate various of Beckett's "riddles," for example, the exact relationship between Molloy and Moran. Rather than tackling specific symptoms, I prefer to try to understand the underlying issues, which I consider to be of much greater import. Thus I approach Beckett's work somewhat impressionistically, believing that thoughtful reflection on the text will give us an insight into the issues that were important to him.

---

46. Pattie, *Samuel Beckett*, 15.

A further issue concerns Beckett's narrators in *Three Novels*. To what extent can their many voices be seen as *representative* of Beckett himself—Molloy, Moran, Malone, the Unnamable? It is a question that has been dealt with at great length in other critical works. P. J. Murphy points out that the question of authorship concerned Beckett right from the outset: "he has persistently sought for a clarification of the essential co-ordinates of the creative act: who is speaking? with what authority?"[47] There are philosophical avenues to explore here—but those are not my concern. Rather, I see Beckett's very questioning as indicative of the issue that lies at the heart of this thesis. A comment, by Josephine Jacobsen and William R. Mueller, proposes the Beckettian use of narrator as an outworking of his exploration of identity:

> Virtually the whole of the Beckett canon is the spiritual or intellectual—certainly the internal as distinguished from the external—autobiography of one man. This man, a mid-twentieth-century Everyman, wears many masks, and he would seem to try them on, one after the other, in an attempt to identify himself.[48]

The vast bulk of scholarly opinion, of which this quotation is only a brief example, concludes—in some form or other—that the Beckett genre is a kind of "autobiographical fiction," as Charlotte Renner has called it.[49] Celia Hunt has summarized autobiographical fiction in this way:

> ... the implied author is a *fictional construct which embodies certain norms and values of the real author at the time of writing*. These values will not necessarily be those which the author has set out to express in the work, nor will they be his norms and values for all time; rather, they will be a projection, or externalisation, to use [Karen] Horney's term, of aspects of the author's psyche into the text—the author's prevailing *personal fiction*—containing elements of his personal truth.[50]

Beckett's narrators, therefore, are fictional constructs, but they embody, I believe, large elements of his "personal truth." Of this I shall have more to say but my approach here is to perceive the narrators as giving substantial insight into Beckett's psyche, while stopping short of claiming *exact* correspondence between Beckett and his narrators.

---

47. Murphy, "Beckett and the Philosophers," 224.
48. Jacobsen and Mueller, *Testament of Samuel Beckett*, 118.
49. Renner, "Self-Multiplying Narrators," 97.
50. Hunt, "Autobiography and the Psychotherapeutic Process," 191–92. Italics as used by the author.

Lewis

Besides *Till We Have Faces*, a range of Lewis's texts shall be consulted. This is not simply because there we find expansion of his thoughts on the self in relation to God, although he wrote much on this subject throughout his life. Rather it is because Lewis's work, unlike Beckett's, reveals a lifelong development in his thinking. In marked contrast to Beckett's constant vacillations, Lewis changed in a progressive fashion. Owen Barfield, Lewis's lifelong friend, said Lewis "changed and continued to change. He developed to a considerable extent after his conversion."[51] The changes that took place in him are highly pertinent to this project; his thought on selfhood was a lifelong process of lived experimentation, partially based upon his Christian faith and partially based upon (varying) degrees of attention to the impact of his own behavior and attitudes. This has not always been observed; for the reader who does not specifically seek out the nuances, there appears to be a strikingly consistent stance on the self throughout his mature writing. Most critics who write on Lewis recognize, at least in passing, the profound impact which Christianity had upon his ideas of the self. But for others, there is an appreciation that his later works suggest a development in thought. *Till We Have Faces*, being a later work, can be interpreted as indicative of a change in Lewis himself. A number of critics, (such as Humphrey Carpenter), comment, usually in passing, that *Till We Have Faces* is a reflection upon Lewis himself acquiring a face.[52] But the profound connectedness of Lewis's ideas on the self and God has not been adequately teased out.

With regard to preliminary comments on my approach to Lewis, I would want to say—necessarily briefly—that a sensitive reading of Lewis involves an understanding of his use of the concept of myth. For Lewis, myth was not *just* a form of fictive entertainment. He said, "The value of myth is that it takes all the things we know and restores to them the rich significance which has been hidden by 'the veil of familiarity.'"[53] Much of his view of myth came initially from George MacDonald, who was for Lewis, the master of myth making. Later, at the time of his conversion to Christianity, his thinking was honed through dialogue with J. R. R. Tolkien and Hugo Dyson. For him, myths are ultimately theological, carrying "gleams of celestial strength and beauty." In *An Experiment in Criticism*, Lewis outlined the characteristics that he believed belonged to

---

51. Barfield, "Lewis and/or Barfield," 106.

52. Carpenter, *Inklings*, 245. Strangely, A. N. Wilson makes next to nothing of *Till We Have Faces*. He hardly refers to it.

53. Lewis, "Dethronement of Power," 137.

myth. 1) Myth is independent of the form of the story in which it is told, and the actual words used. 2) There is little use made of suspense or other such narrative features. 3) The reader does not project him/her self into the story. 4) The setting is always "fantastic," never realistic. 5) Myth is always grave, never comic. 6) The effect is awe-inspiring and the experience contains a numinous quality. Unlike allegory, myth cannot be tied down to a single interpretation; rather, it dilates the mind with implication.[54] For this reason, Lewis claimed, it is more akin to music than to poetry.

> It goes beyond the expression of things we have already felt. It arouses in us sensations we have never had before, never anticipated having, as though we had broken out of our normal mode of consciousness "and possessed joys not promised at birth." It gets under our skin, hits us at a deeper level than our thoughts or even our passions, troubles oldest certainties till all questions are re-opened, and in general shocks us more fully awake than we are for most of our lives.[55]

In *Spenser's Images of Life*, Lewis referred to Macrobius' comment that great truths need to be treated "mythically (*per fabulosa*) by the prudent."[56] In his last novel Lewis tried to convey truths *per fabulosa*. As Lewis wrote to his friend Arthur Greeves, "the 'doctrines' we get *out of* the true myth are of course *less* true: they are translations into our *concepts* and *ideas*."[57] God and selfhood—P/personhood—of all subjects, seem to suffer most when approached "doctrinally." It is my sincere hope that in trying to explicate an aspect of *Till We Have Faces*, I shall in no way diminish its "almost unlimited mythic quality."[58] But I hope that in teasing out some of the apparently unlimited implications of *Till We Have Faces*, a clearer reading of the myth itself can be achieved. In this sense of multiple interpretations, my reading of both writers has been to consider them both as purveyors of myth, and to try to understand the underlying issues.

In laying bare these underlying issues, I am addressing an area that has only been tangentially explored in the work of both these writers. That is not to say that critics have not addressed the question of the self in either body of work. The concern is too central in both *oeuvres* for critical atten-

---

54. Lewis, *Experiment in Criticism*, 43.

55. Lewis, *George MacDonald*, 28–29.

56. See Lewis's comments on the veiled Venus in *Spenser's Images of Life*, 43. There seems to be an obvious connection with the veiled Orual.

57. Lewis, *Letters of C. S. Lewis*, 289.

58. The phrase is used by Clyde Kilby in "Till We Have Faces: An Interpretation," 181.

tion to have passed by. But the intimate connectedness of self to God has not been explored. In Beckett's work, in particular, the vexed question of the self (or the subject) has been the cause of much spilt ink. Laura Barge is the critic who has come closest to connecting ideas on God and the self in Beckett's work. But the *integral* nature of the connectedness between the two seems to be increasingly elusive.

Poet: Lens or Paradigm?

Some further comments need to be made at this stage with regard to the method that is used in this book. It is not a piece of literary criticism; I do not seek to protect the work of art. Rather, I am seeking to explore how the works of art express the outworking of a stance; in one sense I am "using" literature in a way that some humanist critics might claim to find offensive—although every reading is surely ultimately a "use." Having said that, I intend no "abuse" of the literature, for my project stands or falls upon its faithfulness to what the authors are saying. If the material does not support the thesis of the "double knowledge" then the truth will out. So be it. It is vitally important that the material is allowed to speak with its own voice.

In that respect I shall suppose that the narrative voice reflects something of the mind of the author. As Dorothy Sayers points out, although a work or body of work may not convey the whole mind of an author, nevertheless it does incarnate an aspect of their mind; "a writer cannot create a character or express a thought or emotion which is not within his own mind."[59] Although qualifications to this statement can—and should—be made for particular cases, it is my judgment that there is no call to do so here; for the purposes of this project, authorial intention shall not be bracketed out. I judge it relevant and shall proceed from that perspective rather than adhering to the notion of intentional fallacy (in other words, that reference to the author's purposes/state of mind/personal situation is a harmful mistake). I should like to align myself with the position outlined in M. H. Abram's *A Glossary of Literary Terms*: "in the exceptional instances . . . where we possess an author's express statement about his artistic intentions in a literary work, that statement should constitute evidence for an interpretive hypothesis, but should not in itself be determinative."[60] In other words, in choosing to disregard the concept of the intentional fallacy, I should hope to illumine the work of an author by reference to

---

59. Sayers, *Mind of the Maker*, 51.
60. Abrams, *Glossary of Literary Terms*, 126.

corresponding statements of intention or belief.[61] In doing so, I position myself, ironically, somewhat differently from both the authors under scrutiny, for each of the two men articulated their belief, or desire, that a text should be free-standing. Indeed, to a large extent I am contravening these authors' own wishes. For Beckett, interiority was inaccessible. Therefore, in raising the whole issue, I am flying in the face of Beckett's own beliefs, which he articulated to Lawrence Harvey; "The obscure inner tensions that give rise to a work of art are unavailable, because the critic is not *dans la peau du tendu*."[62] There is much of value in his sense that we cannot ever fully know a person, and that we can never, for example, be fully sure of another person's motivation—a fault for which he chides Balzac.[63] Whilst conceding that this is, in an ultimate sense, true, there is, nonetheless, a sense in which I would want to disagree. Beckett had his own reasons for seeking to protect his psychic privacy, the large part of which was, I think tied in with the very issues which I am seeking to address in this thesis.[64]

So too for Lewis. Certainly for a substantial part of his mature life, he opposed what he called the "personal heresy"—the reading of an author through his work. He proposed that "the poet is not a man who asks me to look at *him*; he is a man who says 'look at that' and points; the more I follow the pointing of his finger the less I can possibly see of *him*."[65] In approaching literature we share the poet's consciousness; we don't study it, according to Lewis. This shall be explored in more detail, but Lewis also had reasons for wishing to hold people at arms length. It is only later in life, I shall argue, that we find him accepting the value of a greater degree of openness—a value that is articulated right at the heart of *Till We Have Faces*. Lewis may have been arguing against the Romantic trend towards the poet as "the paradigm human being," but I would want to argue that a study

---

61. This is not because I accept the humanistic assumption that the individual is the source of meaning. In other words, I am not rejecting the "death of the author" because I would wish to propose the author as authority—and here I *do* use Lewis—but the author as "trying to embody in terms of his own art some reflections of eternal Beauty and Wisdom." (C. S. Lewis, "Christianity and Literature," 9). The author shares what he has received. The reader can be enriched by participating in their perspective, as Gadamer has most clearly articulated. This project goes beyond an act of humanistic literary criticism, where origins and context are taken into account, and argues that a writer's expression of meaning is articulated both by their written texts and by the texts that are their lives.

62. Harvey, "Samuel Beckett on Life, Art, and Criticism," 545–62.

63. See comments by Rabinovitz, "Beckett and Psychology," 65–79.

64. Interestingly, Beckett himself paid close attention to any possible connections between the life and work of a philosopher. P. J. Murphy cites Lawrence Harvey on this in "Beckett and the Philosophers," 228.

65. Lewis, "Personal Heresy in Criticism," 15.

of a writer's life and work is not automatically and invariably wrong.[66] Whilst I should seek to extend to both writers what George Steiner calls *cortesia*—a certain courtesy when trying to ascertain intentions and motivations—I nonetheless believe we can more easily enter into an understanding of the poet's consciousness by studying the poet.[67] To posit otherwise (and here I also have in mind the post-structuralist concept of the author as the empty site traversed by discourses) is a symptom of fragmentation and dis-unity. As E. M. W. Tillyard put it in his rejoinder to Lewis; "If you wish to see God in poetry, you can see Him as readily in the mind of a human being as in a piece of silk."[68]

Studies in Words: Definitions

This book uses two words over which much ink has been spilt: "self" and "mysticism." Neither word can be easily defined, and it would not be advisable to proffer any definitive explanation, particularly at this early stage. In seeking to understand what these writers are saying, it will be best to let their voices be heard on the two words that connote the subjects that lie at the heart of this project. For each writer the connotations are different, but in the exploration of these differences the project consists. Moreover, while it is not my task to explore nor even to locate the concepts in particular ideologies I would, in the course of the project, want to draw upon some of the insights granted by the many disciplines that do engage with the terms. This, I hope, will take us some way towards a fuller understanding, and avoid perhaps, some of the dangers of fragmented knowledge. As with so much else in this project, it is my intention that these nuances should unfold as we see them "embodied," as it were, by these writers. Beckett was living in France, (having studied French and Italian) when he wrote *Three Novels* and his understanding of the concept of the self will undoubtedly reflect that milieu, whereas Lewis's understanding may retain more of the classical education, with Romantic elements as well as contemporary British influences. But even to use such broad brush generalizations is to oversimplify; both had complex relationships to the various strands within the Enlightenment, Romanticism and Modernism and it is not possible in the scope of this work to outline the historical and philosophical underpinnings of these many and varied influences upon the two men. Rather, I shall confine my comments to some of the specific influences that can be detected in their work.

66. See also C. Taylor, *Sources of the Self*, 481.
67. Steiner, *Real Presences*, 171.
68. Tillyard, "Personal Heresy in Criticism: A Rejoinder," 20.

With regard to the "self," to begin—or even to end—with a definition of the word would be too limiting. Charles Taylor, in his *Sources of the Self* has spelt out most thoroughly the complexities of the woven strands which may constitute the fabric of the "self." Like Taylor, I perceive the terms "self," "person" and "subject" as interchangeable. But I use the term "self" in deliberate preference to other related terms, such as "identity" and "agent." These I have generally avoided, unless the context has required it, largely because the writers themselves do not tend to use them, but partly because they often carry specific connotations that are not necessarily helpful to this project. The word "self" spans eras and disciplines and remains sufficiently open to cover the concept that I wish to explore.

Equally, the word "mysticism" shall be best served by allowing it to unfold. Once again the great diversity of interpretations prohibits any attempt at a clear outline here, but it may be helpful to sketch a little of the immediate background for Beckett and Lewis. Both authors seem to have been attracted by that which is beyond human consciousness. Both in differing ways showed familiarity with Platonic elements of mysticism. This could be somewhat loosely described as the soul's attempt to reach union with the Divine, through specific acts of withdrawal, contemplation and purification. At the end of the nineteenth century there was an upsurge of academic interest in the concept, focusing upon the theoretical issues that dominated at the time, including questions about the mystic as a member of the elite and the relationship between apophatic and cataphatic approaches, amongst others. Such concerns can be seen in the writings and lectures of William James, W. R. Inge, K. E. Kirk, Baron Von Hügel, and Evelyn Underhill to name some who wrote in the English language.[69] It is highly likely that Beckett and Lewis were familiar with and read these writers; we certainly know that they both read at least some work by Inge. Moreover, the interest in mysticism in France was, according to Bernard McGinn, "truly remarkable" in the 1920s and 1930s and likely surpassed that in Britain, extending far beyond theological circles.[70] As the book unfolds, I shall attempt to disentangle some of the elements more pertinent to the thinking of Lewis and Beckett, for both in their very different ways sought to engage with these concepts in their articulation of the self, not least because those who claimed insight into the divine often had much to say about the self. And so we find ourselves brought full circle to where we began. Let us break out of this circle then, by turning to the work and life of Samuel Beckett, and exploring the interconnectedness—

69. McGinn, *Foundations of Mysticism*.
70. Ibid., 280.

or otherwise—of his writing on the self, and his writing about God. It only remains to point out that the division of the chapters is slightly different for the two men. In the section on Beckett, theology is dealt with quite separately from self, whereas in the section on Lewis self and theology are together. This is what the material itself seems to require, and given the premise of the project, it is perhaps not so very surprising.

CHAPTER I

I'll Sprout a Head at Last, All My Very Own

Beckett—Self and Psychology

To and Fro in Shadow: Beckett and the Self

neither

To and fro in shadow from inner to outershadow
from impenetrable self to impenetrable unself by way of neither
as between two lit refuges whose doors once neared gently close,
   once turned away from gently part again
beckoned back and forth and turned away
heedless of the way, intent on the one gleam or the other
unheard footfalls only sound
till at last halt for good, absent for good from self and other
then no sound
then gently light unfading on that unheeded neither
unspeakable home[1]

"You were there before me, but I had departed from myself. I could not even find myself, much less you."
Augustine Confessions 5.2

The Only Theme: Beckett and the Self

THE IDEA OF THE self was of central importance to Beckett and this chapter shall focus on the Beckettian sense of the self and the psychological factors that may have been influential in this regard. John Fletcher

---

1. Beckett, *Complete Short Prose*, 258.

has observed of Samuel Beckett's work, "it can in fact be safely said that the last novels are chiefly concerned with the investigation of the pronoun 'I.'"[2] In an unusually clear piece of communication, Beckett told Morton Feldman in 1976 that there was only one theme in his life, "To and fro in shadow, from outer shadow to inner shadow. To and fro, between unattainable self and unattainable non-self."[3] Beckett, on some cognitive level, would seem to have rejected the idea of a stable sense of self, portraying instead one that is constantly modified, only discernable retroactively. His early reading of Giambattista Vico, may have contributed to the development of what Charles Taylor calls an expressivist sense of the self, in which the emphasis is upon an organicist approach rejecting compartmentalization.[4] In his essay on *Proust*, Beckett speaks of the self as volatile, capricious, inconstant—it cannot be reduced to a single concept or substance. "The individual is the seat of a constant process of decantation, decantation from the vessel containing the fluid of future time, sluggish, pale and monochrome, to the vessel containing the fluid of past time, agitated and multicolored by the phenomena of its hours."[5] The image of decantation conveys Beckett's perception of the fluidity of being at this early stage in his work—the individual as experiencing "an unceasing modification of his personality, whose permanent reality, if any, can only be apprehended as a retrospective hypothesis."[6] Both Proust and Joyce (another influence on Beckett) are cited by Charles Taylor as being amongst the moderns who attacked the idea of a single, unitary identity, proposing instead an altogether more fluid sense of identity.[7] In *Dream of Fair to Middling Women*, we find the Mandarin saying "The reality of the individual . . . is an incoherent reality, and must be expressed incoherently"—a statement which I take to represent the thinking of Beckett himself.[8] Not only does he tend to emphasize the mutability of the individual, but any attempt to reach a summation is decisively rejected. Again, in *Proust* we read; "Life is habit. Or rather life is a succession of habits, since the individual is a succession

---

2. Fletcher, *Samuel Beckett*, 168.

3. Knowlson, *Damned to Fame*, 631. The text entitled "neither" was posted to Morton Feldman shortly after.

4. Sass, "Self and Its Vicissitudes." Here Sass summarizes what C. Taylor wrote in *Hegel*.

5. Beckett, *Proust*Three Dialogues*, 15.

6. Ibid., 15.

7. C. Taylor, *Sources of the Self*, 463.

8. Beckett, *Dream of Fair to Middling Women*, 101.

of individuals."⁹ (It is worth noting that such a sense of fluidity of the self is a particularly French emphasis.¹⁰)

Here already is the basis for the structure of the *Three Novels*, wherein the narrators bleed into one another, each displaying elements of continuity and discontinuity, particularly in the case of Molloy/Moran. Molloy speaks of passers-by "hard to distinguish from yourself" and of "a mist which rises in me everyday and veils the world from me and veils me from myself."¹¹ Self-definition is sought but remains elusive—"wrapped in a namelessness often hard to penetrate."¹² With Moran as the narrator in the second part of the novel, we find a further blurring of distinction, this time between him and Molloy. Critical speculation on this is inevitable given such statements as Moran's comment on Molloy, "He had only to rise up within me for me to be filled with panting."¹³ Charlotte Renner, however, goes beyond the mere puzzle presented by Beckett. Whilst accepting that Moran becomes (in some sense) Molloy through a reversal of chronological order, she suspects, and I think rightly so, that it stems from "Beckett's definition of the self . . . as 'a constant process of decantation' of the 'fluid of future time' into the 'fluid of past time.'"¹⁴ In *Molloy* we would appear to have one of Beckett's many experiments with the fluidity—or otherwise—of the individual. Elsewhere, he raises the difficult issue of the danger of the subject as object under surveillance, whereby the subject becomes conscious of perception, and "the object loses its purity and becomes a mere intellectual pretext or motive."¹⁵ He is only too aware that his attempts to capture the elusive "I" look somewhat like the kitten trying to catch its own tail to which he refers in "Dante...Bruno.Vico..Joyce."¹⁶ So we see that already in 1929, there were indications that Beckett was far from content with the idea of a fixed self—or even the self of the existentialists which could change progressively through time or be self-consciously created by the authentic individual—and his work goes on to exemplify his criticisms of these concepts.

But the acknowledgment and awareness of fluidity and elusiveness do not eliminate the problem of "the self" for Beckett, nor for the reader of

---

9. Ibid., 19.
10. Jerrold Seigel argues this in ch. 6 of *Idea of the Self*.
11. Beckett, *Three Novels*, 8 and 29.
12. Ibid., 31.
13. Ibid., 113.
14. Renner, "Self-Multiplying Narrators," 104.
15. *Proust*, 75.
16. Beckett, "Dante...Bruno.Vico..Joyce," 33.

his work, and the issue of identity remains a central concern. John Fletcher, for example, is one early critic who has pointed out that such questions of identity intensify, becoming the overriding preoccupation of Beckett's fiction from *Malone Dies* onwards.[17] Unable to finally dispense with the notion of some core essence, Beckett does not rid himself of a sense of an essential self, as Iain Wright concedes.[18] Each of the narrators in the *Three Novels* articulates, implicitly or explicitly, Malone's express need "to look at myself as I am."[19] But the hope is no sooner uttered than the possibility of fulfillment is negated in that characteristically Beckettian way. For example, at the end of *Molloy*, at the point at which Moran returns home, and is, in one sense closest to becoming Molloy, we find him claiming "I not only knew who I was, but I had a sharper and clearer sense of my identity than ever before, in spite of its deep lesions and the wounds with which it was covered. And from this point of view I was less fortunate than my other acquaintances. I am sorry if this last phrase is not so happy as it might be. It deserved, who knows, to be without ambiguity."[20] Ambiguous the phrase certainly is; for one thing, the text has demonstrated little that may be called self-knowledge on the part of Moran, and the reader is left uncertain as to the level of irony consciously employed by Beckett here.

Moreover, Beckett himself has articulated a sense of dualism of the inner and outer self; in an interview with Lawrence Harvey, Beckett told him that the authentic self is not the same as the self that is visible in the outside world. "The deeper self is a being somehow stunted, undeveloped, but more real, more authentic than the public man, who seems closer to the second or third person than to the first."[21] Rubin Rabinovitz tries to synthesize the two emphases suggesting that Beckett's "road to self-discovery is littered with images of the self that are discarded in the pursuit of new ones that promise to be superior."[22] Wolfgang Iser puts it most succinctly: "Subjectivity in *Malone Dies* is presented in the form of a ceaseless dialectic that is never synthesized."[23]

One interpretation of the attitude that may underlie such ambiguity is to perceive Beckett as being entirely ironic. This interpretation, put forward by Shira Wolosky, is that the "universally accepted" reading of Beckett on

17. Fletcher, *Novels of Samuel Beckett*, 168.
18. Wright, "What matter who's speaking?" 59–86.
19. Beckett, *Three Novels*, 189.
20. Ibid., 170.
21. Harvey, *Samuel Beckett, Poet and Critic*, 556.
22. Rabinovitz, "Beckett and Psychology," 11, 12, 65–79.
23. Iser, "Subjectivity as the Autogenous Cancellation of Its Own Manifestations," 75.

an existential quest, "desperately pursuing an idea of self as pure essence, yet always being defeated in his attempts to achieve it," is a misreading of his repeated questioning of such a notion of essential selfhood.[24] Wolosky argues that although Beckett's "whole textual venture centers in selves that do nothing except seek themselves in some absolute, self-centered purity, that his fictions *intentionally* do so in ways that call this very project into question."[25] His texts, she argues, purposefully show how the defeat of the pure self is evidenced through the failure of Beckett's narrators to establish a self by figuration. For her, it is ultimately Beckett's aim to show up the falsity of a particular notion of the self—the essential self:

> Beckett indeed scrupulously adopts traditional notions of a pure, unitary self, one beyond time, space, extension, essential, interior, and, as is often claimed, transcending "physical and material life" to "exist in nonmaterial dimension." But his texts—through comedy, parody, tediousness, and the macabre—show this definition to be both quixotic and undesirable. The endless effort to attain the pure self is endlessly defeated.[26]

Wolosky may be correct to say that Beckett's selves are neither pure nor unitary—already in *Proust* we have ample evidence that he clung to no such concept. (One cannot help but wonder who does propose such a pure unitary self). But I have already stated my position that a reading that overemphasizes Beckett's use of irony is to go against the grain of his work. There is no suggestion of irony or parody when Beckett cites—and prefaces—Proust's comment:

> We cannot know and we cannot be known. "Man is the creature that cannot come forth from himself, who knows others only in himself, and who, if he asserts the contrary, lies."[27]

The weakness of the idea of "unitary, unmediated, self-identity" is exposed in Beckett's fiction, not primarily by single ambiguous, or unambiguous, statements, but by the weight of his work as a whole.[28] A succession of

---

24. Wolosky, *Language Mysticism*, 72.

25. Ibid., 74.

26. Ibid.

27. Beckett, *Proust*, 66.

28. Nor was he alone in this at the beginning of the twentieth century. As Charles Taylor puts it: "And so a turn inward, to experience or subjectivity, didn't mean a turn to a self to be articulated, where this is understood as an alignment of nature and reason, or instinct and creative power. On the contrary, the turn inward may take us beyond the self as usually understood, to a fragmentation of experience which calls our ordinary notions of identity into question . . . or beyond that to a new kind of unity, a new way of inhabiting time, as we see, for instance, with Proust." *Sources of the Self*, 462.

narrators demonstrate not only their desire to make their own acquaintance, as the narrator of *The Unnamable* would put it, but also their failure to do so. Malone himself disintegrates at the end of *Malone Dies*, only to reappear as the bodiless narrator whose stated aim is to pay a little attention to himself, and to get beyond words to silence in *The Unnamable*. The weakness in Wolosky's argument is that a close reading of the trilogy and other passages in *Proust* reveals an author who is painfully aware of the problems, even the impossibility, of his task, yet is somehow *compelled* to embark and keep going. As the narrator of *The Unnamable* makes us so painfully aware, the nature of the self is ineffable, yet the self must needs "eff."

> It's of me now I must speak, even if I have to do it with their language, it will be a start, a step towards silence and the end of madness, the madness of having to speak and not being able to, except of things that don't concern me, that don't count, that I don't believe, that they have crammed me full of to prevent me from saying who I am, where I am, and from doing what I have to do in the only way that can put an end to it, from doing what I have to do.[29]

The text in its entirety is well encapsulated in the closing words, "I can't go on, I'll go on." Aware of the incoherence of the individual, aware of the ceaseless modification that takes place, the decantation of past and future times, Beckett still seems compelled to pursue, to "eff," in a way that belies the intellectual statements made in *Proust*. As Hugh Kenner points out, the compulsion reaches to the very structure and grammar of *The Unnamable*, as punctuation is abandoned, and statements are negated as soon as they are uttered: "This 'I' requires a name but does not receive one; panic is mounting; sentences grow longer and longer; the need is to be formed and defined and named, the anticipation is always of rebirth, the horror is when the birth occurs."[30] The final "babble" as the narrator of *The Unnamable* itself calls it, is a litany of yearning—for birth, for life, for death, for a voice, for silence, for stories, for cessation of seeking, for embodiment, for limbs, for a head, for a countenance.

It is precisely because of this sense of mounting panic that I want to argue that Beckett's oeuvre is ultimately something other than a deconstruction of the Enlightenment concept of the unitary self. The critical discussion about such philosophical influences on Beckett continues. Through the years of Beckett criticism, many and various influences have been perceived as influential upon Beckett's thinking; Vico, Descartes,

---

29. Beckett, *Three Novels*, 324.
30. Kenner, *Reader's Guide to Samuel Beckett*, 112.

Kant, Hegel, Schopenhauer, and Kierkegaard. For example, the Cartesian influence, (which is explicit in Beckett's early poem "Whoroscope" about Descartes) has been found throughout the body of his work. John Fletcher is one of a number of critics who has attributed Beckett's extreme separation of mind and body to the influence of Descartes.[31] But P. J. Murphy argues that Beckett adopts a Spinozist maneuver, of playing off against each other Aristotelian and Cartesian notions of mind-body relations.[32] In Beckett's novel *Murphy* (1938), the self-enclosed character of Murphy's mind is specifically indebted to Spinoza's thought. *Watt* (written 1943), on the other hand, is a Kantian novel, written after Beckett had bought the complete works of Kant. P. J. Murphy believes that Kant, although largely overlooked by Beckett's critics, was more influential than philosophers such as Hegel and Schopenhauer, who have received more critical attention. There is undoubtedly much work to be done here. And yet, even P. J. Murphy's excellent critique admits that, despite the philosophical nature of the questions, Beckett found such philosophical systems too "reasonable." As he told Michael Haerdter:

> The crisis started with the end of the seventeenth century, after Galileo. The eighteenth century has been called the century of reason, *le siècle de la raison*. I've never understood that; they're all mad, *ils sont tous fous, ils déraisonnent!* They give reason a responsibility which it simply can't bear, it's too weak. The Encyclopedists wanted to know everything . . . but that direct relation between the self and—as the Italians say—*lo scibile*, the knowable, was already broken.[33]

At some point after writing *Watt* (and therefore before *Three Novels*) Beckett stated that he no longer read philosophers; Molloy and all that followed were conceived out of that admission of his own ignorance.[34] In the end, P. J. Murphy does not attempt to locate Beckett in any particular philosophical tradition. Despite his engagement with philosophy, Beckett did not embrace the limitations of such thought. The narrator of *The Unnamable* comments, "They must consider me sufficiently stupefied with all their balls about being and existing." I conclude this along the same lines as Hugh Kenner:

---

31. Fletcher, *Samuel Beckett's Art*, 126–31.
32. Murphy, "Beckett and the Philosophers," 226.
33. McMillan and Fehsenfeld, *Beckett in the Theatre*, 230–31.
34. See Gabriel d'Aubarède, *Nouvelles littéraires* (Paris, 16 February, 1961). Cited by P. J. Murphy, "Beckett and the Philosophers," 229.

> It is that structure, shaped, sometimes self-canceling if it pleases him, that he has laboured to perfect, draft after draft. And like all of us, he has habitual attitudes. After years of familiarity with his work, I find no sign that it has ambitions to enunciate a philosophy of life.[35]

Equally, it is not possible to find any single ideology of the self, despite the influence of/reaction against Vico or Descartes or Kant or whoever. Rather than demonstrating—or deconstructing—a philosophy of the self, Beckett's concern with the self is a profoundly felt need to articulate. For articulation seems to be his way of attempting to find and maintain a sense of the self. The narrator of *The Unnamable* puts it this way:

> So it is I who speak, all alone, since I can't do otherwise. No, I am speechless. Talking of speaking, what if I went silent? What would happen to me then? Worse than what is happening? But fie these are questions again. That is typical. I know no more questions and they keep on pouring out of my mouth. I think I know what it is, it's to prevent the discourse coming to an end . . . perhaps I shall be obliged, in order not to peter out, to invent another fairy-tale, yet another, with heads, trunks, arms, legs and all that follows, let loose in the dubious round of imperfect shadow and dubious light.[36]

Behind the articulations of the narrators in the *Three Novels* is the desire to write, in order to acquire and maintain a sense of ontological significance. All else, I would argue, is secondary to this, dominated by the fear of petering out. Daniel Albright summarizes it by saying; "It is as if the imagination were a faculty given to mankind to assuage the pain of being unable to know who we are, as if all novels or paintings spring from our incapacity for real autobiography, real self-portraiture. Narcissus, like Wilde's Caliban, rages because he cannot see any image on his film of water except that of his own face, a face that is not quite his own."[37] It is far from a post-structuralist *jouissance*. Iain Wright points out just how much Beckett's work goes against the grain of the "liberation" claimed by such readings:

> This free-play in the flux of discourse, this deconstruction of the logocentric illusions underlying the whole of Western man's utterance about himself since the pre-Socratics, this expunging of

---

35. Kenner, *Reader's Guide to Samuel Beckett*, 38.
36. Beckett, *Three Novels*, 307.
37. Albright, *Representation and the Imagination*, 9

> origins and foundations, this *mise en abime*, is supposed to be experienced as a liberation, a discovery of erotic *jouissance* . . . There is a rather complicated irony at work here, an irony which derives from the fact that, while Beckett's narrators are ceaselessly at work in a deconstructionist activity—foregrounding their own textuality, decentring the texts they inhabit, subverting subject positions, denaturalizing language—the issue is misery and meaninglessness, and that activity is what they seek continually but unsuccessfully to escape *from*, back into the world of solid foundations, solid signifieds.[38]

Wright goes on to perceive the central issue for Beckett's narrators as the problematic of the subject in language. (P. J. Murphy also perceived this as Beckett's abiding concern, how language relates to reality.) But language, although inextricably tied to "the struggle to discover 'I'" is only a symptom. The source of Beckett's narrator's compulsion to speak lies deeper. Malone says, "Live and invent . . . Live and cause to live . . . After the fiasco, the solace, the repose, I began again, to try and live, cause to live, be another, in myself, in another, how false all this is."[39] The need to invent is the struggle to live. The sense of failure can be sensed through the very arbitrariness of the naming of Malone's invented characters. Sapo becomes Macmann because Malone "cannot stomach" the name Sapo any longer. Even Malone's name is not fixed. At one point he refers to the whole sorry business of Malone, "since that is what I am called now." Beckett's attempt to create characters is inextricable from his attempt to create a sense of self, and both character and sense of self disintegrate into the most lifeless of substances, ash:

> And it was, though more unutterable, like the crumbling away of two little heaps of finest sand, or dust, or ashes, of unequal size, but diminishing together as it were in ratio, if that means anything, and leaving behind them, each in its own stead, the blessedness of absence.[40]

The Hegemony of the Inner Life

The crucial factor, I believe, which is integral to the circuitous repetitiveness of his later fiction, lies in Beckett's decision in 1945 to abandon any inclination towards ordering the outside world, and to deal, henceforth,

---

38. Wright, "What Matter Who's Speaking?" 71.
39. Beckett, *Three Novels*, 194–95.
40. Ibid., 222.

with the darkness of the inner self. He told Knowlson in 1989 of his decision to take a different literary path from James Joyce:

> I realised that Joyce had gone as far as he could in the direction of knowing more, (being) in control of one's material. He was always adding to it; you only have to look at his proofs to see that. I realised that my own way was in impoverishment, in lack of knowledge and in taking away, subtracting rather than adding.[41]

In effect, Beckett would seem to have given himself permission to explore that area that had such a draw for him, (as is evidenced in his *Proust* comments), but which he had tried to keep in abeyance. Back in 1932 he had signed, along with other artists, a manifesto entitled "Poetry is vertical" which began, "In a world ruled by the hypnosis of positivism, we proclaim the autonomy of the poetic vision, the hegemony of the inner life over the outer life."[42] But it would seem to have been in 1945 that Beckett consciously allowed the "hegemony of the inner life" to dominate his writing. Beckett told Deidre Bair, that, having become aware of his own stupidity, "I began to write the things I feel."[43] Knowlson tells us that Beckett spoke of it in terms of the darkness of the inner world, which was to be his most precious ally; including ignorance, folly and failure. Henceforward he would draw "on his own inner world for his subjects; outside reality would be refracted through the filter of his own imagination; inner desires and needs would be allowed a much greater freedom of expression; rational contradictions would be allowed in; and the imagination would be allowed to create alternative worlds to those of conventional reality."[44] As Knowlson comments, the ground had been well prepared for this by a number of factors; psychotherapy, dissociation from Joyce, freedom from Ireland and his mother, the war years. In *Proust* he had already voiced his inclination towards "contraction":

> the only possible spiritual development is in the sense of depth. The artistic tendency is not expansive, but a contraction . . . The only fertile research is excavatory, immersive, a contraction of the spirit, a descent. The artist is active, but negatively, shrinking from the nullity of extracircumferential phenomena, drawn in to the core of the eddy. He cannot practice friendship, because friendship is the centrifugal force.[45]

41. Knowlson, *Damned to Fame*, 352.
42. *transition*, 21 (Paris, 1932), 148–49.
43. Pattie, *Samuel Beckett*, 30–32.
44. Knowlson, *Damned to Fame*, 352–53.
45. Beckett, *Proust*, 64–66.

But David Pattie is correct to say that from this point on the change in Beckett's work was dramatic. This was partly, no doubt, due to his experiences during the war, and his choice to write in French, but surely also it was due to this permission to take an inward turn, to write out of this sense of failure and contraction. Laura Barge describes it as the turn to the microcosm rather than the macrocosm. The *Three Novels*, written in the early 1950's, exemplifies this new interiority, demonstrating a rapid acceleration into a world that is constantly in the first person, in the form of monologue; there is little that resembles the traditional plot and characterization disintegrates. It is the novel of introspection *par excellence.*

Self-referentiality becomes more marked; Steven G. Kellman locates this within a particularly French tradition of reflexivity. "*Molloy, Malone Muert* and *L'Innomable* are thoroughly conscious of their status as works of literature, of their place in literary history and of their relationships to one another. Each is a first person account and the narrator of each novel explicitly presents himself as a writer. Molloy, in his mother's bed, scribbles the pages that we read; Moran, at the behest of Youdi, writes a report on his activities; Malone creates his world by means of his pencil and his exercise book; and the narrator of *The Unnamable* admits: "It is I who write, who cannot raise my head from my knee."[46] The reader is propelled back to the first page of the text after he has read the last.[47] The primary intertextuality to be found in the *Three Novels* is intratextuality. There is little by way of meaningful reference to the world outside of the world that the novelist is creating by way of the narrator.

Indeed, the entire emphasis becomes thrown onto this kind of individual self-making. Beckett's narrators speak in order to maintain *any* sense of themselves; their project becomes not just an attempt to locate a sense of self, but an attempt to take hold of a basic sense of self-presence. The narrator of *The Unnamable* is particularly insistent upon this with his; "Talking of speaking, what if I went silent? What would happen to me then? Worse than what is happening? . . . Perhaps I shall be obliged, in order not to peter out, to invent another fairy tale, yet another, with heads, trunks, arms, legs and all that follows . . ."[48] As another consequence of this interiority, language becomes more and more foregrounded. The voice is

---

46. Kellman, *Self-Begetting Novel*, 130.

47. Charles Taylor would say that Beckett was far from alone in this turn to interiority; "There is a new reflexive turn, and poetry or literature tends to focus on the poet, the writer, or what it is to transfigure through writing. It is amazing how much art in the twentieth century has itself for its subject, or is on one level at least thinly disguised allegory about the artist and his work." *Sources of the Self*, 481.

48. Beckett, *Three Novels*, 307.

more than the means of self-reflection; it is essential for the existence of the self; "I'm in words, made of words, others' words."[49] The narrative becomes the potential means by which the self is posited, hence the desire to go beyond story and the inability to do so; "there's a story for you, I thought they were over, perhaps its a new one, lepping fresh, is it the return to the world of fable, no, just a reminder, to make me regret what I have lost."[50] H. Abbott Porter has argued that Beckett is writing "autography," that is, that his work is neither fiction nor autobiography, but an attempt to create the self in the moment of writing.[51] For him, Beckett's work "is writing governed not by narrative form or any species of tropological wholeness but by that unformed intensity of being in the present which at every point in the text seeks to approach itself."[52] Despite an apparent contradiction with Beckett's awareness of the slipperiness of the subject as object, this nonetheless rings true; contradiction is, of course, grist to Beckett's mill. But his early instinct proves to be correct. Self-reflexivity seems to provide no satisfactory sense of identity. Laura Barge has clearly traced the complexities, and failure of this attempt at self-composition through narrative in *God, the Quest, the Hero*.[53] As she points out, *Malone Dies* demonstrates the loss of permanent and reliable identity in the characters referred to, "Malone (and all the subsequent heroes who engage in the quest to tell a story) cannot construct art that will authenticate the self as artist."[54]

Between Unattainable Self and Unattainable Non-Self

Beckett's characters do not engage in self-reflexivity blithely. A vacillation between the compulsion to reflect upon his interior world, and a fear of the same is evident. This fear of self-reflexivity is evidenced in a number of ways. Moran, speaking of such explorations, comments:

> And doubtless, I should have gone from discovery to discovery, concerning myself, if I had persisted. But at the first faint light, I mean in these wild shadows gathering about me, dispensed by a vision or by an effort of thought, at the first light I fled to other cares. And all had been for nothing. And he who acted thus was a stranger to me too.[55]

49. Ibid., 386.
50. Ibid., 407.
51. Porter, *Beckett Writing Beckett*.
52. Ibid., 18.
53. Barge, *God, the Quest, the Hero*, 230.
54. Barge, "Beckett's Questing Hero," 56.
55. Beckett, *Three Novels*, 149.

Such thought is hard; indeed, Malone suggests that thought alone will not lead to the desired end; "Somewhere in this turmoil thought struggles on, it too wide of the mark. It too seeks me, as it always has, where I am not to be found."[56] By the end of *The Unnamable* the narrator is still speaking of the need to *start* speaking of the self; "Perhaps it is time I paid a little attention to myself, for a change. I shall be reduced to it sooner or later. At first sight it seems impossible."[57] The overriding sense is that of a person torn almost equally by desire *and* by fear and inability, one who has told stories at times precisely in order to avoid introspection. The narrator in *The Unnamable* speaks of the "alleviations of flight from self."[58] He says of Mahood, "It is I invented him, him and so many others . . . in order to speak, since I had to speak, without speaking of me, I couldn't speak of me, I was never told I had to speak of me."[59] And in an interview with John Gruen in *Vogue* magazine in 1969, Beckett commented that self-perception is the most frightening of all observations for a human; "He must know that when man faces himself, he is looking into the abyss."[60] There may be an element of self-contempt too; Moran speaks of what he is "condemned to be." Josephine Jacobsen and William R. Mueller refer to it as an "acute self-revulsion," indicating the dual role of oppressor and victim that can be traced in the narrators.[61] This self-aversion may be manifested, for example, in the yearning for inception, captured in startling birthing images. Malone, in speaking of himself as an "old foetus" who shall be dropped "with the help of gangrene," despairs; "I shall never get born and therefore never get dead."[62] The desire for birth coincides with the simultaneous desire for death.

There is an astute awareness in Beckett's comment on his early protagonist, Belacqua, in *Dream of Fair to Middling Women* (written in the early 1930s), that "the emancipation, in a slough of indifference and negligence and disinterest, from identity, his own and his neighbour's, suits his accursed complexion much better than the dreary fiasco of oscillation that presents itself as the only alternative."[63] For Beckett could only see these two options; the "dreary fiasco of oscillation" or the emancipation from identity.

56. Ibid., 186.
57. Ibid., 300.
58. Ibid., 367.
59. Ibid., 395.
60. Gruen, "Samuel Beckett talks about Beckett," 210.
61. Jacobsen and Mueller, *Testament of Samuel Beckett*, 143–45.
62. Beckett, *Three Novels*, 225.
63. Beckett, *Dream of Fair to Middling Women*, 121.

"To and fro, between unattainable self and unattainable non-self."[64] Non-self and the desire for emancipation recurs in *Proust*. Beckett's desire was at least partially fed by the reading of his early twenties, whereby he became interested in the ability to "expunge his consciousness" or to "troglodyse," as he puts it in *Dream of Fair to Middling Women*. It may well have been fed by his own reading of Christian sources. We know, for example, that he had read *Confessions*: notes from that text, jotted down in his *Dream* notebook, include such phrases as "hesitating to die to death and to live to life."[65] Part of the import behind Augustine's phrase is the New Testament concept that involves a kind of death to the old self, and a putting on of the new self.[66] Of course, Beckett as a low-down, low-church Protestant, (as he put it on two occasions in *Dream of Fair to Middling Women*) had some familiarity with the Bible, and in his early adult years he would seem to have gained familiarity with spiritual writers or mystics such as Teresa of Avila, John of the Cross and Julian of Norwich, even if only through reading about them second-hand in the work of W. R. Inge, which we know he read from the notes in the *Dream* notebook.[67] It is highly likely that Beckett would have been familiar with such phrases as "To arrive at being all, desire to be nothing" by John of the Cross. The embracing of "nothingness" in order to embrace spiritual growth is evident even so far as the end of the trilogy. Gabriele Schwab has put Beckett's perception in this way:

> Just as negative theologies attempt to clear consciousness of every trace of representation of God in order to approach God and pure nothingness, the Unnamable tries to clear his consciousness of his self in order to experience himself in silence as pure nothingness—hence his dream of ultimate silence and "an empty mind at peace."[68]

But an interesting change can be charted within *Proust* and the trilogy. In *Proust* we find a fairly explicit reference; "this reluctance to die, this long and desperate and daily resistance before the perpetual exfoliation of

---

64. Knowlson, *Damned to Fame*, 631.

65. Beckett, *Beckett's Dream Notebook*, entry 156.

66. For example, Col 3:9–10. Paul tell the Colossians to rid themselves of old ways of behaving, "since you have taken off the old self with its practices and put on the new self, which is being renewed in knowledge in the image of its Creator." It is interesting to note that this is the most common image of this kind in the New Testament, rather than any general exhortation to put the self to death.

67. Inge, *Christian Mysticism*.

68. Schwab, *Subjects without Selves*, 155.

personality."[69] It would seem that Beckett's interpretation of the concept of the death of the self is that of exfoliation, or as the OED puts it, the stripping of the self.[70] In *Molloy*, Moran speaks of "a growing resignation to being dispossessed of self" in the context of "clawing towards light and countenance I could not name, that I had long known and long denied."[71] The ambiguity of the phrases, and the quasi-mystical context of it, suggest that the idea is not fully clear in the mind of Beckett. Moran's killing of a man who physically resembles him shortly after leads Hélène Baldwin to deduce that *Molloy* is the account of a man who is on the negative way; one who has spiritually put to death his "old" man, but is not yet transformed.[72] Such a deduction is not entirely unjustified, given the allusiveness of the passage, but it bespeaks an optimistic interpretation of a passage that is shrouded in uncertainty. Likewise, a passage in *Malone Dies* is similarly hard to decipher. There Malone lies in his bed, speaking of some kind of non-physical death; "It is there I die, unbeknown to my stupid flesh."[73] By *The Unnamable* the general yearning for emancipation—from the madness of having to speak—permeates the entire text, but there is little which resonates with explicit reference to spiritual death. There is a strong sense that Beckett has given up on this idea which once had such appeal to him, but which seemed so unattainable—and so painful—and seeks solace in utterance and the "wordy-gurdy," hoping that he can finally exhaust words and come to the peaceful silence of his longings.

By the end of *The Unnamable* the incoherent individual is trapped in his own words and we are reminded of Augustine's fascination with the inaccessibility and alienness of the speaking mind to itself. Beckett has deconstructed, with consistency, the idea of coherence in the unitary self, and has presented the gamut of problems entailed in broaching the idea, whether they be emotional or cognitive. "I shall not say I again, ever again, it's too farcical."[74] *The Unnamable* could be said to express the fundamental principle of all introspection. Wolfgang Iser summed it up as follows:

---

69. Beckett, *Proust*, 25.

70. The OED (Clarendon, 1989, 5:532) definition hinges upon the stripping of a bone, or of leaves. The intention would seem to be purgative—in order to facilitate health—although there is little in Beckett's *oeuvre* to convey this sense. It is interesting to note the difference here with the thinking of C. S. Lewis on the "death of the self" which is closer, I think, to the dictionary sense of exfoliation.

71. Beckett, *Three Novels*, 148–49.

72. Baldwin, *Samuel Beckett's Real Silence*, 50–55.

73. Beckett, *Three Novels*, 186.

74. Ibid., 355.

> Once the conscious mind turns its attention to its own activities, it no longer functions as a means of translating outside data into comprehensible images; instead it focuses upon the projections and assumptions inherent in this process. But if these are shown up as preconditions for the functioning of consciousness, then the resultant image of the self will in fact be only an image of a preconditioned and so restricted manifestation of the self. As the heightened consciousness reduces all its images of the self to their nonrepresentative individuality, the self can only experience its own reality through an unending sequence of unintegrated and unintegratable images.[75]

And yet he writes on, unable to stop. Beckett's predicted "dreary fiasco of oscillation" has played itself out before our eyes. Unable to find emancipation by any means, he has exemplified E. D. Starbuck's observation, that the attempt to eradicate the self by means of the will is to leave the imperfect self the thing most emphasized.[76] He has illustrated Kierkegaard's multi-dimensional despair:

> To despair over oneself, in despair to will to be oneself, in despair to be rid of oneself, in despair to will to devour oneself is the formula for all despair, to which also the other form of despair, in despair to will to be oneself, can be traced back, just as the above, in the despair not to will oneself, to will to be rid of oneself, is traced back to: in despair to will to be oneself.[77]

Beckett's narrator babbles on, fragmented and disembodied, hoping for a door, for limbs, for a head, above all, for a countenance—even the name that he does not have. Despite the urgency of the rhetoric, there seems little hope, even retroactively. "We cannot know and cannot be known," was his conclusion in *Proust*, and by the end of *The Unnamable*, we have seen the solipsistic outworking of this stance.

And on Myself Too I Pored: Psychological Factors

In order to understand Beckett's approaches to the self, we shall turn next to psychology and psychoanalysis. This may shed some light upon his distinctive traits; for example, is it possible that he has a particular—psychological (for want of a better word)—tendency to struggle with an

---

75. Iser, "Subjectivity as the Autogenous Cancellation," 80.

76. Starbuck, *Psychology of Religion*. Cited by William James, *Varieties of Religious Experience*, 208–11.

77. Kierkegaard, *Journals and Papers*, 1:349.

elusive sense of the self? We shall also address his awareness of and knowledge about things psychological, for that too has a bearing on his writing. More recent psychoanalytical approaches to Beckett have made much of the connections with psychoanalysis. J. D. O'Hara's *Samuel Beckett's Hidden Drives* (1997) demonstrates the likelihood of a strong Freudian influence. Phil Baker's *Beckett and the Mythology of Psychoanalysis* (1997) is specifically dedicated to the exploration of psychoanalytic and quasi-psychoanalytic material found in the work and he plausibly argues that Beckett's earlier writing is indeed littered with the debris of psychoanalytic discourse. Thomas Cousineau, in a more psychoanalytic reading in *After the Final No: Samuel Beckett's Trilogy* uses the lens of Gilles Deleuze and Felix Guattari and their "schizo-analytical method." Such labels are inviting, given the allusiveness of Beckett's work, and the undoubted, although not uncritical, interest in psychoanalysis that he displayed.

Negation of Living: Beckett and Psychoanalysis

Beckett's own temperament as a young man was one of marked introversion, given over to much self-scrutiny, leading him to enter psychoanalysis in order to better understand his own symptoms, and the causes of them. We also know of his visits with a doctor friend, Geoffrey Thompson, (whilst living in London) to the Bethlem Royal Hospital where he learnt much about mental disorders. He was deeply interested in Jung and Freud, (having heard Jung lecture in 1935), although according to J. D. O'Hara, Beckett came to prefer the work of Freud. "He responded to the sense of a fragmented psyche with hostile and inaccessible parts, the sense of an internal judge, the sense of voices within the mind . . ." comments J. D. O'Hara.[78] Likewise, Freud's idea of the repressed unconscious as the residue of early relationships, reverberates more with the work of Beckett than Jung's collective unconscious, although there is no doubt that Beckett was very interested in the idea of the unconscious.[79] Beckett was also friendly with the daughter of James Joyce, Lucia, who was diagnosed in 1932 with what was then believed to be schizophrenia. And he read widely on psychology and psychoanalysis; Knowlson points out that his detailed notes on various psychological textbooks still exist.[80]

Perhaps most significant of all for its impact upon the trilogy, indeed upon Beckett's whole life, was the fact that he experienced psychotherapy

---

78. O'Hara, *Samuel Beckett's Hidden Drives*, 2.
79. Knowlson, *Damned to Fame*, 218.
80. Ibid., 177–78.

in London with Dr Wilfred Ruprecht Bion from 1933 to 1935.[81] In January 1934, he wrote to Morris Sinclair; "Three times a week I give myself over to probing the depths with my psychiatrist, which has already, I think, done me some good, in the sense that I can keep a little calmer, and thst the panic attacks in the night are less frequent and less acute. But the treatment will necessarily be long, and I may have months more of it yet. I'm not complaining, I regard myself as very fortunate to have been able to embark upon it, it is the only thing that interests me at the moment, and that is how it should be, for these sorts of things require one to attend to them to the exclusion of virtually anything else."[82] Although we have no specific knowledge of the content of those sessions, we do know certain of Bion's emphases. His analysis was distinctive in style. Steven Connor describes it as inhabiting the "looped, interrupted, convoluted duration of the modernist or postmodernist text," rather than the more typical forward movement defined by the desire to retrieve the past.[83] Here Beckett and Bion may have been of mutual influence on each other. Connor concludes that Bion's principle of a narrative progress achieved through subtraction, denial and disaggregation becomes the engine of Beckett's written work. Bion's approach was somewhat eclectic, borrowing from different sources such as Freud or Melanie Klein; he did not follow a particular school of thought.[84] He encouraged Beckett to pay attention to his dreams, and, according to Joan and Neville Symington, he believed that there was an ultimate truth which cannot be known directly, but to which mystical experience has approximated most closely. His approach was "geared to facilitating mystical experience" by focusing on those defenses which a client would put up against those experiences.[85] As Knowlson points out, he was interested in the processes of artistic creation:

> . . . he probably helped Beckett to see how his solipsistic attitudes could be mined fruitfully in his writing. By externalizing some of the impulses of the psyche in his work—the feelings of frustration and repressed violence for example—he would find it easier to

---

81. The specific dates (and even the number of sessions per week) vary in the different accounts.

82. Samuel Beckett, letter to Morris Sinclair (January 27, 1934), *Letters of Samuel Beckett*, 1:182–83.

83. Connor, in "Beckett and Bion," a paper given at the Beckett and London Conference, Goldsmiths College, 1997. Online: http://www.bbk.ac.uk/eh/eng/eng/skc/beckbion.

84. Symington, *Clinical Thinking of Wilfred Bion*.

85. Ibid., 177–78.

counter the self-absorption that had become morbid and destructive in his personal life. The writing thus became essential to his later mental and physical well-being.[86]

It is highly probable that Beckett's writing was heavily indebted to those years with Wilfred Bion, as Steven Connor explains.

> I think an argument could be made that the transformation in Beckett's life and writing begins with the period of quite intensive analysis which he underwent with W. R. Bion in 1934-6. Neither Cronin nor Knowlson devote much space to this encounter, possibly because however absorbing and exacting the analysis might have been (nearly two years of weekly sessions, though Beckett remembered it in later years as lasting only about six months), Beckett himself had little to say about it in his many letters to Thomas MacGreevy of the period, and, in fact, he broke off the analysis prematurely . . . However, the evidence of one or two letters to MacGreevy seems to indicate that during these years, Beckett was beginning a process of giving birth to himself . . . The acknowledgment rather than the disavowal of his own melancholy ambivalence, an acknowledgment that perhaps could not be complete until after the War, would be a crucial stage in delivering Beckett from an art of mutilating rage into one of maimed mercy.[87]

It may be this process which gave rise to the form which the *Three Novels* takes. Adam Phillips has spelt out that autobiography is a process of finding a shape for the story of the self, with a beginning, middle and end whereas in psychoanalysis, however, the story of the self is deconstructed and becomes unreadable, in order to be read and interpreted.[88] That is not to say that the trilogy is pure autobiography. As Sinéad Mooney points out, to do so would be simplistic, not least because the novels are the "reverse of self-revelatory." But, as she continues, "all three novels play with autobiography, and *The Unnamable* in particular, flirts with the prurient idiom of the confessional narrative before rejecting it violently."[89] This is more in keeping with the writing of one's life as a means of self-analysis, without chronology or structure, rather than strict autobiography—John Sturrock uses the term "autopsychography"—and would seem to be part of an attempt to gain insight.[90]

86. Knowlson, *Damned to Fame*, 181.
87. Connor, "How He Was: Samuel Beckett's Lives," 121–26.
88. Phillips, *On Flirtation*, 68.
89. Mooney, *Samuel Beckett*, 23.
90. Sturrock, *Language of Autobiography*, 258.

This method of self-analytic autobiography had been articulated by Karen Horney, and may well have been read by Beckett himself, for she appealed to a wide public in the 1940s and 50s.[91] She believed that we are "more familiar with ourselves than any outsider can be" and self-analysis is possible, if somewhat more demanding because of the resistances which may be put up.[92] For Horney, self-knowledge is achieved through the free association of what one really feels, giving as much free range to the feelings as possible and keeping the reasoning faculty very much in abeyance.[93] Celia Hunt points out that this exercise is most valuable when the material is allowed to emerge as freely as possible, so that themes or characters are allowed to "take on a life of their own," even if the subject matter is unattractive to the writer—in other words, "personal truth" is sought through the imagination.[94] Significantly, Hunt tells us that this self-analysis is a form of psychotherapy that puts emphasis upon the "present configuration of the personality rather than on retrieving the past."[95] For psychoanalysts, in theory, this would then form the basis for re-evaluation and insight. Freud, although he subjected himself to self-analysis, privately admitted doubts about the efficacy of self-analysis; "My self-analysis is still interrupted. I have now seen why. I can only analyze myself with the objectively acquired knowledge (as if I were a stranger): self-analysis is really impossible, otherwise there would be no illness . . ."[96] This stage may also have eluded Beckett. Despite the profound impact of psychoanalysis upon him, Beckett did not return to analysis, with Bion, or with anyone. Didier Anzieu, a French psychoanalyst, makes explicit the idea that Beckett's writing of the *Three Novels* was heavily influenced by both the analysis—and the apparently abrupt termination of it in 1935:

> The originality of Beckett's narrative writing derives from the attempt (unacknowledged and probably unconscious) to transpose into writing the route, rhythm, style, form and movement of a psychoanalytic process in the course of its long series of successive sessions, with all the recoils, repetitions, resistances, denials, breaks and digressions that are the conditions of any progression.[97]

---

91. Horney, *Self Analysis* and *Our Inner Conflicts*.
92. Horney, *Self Analysis*, 145–50.
93. Ibid., 186, 248–49.
94. Hunt, "Autobiography and the Psychotherapeutic Process," 192.
95. Ibid., 181.
96. Freud, *Origins of Psychoanalysis*, 234.
97. Anzieu, translated by Steven Connor, in "Beckett and Bion," para 8.

Unconsciously or consciously, the termination may have been a protective gesture on the part of Beckett; "self-analysis," according to Anzieu, would have involved less negative transfer. "In Beckett's self-analysis, the analyst is physically absent but psychologically present . . . he is embodied by the messenger who comes (each week?) to fetch the narrator's pages . . . In this way, he approaches ever closer to a voice that speaks from the deepest recesses of his being, arriving finally at the Unnamable."[98] Here too the remarkable influence of Bion remained, according to Connor, in that the very sense of physical dissolution in that text is similar to that described by Bion in his "Notes on the Theory of Schizophrenia."[99]

Ultimately, as Katherine Martin Gray has spelt out, Beckett was highly ambivalent, if not hostile to the institutionalized practices of psychoanalysis and psychology.[100] But his *oeuvre* bears the marks of that inner and isolated depth plunge which is ultimately an attempt at that kind of self-knowledge. For, on certain levels, psychoanalysis is a discipline that encourages a realization of the self. Horney, for example, wrote emphatically on the idea of the self—"that central inner force, common to all human beings and yet unique in each, which is the deep source of growth."[101] She comments that the goal of psychoanalysis is the outgrowing of the destructive forces within which prevent growth. "The way toward this goal is an ever increasing awareness and understanding of ourselves. Self-knowledge then is not an aim in itself, but a means of liberating the forces of spontaneous growth."[102] This is not the language of Freud, Jung—or Beckett, for that matter. But self-knowledge is the counterbalance to the neuroses of which psychoanalysis does speak. And fundamentally it underlies Beckett's quest. The narrator of *The Unnamable* refers to personal self-knowledge, "For on the subject of me properly so called, I know what I mean, so far as I know I have received no information up to date."[103] The repetition of "know" is hardly accidental.

But knowledge requires some kind of recognition; without that there can be no genuine knowledge. It is, in fact, recognition that Beckett seems to be seeking. "Shall I come upon my true countenance at last, bathing in a

---

98. Anzieu, "Beckett and the Psychoanalyst," 23–34, 28.

99. Connor, "Beckett and Bion," para 16.

100. Gray, "Beckettian Interiority," 95–103. She makes particular reference to Beckett's plays and suggests that even the use of the word "self" privileges the coherence of a subject in a way that is misleading for those attempting to follow Beckett's thought.

101. Horney, *Neurosis and Human Growth*, 17.

102. Ibid., 15.

103. Beckett, *Three Novels*, 336.

smile?"[104] But the most he can muster is the heavily ironic, "He who seeks his true countenance, let him be of good cheer, he'll find it, convulsed with anguish, the eyes out on stalks."[105] Beckett's narrators achieve no such recognition—or in Aristotelian terms *anagnorisis*, the change from ignorance to knowledge—and there seems little evidence that Beckett made any such discovery.

One important aspect which psychoanalysis has bequeathed to our understanding is the importance of early relationships. Undoubtedly addressed in Beckett's psychoanalytic sessions, although we have no details, was Beckett's relationship with his mother, May Beckett. Certainly, his medical friend, Geoffrey Thompson, is cited by Knowlson as saying that the key to understanding him is found in his relationship with his mother. Knowlson refers both to May's high, even strict, standards, and to Beckett as "having umbilical dependence" on his mother; Beckett, in turn, has spoken of her "savage loving."[106] Knowlson also comments that Beckett's mother may have contributed to later feelings of superiority and isolation; "by setting him on a pedestal as a child, she had fostered his sense of superiority, while at the same time smothering him claustrophobically and demanding conformity to her own rigid (and for him, unacceptable) standards and values."[107] In avoiding being smothered, Beckett's choice would seem to have been for isolation—Knowlson refers to a point in the mid-1930's when Beckett saw no-one in London, where he was living at the time, except Bion, and his good friend, Thomas MacGreevy. A letter to MacGreevy written in 1935 indicates Beckett's own reaction to this development:

> For years I was unhappy, consciously and deliberately ever since I left school and went into T.C.D. [Trinity College, Dublin], so that I isolated myself more and more, undertook less and less and lent myself to a crescendo of disparagement of others and myself. But in all that there was nothing that struck me as morbid. The misery and solitude and apathy and the sneers were the elements of an index of superiority and guaranteed the feeling of arrogant

---

104. Ibid., 338.
105. Ibid., 347.
106. Beckett, letter to Thomas McGreevy (Oct. 6 1937), *Letters*, 1:552.
107. Knowlson, *Damned to Fame*, 180. Patrick Wakeling goes so far as to say that Beckett and his mother were "enmeshed" and that "only by surrendering his identity could he gain his mother's approval." According to Wakeling, Beckett's entire concern, "both as a person and as a writer, has been to protect his 'true' inner self against what he has genuinely always felt to be the terrifying threat of engulfment." Patrick Wakeling, "Looking at Beckett—The Man and the Writer," 5–17.

"otherness," which seemed as right and natural and as little morbid as the ways in which it was not so much expressed as implied and reserved and kept available for a possible utterance in the future. It was not until that way of living, or rather negation of living, developed such terrifying symptoms that it could no longer be pursued, that I became aware of anything morbid in myself.[108]

It is significant that Beckett's reply to MacGreevy was in response to his suggestion that he read Thomas à Kempis' *Imitation of Christ* in order to calm his physical symptoms of black moods and a heart that Beckett described as "bubbling." Beckett rejected what he saw as leading to "an abject self-referring quietism" which was unhelpful for someone of his temperament; "I cannot see that it allows of any philosophical or ethical or Christlike imitative pentimenti, or in what way they could redeem a composition that was invalid from the word 'go' and has to be broken up altogether."[109]

Knowlson argues that it was Bion who helped Beckett "to counter his self-immersion by coming out of himself more in his daily life and taking a livelier interest in others."[110] In effect, Beckett's change in behavior would seem to have prevented him from continuing in a solipsistic spiral of isolation and morbidity; Knowlson says, "the evidence of his friends suggests that what may have been a search for a tolerable *modus vivendi* evolved into a far more natural, spontaneous sharing in the problems, pains and sufferings of others."[111] This impression is confirmed by a reading of his letters, which suggest a subtle but clearly discernable shift away from self-absorption towards an increasing interest in the arts.

He Who Acted Thus Was a Stranger to Me Too: Psychological Profiles

Despite his conscious effort to take a livelier interest in others, it is also evident from one letter, that Beckett was somehow willing to accept his own psychological make-up. "I realize how lost I would be bereft of my incapacitation," he wrote to Thomas McGreevy.[112] In that vein, he had given himself permission to allow his inner life to dominate his writing. That inner turn becomes clear in the *Three Novels*, as we have already noted. Beckett had criticized the scientific method or "philosophical language"

---

108. Samuel Beckett, letter to Thomas MacGreevy (January 25, 1931), *Letters*, 1:62.
109. Ibid., 259.
110. Ibid., 181.
111. Ibid.
112. Beckett, letter to Thomas MacGreevy (February 14, 1935), *Letters*, vol. 1, 250.

(by which he means the language of logicians and scientists) in his first published essay, "Our Exagmination," but by the writing of *Molloy*, had given up abstract studies of the mind—and considered himself free to study not so much the laws of the mind but those of his own mind.[113]

The consequences of this turn to introspection take us towards a disjointed world, where everything fragments, "endlessly collapsing." In fact, there is much in the *Three Novels* that is more like the product of a fragmented mind, than one that is coolly assessing various interpretations of a fragmented mind. Despite Beckett's reluctance to allow precedence to any psychological theories, it may be informative to consider some of those that come closest to describing the mindset of Beckett's narrators. Whilst Knowlson, (unlike Deidre Bair in a previous biography), does not represent Beckett as a tormented schizoid character, it may be fair to say that there is enough in his biography to suggest that Beckett may have had traits that could have culminated in schizoid tendencies.[114] G. C. Barnard, whose 1970 study was the first psychological study on Beckett, indicated his belief that many of the existential humanist critics (such as Hugh Kenner, R. N. Coe, and John Fletcher) "fail to deal adequately with the psychological and purely human aspects, and notably they entirely ignore the part played by schizophrenia in the novels" which in effect leads them away from a full understanding of the work.[115] Barnard is not alone in suggesting that schizophrenia and related illnesses resonate strongly with Beckett's concerns and even his style of writing. Steven Connor points out how various features of the *Three Novels* are very much in keeping with the theory that Bion addressed in his work. Connor is quick to point out that he is not proposing that Beckett "presented in his analysis the kind of symptoms which Bion was later to describe as psychotic. Nor is the drama of 'inchoation,' to use a Beckettian word of Bion's, itself contained within the frame constituted by the work as a whole."[116] However, this simulation of a soul in hell is "strangely fragile, since the writing seems so often to erupt out of its containment, swallowing its frame, as it were, and drawing it inwards into its process of ceaseless evacuation."

It is the fragile border, the eruption out of the simulation of the soul in hell that is of particular interest here, for the simulation takes us remarkably close to the state itself. It is a difficult area; much of the difficulty—and

---

113. Beckett, *Three Novels*, 13.

114. Deidre Bair's biography has been largely discredited due to its many factual errors about Beckett's life.

115. Barnard, *Samuel Beckett: A New Approach*, xi.

116. Connor, "Beckett and Bion," para 26.

most critics continue to shy away from any engagement of this issue—may lie in the fact that schizophrenia and related personality types are not fully understood, to the extent that the relationship of schizoid tendencies to full blown schizophrenia remains controversial, and both the origins and development of either seem, ultimately, to be open to question.[117] Therefore, no definitive diagnosis can be decreed in this project, although, alongside Barnard, I would suspect that the disavowal, or omission of the psychological is one that is detrimental to the understanding of Beckett and his work. In considering issues such as his attitude to the self and to God, I would see such factors as having a significant, even central role. As a consequence, I shall endeavor to explore them, without making any attempt at diagnosis.

A study by one man is particularly suggestive for a "reading" of Beckett. Louis A. Sass in his book on schizophrenia and related psychological disorders, *Madness and Modernism*, says that Beckett was a markedly schizoid person and that his characters often resembled schizophrenics.[118] Sass's argument resonates with Beckett's trilogy. In order to consider this a little more, let us consider the characteristics involved in the schizoid and schizophrenic personalities.[119] The "schizoid" personality has a textbook definition as follows:

> . . . patients with schizoid personality disorder do not appear to desire or enjoy social relationships and usually have no close friends. They appear dull, bland and aloof and have no warm tender feelings for other people. They rarely report strong emotions, are not interested in sex, and experience few pleasurable activities. Indifferent to praise, criticism, and the sentiments of others, individuals with this disorder are loners and pursue solitary interests.[120]

The most prominent characteristics of schizoid persons, according to Sass, are as follows: an apparent asociality and indifference; disharmony with the body and the environment; duality of cognitive style, which encompasses

117. Mary Boyle, *Schizophrenia*, for example, has argued that the concept of schizophrenia is a useful one in the face of incomprehensible behaviour, as it gives the impression of knowledge and therefore maintains credibility.

118. Sass, *Madness and Modernism*, 367. In this thorough study, Sass acknowledges that schizoid characteristics and schizophrenia may be a complex interaction of biology and culture but he argues that schizophrenia is peculiar to modernity and that the "inner turn" is central to this. In turn, schizophrenia feeds into modernity and postmodernity—for example, he sees schizophrenic characteristics in the work of Jaques Derrida, amongst others.

119. We shall not consider schizotypal personality disorder for the sake of simplicity.

120. Davison and Neale, *Abnormal Psychology*, 283.

both excessive doubting and extreme obstinacy; interest in the abstract, metaphysical or technical.[121] Apparent detachment may mask extreme sensitivity, although there is often a rift in the sense of connectedness to the world, and within the person, so that there is a sense of a hidden inner self and a public outer self.

Schizophrenia is not a simple development of the schizoid state, despite the similarities. I shall, for the sake of simplicity, use a definition based on DSM III, which Sass also uses:

> The symptoms of schizophrenia are typically divided into positive and negative types. Positive symptoms refer to behavioural excesses, such as delusions, hallucinations, and disorganized speech. Negative symptoms refer to behavioural deficits, such as flat affect, avolition, alogia, and anhedonia . . . Schizophrenia is typically divided into subtypes, such as paranoid, catatonic, and disorganized . . . (which) reflect the considerable variations in behaviour found among people diagnosed with schizophrenia.[122]

There is a good case for arguing that the characters that people many of Beckett's works demonstrate schizophrenic tendencies. Barnard has set out this case, arguing that the characters in *Murphy, Watt,* and the *Three Novels* all demonstrate clear signs of being schizophrenic, with their withdrawal, catatonic phases, bizarre physical postures and behavior, even their inner voices. In *Molloy*, he argues, Beckett "has delineated a considerable portion of the whole schizophrenic picture, starting with the precariously integrated and impoverished ego about to break down, continuing through the subjective experience of acute mania and ending with a phase of depression and apathy, partial convalescence and greatly diminished personality."[123] Moran too has symptoms, including an acute catatonic phase, and Malone is really a further development of this one disintegrated ego. In Barnard's view, *Three Novels*, "presents one man whose various schizophrenic phases are described under the names of Sapo, Moran, Macmann, Molloy, and Malone, with the Unnamable and Pim as his postmortem states."[124] Certainly, this interpretation goes some way to explaining the rather loose use of characterization in the *Three Novels*. Likewise, the texts are pervaded by some of the behavioral characteristics which accompany schizophrenia; the obsession with specific material objects, for example, which recurs throughout *Molloy* and *Malone Dies*; the hearing of voices, so explicit in

---

121. Ibid., 76–78.
122. Ibid., 360.
123. Barnard, *Samuel Beckett: A New Approach*, 38.
124. Ibid., 54.

Molloy, but recurring elsewhere too; the defiance of traditional conventions, an antinomianism sometimes scatological in nature, is evident in various incidents, such as Mahood finding his family all dead as a result of sausage poisoning.[125] (Even the characteristically sardonic throwaway comments of Beckett could be attributed to schizoid tendencies, as when Molloy speaks of his mother "I don't think too harshly of her. I know she did all she could not to have me, except of course the one thing, and if she never succeeded in getting me unstuck, it was fate that ear-marked me for less compassionate sewers."[126]) The whole question of whether or not *The Unnamable* is spoken by one alive or dead, is certainly less angst-ridden if one accepts these parameters, for R. D. Laing points out that there is a precariousness to the schizophrenic individual's subjective sense of his or her own aliveness—a question which is present to the narrator even in *Malone Dies*.[127] So too Wilfred Bion emphasized the importance of understanding the conflict between the life and death instincts in the schizophrenic person.[128] In short, the radical interiority of *The Unnamable* would be in keeping with the breakdown into psychotic dysfunctionality.

Possible connections could also be drawn with regard to Beckett's use of language. The narrator of *The Unnamable* uses language very much in keeping with the analysis of schizophenic language made by Sass.[129] Unending sentences, lack of contextual clues, preoccupation with the ineffable, hyperabstraction coupled with apparent concreteness, repetition and a sense of the inadequacy of language; these are amongst the characteristics of the language of a schizophrenic. Indeed, Sass refers to the famous speech by Lucky at the end of Act I in *Waiting for Godot* as the *ne plus ultra* in modern literature of the nonsense speech that characterizes a schizophrenic who is overwhelmed by the inadequacy of language. Interestingly, based on his experience with schizophrenics, Sass would perceive such glossomania as potentially highly intentional, even to the extent that it is *intended* to sever social bonds. Whatever the purpose of glossomania—and we can only speculate—*Three Novels* is increasingly dominated by those linguistic characteristics which Sass delineates as integral to schizophrenia. Connor

---

125. This kind of antinomianism is touched on by Sass, *Madness and Modernism*, 103–9.
126. Beckett, *Three Novels*, 18.
127. Laing, *Divided Self*, 95–96.
128. Symington, *Clinical Thinking of Wilfred Bion*, 146.
129. Sass, *Madness and Modernism*, 176f. Although recent work on schizophrenic language questions earlier distinctions made, I believe that these general comments remain valid.

too points out just how close Beckett's use of language comes to Bion's discussion in "Notes on the Theory of Schizophrenia."[130]

Importantly, the question of the self is central to the schizophrenic spectrum of illnesses. Schizophrenia is a dissociative state. From a psychological perspective, dissociation is when parts of the psyche are "split-off" or fragmented. The narrator in *The Unnamable* searches most intensely for a place, in close conjunction with his expressed desire for a head, a body, and the silencing of his own voice. It is an image of extreme interiority, which conveys a supreme disconnectedness from and devaluation of the external world of places and people. We have noted that the external world falls away more and more in Beckett's work. Equally evident in his work is the narrators' strange detachment from themselves, one example of which can be seen in these words by Moran:

> And on myself too I pored, on me so changed from what I was. And I seemed to see myself ageing as swiftly as a dayfly. But the idea of aging was not exactly the one which offered itself to me. And what I saw was more like a crumbling, a frenzied collapsing of all that had always protected me from all I was always condemned to be. Or it was like a kind of clawing towards a light and countenance I could not name, that I had once known and long denied . . . and all had been for nothing. And he who acted thus was a stranger to me too.[131]

This is entirely in keeping with the schizoid sense that the outer self has become increasingly independent and removed, like an actor playing a part.[132]

> Disconnection—the sense of being cut off from external objects and other people is not the only form of separation experienced by the schizoid individual . . . Typically, such a person's existence is also riven in a second major way . . . where consciousness focuses on the self not as a knowing centre . . . but as an actor in the world and a potential object of awareness for others.[133]

Sass perceives such aspects of acute self-consciousness as elements of what he calls "hyperreflexivity," for him the master theme of schizophrenic consciousness. This is of significance with regard to Beckett in two major ways. Firstly, this "wholesale reflexivity' leads to the "dissolving of anchored

---

130. Connor, "Beckett and Bion."
131. Beckett, *Three Novels*, 148–49.
132. See Sass, *Madness and Modernism*, 102.
133. Ibid., 90–97.

vantage points" and leads to a universal "institutionalization of doubt."[134] This can be seen in Beckett in a whole range of ways, but perhaps most pertinent to his ideas on the self, it involves a heightened sense that one is always open to the perception of others, with the concomitant ambiguity which may accompany this. This goes far beyond normal self-consciousness. R. D. Laing in *The Divided Self* puts it in this way; "An understanding of self-consciousness in some such terms eludes, I believe, the central issue facing the individual whose basic existential position is one of ontological insecurity and whose schizoid nature is partly a direct expression of, and occasion for, his ontological insecurity, and partly an attempt to overcome it . . ."[135] In effect, for the ontologically insecure person, the perception of others is a reassurance that he or she exists. In line with this we note Beckett's constant desire to be perceived; *esse est percipi,* "to be is to be perceived." Anthony Giddens suggests that feelings of invisibility are linked to early relationships with parenting figures; the child who has not developed an early sense of ontological security may struggle with paralysis of the will, feelings of engulfment and an inability to make those "leaps of faith" which practical engagement involves.[136] If it is a great leap for such a person to grasp a sense of their own reality, how much more likely is it that doubt will dominate metaphysical questions? For Beckett, the whole question of being perceived by God—so powerfully expressed in *Waiting for Godot,* but also articulated in *Three Novels*—may well be linked to his heightened ontological need for a perception which goes beyond the purely visual, just as his radical doubt will affect his ability to have faith in such a figure in the first place. R. D. Laing summarizes such tendencies succinctly:

> . . . in its detachment it (i.e. the schizoid self) is constantly subject to (as it feels) the threat of an implosive or engulfing "reality," and whereas it is preoccupied by itself and its own objects, it is still hyperacutely aware of itself as an object in the eyes of others . . . For the schizoid individual direct participation "in" life is felt as being at the constant risk of being destroyed by life, for the self's isolation is, as we said, its effort to preserve itself in the absence of an assured sense of autonomy and integrity.[137]

The second pertinent aspect of hyperreflexivity is exhibited in one's self-perception, in exigent introspection. It is an inwardness that entails acute

---

134. Ibid., 371–72. Here Sass makes reference to points made by Anthony Giddens in *Consequences of Modernity.*

135. Laing, *Divided Self,* 115.

136. Giddens, *Modernity and Self-Identity,* 2–3.

137. Laing, *Divided Self,* 95.

self-consciousness. This may help explain why, despite his acknowledgement of the impossibility and futility of perpetual self-observation in *Proust*, Beckett remained fixated with the self. It is a self *incurvatus en se* which Sass calls "a vertiginously self-referential abyss." He cites Wittgenstein's comments on William James' attempts to find the "self of selves"; "And James' introspection showed, not the meaning of the word "self" . . . nor any analysis of such a thing, but the state of a philosopher's attention when he says the word "self" to himself and tries to analyze its meaning."[138] This self-enclosed self is largely separated from contextual influences. In Beckett's characters we perceive a detachment from their external surroundings.[139] The *Three Novels* play with and point us beyond the concept of the disembedded self of the Enlightenment; his narrators uproot themselves, or are without specific location (with the exception of Malone). A. Alvarez has written of Beckett's "placeless" novels as being tied in with his "spirit of negation."[140] *Three Novels* resounds with what J. D. O'Hara calls Beckett's sense of exile; his narrators tend towards predominantly solitary existences.[141] It is only post-trilogy, that his characters tend to be found in pairs. Beckett's favored image is that of living in the borderlands and his narrators are profoundly homeless. In *Three Novels*, the only narrator to be described in his own home is Moran; the rest are displaced and restless, alienated. The specificity of Molloy's mother's room disintegrates into the remarkably unsituated "space" of the narrator of *The Unnamable*. By the concluding monologue, the raving voice depicts an interiority which has few external referents, and in which the desire for the implicitly connected "I," "silence," "solitude," and "place," becomes particularly urgent; ". . . if only I could feel a place for me, I've tried, I'll try again, none was ever mine . . ."[142] While it could be said to stem from Beckett's own experience of uprootedness from Ireland, and from his experiences with the Resistance during the war, this does not seem to be an adequate explanation. Such uprootedness does not fully explain the extent to which Beckett's narrators spiral into an increasing disembodiment which would seem to be a

---

138. Sass, *Madness and Modernism*, 223. I can find no evidence that Beckett had read William James, although it seems likely that he might have, given his interests.

139. This is clearly documented by Rubin Rabinovitz in "Self Contained: Beckett's Fiction in the 1960s," 50–64.

140. Alvarez, *Samuel Beckett*, 49.

141. O'Hara, *Samuel Beckett's Hidden Drives*, 280. O'Hara refers to "Beckett's continuous concern with the primary cause of these metaphoric exiles from heaven, God, home, the Earthly Paradise, and so on."

142. Beckett, *Three Novels*, 399.

particularly intense version of Zygmaunt Bauman's vagabond, or of the 'homelessness' of the modern mind as portrayed by Peter Berger *et al.*[143]

Three Novels does inevitably raise serious questions about the possibility of the disembedded self, severed from body, place, language, and other selves—all that is particular about human beings. Where this is most extreme, in *The Unnamable*, the yearning to be "embedded" is most obvious; as the narrator says, "I wanted myself, in my own land for a brief space, I didn't want to die a stranger in the midst of strangers, a stranger in my own midst."[144] At the very point where his narrator is least embodied and least situated, there we find vocabulary that conveys excess of longing for embodiment and emplacement. Shira Wolosky once again perceives this as an outworking of Beckett's intentions; that he *set out* to convey the impossibility of selfhood without relation, communication and location. For her, then, Beckett achieves his aim: "Beckett, then, does not fail to attain to some true self beyond time, space, and language. His writing instead shows the failure of this notion of the self. In this it reasserts expression and representation as exactly the conditions that make selfhood possible."[145] Once again, Wolosky credits Beckett with succeeding in that to which there is no evidence that he aspired.

Martha Nussbaum also misinterprets this aspect of the trilogy. She attributes the negation of the particular in Beckett's writing to the influence of religion—specifically, Christianity. "The complete absence in this writing of any joy in the limited and finite indicates to us that the narrative as a whole is an expression of a religious view of life."[146] It is on this basis that she argues against what she perceives to be the flawed Christian aspiration that Christians may transcend their humanity. But to argue thus is a refusal of the particular account given in *Three Novels* (and Christianity, although more of that at a later stage). To suggest that Beckett's trilogy is representative of Christianity is to refuse to hear Beckett's own voice. When Beckett's narrator in *The Unnamable* speaks of "that foul feeling of pity I have so often felt in the presence of things" he is not speaking of his attitude to things in contrast to his attitude to God; he is speaking of his preference for these things ("little portable things in wood and stone") above "the society of nice people" or "the consolations of some religion or other."[147] There is irony here, but it still does not stretch to support Nussbaum's

---

143. Bauman, *Postmodern Ethics*, 240. Berger et al., *Homeless Mind*.
144. Beckett, *Three Novels*, 396.
145. Wolosky, *Language Mysticism*, 88–89.
146. Nussbaum, *Love's Knowledge*, 309.
147. Beckett, *Three Novels*, 247–48.

claims. (Indeed, there is a profound irony in Nussbaum's negation of the particularity that constitutes Samuel Beckett.) *Three Novels* is more suggestive of the wider sense of disconnectedness of the "interiorized" mentality than it is of any profoundly Christian sense of the created order; rather, it is to the contrary, as we shall see.

Of pertinence to this discussion is Beckett's paradoxical self. Dualities and paradoxes lie at the heart of the schizoid mentality—just as they do in Beckett's work. And it is a particular form of paradox; seen clearly in Beckett's "I can't go on, I'll go on." It is closer to aporia, or a gap in logic that cannot be resolved.[148] Beckett expressed concern for form over content. In a number of interviews, Beckett cited a quotation that he believed to be from Augustine, although subsequent scholarship has been unable to locate it in the exact form that Beckett used. "I am interested in the shape of ideas even if I do not believe in them. There is a wonderful sentence in Augustine. I wish I could remember the Latin. It is even finer in Latin than in English. 'Do not despair; one of the thieves was saved. Do not presume; one of the thieves was damned.' That sentence has a wonderful shape. It is the shape that matters."[149] In a similar vein, he told Charles Juliet, ". . . You can't even talk about truth. That is part of the general distress. Paradoxically, it's through form that the artist can find a kind of solution—by giving form to what has none. It is perhaps only at that level that there may be an underlying affirmation."[150] Beckett's form is dialectic without any prospective of synthesis. As the narrator in *The Unnamable* puts it; "What am I to do now, what shall I do, what should I do, in my situation, how proceed? By aporia pure and simple? Or by affirmations and negations invalidated as uttered, or sooner or later?"[151] Prior to that, some annoyance was expressed at being "back at my old aporetics."[152] Leslie Hill articulates it as follows:

> Aporia, in Beckett's writing, is a figure of indifference, of differences articulated and then suspended. To the extent that it creates not significance but further aporia it is circular in its implications, returning its proponent, or victim, to the very space which he or

---

148. This definition is in keeping with the more modern (or postmodern) definition of the word, as by the French deconstructionists. I do not know if Beckett was amongst the first to use it in this indeterminate way. We shall observe it in its more ancient, Aristotelian usage when we are considering Lewis's work.

149. This is cited by Harold Hobson, "Samuel Beckett, Dramatist of the Year," 153–55.

150. Juliet, *Conversations with Samuel Beckett*, 149.

151. Beckett, *Three Novels*, 291.

152. Ibid., 181.

she would wish to resolve. Its typical form is of a dualistic relation stated and then effaced, or, conversely, of unity posed and then divided against itself.[153]

Although Hill does not make the connection between Beckett's use of aporia and the schizoid outlook, others do. For example, Barnard calls Beckett's style "the schizophrenic dichotomy of simultaneous assertion and denial of existence."[154] And Laing draws the explicit link to the sense of selfhood in the schizoid person:

> In this region everything is paradoxical . . . the self dreads as well as longs for real aliveness. The self dreads to become alive and real because it fears that in so doing the risk of annihilation is immediately potentiated. "Self-consciousness" is implicated in this paradox.[155]

It is possible, therefore, to conjecture that Beckett's "yesses and noes," his profound inability to speak without subsequent negation, is closely linked to this aspect. Wolfgang Iser speaks of subjectivity in *Malone Dies* as "a ceaseless dialectic that is never synthesized" and goes on to comment that it is very hard to unravel the paradox of this, whereby the narrators find it impossible to find their own identity, yet through this impossibility are able to discover something of their own reality.[156] It seems overly optimistic, however, to suggest that Beckett's narrators do progress beyond the indeterminate stasis that we have observed.

Beckett's extreme use of "contradictories" could be closely aligned to a profound ontological insecurity, in keeping with the hypothesis of Laing. Sass also speaks of the paradoxical or contradictory as characteristic of schizophrenia and uses a phrase by Beckett to describe the state as found in various postmodernist avantgarde works; "imagination imagining itself imagine" is indicative of the "vertiginously self-referential abyss" found in the *mise en abyme* emblem there, which plays out as "a paradoxical combination of self-constitution and self-cancellation, a process in which categories are 'torn apart' by their own self-referentiality."[157] Christopher Lasch

---

153. Hill, *Beckett's Fiction*, 65.
154. Barnard, *Samuel Beckett: A New Approach*, 133.
155. Laing, *Divided Self*, 119.
156. Iser, "Subjectivity as the Autogenous Cancellation," 75 and 79.
157. Sass, *Madness and Modernism*, 325, 225, 228. Beckett's use of story-within-story in *Malone Dies* and *The Unnamable* are further examples of the mise-en-abyme. The image most commonly used in connection with reflexivity, is, unsurprisingly, that of the mirror—Jacques Lacan's mirror stage is immediately pertinent here—receiving inadequate mirroring as an infant leads to a perpetual need to form the separate identity that has not been formed.

comments on the self-consciousness of such art; "Novelists and playwrights call attention to the artificiality of their own creations and discourage the reader from identifying with the characters. By means of irony and eclecticism, the writer withdraws from his subject but at the same time becomes so conscious of these distancing techniques that he finds it more and more difficult to write about anything except the difficulty of writing."[158]

The term that Lasch uses to describe this phenomenon is narcissism. Indeed the narcissistic personality disorder could be another possible way of perceiving Beckett's condition. At first glance the narcissistic personality disorder and the schizoid personality disorder would seem to be quite different conditions, especially if reading the summation from DSM III.[159] However, there would seem to be some room for maneuver; for example, Sam Vaknin points out that narcissism and schizoid personality disorders have much in common and that British psychoanalysts tend to use the term "schizoid personality disorder" where American analysts may use the term "narcissism."[160] In other words, differing diagnoses are applied to essentially similar patients because of very different conceptual premises and ideological affiliations. Less clinical approaches have less difficulty. For example, Christopher Lasch (whilst wishing to make clear that full schizophrenia is by no means simply an exaggerated form of narcissism) says schizophrenia "shares with narcissistic disturbances a breakdown in the boundaries between the self and the world of objects" and points out that schizophrenia is a narcissistic disorder.[161] Beckett himself revealed a particular interest in the myth of Narcissus and various psychoanalytically oriented critics have drawn attention to this presence in his texts. For example, Daniel Katz, in a psychoanalytic piece, has drawn attention to Beckett's use of the figure of Narcissus in his early works. For Katz, "Beckett's reading of Narcissus places no emphasis on self-love or successful egotism; rather, Narcissus is the figure of the refusal to take an object, the refusal to accept the location of erotic satisfaction, or even investment, outside of oneself."[162] Thus, Belacqua, in *Dream of Fair to Middling*

158. Lasch, *Culture of Narcissism*, 96–97.

159. "The essential feature of this disorder is a pervasive pattern of grandiosity (in fantasy or behaviour), hypersensitivity to the evaluation of others, and lack of empathy that begins by early adulthood and is present in a variety of contexts." *Diagnostic and Statistical Manual of Mental Disorders*, 349–51.

160. Vaknin, *Malignant Self-Love—Narcissism Revisited*. Vaknin, who claims to be both schizoid and narcissistic himself—clinically speaking—cites many respected psychologists (Freud, Klein, Fairbairn, Guntrip) to defend his argument.

161. Lasch, *Culture of Narcissism*, 171–72.

162. Katz, "'Alone in the Accusative': Beckett's Narcissistic Echoes," 57–71, 63–64.

Women, is portrayed as making the error of loving the Alba, when he can no longer see himself reflected in her eyes.[163] Whether the reference is to the original myth, or psychoanalytic use of it—note that Freud wrote "On narcissism" in 1914, and even connected it to schizophrenia—there can be little doubt that Beckett was drawn to the concept. It may be that the possible similarities (and dissimilarities) between narcissism and schizoid personalities provide an area ripe for exploration.

But, as John Pilling and others have pointed out, it would seem wisest to stop short of either attributing any single theory as particularly influential on the work of Beckett, or of labeling his own psyche with any single diagnostic state. Pilling puts it, "What is certain is that neither psychology nor psychoanalysis constitute, for Beckett, a total answer to the condition of man . . . But equally, as one of his characters says, 'I'd like to be sure I left no stone unturned before reporting me missing and giving up.'"[164] In the interest of leaving no stone unturned, I have tried to reveal pertinent psychological stepping-stones leading in the direction of understanding Beckett's sense of self. But before leaving psychological considerations, it may be worth pointing, albeit briefly, to ways out of the abyss. It seems to me that Anthony Giddens—who manifests a degree of caution towards labels such as "schizoid" and "narcissistic"—is getting at the crux of the matter when he emphasizes the flipside of ontological insecurity, the basic sense of trust which is damaged in the infant; "The feelings of unreality which may haunt the lives of individuals in whose early childhood basic trust was poorly developed may take many forms. They may feel that the object-world, or other people, have only a shadowy existence, or be unable to maintain a clear sense of continuity of self-identity."[165] Could it be that this is Beckett's abyss? Giddens speaks of those afflicted as feeling unable to "go on." Various psychoanalytical theorists such as Heinz Kohut and Jaques Lacan have spoken of the failure of adequate "mirroring" in childhood, which leads to self-depletion.[166] Donald Capps, in his book, *The Depleted Self: Sin in a Narcissistic Age*, uses Heinz Kohut's thinking on inadequate mirroring as a contributory factor to the development of narcissism (and Jacques Lacan's emphasis is similar). Paul Tournier also

---

163. Katz points out that this passage is heavily influenced by a passage from Canto 3 in Dante's *Paradise*, although in this passage Dante is cured of the self-absorption, if not yet fully able to trust his other-oriented gaze.

164. Pilling, *Samuel Beckett*, 131.

165. Giddens, *Modernity and Self-Identity*, 43. Lasch points out that the narcissist's mother may be both devouring and indifferent or aloof (176)—a description which would seem to be in line with Beckett's feelings about his mother.

166. For Kohut, the primary pathologies of our time are self pathologies.

concurs that childhood emotional injury can give rise to doubts about one's own existence.[167] But Capps makes the point that the depleted self is not solely restricted to inadequate early childhood mirroring. Rather, he points towards even the adult need for an ongoing, mutual mirroring that cannot be found in private introspection.[168] "Without mirroring, there can be no self; the light of the self depends on the mirroring it receives from without."[169] Capps, in effect, takes the insight from psychoanalysis, and shows how profoundly applicable it is to both child and adult. Conversely, Beckett's attempt to write the self reverberates with the distortions of the hall of mirrors that proceed from the attempt to self-reflect. But we are left with the question—what *kind* of mirroring could have called the adult Beckett out, through the door, beyond childhood, beyond autonomy, beyond self-scrutiny, and beyond the distortions of self-reflexivity? And what of J. D. O'Hara's conclusion, at the end of his book on depth psychology in Beckett's work, "The cause is lack of love. It sends its victims into themselves and out to the world in search of the love they need but do not deserve. They seek nectar with a sieve, their rational mind"?[170]

In the end we cannot be prescriptive, only suggestive of the resonances. It is certainly possible to see in Beckett's characters traits that are resonant of narcissism and the schizoid/schizophrenic family of disorders. There is still much work to be done in this area of psychology, clearly, but a reading of the *Three Novels* would seem to lend weight to the view put forward by Sass that whilst schizoid characteristics and schizophrenia may be a complex interaction of biology and culture, there are indications of strong connections with the "inner turn" of modernity (and beyond). For example, Sass sees schizophrenic characteristics in the work of Jacques Derrida, amongst others.[171] It may be, as Sass suggests can be the case, a peculiar symbiosis that is a consequence of personal appropriation of certain cultural trends.[172] It is interesting to set all of this alongside Anthony Gidden's comments—as Sass does—on modernity's wholesale reflexivity, which fosters, he argues, social withdrawnness, cognitive wavering and incertitude, a sense of being a divided self, and a predilection to overly abstract modes of thought.[173] Could it be that at the heart of this strangely

167. Tournier, *Place for You*, 101–11.
168. Capps, *Depleted Self*.
169. Ibid., 31.
170. O'Hara, *Samuel Beckett's Hidden Drives*, 280.
171. Carl Jung believed that schizophrenia is of a primarily psychological origin, rather than physical.
172. Sass, 372.
173. Giddens, *Modernity and Self-Identity*, 43.

amorphous malaise that Giddens, Sass, Lasch, and others are all trying to convey, lies the inner turn in its peculiarly modern form? Charles Taylor is emphatic that the distinctly modern inner turn, which he calls, "radical reflexivity," involves a disengagement from an objective order, that has, ironically, both objectified the self, and, at the same time, given place to a radical subjectivity.[174] "The turn to oneself is now also and inescapably a turn to oneself in the first-person perspective, a turn to the self as a self. That is what I mean by radical reflexivity. Because we are so deeply embedded in it, we cannot but reach for reflexive language."[175] It is this that Taylor sees as one of the "fundamental themes" of modern culture.[176] Could it be that Beckett's trilogy shows us aspects of human nature writ large? Is it possible that such radical reflexivity, points us eventually towards the world of Beckett's narrators? "I'm not outside, I'm inside, I'm in something, I'm shut up . . ."[177] If this is so, then it would seem that psychological health is inextricably linked to connection with the "other." As Walter Brueggemann points out, "This 'other' is endlessly inscrutable mystery and endlessly problematic to us, for we can neither escape from that other, nor are we able to seduce, capture, or possess that other who always stands free from and over against us."[178] But this "principle of alterity," as Brueggemann calls it, seems to be essential to our well-being. And to the question of the "other" we now turn. Is it sufficient to engage only with human others, or is a divine Other—or God—integral to our sense of selfhood? And, in particular, what does Beckett make of the divine Other, and does this appear to have any impact upon his sense of self?

174. C. Taylor, "Inwardness and the Culture of Modernity," 88–110. Taylor sees Augustine's inward turn as tremendously influential in the West, although here he speaks most specifically of the secularised inner turn, where there is no givenness to the self.

175. Ibid., 103.

176. Ibid., 106.

177. Beckett, *Three Novels*, 410.

178. Brueggemann, "'Othering' with Grace and Courage," 1. The Old Testament scholar outlines how the Object Relations Theory is particularly congenial to scriptural notions of alterity, or what he calls, the demanding reality of covenant, in that "othering" must begin here. The Old Testament, he argues, affirms this concept.

CHAPTER 2

God, Fomenter of Calm

Beckett—Theology

My master then, assuming he is solitary, in my image, wishes me well, poor devil, wishes my good, and if he does not seem to do very much in order not to be disappointed it is because there is not very much to be done or, better still, because there is nothing to be done, otherwise he would have done it, long ago, poor devil ... No, we have no conversation, never a mum of his mouth to me. He's out of luck, that's certain, perhaps he didn't choose me. What he means by good, my good, is another problem. He is capable of wanting me to be happy, such a thing has been known, it appears. Or to serve a purpose. Or the two at once! A little more explicitness on his part, since the initiative belongs to him, might be a help, as well from his point of view as from the one he attributes to me. Let the man explain himself and have done with it. It's none of my business to ask him questions, even if I knew how to reach him. Let him inform me once and for all what exactly it is he wants from me, for me ... If he wants me to say something, for my good naturally, he has only to tell me what it is and I'll let it out with a roar straightaway. It's true he may have already told me a hundred times. Well, let him make it a hundred and one, this time I'll try and pay attention. But perhaps I malign him unjustly, my good master, perhaps he is not solitary like me, not free like me, but associated with others, equally good, equally concerned with my welfare, but differing as to its nature.[1]

The Unnamable

---

1. Beckett, *Three Novels*, 312–13.

The Specter of the Divine: Beckett's Idea of God

Joseph Long has pointed out that certain texts by Beckett are haunted by other voices: "they speak of fall and redemption, of hope and despair."[2] The same could be said of the trilogy. Predominantly, Long says, the texts are "theological space"; concerned with the writing of an absence. I want to argue that this very absence is intimately tied in with the absent self that we have just explored. As with self, so with God. In this chapter we shall look at Beckett's idea of God—or his "theology"—and how this connects with his idea of humanity, or his anthropology, and how this in turn connects with his sense of the self.

Various critics have perceived Beckett's idea of God as being consistent with a wide range of beliefs or attitudes, from orthodox Christianity to Manichean dualism, from Zen Buddhism to Jungianism and nihilism, even blasphemy.[3] Elements of each can be found in his work—to greater or lesser degrees—as we shall see. It is another facet of the "no stone unturned" approach of Beckett. As Paul Davies has put it, with regard to Beckett's search for the self, "The question, as Beckett saw, is not the province of the psychologist alone. Perhaps Jung also appealed to Beckett precisely because he refused to exclude the arts, music, religion, alchemy, cosmology, and myth from his investigations of human identity, and indeed increasingly saw that the greatest need of our time was to give those things a central place in psychological work . . ."[4] As numerous critics have suggested, Beckett's concerns and questions have an essentially religious dimension. Laura Barge says, ". . . it is not surprising that critics interested in the religious aspects of Beckett's writings agree that there is something important about the sacred, about God, being said . . . Beyond this initial consensus, however, little agreement is reached concerning exactly what is being said. Instead, uncertainty, perplexity, and diversity of opinion lead to questions for which any possible answer resonates with contradiction—an echo of the yes/no dialectic that so consistently orders the structures of Beckett's rhetoric and content."[5]

With this in mind, what is there that we can say about Beckett's idea of God as seen in *Three Novels*? Does he attempt to fill the "space" to

---

2. Long, "Divine Intertextuality," 156.

3. Whilst many critics have made this one element of their study of Beckett, certain critics have focused on this aspect. Of these, two are particularly valuable: Mary Bryden's study is extremely thorough, and the work of Laura Barge consistently points towards the gap between Beckett's metaphysics and what she calls "Christian thought".

4. Davies, *Ideal Real*, 20.

5. Barge, "Beckett's Metaphysics and Christian Thought," 34.

which Long refers? The opening passage seems to demonstrate, in many ways, something of the complexity of Beckett's attitude towards a divine being. Not abstract but not personal either, the master, (a character never formally introduced to us) is a solitary enigma, who may—or may not—have the narrator's good at heart. Only partially potent (for he did not choose the narrator) yet powerful enough to attribute points of views; decidedly poor at communication, although the narrator may, in fact, just not have been listening. Solitary, in all likelihood, although if in contact with others perhaps not functioning in harmony with them. The passage reverberates with a felt disappointment in this being, the master. "God, fomenter of calm. I never believed, not a second," the narrator of *The Unnamable* says.[6]

It is hardly surprising that some see Beckett as an atheist. The problem may well lie in the difficulty of the task; Beckett's inherent opposition to the spirit of "system" compounds his contradictions and negations, and his allusive, even cryptic, manner, results in a rather complex meshing of statements. But is it accurate to say that Beckett is totally opposed to the idea of God? Does he reject this idea and then move on, to an alternative, or beyond? John Pilling denies the possibility of attributing to Beckett any simple atheism; he "continued to be obsessed, personally, by the fundamentally religious questions concerning the existence of God, His justice and mercy, and the afterlife."[7] Mary Bryden, in her very thorough consideration of the subject, posits that it is not possible to conclude Beckett's own religious positioning or non-positioning, but that it is fair to say that the idea of a Godhead, "clings like bindweed . . . He is by turns dismissed, satirized, or ignored, but he, and his tortured son, are never definitively discarded."[8] It was, as this citation implies, primarily the God of Christianity with whom Beckett took issue, for, as he himself said, it was the "mythology with which I am perfectly familiar."[9] He went on to say, "And so I use it."

Is it then simply a matter of utility? Mary Bryden comments that "Beckett often accesses scriptural or devotional literature purely for its evocative power, its pithiness, or its phonetic appeal, and this must be borne in mind when considering his use of scriptural material."[10] But that is not to say that Beckett's theological ponderings are solely functional or

6. Beckett, *Three Novels*, 105.
7. Pilling, *Samuel Beckett*, 117.
8. Bryden, *Samuel Beckett and the Idea of God*, 1–2.
9. Duckworth, *Angels of Darkness*, 18.
10. Bryden, *Samuel Beckett and the Idea of God*, 34.

grist for his artistic mill. References to some sort of divine figure are too pervasive in Beckett's oeuvre, and the tone too perplexed to allow for such dismissal. Bryden points us towards Beckett's reply to Charles Juliet, upon his query in 1977, as to whether or not he had been able to rid himself of the influence of religion, "in my external behaviour, no doubt . . . but as for the rest . . ."[11]

Others see Beckett as revisioning the traditional deity of Christianity. Spyridoula Athanasopoulou-Kypriou is one such, arguing that a demarcation is to be found between those critics who perceive Beckett as adhering to a metaphysical quest, and those who "realize that Beckett is haunted by metaphysics because people are haunted by it."[12] He perceives Beckett as seeking to liberate people; his abiding concern is with "people's metaphysical anguish and emptiness after God and traditional metaphysics have lost their effectiveness." But to state this is to blur certain distinctions that need to be made; whilst it may be fair to say that Beckett perceived people as being haunted by metaphysics (most clearly evidenced in *Waiting for Godot*, for example), is it accurate to state that Beckett's intention was to liberate? Can that be seen, for example, in the opening passage of this chapter? Is it a passage that would liberate those who are haunted by a specter of a God, or is it symptomatic of one who is still haunted? "If he wants me to say something, for my good naturally, he has only to tell me what it is and I'll let it out with a roar straightaway." John Pilling has called Beckett "God-haunted."[13] Colin Duckworth puts it equally unequivocally; "intellectually, he rejects him, but psychologically he needs him." He goes on to say, "Beckett inadvertently, repeatedly, variously and unforgettably, represents to us the spiritual ambivalence that characterizes modern post-Christian society."[14]

But who is the God who haunts Beckett? The deity of *Three Novels* is a fickle deity, one who dictates the human destiny, albeit with dubious motivation, whilst remaining incommunicative, despite promises to the contrary. The images used to convey him tend to be controlling models; the master, the employer. His "delegates"—"low types," "their pockets full of poison and antidote"—give the narrator of *The Unnamable* "the low-down on God." "They told me I depended on him, in the last analysis. They had it on the reliable authority of his agents at Bally I forget what, this being the place, according to them, where the inestimable gift

11. Ibid., 1. Originally in Juliet, *Rencontre avec Samuel Beckett*, 50.
12. Athanasopoulou-Kypriou, "Samuel Beckett Beyond the Problem of God," 34–51.
13. Pilling, *Samuel Beckett*, 1.
14. Duckworth, "Beckett and the Missing Sharer," 141.

of life had been rammed down my gullet."[15] His arbitrary ways are to be considered "grace" by believers. Humans are pawns; the deity is the oppressor; life is unwelcome, a burden to be endured, like a pensum given at birth. Even the devotees are unable to explain him. Gaber says that his employer "doesn't know what he says . . . Nor what he does."[16] Perhaps that is why he does not communicate to those—like the narrator of *The Unnamable*—who wait and wonder. "I have spoken for my master, listened for the words of my master, never spoken, Well done, my child, well done, my son, you may stop, you may go, you are free, you are acquitted, you are pardoned, never spoken."[17] The God that Beckett portrays has something akin to personal qualities, but there is no sense of presence, or engagement between God and Beckett's characters. Ultimately, as Bryden puts it, for Beckett's narrators, God does not sufficiently exert himself.[18]

For these reasons perhaps, Beckett's characters often veer towards outright hostility towards such a God. Moran, in particular, chooses to reject this divinity. He states his desired independence from his employer; "All is tedious, in this relation that is forced upon me. But I shall conduct it my own way, up to a point. And if it has not the good fortune to give satisfaction, to my employer, if there are passages that give offence to him and to his colleagues, then so much the worse for us all, for them all, for there is no worse for me."[19] It is a bleak choice. "There are men and there are things, to hell with animals. And with God."[20] Amongst his theological questions, he wonders, "Might not the beatific vision become a source of all boredom, in the long run?"[21] God is, in effect, rejected as demanding yet simultaneously is not a source of stimulation; forceful but insensitive; capable but inactive.[22] Yet this rejection it is not without trepidation, "And this with hatred in my heart, and scorn, of my master and his designs"; later, he comments (with reference, as I take it, to those preceding paragraphs), "And in writing these lines I know in what danger I am of offending him whose favor I know I should court, now more

15. Beckett, *Three Novels*, 298.
16. Ibid., 94–95.
17. Ibid., 310.
18. Bryden, *Samuel Beckett and the Idea of God*, 130.
19. Beckett, *Three Novels*, 131.
20. Ibid., 165.
21. Ibid., 167.

22. Lance St John Butler comments that Beckett's later texts (1960's or so) tend to be less blasphemous and scatological but the ambivalence towards God continues throughout. *Samuel Beckett and the Meaning of Being*.

than ever. But I write them all the same, and with a firm hand weaving inexorably back and forth and devouring my page with the indifference of a shuttle."[23] Moran's defiant stance, although decidedly the most hostile of the narrators in the trilogy, is echoed elsewhere. Malone comments, "For obscure reasons known who knows to God alone, though to tell the truth God does not seem to need reasons for doing what he does, and for omitting to do what he omits to do, to the same degree as his creatures, does he?"[24]

The idea of a Son of God is equally difficult for Beckett to accept. A few brief references in *Malone Dies* convey something of the timbre of this. MacMann implies that one Christ "was more than sufficient" when faced with Moll's two crucifix earrings (not to mention her tooth, also carved to represent "the celebrated sacrifice").[25] Malone cannot still the sound of the song that was "to the honor and glory of him who was the first to rise from the dead, to him who saved me, twenty centuries in advance. Did I say the first? The final bawl lends color to this view."[26] As Pilling points out, Beckett's Christ is "a singularly unattractive figure in many ways."[27] He goes on to say, "Jehovah in fact becomes preferable to Christ, not simply because of the quality of his jokes . . . but because he is a more comprehensive figure, cruel and worldly as well as mystically remote . . . Certainly, from Beckett's point of view, it seems true to say that Christ's Love is resistible almost because of its greater flexibility, whereas Jehovah's Law must be either accepted or rejected wholesale."

In fact, Christ's role in Beckett's universe is very uncertain. As Barge points out, he has no salvific function:

> Possessing no divinity, he epitomises all men as he experiences the cruel betrayal of the Father/God who abandons him—in his innocence and goodness—to the cross and eternal death. Unlike many other twentieth-century writers, however, Beckett and his protagonists seem to entertain no delusions concerning the inadequacy, or even impotence, of such a Christ figure. They apparently understand that a merely human Christ can function as a scapegoat, but not as a savior, a deliverer offering redemption.[28]

23. Beckett, *Three Novels*, 132–33.
24. Ibid., 245.
25. Ibid., 263–64.
26. Ibid., 208.
27. Pilling, *Samuel Beckett*, 120.
28. Barge, "Beckett's Metaphysics and Christian Thought," 20, 1, 42–43.

It is, as Bryden notes, a Christ who functions only in kenotic mode, emptied and made destitute.[29] The efficacy of the death of Christ is significantly absent, although the crucifixion itself is a frequent image in Beckett's work, as Mary Bryden so thoroughly delineates in her introduction to *Samuel Beckett and the Idea of God*. She notes in particular that many of those references to Christ are in a significantly trauma-free context. But, she continues,

> . . . if Beckett's visual and textual treatment of crucifixion can seem casual and even dismissive, the sheer weight of crucifixion references to be found in his writing seems to demonstrate the iconic power they maintain in his consciousness . . . the lingering over other elements of the crucifixion in his fictional writing seems to indicate a more long-lasting preoccupation with the spectacle than a simple image-flare.[30]

Perhaps, ultimately, it is as the supreme embodiment of suffering, that subject so central to his thought, that the crucifixion captures the imagination of Beckett. It exemplifies the arbitrary dealings of God with humankind, rather than carrying any significance, literally or symbolically, of a more profound spiritual purpose. One critic who has attempted to perceive greater significance in Beckett's treatment of Christ is Jane Walling, who has tentatively suggested that Beckett's characters are confronted, by means of the Crucifixion, with the necessity of the development of a self-conscious self: that Beckett is responding, on some level, to an esoteric Christian archetype, and that there is a sense in which the death of Christ leads to a self-realization.[31] For her, it is a question of activating one's own inner Logos; "The self may come to realize that its reality resides *not* in the various self-images and narratives which it strives to produce and project but precisely in the *process or activity* of production, and it is this activity which represents the kindling of the divine spark or the activating of the inner Logos. In other words, Beckett's characters may not be able to say 'I am' with the conviction of Christ but they may be able to experience the individual activity of their own 'I am.'"[32] Walling speaks also of a contrast which is central in Beckett's work, "between, on the one hand, the experience of loss, absence and isolation and, on the other, experience of a qualitatively different nature" which she speaks

---

29. Bryden, *Samuel Beckett and the Idea of God*, 140.
30. Ibid., 144–45.
31. Walling, "'Dim Whence Unknown,'" 105–18.
32. Ibid., 115.

of as a "post-Crucifixion" vitality and inventiveness. The connection she draws between the death of Christ and the activation of the inner Logos may be theologically interesting but questions must be asked about her basis for speaking of a post-Crucifixion vitality in Beckett's work. There is no reference to the resurrection; the emphasis is all upon Good Friday, or, as Jacobsen and Mueller point out, bewildering Holy Saturday, when the only option was to wait, enduring without answers.[33] Granted, there are moments of intense beauty, particularly in *Malone Dies,* but their elegaic quality could not be confused with vitality, and they usually dissolve into despair. As Malone says, "For even as I said, How easy and beautiful it all is! in the same breath I said, All will grow dark again."[34] The most consistent note in Beckett's work is the pained cry of the wronged.

Beckett's view of humanity is profoundly connected to his perception of God; this negligent God pays no attention to the human plight. Beckett's outlook is dominated by this extreme sensitivity to pain and suffering. Much has been said about his bleak vision, his "negativism that knows no haven."[35] He has been applauded for his honesty, his dogged refusal to allow for any substitute vision, any panacea that will deflect from looking at the mess. Jacobsen and Mueller have commented that, "The pleasure of reading Beckett, in even his grimmest moments, is the pleasure in fidelity of an artist to his truth."[36] Beckett's truth is certainly grim. Character after character demonstrates the belief that humans are abandoned to their wounds and their grief, not just unaided by any divine potentate, but apparently the objects of sport: "The essential is to go on squirming forever at the end of the line, as long as there are waters and banks and ravening in heaven a sporting God to plague his creature . . . Nothing to do but stretch out comfortably on the rack in the blissful knowledge you are nobody for all eternity."[37] Judged and punished for crimes as yet unknown, apparently guilty only of having been born. This idea of the Spanish playwright, Pedro Calderón de la Barca (probably accessed by Beckett through the work of Arthur Schopenhauer) is to be found in *Proust*:

---

33. Jacobsen and Mueller, *Testament of Samuel Beckett*, Appendix, "To Wait or Not to Wait: The Enduring Saturday of Samuel Beckett."

34. Beckett, *Three Novels*, 224.

35. Karl Ragnar Gierow, secretary of the Swedish Academy, when awarding Beckett the 1969 Nobel Prize in Literature.

36. Jacobsen and Mueller, *Testament of Samuel Beckett*, 31.

37. Beckett, *Three Novels*, 338.

> Pues el delito mayor
> Del hombre es haber nacido.³⁸

"For the greatest crime of man is that he was born." Equally, procreation, and even consenting to live are crimes. As Malone reflects, "And no doubt he would have wondered if it was really necessary to be guilty in order to be punished but for the memory, more and more galling, of his having consented to live in his mother, then to leave her. And this again he could not see as his true sin, but as yet another atonement which had miscarried and, far from cleansing him of his sin, plunged him in it deeper than before."³⁹ In *The Unnamable*, the very compulsion to speak, to tell, is a pensum for having been born.⁴⁰

Critics have tried to attribute this to the influence of various strands of Christianity. Anthony Cronin postulates that Beckett's Low Church Irish Protestantism so near to Calvinism has something to do with this strong sense that being is an offense—although he does not substantiate his reasons for this.⁴¹ Martha Nussbaum traces Beckett's people's excremental vision directly to their "Christian world." "We want not only to say that these people feel guilt at original sin; we want to say also that it is guilt at a parental sexual act that is seen as immersing the mother in excrement and causing the birth of the child through excrement."⁴² But Beckett's perception of sin is hardly resonant with Christianity, *especially* Augustine's—he who so often gets blamed for such an excremental vision.⁴³ Beckett is much closer to a dualistic way of thinking. His narrators refer to their bodies in detached, even disgusted ways. Malone refers to

---

38. Beckett, *Proust*, 67.
39. Beckett, *Three Novels*, 239–40.
40. Ibid., 310.
41. Cronin, *Samuel Beckett: The Last Modernist*, 376.
42. Nussbaum, *Love's Knowledge*, 298.

43. It is the willed refusal of trust, the denial of grace, which ultimately became central to Augustine's concept of sin. Robert Markus has pointed out that Augustine's re-reading of Paul in the mid-390's led him away from his belief in human self-determination towards the beginning of this theology of grace that he would deploy against Pelagius. In his fifties, Markus argues, Augustine shifted from his more hierarchical understanding of sin as a breach of the order inscribed into the universe by God, towards a different emphasis: "The aim of the whole discussion of sin and pride in Book XIV of the *City of God* is to shift the stress from sin as the result of the soul's entanglement in the flesh to sin as the result of the will's own decision. Augustine registers the shift by the strenuous effort he makes to establish that the biblical category of the 'flesh' is not sensual indulgence, not a case in other words, of the superior allowing itself to be seduced by the inferior, but a fault within the mind itself. Sin is a matter of pride rather than sensuality." Markus, *Conversion and Disenchantment in Augustine's Spiritual Career*, 32.

his aging body as "impotent" in its uselessness; later, he refers to his feet as "leagues away."[44] There is a radical separation between the mind and the body, often referred to by critics as his Cartesian dualism. But this dualism is, as Alice and Kenneth Hamilton (amongst others, such as John Pilling), have pointed out so thoroughly, a form of Gnosticism, specifically, Manicheaism.[45] To this we shall return.

Innocent humanity, therefore, is trapped in the mess hoping desperately to be perceived and acknowledged; "some kind of assurance that I was really there, such as a kick in the arse, for example, or a kiss, the nature of the attention is of little importance."[46] Here, as we have seen, ontological insecurity may be contributing towards the Beckettian perspective, an intensification of the basic human desire to be recognized. A sense of invisibility is starkly conveyed by the way in which Beckett's locations in the *Three Novels* become less and less available for perception, and more and more hidden in room, womb or tomb. Significance is not bestowed through relationships with other humans either. As Jacobsen and Mueller put it, "the dominant tone in Beckett is loneliness, the haunting sense that persons can never really come together, never really know each other . . . a man's soul, try as it will, cannot quite make the ecstatic leap into the soul of another."[47] Fathers are violent towards their offspring; men are uncertain of the meaning of love; glimpses of unexpected tenderness are occasional but rare. And yet, somehow, ultimately they are yoked together, unable to exist in splendid isolation.

His Voice is There, in Mine, But Less, Less: Beckett's Influences

From what source, or sources, did Beckett derive his image of, and therefore (in some sense, at least) attitude towards, the divine and the human? Despite the difficulty that would be involved in answering those questions definitively, they require to be addressed, however tentatively. For Beckett's idea of God must have some external derivations, insofar as any idea of God is the product of various influences—and choices too—whether conscious or unconscious. What external influences informed

---

44. Beckett, *Three Novels*, 186.
45. Hamilton, *Condemned to Life*, and Pilling, *Samuel Beckett*.
46. Beckett, *Three Novels*, 342.
47. Jacobsen and Mueller, *Testament of Samuel Beckett*, 122–24.

Beckett's sense of this deity, and what led to his lambasting the divine for both 'perverse absence' and "surveillant presence" (as Bryden puts it)?[48]

Dirty Low Church Protestant?: Beckett's Childhood Influences

The particular version of the "mythology" with which Beckett was so perfectly familiar, the Protestantism of Ireland, was a heritage that held little appeal for him, although that does not negate the possibility of its impact upon him. Rodney Sharkey, in writing of Beckett's Irishness in relation to his search for identity, comments that,

> . . . the implied notion that Protestant/Huguenot is a superior code to the Catholic/Gaelige model was riddled with contradiction for the young Beckett. The contradictory cold austerity and yet clinical nature of the "savage loving," combined with pressure to conform to Protestant ethics such as lineage, involvement in the family business (with its encumbent social properties) forced him away from this potential identity.[49]

Despite the probable truth that is articulated in this statement, I am inclined to agree with Martin Esslin, who argues that questions of national identity are "far from providing a complete explanation for the deep existential anguish that is the keynote of Beckett's work."[50] Likewise, it would seem too dogmatic to argue, as Sinead Mooney (and Declan Kiberd) have argued, that Beckett's "seemingly endless repetitions of the same non-narrative in ever-decreasing hope of some eventual expiation" can be traced *primarily* to the Protestant uncertainty of being shriven.[51]

---

48. Bryden, *Samuel Beckett and the Idea of God*, 2.
49. Sharkey, "Irish? Au Contraire!," 1–2.
50. Esslin, "Samuel Beckett: The Search for the Self," 29–30.
51. Mooney, "'Integrity in a Surplice': Samuel Beckett's (Post-)Protestant Poetics," 223–37. Various other critics have commented on the impact that Protestantism had on the *form* of Beckett's work. For example, it is the Protestant "issueless confrontation with conscience" and the Protestant emphasis on personal testimony that Hugh Kenner perceives as contributing so strongly to Beckett's monologues. "When the Reformers abandoned the sacramental universe . . . and when Faith, not Works, and Faith moreover attested to by an experience, became the note of salvation, then the literature of Reformed Christianity became narrative, confessional, and embroiled in the retracing of conscience, or else with testimony to the all-important Experience. These are by no means exclusively Protestant categories, but we may still usefully say that Beckett's visions of endlessness—the men who wait and wait, the minds that re-enact and re-enact, the people locked by memories of choices once taken, powerless unless some power choose to act upon them—correspond to a habit of mind that since the seventeenth century has received a specific religious shaping, so that Beckett's Protestant upbringing is perceptible in the midst of the

Is it fair to attribute Beckett's entropy specifically to the absence of human absolution? And can this be applied to all who live without such absolution? What would appear to be much more likely is that Beckett's paralysis stems from his particular temperament and experiences, exacerbated, perhaps, by the notion of God which he absorbed in his youth, and ultimately leading to his desire to disengage from such.

Of Beckett's childhood ecclesial experience, we know that he attended Tullow Church with his mother; his father preferred walking in the mountains, as Beckett told Knowlson.[52] We have no positive records of Beckett's own church experience. It is worth noting that the narrator of *The Unnamable* mentions two hymns: "Safe in the Arms of Jesus" and "Jesu lover of my soul, let me to thy bosom fly." The tone is skeptical, and it is more than plausible that in his youth Beckett very deliberately rejected the sentimentalized images and what he may have perceived as false security. Safety in the "arms of Jesus," "on his gentle breast" were concepts entirely foreign to Beckett's psyche.[53] There was no attraction for him in taking shelter under "the shadow of Thy wing."[54] It may be, however, that certain other crucial elements of Beckett's oeuvre reflect his Protestant background. For instance, and perhaps most significantly, Sinead Mooney, in aligning his Protestantism with Puritanism, argues that Beckett's inner turn was a puritan probing, an examination of conscience. She speaks of his advocating "distinctively Protestant poetics, pushing for a poetry of self-perception."[55] For Beckett, certainly, self-knowledge is a primary function of art, (as evidenced by his castigation of the poets of the Celtic Revival for their "flight from self-awareness"), just as for the

---

agnosticism into which he passed without, he says, any crisis" (Kenner, *Reader's Guide to Samuel Beckett*, 134). Be that as it may—and who is to say definitively that Protestantism has not fed into these aspects of Beckett?—neither Kenner, nor Junker, nor Bryden, nor any critic whom I have read, has tried to ascertain the nature of the influence of Beckett's Protestant background upon his image of God.

52. Knowlson, *Damned to Fame*, 24.
53. The first verse of "Safe in the arms of Jesus" is as follows:
    "Safe in the arms of Jesus,
    Safe on his gentle breast,
    There by his love o'ershadowed,
    Sweetly my soul shall rest."
54. "Jesu, Lover of my soul" speaks of God as a refuge in the storms of life:
    "All my trust on Thee is stay'd,
    All my help from Thee I bring;
    Cover my defenceless head
    With the shadow of Thy wing."
55. Mooney, *Beckett and Religion*, 228.

Puritans, not art *per se*, but the writing of journals and diaries for self-knowledge was a highly intentional act, usually autodidactic in intention, with the ultimate aim of the mending of faults. As Owen Watkins puts it, "One characteristic of the Puritan approach to these problems was the way in which a personal identity was formulated primarily through its relationship with God . . . Only when it began to know its alienation from God did the soul begin to know itself. And it was through the long experience of change from alienation to reconciliation that a true self-image could be built up step by step."[56] In many instances there are records by individual Puritans of long periods of distressed spiritual struggle, as they grappled with possible reprobacy, recorded when the writer was unable to find solace or assurance apart from sustained meditation upon scripture. Interestingly, a collection of testimonies assembled in Dublin in 1653 has reference to solace from such doubts as being in the form of visions, dreams and interior voices.[57] Beckett's desolation, however, lies in the absence of available solace, no less than in the lack of certainty that any such redemption is possible—unlike the Puritans, who were more concerned about their own inadequacy, rather than that of God. That God and self are linked proved to be ultimately more nebulous for Beckett than for the seventeenth century Puritan.

Beckett's inclination was perhaps even closer to a kind of Quaker spirituality, with its rejection of the outer formalities of religion, the downplaying of the rational and the embracing of the inward turn and the subjective.[58] For Beckett, as for the Quakers, personal experience was the final authority, rather than the scripture that the Puritans relied upon. He claimed that his mother brought him up to be "almost a Quaker"—and indeed, Knowlson comments that there was a "Quaker background" on Beckett's mother's side of the family.[59] It is interesting to note how many similarities and dissimilarities could be found in Beckett's work and the following description of Quaker journals:

---

56. Watkins, *Puritan Experience*, 227.

57. Ibid., 42.

58. Owen Chadwick points out that George Fox's cast of mind would seem to have been remarkably similar to medieval mystics such as Johannes Tauler and the author of the *Cloud of Unknowing* and especially the early radical Protestant mystics such as Jakob Boehme—all mystics who resonate with Beckett, according to critics such as Buning, Esslin and Pilling. Chadwick, *Reformation*, 242.

59. Knowlson, *Damned to Fame*, 3. That he was brought up 'almost a Quaker' is cited by Richard Coe, in *Beckett*, 9.

> The unique contribution which the Quakers made to the Puritan autobiographical tradition was the expression of a powerful mystical experience which was associated with a passionate concern for purity of heart . . . They wrote because they felt they had to, and this guaranteed freedom from one kind of dullness, although too often it led in the first place to an intolerable profusion of extravagant language; but the fact that they were striving to express a first-hand experience that was essentially worth communicating sometimes caused them to triumph over sectarian jargon, over-worked images, and an all but fatal disorderliness of sentence structure.[60]

However, Deirdre Bair suggests that May Beckett's religious rigidity was "governed by the rote performance of ritual observance and not by any true belief. This dichotomy between practice and belief bothered the constantly curious Sam from his earliest memories of religious practice."[61] In fact, May Beckett attended a Moravian Mission school in Ballymena, thus introducing another yet strand of Protestantism, pietism. It may be that Beckett picked up from her his asceticism, as evidenced in *Proust* and demonstrated throughout *Three Novels*, even if he rejected her emphasis upon orthopraxy.[62] It is, however, almost impossible to speculate whether or not his desire for immediate communing with God was influenced by a pietistic strain that, as Max Weber points out, valued this over and above future salvation.[63]

Undoubtedly, regular childhood exposure to scriptural passages, through church and personal reading, was formative of Beckett's linguistic *metiér*. As he told Charles Juliet, "the Protestants are very fond of the Old Testament" and, whatever the validity of this, it is unequivocal that his concept of God is dominated by judgment rather than mercy.[64] Ambivalence, as always, is tangible in his utilization of Biblical material and language; certain passages contain imitations, sometimes parodic, of biblical accounts, whilst others contain wistful echoes of scriptural ideas. Thus, to give just one example of the latter, in *The Unnamable*, the narrator refers to Obidil, "whom I so longed to see face to face, all I can say with regard to him is this, that I never saw him, either face to face or

---

60. Watkins, *Puritan Experience*, 204. Perhaps it is not just in the content of his work that Beckett could be described as Quaker—his "all but fatal disorderliness" may stem from this trait in his genes.

61. Bair, *Samuel Beckett*, 18.

62. Knowlson, *Damned to Fame*, 5.

63. Weber, *Protestant Ethic and the Spirit of Capitalism*, 138.

64. Juliet, *Conversations with Samuel Beckett and Bram Van Velde*, 167.

darkly, perhaps there is no such person, that would not greatly surprise me."[65] The allusion is a biblical one: "For now we see through a glass, darkly; but then face to face" (1 Cor 13:12) and variations of this are to be found in *Dream of Fair to Middling Women* and elsewhere. It was an image that seemed to hold particular resonance for Beckett.[66] On the other hand, the account of Moran and his son in *Molloy* has verbal parallels with the Biblical account of Abraham and Isaac, but without conveying the spiritual import that is to be found in the original. We have the father, the son, the journey, the knife, but we have no intervening God, who acts in response to human faith, as we do in the biblical record. Mary Bryden sums up part of the ambiguity: "If Beckett uses both the Old and the New Testaments extensively within his own early writing, it is usually not to enshrine or venerate them, but rather to wring ironic or deviant readings out of them. This is not to say that he consistently undermines or parodies them, for Beckett is too alive to the strength and poetry of many elements within that complex of literatures which constitute the Bible to target them simplistically or homogenously."[67] But the strength and poetry of the scriptures remains at the level of the poetic—for Beckett, scripture carries no salvific facility. For him, ultimately, there was little efficacy in the Protestant beliefs of those around him. As he told Tom Driver; "My brother and mother got no value from their religion when they died. At the moment of crisis it had no more depth than an old school tie . . . Irish Catholicism is not attractive, but it is deeper."[68] Divine presence and intervention were of crucial importance for Beckett if he were to believe, and this proved elusive. In *Molloy*, for example, Moran is concerned with the effectiveness of the Eucharist, which he has taken after drinking beer:

> The host, it is only fair to say, was lying heavy on my stomach. And as I made my way home I felt like one who, having swallowed a painkiller, is first astonished, then indignant, on obtaining no relief.[69]

65. Beckett, *Three Novels*, 162. The biblical echoes here are surely as strong as—if not stronger than—the potential Freudian echoes of Obidil/libido, to which so many critics have made reference.

66. And for Lewis too, as we shall see.

67. Bryden, *Samuel Beckett and the Idea of God*, 35. This, however, is a far cry from the argument of Sinead Mooney who wishes to argue the Beckett's "spectrally suggestive nakedness of style is also bedded, as has been frequently observed, in the sonorous plainness of the King James Bible." (Mooney, "Integrity in a Surplice," 232)

68. Tom Driver, "Columbia University Forum," Summer 1961, 220.

69. Beckett, *Three Novels*, 102.

The palliative does not function as expected; there is no "relief" to be discerned. It does not matter that Moran does not specify what alteration would have been welcome; what is crucial is the perception of the lack of efficacy of the Eucharist. Here, as so often, Beckett worries away at the non-intervention of a God who is perceived as competent to intervene. Mary Junker comments that (alongside Beckett's cherishing of the Protestant conscience, and his scorning of the Protestant work ethic) familiarity with Biblical texts colors his sense of God; but it is a God who remains markedly absent. She cites Richard Kearney, "The God of the Bible is, for Beckett, a God of paradox and apocalypse, a *Deus Absconditus* who sends mysterious messengers, perhaps even his son, but never comes Himself."[70]

Beckett's exposure to suffering had a significant part to play in the development of his ideas about God. Deaths from tuberculosis in his family impacted him as a young adult, and later his exposure to war further heightened his sense of human misery. Knowlson states that "it was on the key issue of pain, suffering and death that Beckett's religious faith faltered and quickly foundered," pointing to student days as the time when this happened.[71] And he cites what may have been a significant event, probably told to him by Beckett himself, when Beckett went to hear a certain Canon Dobbs preaching on the subject of pain. "The only thing I tell [my parishioners] is that the crucifixion was only the beginning. You must contribute to the kitty."[72] How can pain make a contribution to anything? Beckett wondered; such thinking seemed to him to be an appalling affront to the suffering of the individual.

A Strait of Two Wills: Differentiation

As a young man, Beckett read, somewhat eclectically, from the writings of numerous theologically strong writers. Mary Bryden deals thoroughly with his allusions to theological concepts in such writers as Augustine, Descartes, and Thomas à Kempis, as well as Julian of Norwich and John of the Cross. Other critics have made more than passing reference to this also. This section, therefore, is intended to look primarily at how those writers may have actually impacted Beckett's view of God, and what implications that may have had.

---

70. Junker, *Beckett: The Irish Dimension*, 22. The Richard Kearney citation comes from *Irish Mind*, 277.

71. Knowlson, *Damned to Fame*, 67.

72. Ibid., 67.

Beckett's familiarity with Augustine's *Confessions* is evident from the *Dream* notebook, wherein he made detailed notes in both English and Latin, at around the same time that he wrote *Dream of Fair to Middling Women*. He told Thomas MacGreevy that he had been phrase-hunting in Augustine's writings and it is evident from the notebook that he had indeed done so with some rigor.[73] For example, Beckett's jottings in his *Dream* notebook, include such phrases as "hesitating to die to death and to live to life."[74] Bryden points out some of the similarities between the two men. A similar sense of struggle between body/flesh and soul/spirit, ("a strait of two wills," as Augustine puts it); a comparable intellectual wrestling with questions of God and humanity; and an inner turn which both took, are amongst the traits which she lists.[75] Each were profoundly driven by the same questions. "Let me know you, for you are the God who knows me, let me recognize you as you have recognized me . . . I wish to act in truth, making my confession both in my heart before you and in this book before the many who will read it," may be the words of Augustine, but the wish for recognition and for self-exploration, the desire to act truthfully, and the awareness of the importance of the affect are common to both men. Both could be said to write *in order* to know themselves. Both seem compelled to make their "confessions."[76] Equally both manifest an awareness of existential restlessness. Both flirted with Manichaeism.

Augustine, like Beckett, had known the dark. As a young man, overwhelmed by grief at the death of a friend, he could perceive only death around him. "I had become a puzzle to myself, asking my soul again and again 'Why are you downcast? Why do you distress me?' But my soul had no answer to give. If I said 'Wait for God's help,' she did not obey. And in this she was right because, to her, the well-loved man whom she had lost was better and more real than the shadowy being in whom I would have her trust."[77] Like Beckett, the youthful Augustine found God to be a "shadowy being."[78] More than that, he called his idea of God a delusion, unable to uphold his burden. "It only fell and weighed me down once more, so that I was still my own unhappy prisoner, unable to live in such a state yet

---

73. Beckett, letter to Thomas MacGreevy (January 25, 1931) *Letters*, Vol. 1, 62.

74. Beckett, *Beckett's Dream Notebook*, entry 156.

75. Bryden, *Samuel Beckett and the Idea of God*, 88–101.

76. James Olney has made some interesting observations on the similarities and dissimilarities between the two in "Memory and the Narrative Imperative: St. Augustine and Samuel Beckett."

77. Augustine *Confessions* 4.4.

78. Ibid., 4.4.

powerless to escape from it. Where could my heart find refuge from itself? Where could I go, yet leave myself behind?"[79] There is much of this desire for "alleviations of the flight from self" in the final pages of the trilogy.[80] Augustine, for a considerable time, retained a Manichean God, utterly transcendent, and uninvolved. It was an answer that had appealed to the young Augustine, for whom God was a "shadowy being" who seemed remote from life and his experiences. Manichaeism, as Peter Brown puts it, "enabled Augustine to be a very austere, 'spiritual' young man, one who had a need to feel lofty."[81] It dispensed with the areas of Christianity which were intellectually particularly problematic; the incarnation of Christ and the presence of God in the physical world; the concept of sin and personal responsibility. It also gave a relatively tidy solution to the issue of suffering which so sorely troubled both men. Augustine speaks of his own anguish while he tried to resolve the issue in some way that was satisfactory to himself; "I was still trying to discover the origin of evil, and I could find no solution to the problem. My ideas were always changing . . . What agony I suffered, o my God! How I cried out in grief, while my heart was in labor!"[82] Like Beckett, Augustine as a young man had wanted to reject a God summed up by Peter Brown as, "a father capable of righteous anger, of inflicting punishment, His unique goodness separated by an unbridgeable gulf from the intimate guilt of His sons."[83]

Temperament may contribute to this perception—the temperament which finds evil morally repugnant. It is a perspective that hinges upon the extreme transcendence of God, lending itself to the pessimistic outlook of life. Evelyn Underhill, with reference to William James' *Varieties of Experience*, puts it this way:

> Such a way of conceiving Reality accords with the type of mind which William James called the "sick soul." It is the mood of the penitent; of the utter humility which, appalled by the sharp contrast between itself and the Perfect, which it contemplates, can only cry, "out of the depths." It comes naturally to the temperament which leans to pessimism, which sees "a great gulf fixed" between itself and its desire, and is above all things sensitive to the elements of evil and imperfection in its own character and in the normal experience of man. Permitting these elements to dominate its field of consciousness, wholly ignoring the divine

79. Ibid., 4.7.
80. Beckett, *Three Novels*, 367.
81. Brown, *Augustine of Hippo*, 50.
82. Augustine *Confessions* 7:7.
83. Brown, *Augustine of Hippo*, 53.

> aspect of the World of Becoming, such a temperament constructs from its perceptions and prejudices the concept of a material world and a normal self which are very far from God.[84]

John Pilling argues convincingly that Beckett consciously and deliberately rejected Augustine over the question of evil. It was, he says, as a consequence of reading Schopenhauer's attack on Augustine's theodicy in *The City of God*. Here Schopenhauer wrote, "If anyone studies the Augustinian theology . . . he experiences something analogous to the feeling of one who tries to make a body stand whose centre of gravity falls outside it; however he may turn it and place it, it always falls over again . . . the contradiction between the goodness of God and the misery of the world . . ."[85] This contradiction resonated with Beckett's own sense of outrage to such an extent that he wrote to MacGreevy in 1930 that Schopenhauer was the greatest attempt at "an intellectual justification of unhappiness."[86] It is a telling phrase. As Charles Taylor puts it, Schopenhauer wanted to "throw off once and for all this terrible burden that Christian civilization has laid on us; to declare reality evil once and for all, and have done with it."[87] *Proust* reverberates with something of the same pessimism, the same sense that the perception of good is outright folly; there Beckett wrote of "the haze of our smug will to live, of our pernicious and incurable optimism."[88]

But Christianity increasingly superceded Augustine's Manichaeism and Neo-Platonism and Christ became more and more crucial to his understanding of both God and the self. In contrast to Beckett's impotent scapegoat, Augustine's Christ is the one who mediates between flesh and Wisdom:

> I began to search for a means of gaining the strength I needed to enjoy you, but I could not find this means until I embraced the mediator between God and men, Jesus Christ, who is a man, like them, and also rules as God over all things, blessed for ever. He was calling to me and saying I am the way; I am truth and life. He it was who united with our flesh that food which I was too weak to take; for the Word was made flesh so that your Wisdom, by which you created all things, might be milk to suckle us in

---

84. Underhill, *Mysticism*, 98–99.

85. Schopenhauer, *World as Will and Idea*, 1:525–26 cited by Pilling, *Samuel Beckett*, 118.

86. Knowlson, *Damned to Fame*, 118.

87. C. Taylor, *Sources of the Self*, 444.

88. Beckett, *Proust*, 15. The phrase "will to live" is Schopenhauer's. The context is the Proustian unceasing modification of the personality over time.

> infancy. For I was not humble enough to conceive of the humble Jesus Christ as my God, nor had I learnt what lesson his human weakness was meant to teach.[89]

Augustine's conclusion—that it takes humility to embrace the humble Jesus Christ—is another pivotal point at which he and Samuel Beckett part company. Christ as God incarnate is an entirely crucial aspect of the Christian concept of God—God who takes the initiative, who reaches out, beyond himself, to become enfeebled before being elevated. For Beckett, the kenosis of Christ is an end in itself. For Augustine, such a self-emptying is only a means to an end. As Augustine puts it in *The City of God*, "Yet man did not fall away to the extent of losing all being; but when he had turned towards himself his being was less real than when he adhered to him who exists in a supreme degree. And so, to abandon God and to exist in oneself, that is to please oneself, is not immediately to lose all being; but it is to come nearer to nothingness."[90] The logical outworking of the choice of the self, is really the loss of the self. "But where was I when I looked for you? You were there before my eyes, but I had deserted even my own self. I could not find myself, much less you."[91] This is something that Lewis will elucidate for us later.

As Bryden notes, "What emerges from Beckett's engagement with Augustine is both a profundity of response and a self-differentiation. Beckett may have admired or been pre-occupied with the *Confessions* but he exploits the work for his own purposes, and clearly demurs from some of the text's 'givens.'"[92] Beckett's conclusions about the nature of God's dealings with humanity differ significantly from Augustine's. And, significantly, Augustine concluded that our desiring nature is a crucial part of creatureliness, whereas Beckett continued always to seek to satiate his desire. Bryden observes that whereas Augustine's struggle culminates in a conforming of his will to that which he perceives to be a divine imperative, Belacqua, in *Dream of Fair to Middling Women*, "cannot." In the end, Knowlson comments, Beckett uses Augustine, not so much because of resonances in their musings, but for rhetorical polish; "He merely uses the quotations to underline the contrasting demands of flesh and spirit and to add levels of philosophical allusion for his own delight and for the pleasure or amusement of the reader."[93]

89. Augustine *Confessions* 7.18.
90. Augustine *City of God* 14.13 (Dyson, 609).
91. Ibid., 5.3.
92. Bryden, *Samuel Beckett and the Idea of God*, 96.
93. Knowlson, *Damned to Fame*, 109.

To and Fro in Shadow: Dante

As Beckett defined his position *contra* Augustine, so too could Beckett be said to set himself in clear contradistinction to Dante, whose *Divine Comedy* is often considered to be the most influential text in the life of Beckett. He read it not just as a young man, but returned to it on repeated occasions throughout his life, concentrating usually on *Inferno* and *Purgatory*. Beckett found *Paradise* "much less compelling reading," as he told Knowlson in 1989.[94] Belacqua, in the short story "Dante and the Lobster" had got stuck on the passage delineating the spots on the moon in the third canto of *Paradise,* a notoriously difficult passage. Bryden comments:

> It is difficult to know whether the deep effect which Dante's *The Divine Comedy* had on Beckett was attributable to its partial echoing of a religious upbringing he had already received, or whether, conversely, Beckett's love of the poem accounts for his frequent advertence to the scenes of expiation and come-uppance which it foregrounds. Perhaps each factor continued to reinforce the other; at any rate, Beckett's rational skepticism, which no doubt obtained with regard to many of the theological concepts expounded in the text, did not provide an obstacle to his emotional and aesthetic response to the poem.[95]

In the *Three Novels*, for example, the most obvious allusion occurs at the beginning of *The Unnamable*. Malone (or possibly Molloy) passes, motionless. The place consists (again, possibly) of pits, set aside for them. Tears stream down the narrator's cheeks, reminiscent of scenes from the *Inferno*. Later, the narrator comments, "From centre to circumference in any case it is a far cry and I may well be situated somewhere between the two. It is equally possible, I do not deny it, that I too am in perpetual motion, accompanied by Malone, as the earth is by its moon."[96] Beckett's imagery has shades of Dante's here, with his references to center and circumference, and his being in perpetual motion, but his reordering of these images often creates the antithetical effect. Bryden comments, ". . . although a similar intensity of physical and mental suffering is perceptible in Beckett's work, the ails which assail human kind are not transactions within a divine economy."[97] In contrast to Dante's carefully ordered

---

94. Ibid., 715 n. 35.
95. Bryden, *Samuel Beckett and the Idea of God*, 149.
96. Beckett, *Three Novels*, 295.
97. Bryden, *Samuel Beckett and the Idea of God*, 149.

cosmos, where sinners are carefully assigned their rightful place (for example, the violent against the self suffer differently from the violent against God, art and nature), Beckett's is not ordered; punishments do not match the "crimes"; there is no sense of a divine justice and there is no prospect of alleviation. Whereas Dante's image of God is of a divinity scrupulously just—almost pettily so, it would seem to an age without such emphasis—Beckett's image of God is a petty, unjust and unscrupulous deity, inexplicable and malicious.

There are many such contrasts. Where *The Divine Comedy* culminates in an attempt to convey paradise through a neologistic extravaganza, a going-beyond of the existing range of vocabulary, *The Unnamable* tells of the desire to do without words altogether—if that will enable some form of self-definition. If Dante envisages a paradise where earthly words are inadequate to describe the deep union of souls with all that heaven holds—and Joan Ferrante lists at least eight Dantean neologisms for this idea—Beckett's text witnesses to his profound wish to be left in peace at last.[98] "It's a lot to expect of one creature, it's a lot to ask, that he should first behave as if he were not, then as if he were, before being admitted to that peace where he neither is, nor is not, and where the language dies that permits of such expressions. Two falsehoods, two trappings, to be borne to the end, before I can be let loose, alone in the unthinkable unspeakable, where I have not ceased to be, where they will not let me be."[99] Beckett's desire to be left in peace, for rest and silence, and self-contemplation, sounds, in effect, more akin to the conditions of Hell in *Inferno*. There Dante's Satan is virtually immobile in a place of isolation and stasis, where the shades are individually entombed in frozen ice (although not in peace). This image is the antithesis of the final stanzas in *Paradise,* wherein "The Love which moves the sun and the other stars" hints at a perichoretic reflection of the triune unity of the Godhead with creation. Heaven is, for Dante, a place of constant, joyful, harmonious movement. As Christopher Ryan points out, *The Divine Comedy* portrays an overall shift from the deep stasis of Hell towards the movement which seems to radiate from the heart of the Trinity: "Constant, light, swift, and above all joyful . . . Dante mounts through the nine heavenly spheres which sweep around ever faster the further they are from the earth and the nearer they are to the Empyrean, God's heavenly dwelling."[100]

---

98. Ferrante, "A poetics of chaos and harmony," 161. The citation from *The Unnamable* is from 334–35.

99 Beckett, *Three Novels*, 334–35.

100. Ryan, "Theology of Dante," 147–48.

Allowing for an element of projection from the differing personalities of the two writers, it remains noteworthy that the final weight of Beckett's work runs contrary to his desire for peace and stillness, both of which elude him throughout. His texts convey a sense of incessant motion, which is bound up with his sense of self. Beckett's "to and fro in shadow" oscillating from impenetrable self to impenetrable unself, surely differs in essence from Dante's vision of heaven as a union of harmonious movement. It is more akin to the purposeless waiting that occurs in the two anterooms to Hell and Purgatory. Bryden has pointed out that Beckett's Belacqua the Indolent—the central character in both *Dream of Fair to Middling Women* and *More Pricks than Kicks*—is in fact constantly on the move. Her comment is noteworthy; "What matters above all to him is to retain his autonomy to *choose* when to move and when to remain stationary."[101] Bryden perceives a likeness between Beckett's characters and the inhabitants of Ante-Purgatory, where "time-filling in an inhospitable space, searching for an indefinable future enlightenment" characterizes them.[102] She argues that it is this that places Beckett's people either in Purgatory, which is in fact a world of imminence, movement and heightened insight, or in Ante-Purgatory, which is still more colored, unstructured, and anticipatory. There is some agreement with Beckett's own comments here. In the early essay, "Dante...Bruno.Vico..Joyce," written when he was twenty-three, Beckett commented (in the context of a comparison between Joyce and Dante), "Hell is the static lifelessness of unrelieved viciousness. Paradise the static lifelessness of unrelieved immaculation. Purgatory a flood of movement and vitality released by the conjunction of these two elements."[103] This purgatorial earth is simply a series of stimulants "to enable the kitten to catch its own tail." Bryden suggests that Beckett locates many of his characters in his dramas in zones akin to Limbo, "where the shades, although not tormented, are left to live in a state of unfulfilled desire."[104] For Dante, desire is characteristic of those who are on pilgrimage; it is the sweet desire that draws them towards God. The desire for the knowledge of God without even eschatological hope of fulfillment is the stuff of Limbo, the eternal state of those who desired knowledge beyond their entitlement. Beckett, however, saw

---

101. Bryden, "No Stars Without Stripes," 547.

102. Ibid., 547.

103. Beckett, "Dante...Bruno.Vico..Joyce," 33.

104. Bryden, *Samuel Beckett and the Idea of God*, 151. But, Bryden acknowledges, "Michael Robinson presents an important caveat in stating that part of the suffering of Beckett's people derives from their uncertainty about their whereabouts in terms of present or potential salvation."

it differently. He told Richard Ellman a comment that Joyce had once made to him: "What runs through the whole of Dante is less the longing for Paradise than the nostalgia for being. Everyone in the poem says 'Io fui'—I was, I was."[105] An eschatalogically oriented desire for God in Dante, becomes in Beckett a desire for a past existence.

There are certain other important aspects of Dante's Purgatory that are entirely missing in Beckett's work. For one of the central thrusts of the second canticle is the emphasis—once again—upon humility, particularly the humility of the intellect. As Virgil points out in Canto III:

> Madness! that reason lodged in human heads
> Should hope to traverse backward and unweave
> The infinite path Three-personed Substance treads.
>
> Content you with the *quia,* sons of Eve:
> For had you power to see the whole truth plain
> No need had been for Mary to conceive;
>
> And you have seen such great souls thirst in vain
> As else had stilled that thirst in quietness
> Which now is given them for eternal pain.[106]

The thirst for knowledge that is ultimately the thirst for knowledge of God, cannot be truly quenched on earth—that way madness lies. Contentment with the *quia,* the fact of God, rather than the "why," is essential. Dante's image of the Proud (*Purgatory,* Canto X), bent under the burden of pride, has some resonances with Beckett's characters:

> Alas, proud Christians, faint with misery,
> So warped of vision in the inward sense
> You trust in your backslidings! Don't you see
>
> That we are worms, whose insignificance
> Lives but to form the angelic butterfly
> That flits to judgement naked of defence.
>
> Why do you let pretension soar so high,
> Being as it were but larvae—grubs that lack
> The finished form that shall be by and by?

Beckett's Worm in *The Unnamable* cannot envisage being other than larva; he has no limbs, no wings to fly, and certainly no sense of a finished

---

105. Knowlson, *Damned to Fame,* 723, footnote 44.
106. Dante Alighieri, *The Divine Comedy II, Purgatory,* Canto X, 89.

form by and by. His desire is for countenance and connection—but both seem elusive:

> Worm, to say he does not know what he is, where he is, what is happening, is to underestimate him. What he does not know is that there is anything to know. His senses tell him nothing, nothing about himself, nothing about the rest, and this distinction is beyond him. Feeling nothing, knowing nothing, he exists nevertheless, but not for himself, for others, others conceive him and say, Worm is, since we conceive him, as if there could be no being but being conceived, if only by the beer. Others. One alone, then others. One alone turned towards the all-impotent, all-nescient, that haunts him, then others . . . The one ignorant of himself and silent, ignorant of his silence and silent, who could not be and gave up trying. Who crouches in their midst who see themselves in him and in their eyes stares his unchanging stare . . . And it's not all. He who seeks his true countenance, let him be of good cheer, he'll find it, convulsed with anguish, the eyes out on stalks. He who longs to have lived, while he was alive, let him be reassured, life will tell him how.[107]

This litany of negations, interspersed with the desire to have truly lived whilst actually alive, would seem to call forth, not just images from *Purgatory*, but Dante's dismal figures in the vestibule of Hell, who run perpetually after a whirling standard, endlessly moving, but goaded to do so by hornets and wasps. Their sin? They "against God rebelled not, nor to Him/Were faithful, but to self alone were true."[108] Their refusal to choose, to remain undecided in life means that they had "never lived." Dante presents them as eternally enduring the consequences of this non-decision. Whatever could be said about Dante's eschatology, this is a remarkably apt image for conveying the interminable restlessness so characteristic of Beckett. Moreover, it highlights the very different emphases on self to which the two writers come. For Dante, the human person is both larva and angelic butterfly—there is, for him, a crucial pupa-like stage, which spans the two. It involves human humility, and divine grace and a willingness to enter deeply into that which cannot be intellectually understood. For Beckett's narrator, human life resembles only a worm-like existence of incessant burrowing and struggling in the muck, somewhere between hell and purgatory.

107. Beckett, *Three Novels*, 346–47.

108. Dante Alighieri, *The Divine Comedy, I, Inferno*, Canto III, 86. Bryden (*Samuel Beckett and the Idea of God*, 150) points out that Beckett was aware of this passage, as evidenced in various texts outside the remit of this study.)

Hope beneath My Feathers: Rejections

Beckett was also familiar with the work of Jeremy Taylor, Bishop of Down and Connor from 1660, a divine whose powerful and passionate imagery had gained him many readers prior to the nineteenth century, when he waned in popularity. Pilling suggests that Beckett read *Holy Living* and *Holy Dying* at least twice; certainly he read them at the time of his father's death in 1933, and possibly again in the mid-30's.[109] Explicit reference to *Holy Dying* is to be found in the early play-fragment *Human Wishes*, based on the life of Samuel Johnson and although outside the remit of this study, it is worth noting that Beckett there seemed primarily interested in Taylor's concentration upon death, much as he preferred *Hell* to *Paradise*. Taylor's stated intention in the Epistle Dedicatory is "I shall entertain you in a Charnel House, and carry your meditations awhile into the chambers of death, where you shall find rooms dressed up with melancholy arts, and fit to converse with your most retired thoughts, which begin with a sigh and proceed in deep consideration, and end in a holy resolution."[110] This could almost be, with the exception of the last phrase, the dedication for the *Three Novels*, with its Charnel House atmosphere and melancholic artistry.[111] Taylor, like Beckett, seemed particularly entranced by the discomfort and transience of this life, and both men demonstrate a determination to make others embrace the same vision; "Here is no place to sit down in, but you must rise as soon as you are set" is paralleled in its moody pessimism by "upon the fairest face is placed one of the worst sinks of the body, the nose."[112] Whether it was primarily such melancholia that interested Beckett, or Taylor's vivid style, (much admired by Coleridge and others), or his erudition with regard to the Classics, we cannot know. His advocation of the spiritual discipline of daily examination of our actions, may also have appealed. Bryden focuses upon the rhetorical impact of Taylor upon *Human Wishes* but his quasi-puritan theology must have impacted, to some extent, Beckett's theological understanding, not least by its life-denying emphasis.[113] Nevertheless, Taylor's was a kind of self-denial that made no allowances for any kind of

---

109. Pilling, *Beckett Before Godot*, 165.

110. J. Taylor, *Holy Dying*, 5.

111. In *Malone Dies* (225), Malone refers to himself as an old fetus, to be born headforemost into the charnel-house.

112. J. Taylor, *Holy Dying*, 41–43.

113. Edmund Gosse does point out that Taylor directed his reader towards an examination of conscience without focus on the laws of terror and punishment, unlike *The Divine Comedy*. Edmund Gosse, *Jeremy Taylor*, 1904).

autonomy, offered no easy consolation, and saw most of human endeavor as "restless in a foolish motion."[114] The world is to be shunned, and the word "self" is most commonly used in the context of purification; "we examine our selves that we may finde out our failings and cure them."[115] The emphasis is upon the failings, and self-knowledge is intended to reveal those more clearly.[116]

In several of these respects, the emphasis of Thomas à Kempis in *The Imitation of Christ* was similar. His emphasis was upon complete self-denial; "Always and at all times, small things as well as in great. I make no exceptions, for I desire to have you wholly divested of self. Otherwise, unless you are wholly stripped of self-will, how can you be mine, or I yours?"[117] We know something of Beckett's response to à Kempis; ultimately he came to recognize it as an unhelpful manual for someone of his temperament. As Bryden puts it: "To modern ears, *The Imitation of Christ* can seem gratingly negative and nominalist. Nevertheless, what has made it such a powerful text for many people—its constant reversal of material and 'worldly' values in favor of spiritual ones—might, on the face of it, seem likely to appeal to Beckett."[118] This was indeed the case. Beckett, in a letter to Thomas MacGreevy in 1935, mentioned three phrases which "seemed to be made for me and which I have never forgotten."[119] The phrases are very telling. All three phrases convey aspirations towards peace and light. "He who knows better how to suffer will hold the greater peace" (Bk 2, ch. 3); "Along the path of peace to the fatherland of everlasting light" (Bk 3, ch. 59). The final phrase is perhaps the most telling of the three; "It is a sign of great purity . . . not to wish for consolation from any creature." It turns up in *Dream of Fair to Middling Women*, when the Alba loses patience with Belacqua, who, interestingly, is in Limbo of the personality, brooding, "too permanently selfish, faithful to himself, trying to be like himself as he fancied himself all the time."[120] Her response to this rejection of consolation is interesting; "The filthy blague! To hell with purity, fake purity, to hell with it and to hell with it."[121] The Alba is articulating what ultimately came to be Beckett's conclu-

114. J. Taylor, *Holy Dying*, 34.
115. Ibid., 66.
116. Ibid., 83.
117. Thomas à Kempis, *Imitation of Christ*, 143.
118. Bryden, *Samuel Beckett and the Idea of God*, 34.
119. Beckett, letter to Thomas McGreevy, March 10, 1935, *Letters*, Vol I, 257.
120. Beckett, *Dream of Fair to Middling Women*, 194.
121. Ibid., 195

sion, in spite of his Belacqua-like flirtation with quietistic withdrawal. His purity was to lie in the refusal of consolations of faith, or of hope. Chris Ackerley points out, "the *Imitation* had a lasting influence upon his thought. He was attracted by its emphasis upon self-effacement, modesty, the uncomplaining acceptance of pain, and by the enchantment of the writing."[122] Yet, as Beckett told MacGreevy, (who had suggested à Kempis to Beckett), such an emphasis could only reinforce his own immersion in self, with "an abject self-referring quietism" which led him further towards a pathological superiority and isolation. Self-abnegation, as he astutely implies, can become self-obsession. He wrote to MacGreevy, "When I cannot answer for myself, and do not dispose of myself, how can I serve? . . . is there some way of devoting pain and monstrosity and incapacitation to the service of a deserving cause? Is one to insist on a crucifixion for which there is no demand?" The questions strike deep at the heart of à Kempis' ideas. Just how valid is harsh denial of the self if it has neither efficacy towards humanity (as à Kempis would have it), nor efficacy within the spiritual plane (as Beckett perceived it)? Beckett could not share à Kempis' sense that all suffering is ultimately transformed into spiritual gain. For him, the effort to "expunge," with the purification that he perceived as necessary, was (another) unnecessary crucifixion. There would seem to be much psychological insight into his refusal to accept à Kempis' insight. Paul Tournier points out that self-surrender cannot take place where the self has not been affirmed.[123] If self-forgetfulness can only take place where there has been a prior affirmation, then Beckett would have had no such capacity.

For him, then, the volitional asceticism, the "ablation of desire" to which he refers in *Proust*, was a daunting and impossible undertaking. Yet the alternative, the acceptance of consolation, as he perceived the acceptance of a faith position, was for Beckett, untenable. Consolation diminishes the intensity of feelings. As his publisher, (and one who knew him personally), John Calder has remarked, "It is the norm of the western world to live as if in a dream, through habit and a disciplined timetable, pushing what is unpleasant outside consciousness. Beckett could not accept membership of that world: he had a compulsion to create his own wounds and rub salt in them. He needed to suffer pain to intensify his consciousness, and paradoxically there is the desire, expressed in much of his work, to reduce the thresholds of pain and feeling in order to suffer

---

122. Beckett, letter to Thomas McGreevy, March 10, 1935, *Letters*, Vol. I, 258. See also Chris Ackerley, "Samuel Beckett and Thomas à Kempis: The Roots of Quietism," 89.

123. Tournier, *A Place for You*, 101–11.

less."[124] To accept any ideology that would diminish the pain, would, at the very least, diminish his ability to enter into his art, more than that, it could diminish his sense of self. But he was left then with a sense of identity that was constructed on a shaky premise, that of continuing the heightened awareness of the pained persona, forged out of a very real sensitivity to suffering, and assisted by his art. Barge cites Beckett's friend, the Israeli painter, Avigdor Arikha, who told the media, "What Beckett is 'doing' is 'being on the edge of being.'"[125]

Consolation, faith, comfort—these would blunt Beckett's sense of life and ontological significance. For many, and obviously complex reasons, Beckett's choice was for autonomy. Drawn to austere texts, perhaps because of his very need to feel pain in order to feel alive, his rejection of these qualities entailed a rejection of God. Like Hampson, he seems to have perceived God as a threat to his sense of selfhood. As Bryden points out, what undergirds the thinking of Thomas à Kempis, the crucial faith perspective—that people should not lean on their own strength but take refuge in God ("hope beneath my feathers")—was a step that Beckett could not take.[126] "For Beckett, this solution is not a radical act of trust, but a crucial handover of autonomy which is impossible to contemplate."[127] God was perceived as being not just distinct from the self, but in direct opposition to it. And so he told MacGreevy (in the same 1935 letter) that he replaced à Kempis' use of God with his own version of a *plērōma*; "I mean that I replaced the plenitude that he calls 'God,' not by 'goodness' but by a pleroma only to be sought in my own feathers and entrails."[128] By this he indicated that from henceforth he would seek "fullness of being" not under the shadow of the wing of God, but in himself. However, this decision did not diminish the need to transcend himself—it simply opened up other areas of influence, to which we now turn.

---

124. Calder, *Philosophy of Samuel Beckett*, 3.
125. Arikha, "Waiting for the Author of 'Waiting for Godot'" 18.
126. Beckett, letter to Thomas McGreevy (March 10, 1935) *Letters*, Vol. I, 257.
127. Bryden, *Samuel Beckett and the Idea of God*, 34.
128. *Plērōma*, meaning "fullness" in Greek, is used in Gnostic cosmology to indicate the dwelling place of the spirit. To this we shall return.

CHAPTER 3

The Soul's Leap Out

Beckett—Mysticism

BECKETT, AS A MAN of his time in Paris in the 1920s and 30s, was interested in mysticism. Gnosticism and Christian mysticism are the particular areas that seemed to have the greatest interest for Beckett and which therefore deserve specific consideration in this chapter. This can be seen, for example, in the concept of *plērōma*. It is used by the Apostle Paul, but it is also a Gnostic idea, and the gnostic understanding of the word had much influence on Beckett, as various critics explicate, including Mary Bryden and the Hamiltons.[1] This then raises the question; how clear was Beckett's understanding of Christian mysticism when he chose to seek fullness of being in himself, rather than in Christianity?

Certain passages in Beckett's work exude an otherworldly dimension, as if the author was informed by some sense of transcendence, or dimension beyond the self and the material. For example, in *Dream of Fair to Middling Women*, Belacqua "felt himself heavenly enflamed as the Cherubim and Seraphim for all the world as though his mouth had been tapping the bung of the heavenly pipe of the fountain of sweetness instead of just coming from clipping the rim of a pint pot of half-and-half. For about two minutes he floated about as Gottesfreund and disembodied as you please. This sudden strange sensation was of a piece with the ancient volatilisation of his first communion, long forgot and never brought to mind . . ."[2] (We know from an interview with Tom Driver, that Beckett acknowledged a religious "emotion" at his first communion, but that he claimed to have had "No more."[3])

---

1. Bryden, *Samuel Beckett and the Idea of God*, 70–71.
2. Beckett, *Dream of Fair to Middling Women*, 184–85.
3. Tom Driver, interview with Samuel Beckett in Graver and Federman, *Samuel Beckett: The Critical Heritage*.

Before investigating Beckett's engagement with writings of the "mystical" kind, it may be best to clarify the situation with regard to psychology, given the confusion which surrounds the area termed "abnormal psychology" and mysticism. R. D. Laing comments that the sense of a loss of selfhood for those with schizoid or schizophrenic tendencies can be tolerated in certain circumscribed situations without too much anxiety, such as listening to music, or in "quasi-mystical experiences when the self feels it is merged with a not-self which may be called 'God,' but not necessarily."[4] In other words, certain non-threatening experiences may be tolerated, but a more encompassing experience would be profoundly threatening. Equally, for Barnard, coming at the topic from a literary critical perspective, the schizoid state is not exclusive of the "mystic" state. For Barnard, Beckett is a mystic but of an unusual type, for he recoils from union lest the self fall into annihilation.[5] Beckett's characters, therefore, do not pass beyond this stage to "true union." For the true mystic the world expands; for the schizophrenic, the external world becomes unreal.[6] Others emphasize this contrast between the schizophrenic and the mystic. Sass speaks with clarity on the vexed issue; he makes particular reference to a certain stage that precedes the schizophrenic break whereby reality seems to be unveiled, and the visual world "looks peculiar and eerie—weirdly beautiful, tantalizingly significant, or perhaps horrifying in some insidious but ineffable way."[7] This phase, the "truth-taking stare" involves, according to Sass, a "conjoint and rather contradictory sense of meaning*ful*ness and meaning*less*ness, of significance and insignificance, which could be described as an 'anti-epiphany.'"[8] It is tied in with the "praecox feeling" of radical alienation that is often considered the single clearest characteristic of the schizophrenic shift from the social, consensual world. Gerald May, speaking as a psychiatrist, clearly distinguishes between the unitive experience, which he perceives as being highly integrative and creative, and any experience connected to a schizophrenic episode, which are much more fragmented and corrosive of self-image.[9] In a more general sense, however, it may be possible, as Kenneth Wapnick suggests, that the search for Union in people with a schizoid inner bent, is an extension of the desire to escape the social world within which he

---

4. Laing, *Divided Self*, 98.
5. Barnard, *Samuel Beckett: A New Approach*, 19.
6. Ibid., 132–33.
7. Sass, *Madness and Modernism*, 44.
8. Ibid., 44.
9. May, *Will and Spirit*, 120–22.

or she is unable to function.[10] It may be that self-enclosure leads to a strong desire for self-transcendence. In Beckett—as in others—it may be that the desire to escape from the self-enclosed world led to the desire for a "mystical" encounter. Laura Barge comments, "if we select a hero at random from almost any novel or piece of fiction by Beckett, we find him afflicted with a similar longing to escape the material of a macrocosm that delivers only unfulfilled desires and disappointed hopes and to enter a microcosm of silence, darkness, and the cessation of all fleshly striving by the human will."[11]

Proceeding then from the perspective that Beckett's personality may have predisposed him towards mysticism, the next step is to try to understand his perception of it. Beckett, as a young man, would seem to have been familiar with the *Encyclopaedia Britannica* (1911) entry on mysticism. For example "Gottesfreund" is one of the subtitles. The definition there is relatively appropriate for Beckett's conception of Mysticism:

> A phase of thought, or rather perhaps of feeling, which from its very nature is hardly susceptible of exact definition. It appears in connection with the endeavour of the human mind to grasp the divine essence or the ultimate reality of things, and to enjoy the blessedness of actual communion with the highest. The first is the philosophic side of mysticism; the second its religious side.

Both "sides" would have appealed to Beckett—the philosophic and the religious (if by that we understand the authors "experience"). Indeed, of the disciplines considered so far—psychology/psychoanalysis, philosophy, theology—it is perhaps the "discipline" (and at this stage it was only a burgeoning one) most likely to appeal to him, for it avoids the "scientific" approach of the other disciplines, and yet it offers some understanding, even experience of "ultimate reality." Certainly, there are a significant number of passages in the Beckett *oeuvre* that are suggestive of some sort of transcendental experience. These passages, often in fairly stark contrast to Beckett's usual tone, carry with them lyrical suggestions of a bleak beauty, of a world that is peaceful, calm, although often without hope. There is a sense of being at a threshold, or at least approaching "the threshold scarcely crossed" to which he alludes at the beginning of *Molloy*.[12] The following extracts from a passage from *Malone Dies* is fairly representative of the nature of these passages:

10. Wapnik, "Mysticism and Schizophrenia," 321–37.
11. Barge, "Beckett's Questing Hero: Mystic or Pseudomystic?" 49.
12. Beckett, *Three Novels*, 8. "The threshold scarcely crossed that's how it is. It's the head. It must have had enough. So that you say, I'll manage this time, then perhaps once more, then perhaps a last time, then nothing more."

> The clouds scud, tattered by the wind across a limpid ground. If I had the patience to wait I would see the moon. But I have not. Now that I have looked I hear the wind. I close my eyes and it mingles with my breath. Words and images run riot in my head, pursuing, flying clashing, merging endlessly. But beyond this tumult there is a great calm, and a great indifference, never really to be troubled by anything again ... The search for myself is ended. I am buried in the world, I knew I would find my place there one day, the old world cloisters me, victorious. I am happy, I knew I would be happy one day. But I am not wise. For the wise thing now would be to let go, at this instant of happiness. And what do I do? I go back to the light, to the fields I so longed to love, to the sky all astir with little white clouds as white and light as snowflakes, to the life I could never manage, through my own fault perhaps, through pride or pettiness, but I don't think so. The beasts are at pasture, the sun warms the rocks and makes them glitter. Yes, I leave my happiness and go back to the race of men too, they come and go, often with burdens. Perhaps I have judged them ill, but I don't think so, I have not judged them at all ... Night, storm and sorrow, and the catalepsies of the soul, this time I shall see that they are good. The last word is not yet said between me and—yes the last word is said. Perhaps I simply want to hear it said again. Just once again. No, I want nothing.[13]

This threshold experience is commensurate with the desire to go beyond the "tumult" and the "catalepsies" of the soul, which yet seem to conflict with the life of this world. "I can't go on, I'll go on" is pertinent here too. Despite Beckett's tendency to protest "no-one knows," he was unable to dispense with the longing for the transcendent. But what elements of mysticism did he absorb?

The *Plērōma*: Gnosticism

Although Beckett articulated a rejection of any external, or at least orthodox Christian *plērōma* in 1935, Gnostic ideas seem to have impacted him strongly.[14] Gnosticism may have appealed to him on a number of levels; the combination of esoteric knowledge with the rejection of the material

---

13. Ibid., 198–99. That Beckett's search for himself is not ended, despite his comment to that effect, is evident from the wider context of Beckett's work. It is interesting to note this temporary effect, especially within this context.

14. Gnosticism in the work of Beckett could be fruitfully explored at greater depth but by the nature of this project the focus must be on Beckett's engagement with specifically Christian mysticism (by which I do not negate the fact that there is some level of overlap between the two).

and the concept of God as being removed from matter, beyond name or predicate, the source of the good spirits, who form the *plērōma*, or realm of light.[15] This knowledge, or gnosis was considered to have a liberating effect; "All Gnostic teachings are in some form part of the redeeming knowledge which gathers together the object of knowledge (the divine nature), the means of knowledge (the redeeming gnosis) and the knower himself."[16] The Gnostic answer to rationalistic questioning would be either silence or lies—two words frequently repeated in *The Unnamable*. Of Beckett's frustration with "rationalism" we are already aware. So too with the constant desire for cessation of being; "It's of me now I must speak, even if I have to do it with their language, it will be a start, a step towards silence and the end of madness . . ."[17] Beckett's narrators' vague, hopeless longing to leave the world is perfectly in accordance with the

---

15. "The essential basic features of Gnosis can easily be extracted from the Gnostic traditions, even if they belong to the teachings of different schools." Rudolph, *Gnosis: The Nature and History of Gnosticism*, 55. The basic and common assumptions of Gnosticism have been particularly well summarized by Clark Emery in a book on William Blake. It is on his twelve points that I shall base my observations (Emery, *William Blake: The Book of Urizen*, 13–14). These include:

- The Gnostics posited an original spiritual unity that came to be split into a plurality.
- As a result of the pre-cosmic division the universe was created. This was done by a leader possessing inferior spiritual powers and who often resembled the Old Testament Jehovah.
- A female emanation of God was involved in the cosmic creation (albeit in a much more positive role than the leader).
- In the cosmos, space and time have a malevolent character and may be personified as demonic beings separating man from God.
- For man, the universe is a vast prison. He is enslaved both by the physical laws of nature and by such moral laws as the Mosaic code.
- Mankind may be personified as Adam, who lies in the deep sleep of ignorance, his powers of spiritual self-awareness stupefied by materiality.
- Within each natural man is an "inner man," a fallen spark of the divine substance. Since this exists in each man, we have the possibility of awakening from our stupefaction.
- What effects the awakening is not obedience, faith, or good works, but knowledge.
- Before the awakening, men undergo troubled dreams.
- Man does not attain the knowledge that awakens him from these dreams by cognition but through revelatory experience, and this knowledge is not information but a modification of the sensate being.
- The awakening (i.e., the salvation) of any individual is a cosmic event.
- Since the effort is to restore the wholeness and unity of the Godhead, active rebellion against the moral law of the Old Testament is enjoined upon every man.

16. Rudolph, *Gnosis*, 77.
17. Beckett, *Three Novels*, 324.

Gnostic sense that this world is alien, and that while in it, people seek to escape the compulsion that lays hold of them. Moreover, the mistrust, even disdain, for the body that Beckett's narrators exhibit, finds clear resonances in Gnostic thought.

Beckett would have come across Gnostic ideas in a number of different sources. For example, his familiarity with Manichaeism may well have come in part through his reading of Augustine's *Confessions*, although Bryden points out that Beckett was particularly interested in Gnosticism and Manichaeism in the 1930's. Notes on *Krapp's Last Tape* refer directly to Mani, originator of Manichaeism; for him, matter was corrupt because of the dual nature of the cosmos; the Demiurge who created it is evil, and embodied humanity is trapped inside this darkness, isolated from the light wherein abides the Father of Greatness. In withholding blame from the "master" and putting it onto "the everlasting third party," Beckett aligns himself with such an interpretation:

> It's all a bubble, we've been told a lot of lies, he's been told a lot of lies, who he, the master, by whom, no-one knows, the everlasting third party, he's the one to blame, for this state of affairs, the master's not to blame, neither are they, neither am I, least of all I, we were foolish to accuse one another, the master me, them, himself, they me, the master, themselves, I them, the master, myself, we are all innocent.[18]

These beliefs, often accompanied (although not always) by asceticism, resonate with Beckett's; as Alice and Kenneth Hamilton comment, "At least with respect to its view of creation, the Manichean myth is better adapted to Beckett's estimate of the human situation than the Christian one."[19] The darkness of this world dominates the Beckettian vision, just as it did Mani's—even down to the denigratory attitudes that he demonstrates towards the flesh or predatory female sexuality (as evidenced, for example, in Lousse or Ruth in *Molloy*).

In addition, Jung's thought was highly influenced by Gnostic ideas, through his friendship with Gilles Quispel.[20] "What made Jung's view

---

18. Ibid., 375.

19. Hamilton, *Condemned to Life*, 52. But, as they point out, Beckett "does not share Mani's prescription for salvation, any more than he adopts the Christian prescription."

20. "One of the persons who kept the Gnostic phenomenon alive was C. G. Jung's close associate, the Gnostic scholar Gilles Quispel, who labored long and hard on relating the ancient gnosis of Valentinus and other teachers to the modern gnosis of analytical psychology. He saw the Gnostic effort as involving deep insight into the ontological self, and thus as analogous to the best in depth psychology. Quispel's major work on the subject, *Gnosis als Weltreligion* (*Gnosis as a World Religion*, published in 1972), explains in detail

radically different from those of his predecessors was simply this: he believed that Gnostic teachings and myths originated in the personal psychospiritual experience of the Gnostic sages. What originates in the psyche bears the imprint of the psyche."[21] (It is worth recalling that Wilfred Bion was interested in the idea of an ultimate truth which cannot be known directly, but which mystical experience has approximated most closely.) Gnosis (Greek for "knowledge") is primarily human knowledge about humanity—including knowledge specifically about oneself. Perhaps another element of the attraction for Beckett was the Gnostic conviction that the inner journey to self-knowledge was important. Kurt Rudolph spells this out:

> It is the act of self-recognition which introduces the "deliverance" from the situation encountered and guarantees man salvation. For this reason the famous Delphic slogan "know thyself" is popular also in Gnosis and was employed in numerous ways . . . In the Book of Thomas (the Contender) Christ says at the very beginning to his "twin brother" Judas Thomas: "Examine yourself and know who you are and how you were and how you shall be . . . You have already come to knowledge, and you will be called 'the one who knows himself,' for he who has not known himself has known nothing. But he who has known himself has already come to knowledge concerning the depth of the All."[22]

The opening of *The Unnamable*, "Where now? Who Now? When Now?" could be said to be Gnostic questions, for they reflect the desire to understand the human predicament.

In Gnosticism, the divine is diametrically opposed to the cosmos, and can only be known through the redemptive power of esoteric knowledge, acquired not by learning or empirical observation but by divine revelation. Beckett may have found the Gnostic "praxis," not just the content, attractive. Unlike early Christians, the Gnostics actively sought mystical experiences; the *plērōma* or fullness of the spiritual world was a site of escape—a world both beyond the planets and attainable, paradoxically, within oneself. Bernard McGinn comments on the mystical elements within Gnosticism—and how they reflected certain elements of Neo-Platonism:

---

the relationship of Jung's model to Gnostic teachings. Quispel, like Jung himself, did not reduce Gnostic teachings to depth psychology, but rather pointed to depth psychology as a key to understanding Gnosticism." Hoeller "What is a Gnostic?" para. 16.

21. Ibid.
22. Rudolph, *Gnosis*, 113.

> Positively, the Gnostic texts display important affinities with many of the key themes found in the Hellenistic mysticism . . . descent and ascent of the soul, negative theology, contemplation and vision of God, divinization and unification with the divine. In the Gnostic sources however, these mystical topoi appear within a mythic pattern in which salvation is achieved through that gnosis by means of which some persons (not all) come to recognize the hidden divine nature of their fallen souls. This seems to be the key to the mystical element in Gnosticism.[23]

Much more esoteric, eclectic and elitist than Christian mysticism, Gnosticism was highly attractive to Beckett.[24] But in the end, as he had told Haerdter, the connection with the self and the knowable was broken.

The Ascetic about Town: Beckett as Mystic

Beckett was also drawn to the Christian mystics, with their strong emphasis upon the immediacy of the human experience of God, beckoning beyond the *Deus Absconditus* of Beckett's Protestant experience towards a sense of divine presence. Like the Gnostics, they seemed have dispensed with the human intermediary and the need to adhere to dogma and creed. Certain critics have suggested that Beckett himself had "mystical" experiences. For example, Hélène Baldwin, in *Samuel Beckett's Real Silence* suggests that the passage cited above is a mystical experience of a partial order, corroborated in her opinion by Malone's subsequent comment, a few pages later, that he does not "depart from (himself) now with the same avidity as a week ago for example."[25] For mystics, she adds, recognize the phenomenon that "the grace of partial or complete union comes quite at random, sometimes frequently, other times at long intervals or not at all, and it seems that Malone's comment might appertain to this randomness of the mystical experience." Although she stops just short of identifying Beckett himself as a mystic, her work thoroughly delineates the many aspects of Beckett's work that could be perceived as having "mystical" connotations, including his use of paradox and negation.[26]

23. McGinn, *Foundations of Mysticism*, 261.

24. McGinn tries to disentangle some of the strands of Neo-Platonism, Gnosticism, and Christianity in the first chapters of *Foundations of Mysticism*.

25. Baldwin, *Samuel Beckett's Real Silence*, 61. Malone's comment is from *Three Novels*, 208.

26. Baldwin, like Beckett himself, demonstrates restricted knowledge of first hand sources; her knowledge of mysticism seems limited to F. C. Happold, Elmer O'Brien, and Rudolph Otto. As a consequence, she is inclined to make somewhat generalised statements, which undermine the complexity of the argument.

In a similar vein, Josephine Sutton Miller makes the unwarranted claim that Beckett's desire to unite with the Godhead stems from a deep-seated sense of antenatal "oneness" to which he wishes to return.[27] Most critics who touch on the subject of Beckett's mysticism, unwilling to go out on such a limb (especially one with so many branches), acknowledge the presence of mystical concepts in his work, but avoid any definitive statement as to Beckett's own state. Shira Wolosky sets out four positions on the matter, based on the apocalypse of language that she observes in *The Unnamable*:

1. Beckett's "nothing" designates a transcendent fullness opposed to the material world from which ascetic withdrawal is urged, making Beckett a kind of Christian mystic.
2. The "nothing" signifies an ultimate transcendence that cannot be attained despite ascetic withdrawal from the material world, making Beckett a failed Christian or a "mystique manqué."
3. The material world is utterly repudiated in the name of a transcendent nothing which is absolutely antithetical to it, making Beckett a Gnostic.
4. At the core of reality, when all appearances have been stripped away, there is only an existential void, making Beckett a secular nihilist. Wolosky points out that the most common "placing," that of failed mystic, shades into the next, that of existential nihilist.[28]

Laura Barge is possibly the clearest spokesperson against Beckett as mystic. In Beckett's work, "no-one can claim for any hero even a measure of success in attaining to the mystical experience or in much of anything else. As Beckett has insisted repeatedly, his art is an art of failure . . . It is safe to say that no hero finds God, authenticates the self, or discovers any meaning in human experience, mystical or otherwise, that can be communicated or expressed in art."[29] In other words, for Barge, Beckett's search is not a mystical one because it is not a genuine search for God;

---

27. Miller, *Samuel Beckett: Mystique Raté*, 29. Miller makes the somewhat unsubstantiated claim that Beckett experienced the "Godhead" and always sought to return to this experience; but she produces little textual evidence of the "experience," nor offers little by way of definition of the term "Godhead." Nevertheless, some of her insights are valid. For example: that the search for God and the self seem inextricable in Beckett; that Beckett's greatest fear may be the failure to find the "Other"; that Beckett could be said to be a "sick soul."
28. Wolosky, *Language Mysticism*, 118.
29. Barge, "Beckett's Questing Hero: Mystic or Pseudomystic?" 49.

ultimately she doubts the validity of the mystic element in Beckett's work. "The formulation of certain questions, however, that are provoked by these propositions leads away from a definition of genuine mysticism towards that of a subtle pseudomysticism that haunts us with its aspirations to be real."[30] The view of Samuel Beckett himself would seem to corroborate such statements; in 1935 he told MacGreevy that he seemed "never to have the least faculty or disposition for the supernatural."[31] Beckett felt that he had failed at mysticism. In *Dream of Fair to Middling Women* he called himself a "dud mystic." Belacqua speaks:

> "Behold, Mr Beckett" he said, whitely, "a dud mystic."
> He meant mystique raté, but shrank always from the mot juste. Guardedly, reservedly, we beheld him. He was hatless, he whistled a scrap of an Irish air, his port and mien were jaunty resignation.
> "John" he said "of the Crossroads, Mr Beckett. A borderman."
> And to be sure he did at that moment suggest something of the ascetic about town. But from that, from the live-and-let-live anchorite on leave, to *dud mystic* was a longer call than we cared immediately to undertake.[32]

This passage, despite its characteristic ambiguity, nevertheless conveys a sense that Beckett's own feeling was one of personal failure; rather than a John of the Cross, he is a John of the Crossroads, an ascetic about town, an anchorite on leave. There are echoes of John 1:14, "we beheld his glory"; but here, rather than the Johannine description of one full of grace and truth, the only one who has seen God at any time (v. 18), we find instead one "whose port and mien were of jaunty resignation." One can only assume that the resignation is to his position as 'dud' mystic, although the level of resignation is, I would suggest, open to question, for it is a theme that never quite disappears in his writings. As Josephine Sutton Miller accurately puts it, parody does not prevent Beckett's

---

30. Ibid., 53.

31. Beckett, letter to Thomas McGreevy (March 10, 1935) *Letters*, Vol. I, 257.

32. Beckett, *Dream of Fair to Middling Women*, 186. The next lines are also pertinent in a number of ways, touching on self-knowledge and citing Augustine, as well as picking up on the "face to face" image:

> "'Give me chastity' he mentioned 'and continence, only not yet.' Nevertheless in the twilight, in the evening, in the black and dark night, after music, with the wine of music, Rhine wine, it was given us to cotton on, to behold him as he was, face to face, even as he sometimes contrived to behold himself. Thus through Nemo came Belacqua to a little knowledge of himself and we (though too late for insertion) to a little knowledge of Belacqua, and by the end of Nemo were forewarned."

spiritual search from being serious.[33] One wonders if it is possible that in his subsequent embracing of failure, he was trying to accommodate himself to this sense of failure at a spiritual level.

Self-Expunging: Beckett's Influences

Other questions can be raised at this point also. Failure is only possible if one has specific targets that one fails to achieve. What were Beckett's expectations? What lay behind his desire to "expunge his consciousness," to "troglodyse" himself?[34] From what sources—other than the *Encyclopaedia Britannica*—did he receive his ideas on mystical experience? Informed guesses may be the best we can manage here, but they are nonetheless pertinent. In order to narrow the focus, and further the project, we shall look at his sources in one particular area—an area that is central to notions of the self in Christian mysticism—that of the death of the self.

Remarkable attention was given to mysticism in France in the 1920s and 30s, not just amongst theologians but also amongst philosophers and psychologists.[35] Whilst the formative conversations of such an environment cannot be known, we do have some ability to establish the writers with which Beckett had first-hand familiarity. For example, throughout the *Dream Notebook* and elsewhere, the language used by Beckett reflects, quite explicitly, the language of his sources. For example, Belacqua, in *Dream of Fair to Middling Women*, "bogged in indolence, without identity" wishes for freedom from consciousness, emancipation; a vocabulary heavily influenced by writers such as Augustine and Thomas à Kempis:

> But the wretched Belacqua was not free and therefore could not at will go back into his heart, could not will and gain his enlargement from the gin-palace of willing. Convinced like a fool that it must be possible to induce at pleasure a state so desirable and necessary to himself he exhausted his ingenuity experimenting. He left no stone unturned. He trained his little brain to hold its breath, he made covenants of all kinds with his senses . . . All for nothing. He was grotesque, wanting to "troglodyse" himself, worse than grotesque. It was impossible to switch off the inward glare, wilfully to suppress the bureaucratic mind . . . How could the will be abolished in its own tension? or the mind appeased in paroxysms of disgust? Shameful spewing shall be his portion. He remains, for all his grand fidgeting and shuffling, bird or fish, or,

---

33. Miller, *Samuel Beckett: Mystique Raté*, 6.
34. These terms can be found in *Dream of Fair to Middling Women* (see 121–23).
35. McGinn, *Foundations of Mysticism*, 280.

worse still, a horrible border-creature, a submarine bird, flapping its wings under a press of water. The will and nill cannot suicide, they are not free to suicide.[36]

In some way, for Belacqua, the expunging of consciousness is intimately connected with the search for identity, and the means—the "willing and nilling"—which Belacqua cannot command, are crucial to the passage across the border, the threshold, which Belacqua so wants to cross. But the will and nill cannot suicide—in other words, for Belacqua the will cannot be renounced, or nulled. The fidgeting leads only to a border creature—words which foreshadow the "borderman" appellation, so specifically applied to Beckett himself later in the book. On one level then, Beckett's mystic tendencies took the form of this attempt to negate the will. By the end of the trilogy, Beckett still has not resolved this issue; "Ah if only this voice would stop, this meaningless voice which prevents you from being nothing . . ."[37] The role of the will in the search for God may well be evidence of the legacy of Augustine; "Myself when I was deliberating upon serving the Lord my God now, as I had long purposed, it was I who willed, I who nilled, I, I myself. I neither willed entirely, nor nilled entirely. Therefore was I at strife with myself, and rent asunder by myself."[38] But it was not just in Augustine that Beckett found this terminology of "willing and nilling." We know too, that Beckett was sufficiently familiar with and fascinated by Thomas à Kempis—who could also be called a mystic—to record in his notebook: "Be there to me one willing and one nilling with thee and let me not will nor nill what thou wilt nor nilt."[39] Other phrases which occur in *Dream of Fair to Middling Women*—troglodytes, *plērōma*, hypostasized Abstraction—are taken from his reading of à Kempis, from which fact we can deduce that Beckett's familiarity with these two writers was first hand.

However, the *Notebook* is quite telling. What we find as we read the *Notebook*, (and Bryden glosses over this fact) is that much of Beckett's ideas on mysticism at this stage, with the exception of *Confessions*, and *The Imitation of Christ,* are in fact derived second-hand from W. R. Inge, whose book *Christian Mysticism* had been published in 1899. This means, in effect, that Beckett's ideas on the death of the self (so far as we can tell) are largely filtered to him through the lens of Inge. Inge considered

36. Beckett, *Dream of Fair to Middling Women*, 122–23.

37. Beckett, *Three Novels*, 370.

38. Augustine *Confessions* 8.0, in the translation with which Beckett was familiar, by E. B. Pusey (1838).

39. Beckett, *Beckett's Dream Notebook*, entry 592.

the self as something to be continually killed—"so that we may rise on stepping stones of many dead selves to higher things."[40] And apophaticism was for him "the great accident of Christian Mysticism," largely Eastern and introduced to Christianity by Pseudo-Dionysius.[41] This goes a long way to explain a fact of which Bryden only seems semi-aware; that, in fact, Beckett's variations upon the mystic's own ideas, are in part, caused by a rather hazy knowledge, influenced by Inge and fleshed out in his youth by his understanding of *Confessions* and *The Imitation of Christ*. Bryden does point out that Beckett's early fiction views the renunciation of will as "an elusive state, to be sought as an antidote to other, more unpredictable pangs as opposed to that renunciation outlined by John of the Cross, which is "something necessarily endured for the sake of a greater potential good."[42] This point is well made. What underlies Beckett's desire to negate the self? It may be here that we see most clearly the complex interplay of factors, including the desire to be delivered from the solipsism of the microcosmic world together with the desire to achieve a kind of Gnostic or mystic transcendence. It becomes evident, from such material, that the issue of Beckett's sources and influences needs a more careful approach, for it would seem that his obsession with negating the will is informed in part by his reading—and misreading—of these.

I Have Not Ceased to Be: Beckett's Diminished Self

Beckett's confusion over the idea of the "death of the self"—to expunge and troglodyse—is crucial to his entire understanding of the self, and consequently, of God. There is an undeniable appeal for him that some kind of mystical expungement will enable him to be freed of linguistic and ideological ambivalence and granted aesthetic and spiritual insight. Moreover, therein may lie the key to the "ablation of desire"—the wisdom of the sages—as described in *Proust*.[43] For him, however, as we have seen, it translates to the exfoliation of the personality, and he remains perpetually caught between the Scylla and Charybdis of desire and incapacity, without the means to expunge. Martha Nussbaum proposes liberation from the desire to transcend human finitude.[44] This desire, she argues, citing Lucretius and Nietzsche, has led us away from the particular and

40. Inge, *Christian Mysticism*, 115.
41. Ibid., 115.
42. Bryden, *Samuel Beckett and the Idea of God*, 99.
43. Beckett, *Proust*, 18.
44. Nussbaum, *Love's Knowledge*.

the human. She lays the blame at the feet of Augustine (primarily because of her interpretation of his understanding of the doctrine of original sin) but it is this issue of "transcending humanity" that is of particular pertinence. The ambiguity of the phrase is one that requires consideration; here, in the context of Nussbaum's writing on Beckett, it acquires negative connotations. Citing Charles Taylor, Fergus Kerr's response to Nussbaum makes a crucial distinction. He argues that the aspiration to transcend humanity, may take "dark and sinister" consequences in certain forms of Christianity, namely the Platonizing or Gnostic forms.[45] And this is certainly so in Beckett, where the transcending of his humanity, becomes ablation, eradication; it is another quest for an apophatic state, this time a negation of the will. It is not a true transcending—and we shall look at this when we look at *Till We Have Faces*—but, as Nussbaum correctly points out, a corruption. Where Nussbaum is wrong, is to take Beckett's corrupted version as the definitively Christian one.

Much of Beckett's discussion of the ablation of desire in *Proust* is based upon the thinking of Schopenhauer, whose consideration of the will has been summarized by John Pilling, as "the less we exercise the will, the less suffering we endure."[46] In Schopenhauer's own words there are those:

> . . . who have overcome the world, in whom the will, having reached complete self-knowledge, has found itself again in everything and who find instead of the restless pressure and effort; instead of the constant transition from desire to apprehension and from joy to sorrow; instead of the never-satisfied and never-dying hope that constitutes the life-dream of the man who wills, we see that peace that is higher than all reason, that ocean-like calmness of the spirit, that deep tranquility, that unshakable confidence and serenity, whose mere reflection in the countenance, as depicted by Raphael and Correggio, is a complete and certain gospel.[47]

But herein lies the problem; for Beckett's interpretation of silencing the will leads to the condition of effective non-existence, and (in direct opposition to Nussbaum's conclusion that Christianity is at fault), is directly linked to Schopenhauer's conclusion that therefore there can be no God, for the contemplation of things beyond the will, are not open to

---

45. Kerr, *Immortal Longings*, 6.

46. Pilling, *Samuel Beckett*, 127. Charles Taylor has pointed out in *Sources of the Self* (443) that Schopenhauer espoused a Buddhist outlook in espousing the escape from the self and the will.

47. Schopenhauer, *World as Will and Representation*, 1:409.

investigation and metaphysics is eradicated. Schopenhauer's inward turn and route to nothingness had obvious intrinsic attraction for Beckett, especially because, for Schopenhauer, the alternative to the "world as will" was immersion in art. The real, which is worthless and degraded, must needs be transfigured.[48] But Schopenhauer's will is more than an aspect of the self; it is actually the source of the self's own being. Ultimately Schopenhauer's argument could be said to undo the inward focusing self and, unable to release himself from the concept of the phenomenal self, Beckett would seem to have parted company with him, as from Proust. But the "naught" continued to grip Beckett.[49] In *Molloy* we find, "For to know nothing *is* nothing, not to want to know anything likewise, but to be beyond knowing anything, to know you are beyond knowing anything, that is when peace enters in to the soul of the incurious seeker."[50] And much later, in 1967, Beckett told Sighle Kennedy:

> If I were in the unenviable position of having to study my work, my points of departure would be the "naught is more real . . ." and the "Ubi nihil vales . . ." both already in *Murphy* and neither very rational.[51]

Naught is more real than nothing, according to Democritus, and "Ubi nihil vales, ibi nihil velis" a citation from Arnold Guelincx, which has been translated and explicated by Chris Ackerley, as "by looking into oneself, one realizes one's essential lack of worth, and by doing so one is led to despise and hence not desire the natural world." In Geulincx's *Ethica* the final realization, after self-inspection, is that one has no value until dead. The complicating factor, however, is this interface between Schopenhauer's ideas and a "Christianized" sense that the will must be subjugated, or negated in the interests of personal holiness, picked up perhaps, from a reading of Inge and à Kempis. As Ackerley points out,

---

48. C. Taylor, *Sources of the Self*, 443–44. Taylor comments that Schopenhauer wished "to declare reality evil once and for all."

49. As Chris Ackerley points out, Beckett rejected the Christian dogma, but not the method of renunciation of the human will. "Where Beckett parts company from Thomas, as he had from Augustine, Descartes and Geulincx, is at this point of transcendental validation. Yet that departure is not a simple affair. Throughout the later works the quietism of à Kempis is implicit not only in the unflinching acceptance of 'the ingenuous fibres that suffer honestly'. . . but also in the enduring impulse towards the 'pryue closet.' For Beckett this was not an option, yet the very impulse towards the realm of calm is thwarted by 'this meaningless voice which prevents you from being nothing'" (Ackerley, "Samuel Beckett and Thomas à Kempis," 90).

50. Beckett, *Three Novels*, 64.

51. Kennedy, *Murphy's Bed*, 300.

this was not so totally rejected by Beckett as he may have implied to MacGreevy and it may only have served to exacerbate his desire to subjugate the will.[52] For this emphasis upon a will that must be eradicated brings about exactly its antithesis; a focus on a volitional subjugation, leading to an emphasis on the self as the focus of attention. William James, in *The Varieties of Religious Experience* refers to E. D. Starbuck on exactly this; "to exercise the personal will is still to live in the region where the imperfect self is the thing most emphasized."[53] If Beckett wanted to give up on desire—be it religious or otherwise—he could not do so by will alone. To the contrary, emphasis upon the self's ability to regulate the will throws the self back upon itself, unable to move beyond itself.[54] As Gerald May says, there is a spiritual narcissism that is a consequence of willfulness.[55] And it is not just religious attempts at self-definition which prove to be problematic—psychological ones do also, as we have seen. Whatever lay behind Beckett's religious/mystical/psychological attempt to expunge the will, the inevitable consequence was an expunging quite contrary to that which he sought.

Affirmations and Negations Invalidated as Uttered: Negative Theology and Postmodernism[56]

In its broad sense, this strain of negative or apophatic theology (also known as the *via negativa*), emphasizes that God, in his radical otherness, is best known by negation and statements of unknowing, because nothing—no images, parallels or symbols, can sufficiently articulate the true being of God. Vladimir Llossky defines it as follows; "The negative way of the knowledge of God is an ascendant undertaking of the mind that progressively eliminates all positive attributes of the object it wishes to attain, in order to culminate finally in a kind of apprehension

---

52. Ackerley, "Samuel Beckett and Thomas a Kempis," 81–92.

53. James, *Varieties of Religious Experience*, 209. James cites Starbuck's *Psychology of Religion*, 64. He gives no publishing details.

54. There are parallels with other areas also. As Iain Wright points out; "Beckett's texts—this is the paradox to which I have been trying to point—deconstruct all their authorial subjects, and the very possibility of being an author, and yet there is no modern writing in which the author, Sam Beckett, is so persistently present, directing us, always, relentlessly, back to the same problematic, badgering us, not to listen to 'language itself'—or not only to that—but to the problem of cognition." Wright, "What matter who's speaking?" 82.

55. May, *Will and Spirit*, 119.

56. Beckett, *Three Novels*, 291.

by supreme ignorance of Him who cannot be an object of knowledge."[57] Pseudo-Dionysius and John of the Cross are characteristic of this approach, which emphasized the conviction that ultimately all knowing of God is likely to be experienced by the human self as an overwhelming darkness that remains grounded in love.[58] Some have argued that Beckett's use of negation—a certain kind of "divesting of the mind," to (mis)use a phrase of Lossky's—can be interpreted as an expression of this tradition.[59] Hélène Baldwin, Shira Wolosky and Marius Buning amongst others, have stressed Beckett's use of the negative or apophatic strain within mysticism as one of the richest veins from which he mined theological and philosophical ideas.[60] Even apart from Beckett's expressed admiration for their "illogisme brûlant," there are those who think that he shared the awareness of the negativistic mystic, as Buning puts it; "the inability to express or eff, resulting from the breakdown of language and meaning, yet both are obsessed by the need to voice the ineffable, and both employ a similar range of metaphors to evoke solitude, stillness, and silence."[61] This kind of claim has become, as Steven Connor puts it, "ever more vigorous in recent years."[62] So much so, Connor says, that, "Beckett has become a centrepiece of attempts to recapture for religion or render as religious the experience of religious doubt, or doubt about religion."[63]

And yet, despite the obvious interest that he has in this area, Beckett conveys his usual ambivalence of mind. The narrator of *The Unnamable*

57. Lossky, *In the Image and Likeness of God*, 13.
58. McIntosh, *Mystical Theology*, 200.
59. Lossky uses the phrase on 14 of *In the Image and Likeness of God*.
60. Buning, "The 'Via Negativa' and its first stirrings in *Eleutheria*." Buning's definition is as follows, "Negative theology . . . is a manner of dialectic or paradoxical expression that contains both affirmation (*kataphasis*, 'speaking-with' or saying) and negation (*apophasis*, 'speaking-away,' or unsaying), with a semantic force of its own, which perforce subverts the normal semantics of being and nothingness." But Buning's definition sounds more like a definition of mystical theology than it does of negative theology.
61. Marius Buning, 45. *Eleutheria* (a play), was written by Beckett in 1947. Buning suggests that it demonstrates the first stirrings of apophaticism in Beckett, although I believe that the fascination was already there in *Dream of Fair to Middling Women* (early 1930s). Buning cites evidence that Beckett was reading Meister Eckhart and the Rhineland Mystics not long before his death, which shows a lifelong interest but also repeats the notion that Beckett had "thorough acquaintance" with the classic negative theology at the time of writing the *Dream Notebook* (48). Whilst this may be true on one level—Beckett's reading of Inge *may* be called "thorough acquaintance"—nevertheless, I believe it important to stress that Beckett's theological reading at the time of his early writings may have been much more limited than Buning suggests.
62. Connor, "Beckett's Low Church," 2.
63. Ibid., 4.

declares: "First I'll say what I'm not, that's how they told me to proceed, then what I am."⁶⁴ In *Molloy* we find one of those (unexpectedly tender) Beckettian passages, and therein we find expression of the attraction of negation:

> What I liked in anthropology was its inexhaustible faculty of negation, its relentless definition of man, as though he were no better than God, in terms of what he is not. But my ideas on this subject were horribly confused, for my knowledge of men was scant and the meaning of being beyond me. Oh I've tried everything and in the end it was magic that had the honor of my ruins, and still today, when I walk there, I find its vestiges . . . I listen and the voice is of a world collapsing endlessly, a frozen world, under a faint untroubled sky, enough to see by, yes, and frozen too . . . It's with your head you hear it, not your ears, you can't stop it, but it stops itself, when it chooses. It makes no difference therefore whether I listen to it or not, I shall hear it always, no thunder can deliver me, until it stops. But nothing compels me to speak of it, when it doesn't suit me. And it doesn't suit me at the moment.⁶⁵

Drawn to the faculty of negation, and crediting magic with his ruins, (from which we should deduce mysticism, given the context and concerns of Beckett), nonetheless, here in the frozen Hell, there is no voice of God breaking through, "no thunder can deliver me," *contra* T. S. Eliot. Although Baldwin perceives this as the beginning of the negative way, when the soul has realized the necessity of the journey away from the world, it would seem more accurate to accept Beckett's own suggestion— that he is "horribly confused." The narrator of *The Unnamable* articulates the tension in this way, "It's a lot to expect of one creature, it's a lot to ask, that he should first behave as if he were not, then as if he were, before being admitted to that peace where he neither is nor is not, and where the language dies that permits of such expressions."⁶⁶ Bryden indicates that Beckett expressed both approval of the apophatic tradition ("I appreciate that this writing does not affirm but proceeds by negation . . .") and, four years later, appeared to disapprove of it ("Negation isn't possible. Any more than affirmation.").⁶⁷ In *Dream of Fair to Middling Women*, probably

---

64. Beckett, *Three Novels*, 326.
65. Ibid., 39–40.
66. Ibid., 334.

67. Bryden, *Samuel Beckett and the Idea of God*, 183. Both comments were made to Charles Juliet. Bryden cites them in greater detail but, like Baldwin, Buning and others, focuses upon the affinity to be found with certain mystics of the *via negativa*.

one of the most obviously mystically influenced of Beckett's texts, we find a particular expression of his fascination with the *via negativa;* "the circular movement of the mind flowering up and up through darkness to an apex, dear to Dionysius the Areopagite, beside which all other modes, all the polite obliquities are the clockwork of rond-de-cuirdom"; a statement in large part derived from Beckett's reading of Inge, as we can tell from the *Dream Notebook*.[68] The *Notebook* demonstrates that Beckett was particularly struck by Inge's description of that spokesperson for negative theology, John of the Cross. However, in reading Inge, Beckett must surely have noted his forcible (even harsh) criticism of St John's emphasis; "Juan carried self-abnegation to a fanatical extreme, and presents the life of holiness in a grim and repellent aspect . . . It is a terrible view of life and duty—that we are to denude ourselves of everything that makes us citizens of the world—that nothing which is natural is capable of entering into relations with God."[69] The knowledge that Beckett was familiar with such a critique would seem to lend support to Shira Wolosky's argument that Beckett's quest is to negate such a negation, were it not for the fact that Beckett's oeuvre conveys not so much the counter-mystic that she proposes, but the *mystique raté* which he himself diagnoses. For the primary concern in Beckett work is towards this "flowering up and up through darkness," as opposed to those "polite obliquities."

In the appeal of the apophatic for Beckett, there are distinct resonances with the work of certain other mid-twentieth century thinkers. For example, Thomas A. Carlson observes a close proximity between classic traditions of negative theology and a more contemporary "negative anthropology" (as he calls it) which he sees operative in the works of certain contemporary thinkers such as Jacques Derrida, often considered the primary spokesperson for deconstruction. Carlson questions whether the radical finitude of human subjectivity and the absence of God in contemporary thought may not only be connected, but whether they may fruitfully be compared to the interplay of God's unknowability and the soul's annihilation in traditional negative theologies.[70] Various others in the literary world have suggested parallels between negative theology and deconstruction.[71] For example, Mark C. Taylor suggests the following:

---

68. Beckett, *Dream of Fair to Middling Women*, 17. *Dream* Notebook, entry 686.
69. Inge, *Christian Mysticism*, 223, 228–29.
70. Carlson, "Poverty and Poetry of Indiscretion," 167–93.
71. Jacques Derrida has made this quite explicit although there are many others who draw the same parallel—too many to list exhaustively.

> Deconstruction directs our attention to critical problems which merit serious consideration: the death of God, the disappearance of the self, the erasure of the (A)uthor, the interplay of absence and presence and of silence and speech, the encounter with death, the experience of exile, the insatiability of desire, the inevitability of delay, the burden of totality, the repression of difference, the otherness of the Other, the subversion of authority, the end of the book, the opening of textuality, and the advent of writing.[72]

Whilst Taylor's parallels are somewhat debatable, it is hard to dispute Terry Eagleton's suggestion that deconstruction has become, in the Anglo-American literary critical sphere, a kind of kenosis, whereby the aim of the game is to get rid of all the cards, and to sit with empty hands, having dissolved away all positive particles of meaning.[73] But as Eagleton acknowledges, it is too simplistic to attribute such a form of kenosis to Derrida.[74] Derrida claimed to have kept his distance from Beckett: "This is an author to whom I feel very close, or to whom I would like to feel myself very close; but also too close. Precisely because of this proximity, it is too hard for me, too easy and too hard. I have perhaps avoided him a bit because of this identification."[75] The deconstructionism of Derrida's

---

72. M. C. Taylor, *Deconstructing Theology*, xix.

73. Eagleton, *Literary Theory*, 127.

74. Eagleton says: "But the widespread opinion that deconstruction denies the existence of anything but discourse, or affirms a realm of pure difference in which all meaning and identity dissolves, is a travesty of Derrida's own work and of the most productive work which has followed from it" (ibid., 128). John Caputo has developed the idea that Derrida's form of kenosis is actually closer to the heart of negative theology than the deconstructionism of his acolytes. He argues that Derrida was himself a "kind of" mystic. Likening him to an Old Testament prophet, Caputo suggests that Derrida cleanses the present with his iconoclastic words and ushers in a deeply messianic apophaticism, concerned with an "ontological erosion of the self, a hollowing out of self-ishness, I-hood" (Caputo, *Prayers and Tears of Jacques Derrida*, 84).

For Caputo, Derrida's interest in the name of God is ultimately restorative; the name of God effaces itself, "in order to point to the possibility of something wholly other, *tout autre*, the advent of *the* impossible, of what is never present, what never collapses into presence, never falls into the gross idolatry of the present" (ibid., 87). But what is coming cannot be known; factually and structurally it is unknowable: "Non-knowing puts faith and passion to the test, stretching them beyond the too limited expectations that knowledge tolerates. Derrida does not propose a learned unknowing, which is but a more oblique and negative way to know something still higher. The 'come!' does not arise from a knower's unknowing, a '*docta*' *ignorantia*, but a lover's unknowing, an *ignorantia amans*, not a learned but a loving, expectant unknowing, which keeps the future open by the passion of its love, the messianic yearning for what is 'to come'" (ibid., 103).

75. Derrida, *Acts of Literature*, 60. It may be of relevance to note that Louis Sass suggests that Derrida's writing exhibits classic symptoms of schizophrenia.

acolytes may be a different matter, however. The distinction highlighted by differences within postmodernism draws our attention towards the need for subtleties when referring to apophaticism. For the term "apophaticism" requires further qualification; differentiations in usage of the term are crucial, although there is no clear distinction made in the English language. The radical apophaticism of absolute unknowing, where there is an absolute refusal to install presence in the silence, is very different to that which perceives the absence of God as only apparent.[76] The latter necessarily complements cataphaticism, or the *via affirmativa*. John Jones, in his commentary on Pseudo-Dionysius, sets it out this way:

> On the one hand, negative theology functions within affirmative theology or, more specifically, metaphysics to express the pre-eminence of the divine cause. Here, if you will, the negations are "super affirmations." On the other hand negative theology provides for mystical unity with the divinity. Here negative (mystical) theology denies all that is and all reference to beings and, by my interpretation, ultimately denies all affirmative theology and hence, all metaphysics.[77]

The latter (and the denial of metaphysics may still be a metaphysical gesture) comes closer to deconstruction of the Anglo-American kind, whereas the former uses negation as a form of affirmation. One example of the latter, from within the mystical tradition, is highlighted by Michael Sells in his *Mystical Languages of Unsaying*. Meister Eckhart, Sells argues, expresses an explicit desire to be "free of God," although many translators and commentators explain this away.[78] Unsaying (as Michael Sells translates "apophasis") in its most radical form, is markedly different from the unsaying which is grounded in an intentional *practice* of unknowing—although there may be some kind of continuum between the two, which would allow for something of the distinction which may be made between Derrida and Beckett. For Derrida, (according to John Caputo) seems to be arguing for an embracing of the *ignorantia amans*, a lover's unknowing, whereas Beckett seemed unable to take hold of a loving, expectant unknowing. For him expectancy and yearning were irritants, the unfortunate inheritance with which the Vladimirs and Estragons and Malones of humanity live—with discomfort, and even delusion. Beckett's unsaying comes closer to

---

76. One could also argue for a third kind of apophaticism that presupposes the presence of God but considers language totally inadequate. Sally McFague, for example, stands within this tradition.

77. Cited in Coward and Foshay, *Derrida and Negative Theology*, 11.

78. Sells, *Mystical Languages of Unsaying*, 1.

denial than it does to an intentional practice of unknowing—as various critics of Beckett have observed. For example, Mary Bryden perceives in Beckett a kind of "atheistic mysticism"; suggesting that Beckett's choice for relinquishment of knowledge is a willed refusal to install presence where there is absence, rather than any definitive profession of atheism.[79] In the end, Connor says, it is a never-quite-negative theology, that will never allow itself to be transformed into positive negativity:[80]

> The inability, or is it refusal, to tolerate either decisive affirmation, or decisive negation that is enacted through the trilogy and reaches it apogee in *The Unnamable* and *Texts for Nothing*, a condition which Beckett names as the purgatorial, forms a close parallel with this mode of never-quite-negative theology that does not want to help itself turning into a theology of the never-quite-negative.[81]

Denys Turner highlights another contrast that occurs within the realm of "apophaticisms":

> . . . it might be noted that if there are points of intellectual convergence in our times between mediaeval and contemporary apophaticisms, there is this at least in which those two cultures differ; that in the Middle Ages, apophaticism was no mere intellectual critique of discourse, but was in addition a practice which was expected to be embodied in a life.[82]

The importance of the element of praxis had not escaped the attention of Beckett—we have already noted the strength of his desire for an experience of God. But the experiential does not equate to the embodiment of which Turner speaks. And if, as Bryden says, ultimately Beckett's apophaticism is grounded in a form of willed refusal, it turns our attention to the question of motivation. The distinction between the apophaticism of absolute unknowing and that of epistemic humility is vital, otherwise the desire for mystical experience may prove unproductive; for desire must be accompanied by faith, and faith, by its very nature, must assume a position of humility. Beckett's thinking is infinitely closer to Neo-

---

79. Bryden, *Samuel Beckett and the Idea of God*, 185. It is a similar instance to that of Beckett embracing the quietism of à Kempis without embracing his God.

80. Connor, "Beckett's Low Church," 15. This article also engages with the question of Beckett and apophaticism in relation to the work of Alain Badiou; but given the nature of the apophaticism of Badiou ("even more aggressively emptied of content," Connor, "Beckett's Low Church," 9), I see no value in pursuing the topic in this context.

81. Ibid., 9.

82. Turner, *Darkness of God*, 8

Platonic and Gnostic asceticism—purification in order to withdraw into the soul and to free the soul from the body and allow for an *experience* of ultimacy—rather than the more specifically Christian idea of purification in order to facilitate untrammelled communion with God. Emphasis is upon the affect—rather than the subject, God. Turner points out that the apophatic tradition rejected experientialism decisively; that in the later Middle Ages it increasingly defined its position in opposition to the psychologistic tendencies of an "experientialist" spirituality.[83]

It is, of course, impossible to ascertain definitively the motivation which underlies Beckett's apophatic tendencies—George Steiner's *cortesia* comes to mind here, but so too does his encouragement to misconstructions, bringing "a patient wealth" to our answerability—and there *are* various hints in Beckett's work, as to his intentions. Some of these we have already explored; the unsatisfactory nature of his own religious background coupled with a genuine desire to transcend himself; likewise, the wish to escape the daily grind. If the underlying reason for embracing apophaticism is prompted by anger at an incomprehensible God who withholds the means for self-authentication, as Laura Barge suggests, then, once again humility fails.[84] But another unexplored motivation remains, as John Pilling so tersely observes: "'Negative mysticism' . . . contains certain attractions, but these are almost all on the side of man rather than God . . . in fact the religious problem is squarely bound up with the aesthetic expression of it."[85] In other words, religious experience—if it came—could be made to serve his art—a motive to which Beckett himself makes explicit reference in some of his early writings. "Poetry is Vertical," the manifesto to which Beckett ascribed in 1932, asserts that the primary reason for seeking "the inner life over the outer life" or any sort of "mystic-gnostic-trance" is to receive an "ecstatic revelation" of images to use in the artistic "construction of a new mythological reality."[86] Sass makes reference to the fact that artists in mid-twentieth century movements such as surrealism and existentialism, actively sought shifts in consciousness in order to facilitate their art, involving techniques which "are very reminiscent of the truth-taking stare; and the experiences they were designed to bring about involve the same qualities of fragmentation and hyperclarity that are characteristic of the *Stimmung*," the *Stimmung* being

83. Ibid., 260.

84. Barge's somewhat unsubstantiated claim is certainly worth considering. Barge, *God, the Quest, the Hero*, 58.

85. Pilling, *Samuel Beckett*, 122.

86. transition, 21, 148–49.

the mood that accompanies the truth-taking stare of the schizophrenic.[87] In schizophrenia proper these experiences of hyperconsciousness Sass calls apophanies, but in "schizaesthesia" (as Eric Kahler has called it), a strong element of volition, can create an apophanous mood, accompanied by a detached hyperconsciousness that decomposes all unities; it is, according to Sass, ultimately a kind of anti-epiphany or *anti*mysticism, a transcendence downward. "Instead of a gathering in of all things or a transcendence to some incorporeal plane, we find the several varieties of alienation so familiar to the modern sensibility: deadness, increased sense of distance between self and world, and a decomposition of all the organic unities of human action and perception."[88] And, as Sass points out, such phenomena may be the result of rather complex combinations of volition and determinism, capacity and incapacity. For Beckett, his state of "horrible confusion" about mysticism may have been compounded (although not necessarily prompted) by his motivation towards a hyperconsciousness that would further his art. In dealing in apophanies rather than epiphanies, his endeavor in *Three Novels* evidences something of this schizoid hyperconsciousness that decomposes all unities. His transcendence downward and inward shifts him increasingly toward the detached, entropic and fragmented microcosm of *The Unnamable*. Beckett believed that no thunder could deliver him from the collapsing world, but it may be that ultimately, he elected to be present at a site of collapse.

The End of the Wordy-Gurdy: Language in Beckett

Much has been written elsewhere on the subject of Beckett's use of language. It is my intention here, with the aid of some of this critical dialogue, to consider and highlight the characteristics of Beckett's language—and his attitude towards it—which are of particular pertinence to the questions of God and the self. In other words, my emphasis is now upon the essentially apophatic nature of linguistic usage in the trilogy, rather than apophatic theology. *The Unnamable*, in particular, is a litany of negation that resonates with the equivocations, cancellations and denials that negative theology and postmodernism would seem to have in common. It is hard to ascertain exactly what Beckett would have said of Derrida's theorizing—certainly, his narrators continually seek escape or release from the project in which they are engaged; as Iain Wright points out,

---

87. Sass, *Madness and Modernism*, 62–63.
88. Ibid., 59.

there is very little *plaisir* in the *texte*.[89] The express desire of the narrators in both *Malone Dies* and *The Unnamable* is to get beyond speech, beyond the "wordy-gurdy" to the real silence: "I want it to go silent, it wants to go silent, it can't, it can't, it does for a second, then it starts again, that's not the real silence, it says that's not the real silence, what can be said of the real silence, I don't know, that I don't know what it is, that there is no such thing, that perhaps there is such a thing, yes, that perhaps there is, somewhere, I'll never know."[90] That this is Beckett's own dilemma is evident in the much-quoted statement to Georges Duthuit, which Iain Wright calls "the foundation of an entire aesthetics of the inexpressible"; "The expression that there is nothing to express, nothing with which to express, nothing from which to express, together with the obligation to express."[91] And yet, as Wright points out, the hope is always there, that the going on will lead to a way out, to the beauty of the skies and to a glimpse of the stars—an echo of the words of Dante at the end of *Inferno*—rather than the downward spiral on which he seems to be embarked.[92]

This quest for silence has been interpreted in different ways. Schwab, as we have seen, sees it as part of the Beckettian search for nothingness; Baldwin sees it as a search for the presence of the divine. Whilst the interrelatedness of such issues should not be denied—as we shall see—it would seem that for Beckett, language was the locus around which other concerns pivoted. Other primary sources and a study of Beckett's influences suggest that language retained an ambivalent—both desired and unwanted—hold over him. In a letter to Axel Kuhn in 1937, Beckett wrote:

> More and more my own language appears to me like a veil that must be torn apart in order to get at the things (or Nothingness) behind it. Grammar and Style. To me they have become as irrelevant as a Victorian bathing suit or the imperturbability of a true gentleman. A mask. Let us hope the time has come, thank God that in certain circles it has already come, when language is most efficiently used where it is being most efficiently misused. As we cannot eliminate language all at once, we should at least leave nothing undone that might contribute to its falling into disrepute. To bore one hole after another in it, until what lurks

---

89. Wright, "What Matter Who's Speaking?" 71.

90. Beckett, *Three Novels*, 408.

91. Beckett and Duthuit, *Proust: Three Dialogues*, 103. Ian Wright's comment is on 84 of "What Matter Who's Speaking?"

92. Wright (83) draws on *Texts for Nothing* for this particular reference, but his point is that Beckett's work throughout is this obsessive reiteration of the downward spiral of Dante's infernal journey.

behind it—be it something or nothing—begins to seep through; I cannot imagine a higher goal for a writer today . . . Is there any reason why that terrible materiality of the word surface should not be capable of being dissolved? . . . On the way to this literature of the unword, which is so desirable to me, some form of Nominalist irony might be a necessary stage. But it is not enough for the game to lose some of its sacred seriousness. It should stop.[93]

It was a goal shared with Fritz Mauthner, the Austrian philosopher of language, with whose work Beckett became familiar in the early 1930s, through reading it aloud to the blind James Joyce, and whose ideas remained influential upon him throughout his life. Linda Ben-Zvi comments that Mauthner's influence on Beckett is nowhere more clear than in this desire to go beyond language, to pursue this "godless mysticism," towards laughter and silence.[94] In doing so, both recognize that failure is at the root of their project, as Mauthner put it in the opening page of his *Contributions towards a Critique of Language*; "I must destroy language within me, in front of me, and behind me step for step if I want to ascend in the critique of language, which is the most pressing task for thinking man; I must shatter each rung of the ladder by stepping upon it. He who wishes to follow me must reconstitute the rungs in order to shatter them once again."[95] Language for Mauthner was of little or no use in his quest; for him—as for Beckett—human experience was unknown and unknowable. The attempt to eff is without basis, and is doomed to failure. For both men, human discourse is the mere semblance of communication.[96] Time and time again Beckett's characters in *Three Novels* demonstrate a sense that their words simply serve to fill time; useful for practical and mundane purposes, but riddled with misunderstandings and inadequacy. The Saposcats, as Malone points out, "had no conversation, properly speaking. They made use of the spoken word in much the same way as the guard of a train makes use of his flags, or of his lantern."[97] There is then, in Beckett, a distrust of the efficiency of language; a Caliban-esque sense that "You gave me language and my profit on't is I know how to

---

93. Beckett, *Disjecta*, 171–72

94. Ben-Zvi, "Samuel Beckett, Fritz Mauthner, and the Limits of Language," 183–200. John Pilling comments that it would be difficult to overstate the relevance of Mauthner's ideas of language for students of Beckett (*Samuel Beckett*, 128).

95. This translation is Ben-Zvi's own, based on the original German text by Mauthner, *Beiträge zu einer Kritik der Sprache*.

96. Ibid., 196.

97. Beckett, *Three Novels*, 188

curse." Wright observes that "Language for Caliban, for the Unnamable, for so many of Beckett's characters, is not only no aid to knowing 'thine own meaning,' it is precisely that which prevents and blocks access to authentic selfhood."[98] It may be salient here to recall Sass's point that the schizoid/schizophrenic mentality often has a particularly heightened sense of the inadequacy of language, especially to convey those aspects that are felt to be inner and private.[99]

The indeterminacy of Beckett bespeaks something of, not mystery, but rather a profound sense of the inadequacy of language. Wolosky—reading Beckett without reference to the influence of Mauthner—points out that most critics *accept* the Beckettian ideal of silence, that language fails Beckett. She argues that if this is because of a perception of the "true" self as essential and interior, beyond representation and beyond language, then in condemning language as inadequate, they are endorsing a notion of reality, truth and selfhood that Beckett's work disputes.[100] For Wolosky the attitude that perceives language as masking the true reality bespeaks a profound ambivalence towards the phenomenal world—a denigration of the phenomenal world because of the inner turn—that she (like Nussbaum) perceives in Augustine, and also in Meister Eckhart. As so often, Wolosky raises valuable questions. However, there is little by way of textual evidence to support Wolosky's claim that Beckett was deliberately moving towards an affirmation of the validity of language. Language throughout his texts remains profoundly divisive, both with regard to the interpersonal and the intrapersonal.[101] It is interesting, for example, to note Mauthner's view that language even failed to unite the two distinct aspects of the self, the inner and the outer. Linda Ben-Zvi comments that Beckett would have found in Mauthner a validation of his sense of a schismatic self, an inner self which is never fully captured by language: "Since the ego has no way of articulating itself, it cannot be verbalized and thus can never be known."[102] For both men, the self has no organ for self-understanding; in this, as in communication with others, language is no aid to unity.

Equally, however—and apparently paradoxically—part of the modern and postmodern shift towards obscurity in literary endeavor is tied

---

98. Wright, "What matter who's speaking?" 81.

99. Sass, *Madness and Modernism*, 187.

100. Wolosky, *Language Mysticism*, 82–83

101. His movement towards the nonverbal signification of the play form demonstrates this. See Esslin, "Towards the Zero of Language," 35–49.

102. Ben-Zvi, "Samuel Beckett, Fritz Mauthner, and the Limits of Language," 193.

up with a focus on, or elevation of language. Despite the indeterminacies, the equivocations and the underminings, there is a real sense in *Three Novels* that Beckett's mystifying, intimidating, antagonizing, impressive wordy-gurdy is the remnant to which he clings; "that's all words, they're all I have," the narrator of the *Unnamable* says, at the end of *Three Novels*.[103] Sass explains this paradox in this way:

> The sources for these literary developments are manifold—including, in addition to the simple desire for self-exploration, the wishes to mystify, to intimidate, to antagonize, and to impress; what has occurred, in any case, is a turning away from communal themes and modes of expression and towards the concerns and processes of the inner life, which have come to seem, at least in many circles, more authentic, more powerful, and more real. ("The writer expresses. He does not communicate. The plain reader be damned," declared one writer in a manifesto published in the avant-garde review *transition*.)[104]

Sass argues that this particular attitude towards language usage in modernity (and beyond) is integrally connected to the turn away from the human community. For him, it is the inner turn which underlies the various modes of schizophrenic speech which he outlines; an inner turn, which, away from social connectedness, throws greater emphasis upon what remains—unlike previous eras when "literary language had only a secondary status, as a way of coding, communicating, and beautifying meanings that were assumed to have a prior existence and to guide the writer's subsequent choice of words."[105] The aim is no longer to communicate. Sass speaks of the "apotheosis of the word," whereby the old relationship with the world that was mediated by words, is replaced by an isolating relationship with language alone.[106] Beckett himself, in his letter to Axel Kaun, used the very same term of Joyce's writing, with the obvious intent of distancing himself from it, although here a doubt creeps in. What if, he asks, Ascension to Heaven and Descent to Hell are somehow one and the same?[107] He may have chosen to utilize a more stripped form of language, but it may be equally apotheosized.

---

103. Beckett, *Three Novels*, 413

104. Sass, *Madness and Modernism*, 195–96. The manifesto is the one to which Beckett signed his agreement in 1932.

105. Ibid., 198.

106. Ibid. See "Languages of Inwardness," 174–209.

107. Beckett, *Disjecta*, 172.

What we find then, simultaneously, is that the denigration and the elevation of language can co-exist—and that they clearly do in both the schizoid outlook and deconstruction—and Beckett. Although both attitudes displace true relationship by setting up barriers to communication yet, crucially, Beckett, like Mauthner, continued the attempt to express the inexpressible—in prose and plays—regardless. And that expression is integral to the sense of self. Witness that closing *locus classicus* that constitutes *Three Novels*:

> I'll go on, you must say words, as long as there are any, until they find me, until they say me, strange pain, strange sin, you must go on, perhaps its done already, perhaps they have said me already, perhaps they have carried me to the threshold of my story, before the door that opens on my story, that would surprise me, if it opens, it will be I, it will be the silence, where I am, I don't know, I'll never know, in the silence you don't know, you must go on, I can't go on, I'll go on.[108]

Even though Beckett's characters despair of either self-articulation or of meaningful communication—of effing—throughout *Three Novels* there remains the sense that language is integral to the ego, that it cannot be dispensed with. Language becomes central to the very existence of the self. As Leslie Hill puts it, "The only stable awareness of being for Molloy comes from this dreamlike thread of self-contemplation in language and its questions; reflexion as an intellectual process is synonymous with self-reflexion in the mirror of language."[109] Self-perception is crucial to our existence—and the vehicle of this is language.

Focusing on the issues around the idea that selfhood requires language to exist, Wolosky says; "without linguistic expression there is no self at all."[110] Problematic though this may be, this *is* ultimately the position to which a reading of Beckett points. Once again Wolosky draws our attention to an important issue; for her, Beckett reasserts expression and representation as exactly the conditions that make selfhood possible.[111] But is it language, or that which language facilitates—relationship—which most reflects and mirrors the self?

---

108. Beckett, *Three Novels*, 414.
109. Hill, "Fiction, Myth, and Identity in Samuel Beckett's Novel Trilogy," 89.
110. Wolosky, *Language Mysticism*, 84.
111. Ibid., 81.

One Alone, Then Others: Relationality

As we have seen, Beckett's fiction presents us with an uneasy sense of relationship. Despite his dominant sense that humans cannot come together, it seems that, perhaps through lived experience at the time of his isolation in London, he came to a place where he perceived the importance of the presence of an "other" to validate the self. It is seen perhaps most clearly in some of the later plays, but it is evident in the *Three Novels*. In *The Unnamable*, for example:

> Worm, to say he does not know what he is, where he is, what is happening, is to underestimate him. What he does not know, is that there is anything to know. His senses tell him nothing, nothing about himself, nothing about the rest, and this distinction is beyond him. Feeling nothing, knowing nothing, he exists nevertheless, but not for himself, for others, others conceive him and say, Worm is, since we conceive him, as if there could be no being but being conceived, if only by the beer. Others. One alone, then others. One alone turned towards the all-impotent, all-nescient, that haunts him, then others.[112]

"One alone, then others," could be reminiscent of Hampson's model for the self, but for the reluctant sense here that the individual is spoken into being by others; "Worm is, since we conceive him." The narrator of *The Unnamable* asks, "Is there a single word of mine in all I say?"[113] It is a begrudging kind of acknowledgement, for the overall sense is that of resentment. His is not a willing openness to connectedness, but a reluctant dwelling amongst others. Nussbaum points out that Beckett's narrators loathe the input of other voices, the "they" to whom they refer. This, she argues, is because of an individualistic streak that comes directly from Christianity. "Isn't it really because they are in the grip of a longing for the pure soul, hard as a diamond, individual and indivisible, coming forth from its maker's hand with its identity already stamped upon it?"[114] There are several issues here. Whether or not this idea of the self is fully Christian is one that I would hope to contest in the course of this book. Equally, the longing for the stamp of identity as an explanation for the individualism of Beckett's narrators is one that seems insufficiently nuanced—Nussbaum allows for no personal factors. But she may not have overstated the point about the Beckettian loathing of interconnect-

---

112. Beckett, *Three Novels*, 346.
113. Ibid., 347.
114. Nussbaum, *Love's Knowledge*, 310.

edness with others. His is a world that is intentionally self-enclosed. For example, Beckett interprets Proust as portraying friendship as damaging and destructive. Friendship is a "centrifugal force" which would serve to distract the artist. Friendship is:

> . . . the negation of the irremediable solitude to which every human being is condemned. Friendship implies an almost piteous acceptance of face values. Friendship is a social expedient, like upholstery or the distribution of garbage buckets. It has no spiritual significance. For the artist, who does not deal in surfaces, the rejection of friendship is not only reasonable, but a necessity. Because the only possible spiritual development is in the sense of depth. The artistic tendency is not expansive but a contraction. And art is the apotheosis of solitude . . . The artist is active, but negatively, shrinking from the nullity of extracircumferential phenomena, drawn in to the core of the eddy. He cannot practice friendship, because friendship is the centrifugal force of self-fear, self-negation.[115]

Mary Bryden points out in her section on "Solitude," which covers the topic in the life, letters, and texts of Beckett, that although he was far from implementing Proust's ideas in his life, he did nonetheless, privilege solitude, silence and stillness. Beckett's narrators, such as Malone and the narrator of *The Unnamable* aspire toward solitude as "a condition in which to attain a mobile exploration of the self."[116] As Malone says, "I feel the old dark gathering, the solitude preparing, by which I know myself."[117]

To what extent the drive to solitude is based on philosophy we cannot know; but on occasions his language clearly reflects the influence of another strand in the mystical tradition, the Neo-Platonic.[118] His work echoes with citations lifted (and often re-written) from his reading, for example, Plato ("the forms are many in which the unchanging seeks relief from its formlessness") and Pseudo-Dionysius ("the all-transcending hiddenness of the all-transcending super-existentially super-existing super-Deity").[119] There are many echoes too of Plotinus, with his strong emphasis

---

115. Beckett, *Proust*, 63–66. Pilling (*Samuel Beckett,* 16) speaks of this passage as the "tantalizing glimpse of a writer unknowingly prophesying his own course."

116. Bryden, *Samuel Beckett and the Idea of God*, 169.

117. Beckett, *Three Novels*, 189.

118. In addition to McGinn's, *Foundations of Mysticism*, see Louth, *Origins of the Christian Mystical Tradition* for details of the relationship between Christian Mysticism and Neo-Platonism.

119. *Three Novels*, 197; *Dream of Fair to Middling Women*, 17.

upon withdrawal into oneself in order to ascend to the One. Eyal Amiran argues that Plotinus' influence on Beckett is actually stronger than that of Plato, because he perceives a "broad conceptual affinity" between Beckett's emphases and the Neo-Platonic ascension of soul to the One.[120] Plotinus' supreme, his One, is a purely intellectual concept. As the soul ascends towards the One, it enters more and more deeply into itself. The drive of the soul from entrapment in the body to the world of the pure forms and unification with the supreme latter is marked by rational inquiry but it is also marked by a mystical experience which transcends reason, as the soul goes into itself and returns to Unity with its source. "This is the life of gods and of the godlike and blessed among men, liberation from the alien that besets us here, a life taking no pleasure in the things of earth, a flight of the alone to the Alone."[121] Plotinus finally dismissed all particularity and multiplicity as illusion, to be cast aside in the flight of the alone to the Alone. And, as Andrew Louth points out, "The One has no concern for the soul that seeks him; nor has the soul more than a passing concern for others engaged on the same quest: it has no companions."[122] The fascination with the mind's pursuit of knowledge, combined with introversion, a rejection of the material and a remote, impersonal deity—these resonate with Beckett's own predilections.

Beckett's portrayal of relationships conveys a somewhat grudging concession of the necessity of walking a little way with one's fellow creature. There is an uneasy conflict between the desire for isolation, and the need for connectedness. Yet there is always, at root, a sense of disunity and disharmony. We are reminded of Jacobsen and Mueller's sense that his people "can never really come together" that they can "never really know each other . . . a man's soul, try as it will, cannot quite make the ecstatic leap into the soul of another."[123] As always, Beckett is not univocal. The uneasy coexistence of most Beckett's couples' suggests that while relationality is necessary, even for self-knowledge ("he exists nevertheless, but not for himself, for others") that ultimately, knowledge of the other is just as elusive as knowledge of self. Shira Wolosky acknowledges, that in Beckett's work, "The more the self attempts to locate itself as a self alone, the less it exists."[124] "Beckett's exercises in 'introspective reflection,' stripping away everything other than self, discover only 'a vanishing specter'

---

120. Amiran, *Wandering and Home*, 125.
121. Plotinus *Enneads* VI.9.II
122. Louth, *Origins of the Christian Mystical Tradition*, 51.
123. Jacobsen and Mueller, *Testament of Samuel Beckett*, 122–24.
124. Wolosky, *Language Mysticism*, 87.

and not self at all."[125] The "vanishing specter" applies not only to the self that is introspective (as Schopenhauer originally used the term) but also to the "others" in Beckett's fiction—and to the God with whom he does not converse.

> Others. One alone, then others. One alone turned towards the all-impotent, all-nescient, that haunts him, then others. Towards him who he would nourish, he the famished one, and who, having nothing human, has nothing else, has nothing, is nothing.[126]

Here we see, very clearly—and in words reminiscent of mystical speech—the spectral world that Beckett inhabits. The subject and the object are indistinguishable, the boundaries collapsed into nothing. It is a spectral dissolution of self, God, world and meaning.

He Neither Is nor Is Not: Apophaticism of God and Self

The linguistic impasse, the contradictory and apophatic use of language, the anthropological solipsism, the attenuation of the will, are evidently inextricably connected. We have seen that both radical deconstructionism and radically apophatic mysticism make some of the same compromises. And the connectedness of this apparent disconnectedness, becomes more apparent the more closely one looks. Ultimately, Beckett's apophatic mood leads towards disunity, diminishment and nihilism. Denys Turner's suggestion proves correct; an apophaticism of language about God, where not located "within an overall theological strategy which is at once and at every moment both apophatic and cataphatic is necessarily accompanied by an apophaticism of language about the self."[127] Where radical apophaticism dominates, radically "apophatic anthropology" is invariably to be found—such authors as John of the Cross, in essence,

---

125. Ibid., 88. For Wolosky, Beckett ultimately re-emerges towards affirmation, having shown that the traditional idea of metaphysical truth is itself essentially nihilistic, which denigrates the phenomenal world, and that his "use of negative tradition is finally ironic, presenting its paradoxically plethoric nothingness as in fact a void. His own negative modes, in contrast, convert nothingness into a fertile source of continuous imaginative effort" (*Language Mysticism*, 131–34). In fact, Wolosky's conclusions bear evidence of a little of this "continuous imaginative effort" that she locates in Beckett—one wonders just how fertile and imaginative Beckett could be said to be—and it is certainly difficult to ascertain at what point Beckett definitively re-emerges towards affirmation. It is more accurate to say that Beckett demonstrates the *need* (rather than the affirmation) of such an emphasis upon the "word as instrument and image of the created world," on the necessity of multiplicity for the self.

126. Beckett, *Three Novels*, 346.

127. Turner, *Darkness of God*, 265.

Turner says, appear to say that whatever may be the proper description of the fullest union of the human self with God, there is no distinction which we are able to make between that "self" and the God it is one with.[128] Thomas A. Carlson, in tracing the link or point of "indiscretion," in certain modern philosophers and medieval mystics, highlights this fact, "For Eckhart and Porete alike, just as the creature cannot see into the emptiness of the nameless God, so the creature, created in the image of God, cannot finally see into itself. The namelessness and incomprehensibility of God are reflected or doubled by the namelessness and incomprehensibility of the self."[129]

Daniel Bulzan, in an article on "Apophaticism, Postmodernism and Language: Two Similar Cases of Theological Imbalance" states that apophatic theology necessarily tends towards deconstruction; the postmodern interest in apophaticism is ultimately the interest of self-recognition. Although he omits to acknowledge that there are kinds of apophaticism—as we discussed earlier—his comments are suitable for the consideration of the radical kind, that which refuses to install presence. For him, radical apophaticism and deconstruction, "(b)oth force language to turn against itself, to function in a sense that is contrary to its natural course." He too, like Carlson, perceives the relatedness of apophatic discourse and apophatic anthropology. "Having been de-ontologised, apophatic theology loses its object and turns, in deconstruction, against ontology."[130] In both the Neo-Platonic ascension towards divinity, and in the *via negativa*, this apophaticism deprives the creature of its createdness. Bulzan draws together the various strands: "the deconstruction of meaning reduces human being to solipsism, individualizing the encounter with language to a point of total isolation and thus eliminating that relationality which is specifically ours by creation."[131]

As I have tried to show, the Sass/Lasch/Giddens hypothesis of extreme interiority in modernity and postmodernity, resonates with this in

---

128. Ibid. Turner lists others such as Meister Eckhart and the author of the *Cloud of Unknowing*, as well as Julian of Norwich, Catherine of Genoa and Teresa of Avila.

129. Carlson, "Poverty and Poetry of Indiscretion," 167–93.

130. Bulzan, "Apophaticism, Postmodernism and Language," 282.

131. Ibid., 286. Bulzan perceives the need for a proper theology of language as "one of the most urgent tasks for a Christianity that is interested in serving people by offering solutions to problems . . . The task would be the articulation of a proper theology of language, one that would confer on it the necessary link with creation and thus would clarify its relationship with ontology, taking also into account its sociability and variability. Such a theology of language would naturally find its place on a trajectory determined by creation and incarnation, also taking into account the fall and redemption."

a variety of ways. For example, it enables us to understand the confusion of the critics when trying to interpret Beckett's treatment of the self, for it may be that this then becomes a blind spot. The critical confusion is telling. Gabriele Schwab points out that Beckett seems afflicted by all three Kierkegaardian variations of the sickness unto death; "despair at not being conscious of having a self," "despair at not willing to be a self" and "despair at willing to be oneself."[132] Schwab has no theological point to make in asserting this; for her, Kierkegaard serves well to make the point that *The Unnamable* demonstrates the transitional space of postmodernism. She reminds us that this tension is far from being an isolated event—rather, Beckett lays bare what is characteristic of our age. "His discourse is motivated not by a desire for either stabilization or disintegration, but for the constant oscillation between the two. By insisting on this tension, the Unnamable produces a discourse that hurls itself against the boundaries of subjectivity . . . Allen Thiher has interpreted this coincidence as a trademark of the postmodern schizotext: 'This view of the separation of language and self is a schizo-comedy that takes desperate delight in its own impossibility. In this respect Beckett's work ushers in the era of the schizo-text that is perhaps the postmodern text par excellence.'"[133]

It is my contention that Beckett's text—modern or postmodern—demonstrates the necessary connectedness of not just language and self, or God and self, but everything: God, language, and self. George Steiner's *Real Presences*, in arguing that a sense of presence or absence and the creation of art are more inextricable than we think, draws much of it together:

> In recent art and thought, it is not a forgetting which is instrumental, but a negative theism, a particularly vivid sense of God's absence or, to be precise, of His recession. The "other" has withdrawn from the incarnate, leaving either uncertain secular spoors or an emptiness which echoes still with the vibrance of departure. Our aesthetic forms explore the void, the blank freedom which come of the retraction (*Deus absconditus*) of the messianic and the divine . . . So we have seen, do post-structuralism and deconstruction. Within Derridean readings lies a "zero theology" of the "always absent." The *Ur*-text is "there," but made insignificant by a primordial act of absence. We think of that Torah imagined by

---

132. Schwab, *Subjects without Selves*, 154.

133. Ibid., 136–38. Although it is not the task of this book to establish if Beckett was in fact modern or postmodern, it is pertinent to ask whether Beckett actually celebrated the fragmentation of the self. Whereas postmodern thinkers do indeed speak of celebrating the demise of the idea of the self, modern writers are characterized by an awareness of the loss, which is less than celebratory. Beckett's tone is that of a modern.

> human speech, by human ambiguities of reference or interpretation and, therefore, out of reach.
>
> It is "in this absence" that we shadow-box or, as German so aptly puts it, "fence against mirrors."
>
> What I affirm is the intuition that where God's presence is no longer a tenable supposition and where His absence is no longer a felt, indeed overwhelming weight, certain dimensions of thought and creativity are no longer attainable.[134]

Steiner sees this absence played out in the master-texts of the age, including—he names them specifically—Beckett's *Endgame*, and in the figure of Malone. For Steiner it comes down to this; "where agnosticism, if not a consequent atheism, is the norm of approved discourse, it is extremely difficult for an artist to find words for his making, for the 'vibrations of the primal' that quicken his work."[135] Rowan Williams, whilst acknowledging the starkness of the contrasts here, affirms the dysfunction that proceeds from the severance of the word from world:

> Steiner's still problematic and controversial essay on *Real Presences* identifies a cultural dysfunction in the breaking of the "contract" between word and world implicit in later modern and postmodern literary sensibility; and he traces a very direct connection between this and the disintegration of the self. Once words have been "disinvested" of their involvement with the fabric of the world, the acid of deconstruction leaks into the very notion of the *speaker* of words. "The ego is no longer itself. More precisely, it is no longer itself to itself, it is no longer available to integration." What lies "at the now vacant heart of consciousness" is a chaos of random others—that is, not speaking and relating others, but "parodistic, nihilistic anti-matter."[136]

To blend the words of Steiner and Williams—*Three Novels* shows an artist whose ego is no longer "itself to itself," who cannot reach beyond the solipsism of parodistic, nihilistic, anti-matter, whose aesthetic form explores and exposes the void of negative theism, and whose struggle is to "find words for his making." More boldly, it seems that where God's presence is no longer felt, the very presence of the person becomes elusive to him or herself. The radically apophaticised self dwells only amongst phantoms, all reduced—divine and human, self and other—to a spectral existence. What happens then, if we replace the "vacant heart of consciousness"

---

134. Steiner, *Real Presences*, 228–29.
135. Ibid., 223.
136. Williams, *Lost Icons*, 176. The citations are from Steiner, *Real Presences*, 99.

with a presence, with a specific, describable and described God? Shall we find any diminishment of the namelessness and the desperation that has pervaded *Three Novels*? Is it possible that a sense of the presence of God would enable a sense of self-presence? What would the antithesis look like? Let us turn to C. S. Lewis to explore the outworkings of his antithetical emphases.

CHAPTER 4

A Warped and Masked Reality

Lewis—Psychology

C. S. LEWIS CHANGED markedly during the course of his life. By his late writings he had developed a very clearly articulated stance on the connected concepts of God and the self. But, as we have already noted, in his early adulthood Lewis's attitudes towards both God and the self were relatively close to those of Beckett. In this chapter I shall trace some of the significant aspects of his life and constitution, before moving on to explore the ideas and influences that shaped his mature thinking. In doing so, I shall be looking at his psychological make-up and his own understanding of psychology, in order to explore his thinking on the self.

In most respects this chapter is preparatory for the next chapter in which Lewis's ideas on the self shall be more thoroughly explored. It is my belief that *Till We Have Faces* can best be understood by understanding Lewis's own experience—a point which E. M. W. Tillyard made in his debate with Lewis; "the biography, the *facts* of personality, the data for the mental pattern of the man's life, may substantially help our understanding of the mental pattern as revealed in his art."[1] For our ultimate concern is to test how Lewis's mental pattern and life sheds light on the idea of the double knowledge. If in Beckett we encountered a God-less, self-less realm, how shall Lewis's emphatic belief in God affect his sense of self?

James Como has said that, "The book Lewis should have written but did not was a systematic study on the self: should have, because at bottom he discussed little else in much of his work and his own self is so prominent in that work; did not, because he failed to quite understand his own self but knew he must escape it."[2] The truth or otherwise of this shall

---

1. Tillyard, "Personal Heresy in Criticism," 16. Of the debate between Lewis and Tillyard we shall hear more later.

2. Ibid., 95.

be implicit in our research, but the indisputable emphasis upon the self, coupled with his lived experience, makes him a highly suitable conversation partner for Samuel Beckett.

Como also warns us that:

> The consideration of C. S. Lewis's self is a very great challenge. He at once hid it absolutely, distorted it, and invented parts of it to parade forth; he repressed, explored and denied it; he indulged and overcame it; certainly he would transform and then transcend it; almost always he used it. And always he coyly warned us against discussing it.[3]

As James Como makes clear in this quotation, Lewis could be said to have experimented with different attitudes to the self, some knowingly, others perhaps less so. There is no simple consistency to his behavior, although I believe that there was a consistency within his developing theorizing about the self. But let us turn first to a consideration of Lewis's self.

"Suffocatingly Subjective": Emotional Make-up and Childhood

Lewis's childhood has been recorded in his own spiritual autobiography and by all his biographers and therefore only salient points need to be highlighted here. Whilst on first reading I may seem to be stressing points that are arbitrary and unconnected, I have chosen points that I believe will help us understand the mature Lewis. It is very far from the whole story—which would be a full biography, of course—but my aim is to provide background for the subject at hand.

Born in Ulster in 1898, Lewis—like Beckett—had an ambivalent attitude towards his homeland, possibly because of the complex relationship he had with his father, and partly because of certain political and religious attitudes that he experienced there. But his ambivalence was tempered by a love of the landscape and a felt benevolence from family and friends.[4] His family attended St. Mark's Church in Dundela, Belfast, where his mother's father, Thomas Hamilton, was the rector. Lewis found church far from stimulating as a child. "I was taught the usual things and made to say my prayers and in due time taken to church. I naturally accepted what I was told but cannot remember feeling much

---

3. Como, *Branches to Heaven*, 54.

4. For example, it is interesting to note this comment in his autobiography; "I think we Strandtown and Belmont people had among us as much kindness, wit, beauty and taste as any circle of the same size that I have ever known." *Surprised by Joy*, 123–24.

interest in it."⁵ It may be that he suffered the same hymns as Beckett did, and found them no more appealing.⁶ Biographers often refer to the austere form of Christianity that was prevalent in the post-Victorian Northern Ireland, and there is some confirmation of this in Lewis's own writing. For example, on 6 December 1931, Lewis wrote to his lifelong friend, Arthur Greeves, highlighting the weaknesses of the kind of nonconformist puritanism with which Greeves was surrounded.⁷ Amongst his criticisms, Lewis said that it denied pleasure to others; permitted the worst pleasures (avarice, gluttony); and it could give no reason for the faith. In *The Pilgrim's Regress*—which is in part autobiography—John, the protagonist, is born in Puritania, a country where lip service is paid to the Landlord (or God) and his rules, and hypocrisy dominates. The rules cultivate in John a fearful attitude to life. In his letter to Greeves however, Lewis states that Greeves' experience is not his own, and that he is "apt to forget" how different Greeves' experience is. In other words, the Puritanism that is so often attributed to his own experience is, in fact, observed by him as an outsider. In fact, he had little sense of guilt as a boy and young adult; "It took me as long to acquire inhibitions as others (they say) have taken to get rid of them . . . I have been a converted pagan living among apostate Puritans."⁸

But Lewis was nonetheless fearful. Whether ultimately his fearfulness stemmed from genetics, upbringing or culture is not for us to decide. Apparently he was not sure himself. One abandoned draft of *Surprised by Joy* indicates this about his childhood:

> It was intolerable and delightful. On the one hand fear played a very important part in it. Giant insects peopled my dreams: that is with me the oldest terror. Nightmares of a more spectral kind came later. On the other hand, those years seem to have been full of extreme pleasure. Unless memory plays me false, none of the pleasures were of an imaginative, much less a spiritual kind. They were all hum-drum and mundane: food, play, merriment.⁹

But it is quite possible that he felt shame, an emotion that is often closely tied to fear—and which could well have stemmed from his early child-

---

5. Ibid., 4.

6. Certainly as an adult, Lewis disliked hymns and the "collective" aspect of church life; one also gets the impression from his writings that he chose to consciously embrace the rituals because he believed that they were God-ordained.

7. Lewis, *They Stand Together*, 431–34.

8. Lewis, *Surprised by Joy*, 52.

9. Lewis, Bodleian Library, Oxford. MS Eng. misc. c1109. folio 2v.

hood experiences.[10] Certainly, it is interesting how often fear and shame are mentioned in *Till We Have Faces*.

There was one particular sensation of which Lewis early became aware, and which had a profound impact on his entire life. His brother had once made a toy garden from twigs and flowers that had struck him then—and later—as beautiful:

> As I stood beside a flowering currant bush on a summer day there suddenly arose in me without warning, and as if from a depth not of years but of centuries, the memory of that earlier morning at the Old House when my brother had brought his toy garden into the nursery. It is difficult to find words strong enough for the sensation which came over me . . . It was a sensation, of course, of desire; but desire for what? Not, certainly, for a biscuit-tin filled with moss, nor even (though that came into it) for my own past. Ιουλιαν ποθω—and before I knew what I desired, the desire itself was gone, the whole glimpse withdrawn, the world turning commonplace again, or only stirred by a longing for the longing that had just ceased. It had only taken a moment of time; and in a certain sense everything else that had ever happened to me was insignificant in comparison.[11]

Even as a young boy, reading Beatrix Potter, or later reading Longfellow's *Saga of King Olaf*, or looking at the low line of the Castlereagh Hills, he felt the call of these other worlds as if he was created *for* another world. This fleeting sense of desire Lewis tended to speak of as Joy, Longing or *Sehnsucht*. The German term specifically means literally "longing" or "yearning," although Corbin Scott Carnell points out in his careful study that Lewis uses the term more broadly.[12] He would also have come across it in the writing of William James, who used the term *Sehnsucht* to refer to the deepened sense of mystical significance which could arise, for example, from a word, a sight, poem or musical sound, or the effects of light on land or sea.[13] Lewis himself speaks of a sense of an "unsatisfied desire that is itself more desirable than any other satisfaction."[14] He came to regard *Sehnsucht* as that which, if followed correctly, should lead us to God. All earthly pleasures were substitutes for the true source of Joy. In

---

10. See Kaufman, *Psychology of Shame*. He suggests that inadequate expression of childhood bereavement can lead to a sense of shame.
11. Lewis, *Surprised by Joy*, 11.
12. Carnell, *Bright Shadow of Reality*.
13. James, *Varieties of Religious Experience*.
14. Lewis, *Surprised by Joy*, 12.

Mere Christianity he says "If I find in myself a desire which no experience in this world can satisfy, the most probable explanation is that I was made for another world."[15] It was this, in large part, which led to his acceptance of Christianity.[16] In *The Pilgrim's Regress* he argues, based on his own experience, "that if a man diligently followed this desire . . . he must come out at last into the clear knowledge that the human soul was made to enjoy some object that is never fully given . . . The dialectic of Desire, faithfully followed, would retrieve all mistakes, head you off from all false paths, and force you not to propound, but to live through a sort of ontological proof."[17] In a 1939 sermon, later published under the title "The Weight of Glory" he expressed it thus:

> . . . The books or music in which we thought the beauty was located will betray us if we trust to them; it was not *in* them, it only came *through* them, and what came through them was longing. These things—the beauty, the memory of our own past—are good images of what we really desire; but if they are mistaken for the thing itself, they turn into dumb idols, breaking the hearts of their worshippers. For they are not the thing itself; they are only the scent of a flower we have not found, the echo of a tune we have not heard, news from a country we have never yet visited.[18]

The youthful sensation became a central element in his adult thought, a theme that weaves throughout all of his writings.

The death of his mother when he was nine years old in 1908, affected him for the rest of his life in a significant number of ways, physical, emotional, and spiritual. Physically, he was sent to boarding school in England immediately thereafter. Emotionally, he seems to have gone underground at this time. His naturally strong emotional make-up seems thereafter to have been treated with fear, not only because of the desire to avoid such pain, but because of the embarrassment he felt at his father's own deeply felt and deeply expressed emotional reaction to his wife's death. Spiritually, the death of his mother may have increased his sense of longing. Ann Loades cites from "The Weight of Glory" to support this idea; ". . . our lifelong nostalgia, our longing to be reunited with something in the universe from which we now feel cut off, to be on the

---

15. Lewis, *Mere Christianity*, 136.

16. For a comprehensive discussion of this whole topic, see Carnell's *Bright Shadow of Reality*.

17. Lewis, Preface to *Pilgrim's Regress*, 15.

18. Lewis, "Weight of Glory," 28–29.

inside of some door which we have always seen from the outside . . ."[19] He himself knew that the loss remained with him. In a letter written in 1953, he told a correspondent "I first met this 'cold blast on the naked heath' at about nine, when my mother died and there has never really been any sense of security and snugness since. That is, I've not quite succeeded in growing up on that point; there is still a sense of 'mammy's little lost boy' about me."[20]

Boarding school was extremely difficult, not just because of the lack of a mother's presence, but because the specific schools to which he was sent could only have exacerbated his loneliness and sense of not belonging. During his years at Malvern, he developed a pessimism and cynicism. Like Beckett, he both maintained that God did not exist—and was angry with him, both for not existing and for creating the world.[21] His times at home were also troubled. His father, although undoubtedly sensitive himself, was not sufficiently sensitive to the feeling of his sons, causing him to form what he called his Little Lea skin (based on the name of his father's house in Belfast).[22] He became intensely secretive, cultivating "a habit of concealment" as a consequence of his father's demands for confidences.[23] "I could not be myself while he was at home," he wrote.[24] His brother Warren, who wrote of the humiliating lack of privacy that their father gave them when they were young adults, corroborates this.[25] It is hardly surprising that he ended up with what he refers to in his autobiography, *Surprised by Joy* as his imaginative inner life, (in opposition to his outer life), and although he dates it back to his days at "Chartres," his second boarding school, I should think that there was much else in his history that led to this split. His time being tutored by William Kirkpatrick from 1914 to 1917, only increased this: "The two hemispheres of my mind were in the sharpest contrast. On the one side a many-islanded sea of poetry and myth; on the other a glib and shallow 'rationalism'. Nearly all that I loved I believed to be imaginary; nearly all that I believed to be real I thought grim and meaningless."[26] Kirkpatrick was a rationalist and an atheist, who grounded Lewis in the classics and

---

19. Loades, "C. S. Lewis: Grief Observed, Rationality Abandoned, Faith Regained," 36.
20. Lewis, letter to Mrs. Sandeman (December 31, 1953) *Letters*, Vol. III, 398.
21. Lewis, *Surprised by Joy*, 89.
22. Lewis, *All My Road before Me*, 109.
23. Lewis, *Surprised by Joy*, 92.
24. Ibid., 97.
25. Lewis, *C. S. Lewis 1898–1963*, folio 88.
26. Lewis, *Surprised by Joy*, 132.

"dialectic"—by which we may presume Lewis meant the Socratic method of conversational argument.[27]

The First World War contributed to the split in Lewis. Lewis devotes little of *Surprised by Joy* to the war, in part explaining away his experience in it by saying that he put it from his mind. "It is too cut off from the rest of my experience and even seems to have happened to someone else. It is even in a way unimportant."[28] Whilst biographers such as Humphrey Carpenter and Walter Hooper tend to accept this, K. James Gilchrist has argued that he was to remain not just physically, but emotionally wounded by it for the rest of his life: "As with his shell fragment, Lewis carried a fragment of his war experience hidden within him, near to his very heart. I believe that fragment represented a wounded element in him that would not be healed in this life, much like the wound in the heel of his character, Ransom, in *That Hideous Strength*."[29] Rather than speaking much about the war, Lewis's letters turn quickly to the subject of literature; it was, as Gilchrist points out, his way of coping in his early years with the many vicissitudes. In fact it had early become central to his existence. Kirkpatrick, who would have come to know Lewis well in the three years he spent in his house, wrote to his father that Lewis:

> . . . has singularly little desire to mingle with mankind, or study human nature. His interests lie in a totally different direction—in the past, in the realm of creative imagination, in the world which the common mind would call unreal but which is to him the only real one.[30]

But Lewis did not just read literature; he wrote it. And his struggle with the war can be glimpsed in his early poetry, where he rails against a malicious God who allows such suffering. Prior to and during his time at Kirkpatrick's and for the duration of the war he was an atheist, partly because of personal struggles with prayer, and partly because he could see no connection between the God of the Christianity of his childhood and the grimness of life. While at Kirkpatrick's he read Schopenhauer and honed the purely rational side of his being, in response to the emphasis of his tutor, thus driving a further wedge between inner imaginative world and the outer, rational world. "I believe in no religion. There is absolutely no proof for any of them, and from a philosophical standpoint

---

27. Ibid., 114.
28. Ibid., 152.
29. Gilchrist, "2nd Lieutenant Lewis," 77.
30. Ibid.

Christianity is not even the best. All religions, that is, all mythologies to give them their proper name, are merely man's own invention."[31]

Although he did not feel free to express this openly to his father, he did express it in his preferred genre, poetry. And like Beckett's *Dream of Fair to Middling Women*, there are indications in Lewis's early work of a tendency towards Manichaeism. *Spirits in Bondage* (published when Lewis was twenty), in his own words to Arthur Greeves, "is mainly strung around the idea that I mentioned to you before—that nature is wholly diabolical and malevolent and that God, if he exists, is outside of and in opposition to the cosmic arrangements."[32] In a number of the poems, there is considerable likeness of thought (though not of style), to that which we have seen to be characteristic of Beckett. Some lines from "De Profundis" demonstrates this:

> Come let us curse our Master ere we die,
> For all our hopes in endless ruin lie.
> The good is dead. Let us curse God most High.
>
> Four thousand years of toil and hope and thought
> Wherein men laboured upward and still wrought
> New worlds and better, Thou hast made as naught.
>
> We built us joyful cities, strong and fair,
> Knowledge we sought and gathered wisdom rare.
> And all this time you laughed upon our care,
>
> And suddenly the earth brew black with wrong,
> Our hope was crushed and silenced was our song,
> The heaven grew loud with weeping. Thou art strong.
>
> Come then and curse the Lord. Over the earth
> Gross darkness falls, and evil was our birth
> And our few happy days of little worth.
>
> Even if it be not all a dream in vain
> —The ancient hope that still will rise again—
> Of a just God that cares for earthly pain,
>
> Yet far away beyond our labouring night,
> He wanders in the depths of endless light,
> Singing alone his musics of delight;

---

31. Lewis, letter to Arthur Greeves (October 12, 1916) *They Stand Together*, 135.
32. Lewis, letter to Arthur Greeves (September 12, 1918) *They Stand Together*, 230.

> Only the far, spent echo of his song,
> Our dungeons and deep cells can smite along,
> And Thou art nearer. Thou art very strong.
>
> O universal strength, I know it well,
> It is but froth of folly to rebel,
> For thou art Lord and hast the keys of Hell.[33]

Like Beckett, Lewis's God at this stage is remote and impersonal. There is no reference to Christ, no divine involvement. The spiritual dualism reflects that other area of dualism in his life, reason and imagination. This anger at a deity reflects a haughtiness of spirit that was common to both Lewis and Beckett as they approached their thirties. Like Beckett, Lewis realized that pride was his besetting sin; he too makes reference to his "Narcissus-like" behavior.[34] Just as Beckett had written to MacGreevy about his arrogance, so Lewis, at roughly the same age, wrote to Greeves, "One out of every three is a thought of self-admiration."[35] "There seems to be no end to it. Depth under depth of self-love and self-admiration. Closely connected with this is the difficulty I find in making the faintest approach to giving up my own will: which as everyone has told us is the only thing to do." Both men felt that relinquishing their own will was crucial to their well-being.

But despite these early—and significant similarities—Beckett and Lewis diverged until they reached almost antithetical positions. And the seeds of this can be seen in the same collection of poems, poems in which we find the genesis of Lewis the theist. As Don W. King has so carefully delineated, there are other poems in the collection, poems that reveal his yearning to experience transcendence.[36] Peter J. Schakel points out that the overall emphasis of *Spirits in Bondage* is a rejection of conventional ideas about God, but which has, nonetheless, not just "enlightened" rationalism on the one hand, but a "deep sense of longing for the world of the spirit on the other" thus providing an early version of the themes of *Till We Have Faces*.[37] At this stage they are in conflict. As in Beckett's work, there is an uneasy tension between blasphemy and belief, and poems teeter on the edge of articulating "a strange god's face," as he puts it

---

33. Lewis, *Poems*, 179.
34. See "Posturing," in *Poems*, 103.
35. Lewis, letter to Arthur Greeves (January 30, 1930) *They Stand Together*, 339.
36. King, *C. S. Lewis, Poet*, 78.
37. Schakel, *Reason and Imagination in C. S. Lewis*, 94.

in "Our Daily Bread." And, with greater clarity than Beckett, he articulates an early sense of the need to transcend himself in *Tu Ne Quaesieris*:

> Yet what were endless lives to me
> If still my narrow self I be
> And hope and fail and struggle still,
> And break my will against God's will,
> To play for stakes of pleasure and pain
> And hope and fail and hope again,
> Deluded, thwarted, striving elf,
> That through the window of myself
> As through a dark glass scarce can see
> A warped and masked reality?[38]

Here is a very clear sense that the striving self leads only to a "warped and masked reality"; that life will only be a round of hope and failure if the will constantly breaks against God's will. Thus, in his twenties, Lewis decided that he could not hope to "achieve" selfhood by any effort of his own. Any attempt to "construct" a self became ideologically anathema for Lewis. The Existentialists, he said, feel *Angst* precisely because of their belief in solitary self-creation.[39] It may be that Lewis is making the same point that Kierkegaard made when he spoke of the despair of self-creation:

> Consequently, the despairing self is forever building only castles in the air, and is always only fencing with an imaginary opponent . . . The self wants in its despair to savour to the full the satisfaction of making itself into itself, of developing itself, of being itself; it wants to take the credit for this fictional, masterly project, its own way of understanding itself.[40]

Lewis's solution, at this point, is the solution of Wordsworth—to be "mingled in the large Divine," to realize that he could not exist within the confines of his own self, and that he must accept a certain "givenness" to his being. He later said that this, "for the man coming up from below" is an advance upon mere materialism, even if the dangers of eroticism and occultism must be traversed. It is to these that we shall now turn as the final factors in this exploration of Lewis's particular constitution.[41]

---

38. Lewis, *Poems*, 220.
39. Lewis, *English Literature in the Sixteenth Century Excluding Drama*, 380.
40. Kierkegaard, *Sickness Unto Death*, 100–101.
41. Lewis, "Christianity and Culture," 28.

Of his dabbling in eroticism and occultism we know very little. On the topic of the erotic, as on so many others, his final ideological stance was one to which he came through a combination of experience and the embracing of Christianity. There are hints from the censored remains of his youthful letters to Arthur Greeves of a taste for the concept of sado-masochism, although there is no evidence that this was ever more than imaginative talk. More significantly, his adulthood was dominated by his commitment to Janie Moore, with whom he lived from 1918 until 1950 when he could no longer look after her. The close relationship was an enigma to all, Mrs. Moore being strangely mismatched in interests and twenty-five years his senior. The various biographers are not agreed about the nature of their relationship, and even his brother had little insight into a relationship that perplexed him. Warren called her "Mrs King" when he wrote:

> My own guess about the whole situation is that it stemmed from my father's refusal, or rather failure, to visit Jack in hospital after he was wounded. Jack imagined that his only parent showed but a tepid affection for him, he had no mother; Mrs King had no son, and a synthetic mother-son relationship developed insensibly between them. But this is only a guess, and the secret lies buried with Jack.[42]

That there was an element of a surrogate mother/son relationship, may well be the case but whatever the reasons, the secrecy with which he clothed the relationship, even to Warren his brother, may have made a significant contribution to what was to become his mature personality. It could also be that Janie Moore was the mysterious element to which Lewis refers when he speaks of his "earlier hostility to the emotions being very fully and variously avenged" in a huge but complex episode in his life to which he is not free to refer.[43] Whatever the reason, it would seem possible that this "episode" kept his heart engaged but in a way that was incommunicable to others, thus adding to his impersonal mode of engaging with others. Whatever the original bond between Lewis and Mrs Moore, the final years would seem have been a commitment enacted by Lewis throughout the vicissitudes of her increasing jealousy and senility.

In his writing about sex however, he exhibited no coyness; as a Christian he advocated either marriage or abstinence. His marriage to Joy Davidman at the age of 57 was puzzling to many but in the end the nature

---

42. Lewis, *C. S. Lewis: 1898–1963*.
43. Lewis, *Surprised by Joy*, 154.

of their relationship was far from enigmatic: "No cranny of heart or body remained unsatisfied," he wrote after her death in *A Grief Observed*, a statement generally taken to be the voice of Lewis himself. It may be, as Gaius Davies suggests, that this was a foretaste of a "healing of harms" for Lewis.[44] But it is inevitable that both of these significant relationships played a large part in the development of his character and thought.

In his autobiography, Lewis indicates that the World, the Flesh and the Devil all enter into his life story.[45] The occult was, for Lewis, a dimension of the supernatural, and all things supernatural had an intense fascination for him. His first exposure through the Matron at his boarding school triggered his desire for the preternatural and the diminishment of his childhood belief in Christianity.[46] The passion for the Occult is, he said, "a spiritual lust; and like the lust of the body it has the fatal power of making everything else in the world seem uninteresting while it lasts."[47] He was in part deterred from pursuing the Occult by his experience of watching Janie's brother, Doc Askins, die in mental anguish. In the end, according to Lewis, he himself was wonderfully protected; partly through ignorance, partly through fear, but primarily through his experience of Joy:

> This ravenous desire to break the bounds, to tear the curtain, to be in the secret revealed itself, more and more clearly the longer I indulged it, to be quite different from the longing that is Joy. Its coarse strength betrayed it. Slowly, and with many relapses, I came to see that the magical conclusion was just as irrelevant to Joy as the erotic conclusion had been.[48]

He continues:

> What I like about experience is that it is such an honest thing. You may take any number of wrong turnings; but keep your eyes open and you will not be allowed to go very far before the warning signs appear. You may have deceived yourself, but experience is not trying to deceive you. The universe rings true wherever you fairly test it.

---

44. Davies, *Genius, Grief, and Grace*, 285.
45. Lewis, *Surprised by Joy*, 136.
46. Ibid., 45.
47. Ibid.
48. Ibid., 137.

And so he began to move away from the "suffocatingly subjective" stance that had been his mode for much of his life.[49] It seems that it is primarily at this point that the divergence of the ways of Beckett and Lewis occurs.

A Road Right out of the Self : Rejection of Introspection

One particularly similar occurrence in their lives serves to demonstrate this divergence, and it is profoundly telling, for it seems to me that the reactions and behavior in this sphere determined—to a very large extent—the respective courses taken by the lives and literary outputs of Beckett and Lewis. Both men kept up lifelong correspondence with a good friend in Ireland, in Beckett's case with Thomas MacGreevy and in Lewis's case with Arthur Greeves. Each of these relationships was a lifelong baring of mind and heart, but there is one fascinating parallel that took place when both men were aged twenty-seven or twenty-eight. In fact, note has already been taken of Beckett's reaction, to a suggestion by MacGreevy in 1935 that he should read Thomas à Kempis. Although Beckett rejected à Kempis's "self-referring quietism," he accepted and acted upon the point that lay behind MacGreevy's recommendation, that he should counter his self-immersion by taking a more lively interest in others. It could be argued that this was a crucial counterpoise to his inner turn of 1945. Lewis, in a remarkably similar event at the age of 28, broached the same subject in a letter to Greeves, expressing his desire to escape what he calls a disease. He reflected upon the process which he had observed in himself whilst writing his narrative poem *Dymer*, which he worked upon—in various guises—from 1916 until 1926 or so;

> . . . The cure of this disease is not easy to find . . . I was free from it at times when writing Dymer. Then I was interested in the object, not in my own privileged position as seer of the object. But whenever I stopped writing or thought of publication or showed the MS to friends I contemplated not that of which I had been writing, but my writing about it: I passed from looking at the macrocosm to looking at a little historical event inside the "Me." The only healthy or happy or eternal life is to look so steadily on the World that the representation "Me" fades away. Its appearance at all in the field of consciousness is a mark of inferiority in the state where it appears. Its claiming a central position is disease.[50]

49. "Suffocatingly subjective" is the phrase used by Lewis to describe his account of his early life and conversion in *Surprised by Joy*.

50. Lewis, letters to Greeves (August 18, 1930) *They Stand Together*, 383–84. The passage is actually taken from a diary extract from March 6, 1926 that Lewis forwarded to Greeves in 1930.

And in another letter in 1930 he confessed, "I catch myself posturing before the mirror, so to speak, all day long. I pretend I am carefully thinking out what to say to the next pupil (for *his* good, of course) and then suddenly realize I am really thinking how frightfully clever I'm going to be and how he will admire me."[51] Even earlier than that we see a glimpse of his determination to avoid introspection. His experience of the mentally anguished death of Doc Askins in the early 1920s was perhaps a clarion call. "Keep clear of introspection, of brooding, of spiritualism, of everything eccentric. Keep to work and sanity and open air—to the cheerful & the matter of fact side of things," he told Greeves.[52]

Philosophy also led him to this position. He taught philosophy at University College, Oxford in 1924/25, and A. N. Wilson suggests that the philosophical attempt to consider virtue was the beginning of a metaphysical turn to his thought.[53] Lewis comments that the teaching of philosophy forced him to clarify the terms which he was using and this in itself was enough to drive him from a watered down Hegelianism to a somewhat abstract use of the term "God."[54] He was "driven back into something like Berkeleyanism"; "the simple, workable, theistic idealism of Berkeley."[55] It was not Berkeley's subjectivism (which so intrigued Beckett; "to be is to be perceived") but his theistic idealism (and perhaps something of the thought that was later to play into Personalism with its emphasis upon the person as the basic concept and unit of value in the explanation of reality). But another text from this time was crucial in his step away from introspection. His reading of Samuel Alexander's *Space, Time and Deity* in 1925 gave him intellectual reasons to set aside introspection other than for purposes of understanding consciousness. He accepted Alexander's distinction between "enjoyment" and "contemplation."[56] Lewis explains it this way; "Enjoyment has nothing to do with pleasure, nor 'Contemplation' with the contemplative life. When you see a table you 'enjoy' the act of seeing and 'contemplate' the table." In other words, a clear distinction must be made between attention to an object and the feelings that arise with regard to that object. For Lewis, the consequences were instantly and "catastrophically" obvious:

---

51. Ibid., (January 30, 1930) 339.
52. Ibid., (April 22, [1923]) 292.
53. Wilson, *C. S. Lewis: A Biography*, 85–87.
54. Lewis, *Surprised by Joy*, 173.
55. Ibid., 173.
56. Ibid., 169f.

> It seemed to me self-evident that one essential property of love, hate, fear, hope, or desire was attention to their object. To cease thinking about or attending to the woman is, so far, to cease loving; to cease thinking about or attending to the dreaded thing is, so far, to cease being afraid. But to attend to your own love or fear is to cease attending to the loved or dreaded object. In other words the enjoyment and the contemplation of our inner activities are incompatible. You cannot hope and also think about hoping at the same moment; for in hope we look to hope's object and we interrupt this by (so to speak) turning round to look at the hope itself. Of course, the two activities can and do alternate with great rapidity; but they are distinct and incompatible.[57]

In this sense, introspection falsifies, or as Lewis puts it, misleads:

> . . . it followed that all introspection is in one respect, misleading. In introspection we try to look "inside ourselves" and see what is going on. But nearly everything that was going on a moment before is stopped by the very act of our turning to look at it. Unfortunately this does not mean that introspection finds nothing. On the contrary, it finds precisely what is left behind by the suspension of all our normal activities; and what is left behind is mainly mental images and physical sensations. The great error is to mistake this mere sediment or track or by-product for the activities themselves.[58]

It may well be for this reason (as Stephen Medcalf has suggested) that Lewis disliked the works of Joyce and other modernist writers who are engaged in trying to catch consciousness through introspection.[59] In *A Preface to Paradise Lost* (1942) he wrote about the critical reaction to "such a work as *Ulysses*":

> In my opinion this whole type of criticism is based on an error. The disorganised consciousness which it regards as specially real is in fact highly artificial. It is discovered by introspection—that is, by artificially suspending all the normal and outgoing activities of the mind and then attending to what is left. In that residuum it discovers no concentrated will, no logical thought, no morals, no stable sentiments, and (in a word) no mental hierarchy. Of course not: for we have deliberately stopped all these things in order to introspect. The poet who finds by introspection that the soul is mere chaos is like a policeman who, having himself stopped all

---

57. Ibid., 170.
58. Ibid.
59. Medcalf, "Language and Self-Consciousness."

the traffic in a certain street, should then solemnly write down in his note-book "The stillness in the street is very suspicious . . ."[60]

In other words, introspection falsifies because the normal constraints are removed.[61] Lewis coupled this aversion to subjectivity with his experience of *Sehnsucht*, realizing that it is the very "otherness" which had drawn him. "Desire is turned not to itself but to its object."[62] Having tried by elimination to capture this Joy, his eventual conclusion was that Joy was not a state, it was a way:

> Inexorably Joy proclaimed, "You want—I myself am your want of—something other, outside, not you nor any state of you" . . . I thus understood that in deepest solitude there is a road right out of the self, a commerce with something which, by refusing to identify itself with any object of the sense, or anything whereof we have biological or social need, or anything imagined, or any state of our own minds, proclaims itself as sheerly objective. Far more objective than bodies, for it is not, like them, clothed in our senses; the naked Other, imageless (though our imagination salutes it with a hundred images), unknown, undefined, desired.[63]

Although this Other was not yet identified with God, Lewis's realization was to form one of the Four Moves which lead to his conversion, and it pointed him radically outward towards the stance on the self which Lewis was to hold to until the mid-50's. In *Surprised by Joy*, published in 1955, he explained that the realization of the need for this stance was a significant part of his conversion to Christianity. His autobiography charts his progression from atheism to Philosophical Idealism, from Idealism to Pantheism and from Pantheism to Theism, before his conversion to Christianity. He says there ". . . one of the first results of my Theistic conversion was a marked decrease in the fussy attentiveness which I had so long paid to the progress of my own opinions and the states of my own mind . . . to believe and to pray were the beginning of extroversion. I had been, as they say, 'taken out of myself.'"[64]

For the next thirty years, he labored to purge himself of any suggestion of what he called the "disease." Lewis, like Beckett had raised the

---

60. Lewis, *Preface to Paradise Lost*, 135–36. Italics mine.

61. We do know that Lewis may have come across something similar to this (the systematically elusive "I") in a discussion group in Oxford with Gilbert Ryle, but I can find no explicit reference to Ryle as having made an impact upon Lewis.

62. Lewis, *Surprised by Joy*, 171.

63. Ibid., 172.

64. Ibid., 181.

question of the danger of the subject as object under surveillance, the attempt to capture the elusive "I" that looks somewhat like the kitten trying to catch its own tail. And it proved to be a crucial turning point for him. It is on this particular point that the two men's lives diverge. Whereas Beckett's "outer turn" took the form of increased contact with others, it also included psychotherapy which is, by nature, a form of therapy that focuses on the interior condition of the patient, thereby throwing him or her back into the posture of reflexivity. And he coupled this with his deliberate choice to write out of an introspective posture. Lewis, instead took a very different path. His thoughts, he said, became centripetal rather than centrifugal.[65] His emphasis upon the Other lead him to value objective meaning, and to reject the subjectivism which he had come to believe was so damaging. The transfer of meaning to the "Subject" rather than an external "Object" became an issue that he targeted again and again. Lewis's emphasis is manifest in his fiction and non-fiction works, as well as his literary criticism. Scott Oury has gone so far as to say that this attention to "the object itself" was the dominant quality of Lewis's life work and thought.[66] For example, in "The Poison of Subjectivism" and *The Abolition of Man* he argued emphatically for objective values; "This whole attempt to jettison traditional values as something subjective and to substitute a new scheme for them is wrong. It is like trying to lift yourself by your own coat collar."[67]

In *The Allegory of Love* (1936 but written several years before) Lewis ruminates upon Augustine's role in a societal inner turn. And in a preface written in 1952 he argues that humans have emptied the universe by this turn to subjectivity:

> At the outset, the universe appears packed with will, intelligence, life and positive qualities; every tree is a nymph and every planet a god. Man himself is akin to the gods. The advance of knowledge gradually empties this rich and genial universe: first of its gods, then of its colors, smells, sounds and tastes, finally of solidity itself as solidity was originally imagined. As these items are taken from the world, they are transferred to the subjective side of the account: classified as our sensations, thoughts, images or emotions. The Subject becomes gorged, inflated, at the expense of the Object.[68]

65. Ibid., 172.
66. Oury, "'Thing Itself,'" 1–19.
67. Lewis, "Poison of Subjectivism," 94.
68. Lewis, Preface to D. E. Harding, *Hierarchy of Heaven and Earth*, 9–10.

In *The Discarded Image*, published in 1964, he summed this up as being "that great movement of internalisation, and that consequent aggrandisement of man and desiccation of the outer universe, in which the psychological history of the West has so largely consisted."[69] But the emptying of the universe will lead to the emptying of the person:

> The same method which has emptied the world now proceeds to empty ourselves. The masters of the method soon announce that we were just as mistaken (and mistaken in much the same way) when we attributed "souls," "selves" or "minds" to human organisms, as when we attributed Dryads to the trees . . . We, who have personified all other things, turn out to be ourselves, mere personifications . . . And thus we arrive at a result uncommonly like zero. While we were reducing the world to almost nothing we deceived ourselves with the fancy that all its lost qualities were being kept safe (if in a somewhat humbled condition) as "things in our own mind." Apparently we had no mind of the sort required. The Subject is as empty as the Object. Almost nobody has been making linguistic mistakes about almost nothing. By and large this is the only thing that has ever happened.[70]

Empty, zero, nothing, nobody; it was as if Lewis foresaw the kenotic impulses of Anglo-American deconstructionism, the zero theology of which Steiner speaks.[71] (It is certainly interesting to note that Lewis was writing this critique at the same time that Beckett was undergoing the Siege in the Room, having made the conscious choice to allow the "hegemony of the inner life" to dominate his writing.[72]) Lewis concludes *The Discarded Image* (1964) with the same point. Literature has undergone a great change since the Middle Ages, a change that elevates the poet, and not the content of his poetry; but in elevating the subject, the subject itself becomes lost:

> In this great change something has been won and something lost. I take it to be part and parcel of the same great process of Internalisation which has turned genius from an attendant *daemon* into a quality of the mind. Always, century by century, item after item is transferred from the object's side of the account to the subject's. And now, in some extreme forms of Behaviourism the

---

69. Lewis, *Discarded Image*, 42.
70. Lewis, Preface to D. E. Harding, *Hierarchy of Heaven and Earth*, 9–10.
71. In *That Hideous Strength* he suggested that the vacuum was in danger of being filled by a concentration upon power, even the *Anima Mundi* of the magicians.
72. Beckett was probably writing *Malone Dies* and *The Unnamable* during 1952.

subject himself is discounted as merely subjective; we only think that we think. Having eaten up everything else, he eats himself up too. And where we "go from that" is a dark question.[73]

"This Construction Me": Lewis's Persona

In emptying the universe of the Object, modernity has performed a kind of kenotic act. But clearly, this was not the sort of kenoticism that Lewis wanted to embrace. It was consistently his choice to try to embrace another, very different kind, one in which he negated himself as subject in order to focus on the Object, or Other. This kenotic impulse shall be explored in the next chapter. It is the consequences that are relevant here. For the outworking of Lewis's emphasis led to a somewhat strange imbalance in his life and writings. Particularly revealing is a series of exchanges with E. M. W. Tillyard, (originally published in 1934/35 in *Essays and Studies of the English Association*). In these, Lewis articulated his rejection of the emphasis found in modern criticism upon the character or personality of the poet, an emphasis which he called the Personal Heresy: "In this paper I shall maintain that when we read poetry as poetry should be read, we have before us no representation which claims to be the poet, and frequently no representation of a *man*, a *character*, or a *personality* at all."[74] He claimed that the reader shared the consciousness of the poet; "I look with his eyes, not at him."[75] The poet therefore should focus not on what is private and personal but what is public, common, impersonal and objective. Tillyard's Rejoinder made a number of points, amongst which he said that he found Lewis "too rigidly concerned with things and too little heedful of states of mind." He stated that a biographical approach may "substantially help our understanding of the mental pattern as revealed in [the artist's] art" when one's own understanding had come to a standstill.[76] To this Lewis replied that, on the contrary, it was because he revered personality that he objected to its use being perverted by inappropriate usage, by a kind of Poetolatry. Perhaps most interesting of all, Lewis made no reply at all to the presentation of a paradox which was ultimately to become central to his own approach. Referring to T. S. Eliot's "Tradition and the Individual Talent," Tillyard proposed that his "continual extinction of personality" was part of a paradox which,

---

73. Lewis, *Discarded Image*, 214–15.
74. Lewis, "Personal Heresy in Criticism," 9.
75. Ibid., 15.
76. Tillyard, "Personal Heresy in Criticism: A Rejoinder," 16–17.

"consists in the poet often producing the most characteristic and personal work through this very process of self-surrender. The more the poet experiences this abandonment of personality, the more likely is the reader to hail the poet's characteristic, unmistakable self. In fact the poet is *ipsissimus cum minime ipse.*"[77] Lewis's reply seems uncharacteristically tangential; James Como speaks of his "vastly over-argued protestations."[78] The problem may have been exacerbated by the terms of the debate; he was arguing for a Christian view in a secular debate. He is only just implicit about his belief that meaning is created by God—and that humans are just sub-creators. About this he was more explicit in "Christianity and Literature," an article published some years later. The primary targets of his criticism, (in this essay and in 'Christianity and Culture') were F. R. Leavis and I. A. Richards who were disproportionately emphasizing the role of the poet *because* of their emphasis upon subjectivity. But in attacking *subjectivism*, Lewis seems to have fallen into the opposite danger to Leavis and Richards. He tried to do away with the Subject entirely. It seems that on this occasion he could not hold together the two sides of the paradox.

It was not just Tillyard who pinpointed a problem with the stance that Lewis took. Owen Barfield, who emphasized throughout the subjective element in perception, had been frustrated by Lewis's emphasis upon the object, refusing any psychological element to perception.[79] Lewis continued to distinguish between the perceiving subject and the perceived object. In 1934 Barfield read Lewis's *Open Letter to Dr Tillyard* and proclaimed it *pastiche*. For him, both then and right into the 50s, Lewis effectively split himself into two, a fact that Barfield went so far as to embody in a poem and present to Lewis.[80] Barfield concluded that this strange state of affairs was somehow in Lewis's own hands; "*Was* there something, at least in his impressive, indeed splendid, literary personality, which was somehow—and with no taint of insincerity—*voulu*?"[81] Lewis, he felt, had developed a persona. Specifically, he ties this to Lewis's attitude on the self:

> What I think is true is, that at a certain stage in his life he deliberately ceased to take any interest in himself except as a kind of

77. Ibid., 7 and 13.
78. Como, *Branches to Heaven*, 114.
79. A series of exchanges between them, called the Great War, has been explored by Lionel Adey in *C. S. Lewis's "Great War" with Owen Barfield*.
80. Barfield, Introduction to *Light on C. S. Lewis*, xiv–xvi.
81. Ibid., xi.

> spiritual alumnus taking his moral finals. I think this was part of the change to which I have referred; and I suggest that what began as deliberate choice became at length (as he had no doubt always intended it should) an ingrained and effortless habit of soul. Self-knowledge, for him, had come to mean recognition of his own weaknesses and shortcomings and nothing more. Anything beyond that he sharply suspected, both in himself and in others, as a symptom of megalomania. At best, there was so much else, in letters and in life, that he found much more interesting![82]

At worst, Barfield suggests, Lewis's refusal to pay any attention to himself led, not simply to a healthy objectivity, but to an unhealthy misunderstanding of object/objectivity and subject/subjectivity. Peter Schakel makes explicit what Barfield implies; "Barfield's concern—and I think it has not been given sufficient attention in considerations of Lewis's work—is that a consciousness of self, and of the inevitability of a degree of subjectivity, is necessary to proper understanding even of 'objective' things, and that Lewis's failure to include self in his thinking was an inhibiting factor in his thought and work."[83] A. N. Wilson comments that Lewis, after his conversion, "did completely change his view, not only of his own personality but of human personality in general." And he perceives it as a negative change, because of the way it played itself out in Lewis's life:

> It is said that when he heard his own voice on the radio . . . Lewis was surprised and in some measure disconcerted. In a similar way he might have been surprised by the figure he cut in prose, or come to that in life. But he was in no sense putting on an act. The strange locutions, the shabby clothes, the combination of kindliness and brusqueness, the strong "personality" but increasing *impersonality* of his conversation and interests, were all part of the same process. It is comparable with the oddness which might visit all our outward appearances if we stopped looking in mirrors. The only contrived thing about it was the initial impulse, which interpreted the New Testament injunction to deny self as to "live without an image of the self." The "image" of C. S. Lewis, which many were to find rebarbative, was not, as they imagined, stage-managed or rehearsed, but it was nonetheless odd for that.[84]

Despite Wilson's somewhat simplified view of the cause of this change, his charge of impersonality serves to reiterate Barfield's accusations.

82. Ibid., xvi.
83. Schakel, *Reason and Imagination in C. S. Lewis*, 89.
84. Wilson, *C. S. Lewis: A Biography*, 147.

Wilson emphasizes that Lewis disliked sharing spoken intimacies with friends, and that he showed no interest whatsoever in a friend's private life whenever they met up; "all that would have been discussed would have been the merits of Layamon as a poet, or the rights and wrongs of cannibalism."[85] Chad Walsh has also spoken of Lewis's outer turn as being primarily an interest in and sharing of ideas: "These comments must be modified when considering certain of Lewis's later books, but in general they ring true to anyone who knew Lewis. He was at the same time remarkably open and remarkably shut. The world of his mind was freely available to friends and public. The world of feelings and intuitions was sparingly shared, or conveyed in such transformed style as to seem divorced from its source."[86] Another who knew him, John Wain, has said that everyone who knew Lewis was aware of this strange dichotomy, "The outer self—brisk, challenging, argumentative, full of an overweening physical energy and confidence—covered an inner self as tender and as well-hidden as a crab's."[87]

The outworking of the dichotomy has been explored by Stephen Medcalf.[88] Medcalf, who argues that Lewis shed one persona (in the late 1920's) in order to create another, lists a substantial portion of Lewis's mature works as being written in the spirit of what he calls Lewis's "Middle-Period Persona." In this list he includes the works that made Lewis best known; the space trilogy, several of his Christian books and a couple of his academic books.[89] Medcalf suggests that Lewis's persona was primarily because of his rejection of introspection. Whilst Medcalf is right to identify such a mid-life persona, he, like Wilson, oversimplifies. To pick up on Wilson's apt image, Lewis refused not only the mirroring of introspection, but he also refused the mirroring which comes from the kind of friendship that allows people to get close enough to speak truth into one's life.

It is possible to speculate that Lewis's shell had developed in response to those factors which we have already explored; a childhood which had

---

85. Ibid., 235.
86. Walsh, *Literary Legacy of C. S. Lewis*, 8.
87. Wain, Encounter 22, 51–54. Published in *Critical Thought Series 1, C. S. Lewis*, 27.
88. Stephen Medcalf, "Language and Self-Consciousness."
89. The other books Medcalf lists are: *The Problem of Pain, Mere Christianity, The Abolition of Man, Miracles, The Screwtape Letters, The Great Divorce, A Preface to Paradise Lost, English Literature in the Sixteenth Century.* He goes on to say, "I am sorry he is best known for this period because, superb as some of these books are and profoundly wise as much of the thought that they embody is, I do not think that they include his very best and am sure they do not include his most original work" (119–20).

been traumatized by the loss of his mother, the unhelpful behavior of his father. Lewis himself said that his shyness of emotions was because he had found his father's vacillating emotions embarrassing.[90] The protective barrier may then have been exacerbated by a number of other factors as he moved into adulthood. Boarding school, life with W. T. Kirkpatrick, the war, and his life as a don may have been further contributory factors. These may not have been helped by the sharing of his life with Janie Moore, which—for whatever reason—was shrouded in mystery. All these may have may have contributed to the development of a kind of Stoicism. (Kierkegaard called this kind of construction of the self, "Stoicism," although he fully knew that it was not "just in the sense of the sect").[91] An emphasis upon reason and virtue, and a detachment from the emotions—*apatheia*—may have taken root in Lewis early, to be further strengthened by his reading of Medieval and Renaissance thought. For example, Boethius' definition of a person—"A person is an individual substance of a rational nature"—is just one example of the way that Stoic thought took root throughout the Middle Ages. Ideologically, of course, Lewis rejected many elements of Stoicism, including Boethius' definition of a person, but like so many other thinkers whom he enjoyed—Aquinas, Calvin, Shakespeare—he incorporated more Stoicism than he was consciously aware of incorporating. *The Abolition of Man*, for example, does not extol the virtuous life, as such, but his argument that natural law is compatible with Mosaic law is essentially Stoic.[92] (It is hardly accidental that the word "persona" meaning specifically "mask" but also "person" dates back to Roman times.) Charles Taylor speaks of the specifically modern variant of Stoicism which has developed 'the disengaged self, capable of objectifying not only the surrounding world but also his own emotions and inclinations, fears and compulsions, and achieving thereby a kind of distance and self-possession which allows him to act "rationally."[93] James Houston highlights the Stoic idea of personhood as one of the most enduring:

> Of all the ongoing theories of human identity, that of the Stoic character has had the greatest persistence, simply because it is the one in which the psychological and physiological traits can be most closely linked within a rational explanation . . . It provides a

---

90. Carpenter, *Inklings*, 59–60.

91. Kierkegaard, *Sickness Unto Death*, 99.

92. For the intertwining of Stoicism with Western Christendom, and a critique of the dangers of this, see Houston, *Mentored Life*, 51–58.

93. C. Taylor, *Sources of the Self*, 21.

"natural" framework of rational habits that give shape, form and continuity to being a "habituated self" that appears cognitively reinforcing. It gives little scope, however, for the contingency of the emotions, other than the sexual, in a more personalized world of self-transcendence.[94]

Whatever the factors that affected Lewis, the consequence was, as Wilson points out, that he kept people at arm's length. He was like a crab, a lobster, a dragon, using his outer coat to protect himself. It was a fact that he himself seemed to be dimly aware of; there is even an implicit suggestion that it was brought to his attention by divine intervention. In retrospect, as he writes of his conversion experience in *Surprised by Joy*, he says:

> Without words and (I think) almost without images, a fact about myself was somehow presented to me. I became aware that I was holding something at bay, or shutting something out. Or, if you like, that I was wearing some stiff clothing, like corsets, or even a suit of armour, as if I were a lobster.[95]

Medcalf traces the use of these images in the late 1940s into the mid-50s and finds them not only in *Surprised by Joy* but in the Narnia tales also and he explicitly connects them to Lewis's own sense that he had a persona that he needed to shed.[96] But the persona did not disappear; quite the contrary, in fact. It is not insignificant that Eustace in *The Voyage of the Dawn Treader* finds that he cannot shed the dragon's skin himself, no matter how he tries to shed the scaley layers. He needs Aslan's help. It would seem to have been so for Lewis; he was unable to shed the protective layer without external help. But it was many years before help came.

The Unknown Depth: Interest in Psychology

It may be that some dim awareness of the complexities of his own being led him towards an interest in psychology. Lewis, like Beckett, was interested in the "new Psychology," or psychoanalysis. According to his diaries he read some Freud and Jung and other books on psychoanalysis in 1922; "we did not swallow it whole (few people then did) but we were all influenced."[97] As a mature adult he believed that it—like Christianity—was a "technique for putting the human machine right"

---

94. Houston, *Mentored Life*, 111.
95. Lewis, *Surprised by Joy*, 174.
96. Medcalf, "Language and Self-Consciousness."
97. Lewis, *Surprised by Joy*, 158.

which overlapped with Christian morality at some points; "and it would not be a bad thing if every person knew something about it."[98] In effect, psychoanalysis can help a person to have neuroses cured—in order to be better placed to make the right moral choices. More than that, psychoanalysis restored the depth in a world wounded by the superficiality of materialism.[99] He maintained this to the end. In the last book he wrote, *Prayer: Letters to Malcolm* he said; "We are greatly indebted to [the Freudians]. They did expose the cowardly evasions of self-knowledge which we had all been practicing from the beginning of the world."[100]

But Lewis had many criticisms to make of Freudian thought, considering it reductionistic. The idea of the super ego, with its suggestion that the conscience was external coercion internalized, was at odds with his own beliefs. He disliked the psychoanalytic emphasis upon repression, for he felt that it diminished human awareness of shame, guilt and sin.[101] He particularly came to dislike the concept of wish-fulfillment, believing that it had, for a while, deflected him from truly understanding the concept of Joy. Freud also spoke of *Sehnsucht*. In a paper published in 1899, Freud spoke of a longing that accompanied him all of his life.[102] But his conclusions were antithetical to Lewis's; we ourselves create objects of desire. In *The Pilgrim's Regress*, Sigismund Enlightenment asks John, "Have you never before imagined anything to be true because you greatly wished for it?" Sigismund argues that such wishes are a pretence to conceal his own lusts from himself.[103] For Freud, God was a Feuerbachian projection. In fact, Lewis came to turn the whole concept on its head, arguing *contra* Freud, that instead of our desire for God being misdirected sexual desire, our desire for sex is more likely to be an aspect of the desiring self which is intended to lead us to God.[104]

On the other hand, Lewis considered Jung's thought on myth and imagery to be more humane and civil, perhaps partly because of Jung's use of archetypes, for he considered Jung's attempt to explore archetypes

---

98. Lewis, *Mere Christianity*, 88–89.
99. Lewis, "Psycho-Analysis and Literary Criticism," 299.
100. Lewis, *Prayer: Letters to Malcolm*, 32.
101. Lewis, *Problem of Pain*, 44–46.
102. Nicholi, *Question of God*, 47.
103. Lewis, *Pilgrim's Regress*, 75.

104. That all literary works may be reduced to wish fulfilment he specifically challenged in "Psycho-Analysis and Literary Criticism." In *Pilgrim's Regress*, Book IV, Lewis points out that it could equally be argued that it is Freudianism that is self-authenticating.

one of history's few attempts to explore the significance of myths.[105] That Jung was influential on his thought can be seen from a simple comment in a letter to a correspondent about *Till We Have Faces*. "I expect some Jungianisms do come in but the main conscious prosework is Christian, not Jungian."[106] Certainly Orual has dreams that are informative, as part of what could be described as her journey of individuation.[107] It is also interesting to note, in passing, in the lecture notes that became *Spenser's Images of Life*, that he comments upon the way in which Jung's archetypes could be seen in *The Faerie Queene*, giving particular attention to potential personas.[108] The idea of the collective unconscious was of great interest to Lewis; that we might have inborn images or archetypes that could be uncovered resonated with his own desires to peer behind the veil of the material world. Dealing with the beginnings and foundations of the mind, "things that from immemorial time have lain buried in the depths," Jung offered back some kind of depth.[109] But in the end, as Lewis explained in "Psycho-Analysis and Literary Criticism," "there are some grounds for suspecting that (Jung's) argument seems plausible not because of its real cogency but because of the powerful emotions it arouses."[110] Lewis had no belief in universal consciousness of the kind that merges all particularity into a unity. In fact, it is his demonic characters who desire this. In *The Screwtape Letters,* Our Father Below feeds on souls that are merged; Weston, in *Perelandra,* believes in the merging of souls, as does Withers in *That Hideous Strength*. They sought unity that would transcend individuality. Ultimately, psychoanalysis proved inadequate for Lewis, despite the potency of its rhetoric. It did not answer the sheer complexities of consciousness. In *Prayer: Letters to Malcolm* Lewis commented that consciousness is really a facade, "the thinnest possible film on the surface of a vast deep." His quarrel with the psychoanalysts was that they underestimated the sheer power of the unconscious; "Their real error lies in underestimating the depth and variety of its contents. Dazzling lightness as well as dark clouds come up . . . and depths of time too. All my past; my ancestral past; perhaps my pre-human past."[111] In

---

105. See "On Stories," in *Of This and Other Worlds*, 25.
106. Lewis, letter to Patricia (March 26, 1963), *C. S. Lewis: Letters to Children*, 107.
107. For more detail on this see Myers, *Bareface: A Guide to C. S Lewis's Last Novel.*
108. Lewis, *Spenser's Images of Life*, 117.
109. Lewis, "Psycho-Analysis and Literary Criticism," 298.
110. Ibid., 299.
111. Lewis, *Prayer: Letters to Malcolm*, 75–76.

short, as he concluded in *The Pilgrim's Regress,* psychoanalysis paid insufficient attention to the trio, Reason, Philosophy and Theology.

There is an interesting paradox at work here, for Lewis's rejection of introspection seems, in the long run to have freed him to become much more aware of the question of consciousness. He became a student of human nature that Kirkpatrick could not have foreseen. David Downing has pointed out that when Lewis gave up introspection as self-therapy, he took it up as a philosophy.[112] Lewis puts it this way in *Surprised by Joy*; "Self-examination did of course continue. But it was (I suppose, for I cannot quite remember) at stated intervals, and for a practical purpose; a duty, a discipline, an uncomfortable thing, no longer a hobby or habit." Consciousness, for him, became an instrument to be explored—measured against his experience of Joy. For he believed that the visitations of desire were "the moments of clearest consciousness we had."[113]

Possibly through his philological studies, and probably through George MacDonald, he came to believe that both consciousness and conscience were intimately linked to each other and to our experience of God.[114] This can be seen in *Studies in Words* (1960).[115] The study there seems to provide a backdrop for his late thoughts on the matter of consciousness: "conscience" (*conscientia, suneidesis*) in the classics only meant knowing what others did not know; conscience was not a guide but a witness with which one was complicit. The New Testament may have contributed to the semantic shift that introduced the concept of the conscience in the role of moral judgment, as an inner lawgiver, almost. "Consciousness" then took the role of the witness. Lewis draws no theological conclusions whatsoever here but the early usage which he delineates—the sense of one being complicit with oneself—seems to correspond to his increasing sense that our consciousness is effectively continuous with the consciousness of God. He further spells out the connection between consciousness and God in layman's terms in an article called "The Seeing Eye," published in February 1963 for an American periodical *Show*. He comments that his effort to obey his conscience was what led to his conversion to Christianity—and a change in his concept of himself:

---

112. Downing, *Most Reluctant Convert,* 161.

113. Lewis, *Surprised by Joy,* 172.

114. We shall see more of the connection between MacDonald and Lewis later in the chapter.

115. Lewis, *Studies in Words,* 181–213.

> Presently you begin to wonder whether you are yet, in any full sense, a person at all; whether you are entitled to call yourself "I" (it is a sacred name). In that way, the process is like being psychoanalysed, only cheaper—I mean in dollars; in some other ways it may be more costly. You find that what you called yourself is only a thin film on the surface of an unsounded and dangerous sea. But not merely dangerous. Radiant things, delights and inspirations, come to the surface as well as snarling resentments and nagging lusts. One's ordinary self is, then, a mere facade. There's a huge area out of sight behind it.[116]

His argument continues that certain people—presumably himself included—may come to the conviction that their contact with the mystery (by which he means God) is at its closest through their own being;

> . . . your contact with that mystery in the area you call yourself is a good deal closer than your contact through what you call matter. For in the one case I, the ordinary conscious I, am continuous with the unknown depth.
>
> And after that, you may come (some do) to believe that that voice—like all the rest, I must speak symbolically—that voice which speaks in your conscience and in some of your intensest joys, which is sometimes so obstinately silent, sometimes so easily silenced, and then at other times so loud and emphatic, is in fact the closest contact you have with the mystery; and therefore finally to be trusted, obeyed, feared and desired more than all other things.[117]

He goes on to say, "Much depends on the seeing eye."[118] It is here we realize that Lewis has just completed a profound turnaround. The man who rejected introspection so wholeheartedly seems to have come full circle. No longer is he banishing the subject and subjectivity in favor of the object—rather he is advocating what he calls in *Prayer: Letters to Malcolm* the subject-object embrace. But the difference is crucial. It is not the conscious mind looking into the unconscious—as in introspection. Now he wishes to allow that which is beyond consciousness to come into contact with consciousness; a kind of supraconsciousness, a living beyond oneself. Lewis could well have echoed Kierkegaard's words "It is perfectly true, isolated subjectivity is, in the opinion of the age, evil; but 'objectivity' as a cure is not one whit better. The only salvation is subjectivity, i.e.

---

116. Lewis, "Seeing Eye," 216.
117. Ibid.
118. Ibid., 217.

God, as infinite compelling subjectivity."[119] There is a kind of subjectivity, both Kierkegaard and Lewis conclude, that includes the engagement of the knower in the knowledge; it is this that is the antidote to the evils of pure subjectivity and pure objectivity alone.

The Reawakened Awareness: Lewis's Changed Stance on the Self

The change in C. S. Lewis has been noted by a number of scholars. Both Schakel and Medcalf—and Wilson too—say something of particular pertinence here, for they pinpoint a change in Lewis's later works, a change that does not seem to have been discerned by Barfield when he speaks of Lewis as lacking in self-knowledge. Schakel puts it this way: "Barfield does not indicate that this attitude changed later in Lewis's life. It appears to me, however, that for the final decade and a half of his life Lewis gradually shifted his emphasis to give fuller consideration to the self and the subjective, simultaneous with and related to an altered emphasis on reason and imagination, all of which leads to a remarkably different tone in his later works."[120] "Consciousness of self, and of self as a necessary aspect of perceiving, thinking and imagining, is a factor that shaped Lewis's works in the last decade of his life, particularly *Surprised by Joy*, which was crucial in preparing the way for *Till We Have Faces* and the subsequent books."[121] Medcalf suggests that the Narnia Books and *Surprised by Joy* bear some marks of this change too. Schakel's interest is in the altered emphasis on reason and imagination; mine on the altered emphasis on self and the subjective, as evidenced in the later work, especially *Till We Have Faces*, but also hinted at in a host of other ways. In fact, the books written in the 60's led to a number of accusations that he was just writing about himself. For example, Tolkien suggested that *Prayer: Letters to Malcolm* was all about Lewis praying and not about prayer.[122] *A Grief Observed* was so very personal that he fell back on a pseudonym, N. W. Clark. *Experiment in Criticism* (1961) could, according to A. N. Wilson also be said to be "not about literature but about Lewis Reading."[123] Schakel delineates his argument there:

---

119. Kierkegaard, *Journals of Soren Kierkegaard*, 184.
120. Schakel, *Reason and Imagination in C. S. Lewis*, 90.
121. Ibid., 151.
122. Wilson, *C. S. Lewis: A Biography*, 289.
123. Ibid., 290.

> He remains a firm objectivist, but does so while granting that objectivism is not so simple and clear-cut in practice as it had seemed to him in the thirties and forties. He attempts to develop an approach which accents the activity of reading, while retaining an emphasis upon the work as object . . . Lewis's distinction is not between a nonsubjective activity (receiving) and a subjective one (using), but between an acceptable kind and degree of subjectivity (one kept in check by contact with external reality) and a kind less acceptable because it is unrestrained by reality.[124]

The self, Lewis learnt, and as Paul Homer points out, "is both a recipient of a host of things and also an active agent. More properly, the self is a relation, not a thing."[125] This new view of the self will receive a thorough exploration in the next chapter.

The change in Lewis would seem to have been wrought in multiple ways and Schakel and Medcalf both delineate reasons for the changes that are evident in Lewis's work. Schakel—to turn to him first—discusses three stages in Lewis's struggle between reason and the imagination, highlighting his initial orientation towards total objectivity; followed by a lessening of reliance upon reason which occurred in the 1940s, connected by Schakel to a number of possible causes including his defeat in debate by G. E. M. Anscombe, in 1948. Lewis's expanded conception of myth through ongoing dialogue with Tolkien and others may also have affected him; for example, Charles Williams had expressed a concern about his emphasis on reason. There is no doubt that his friends had a great influence on him. Even Barfield's views on consciousness would seem to have hit home. Lewis's move away from a mechanical approach to the objective may have been in part due to Barfield's discourse on "consciousness."[126]

Medcalf's concern is closest to the issues at the heart of this project, for he looks specifically at the change in Lewis's persona and how he acquired "immediacy." He incorporates the dissolution of Lewis's emphasis upon reason, but considers the fact that his change in style came from more than just a shift in his consideration of subject-object relations but from a personal change, which, he says, was spontaneous and internal, sometime around 1955. He acknowledges that Lewis's relationship with Joy Gresham may have been important, but concludes that the primary instrument of change was the writing of his autobiography, which was

---

124. Schakel, *Reason and Imagination in C. S. Lewis*, 166–67.
125. Homer, *C. S. Lewis: The Shape of His Faith and Thought*, 86.
126. Schakel, *Reason and Imagination in C. S. Lewis*, 148f.

published in 1955. Certainly, it is undoubtedly true that the writing of the autobiography would seem to have been a major factor, as we shall see in the next chapter. But the importance of his relationship with Joy should not be downplayed. And there were many other factors that contributed to the change in Lewis. In this I take my lead from *Till We Have Faces* which shows Orual forced into recognition of her own behavior by a thoroughly comprehensive series of events, a series which I think reflects Lewis's own experience of long years of stoic efficiency, suddenly sluiced away (to rework an image used by Wilson).

It may be, however, that the seeds of the change occurred not so long after he adopted his extreme position on introspection. At conversion, he began to pray, and having done so, he found that he need not be quite so frightened; ". . . since I have begun to pray I find my extreme view of personality changing. My own empirical self is becoming more important," he wrote to Barfield in 1935, "and this is exactly the opposite of self-love."[127] This may be the beginning of a turnaround, although he maintained his extreme emphasis upon objectivity over the next 15 years or more. In 1940 Lewis chose to start taking confession and shortly thereafter he sought spiritual direction. Of these interactions we know nothing but as relationships that require honesty and openness—Medcalf's "immediacy"—they may have prevented him from truly becoming lost in his persona, just as, at a basic level, the Fox and Bardia do for Orual. So too, the debate with Elizabeth Anscombe in 1948 may have had far-reaching consequences for Lewis, because so much of his being was tied into the contentious persona who loved to be victorious in debate—not least in the area of Christian apologetics. George Sayers says that it was the debate with Anscombe that stopped Lewis writing the somewhat contentious "theological" books that he had written to date.[128] Certainly, he wrote no more after that date. It may also be that even the poem that Barfield wrote about him struck home with this sensitive man—more than Barfield ever realized. In a letter dated 4 April 1949, Lewis replied to Barfield "I hope I'm not Andromeda too . . . the passage you mention does now come back to me."[129]

127. Lewis, letter to Barfield, (December 9[?], 1935), *Letters*, Vol. II, 172–73.

128. Sayers, *Jack: C. S. Lewis and His Times*, 186–87.

129. Lewis, letter to Barfield, April 4, 1949. Bodleian Library, MS facs.c.53. The letter as published in *The Collected Letters of C. S. Lewis*, Vol. II, 929 does not have the line, "I hope I'm not Andromeda too." In *Light on Lewis*, xv, Barfield states that Lewis had completely forgotten that the poem was about him, but this letter seems to imply otherwise.

However, the real changes would seem to have come about in the late 1940s and early 50s. Janie Moore died in 1951 after a prolonged period of ill health. Lewis had found the last few years of her life difficult, as she had been particularly demanding in her incapacitated state. Wilson comments, "Now that she was dead, Jack was ready to start his life all over again. The children's books written at this period were more than an imaginative return to his own childhood. They were a sluicing of the system which, together with his regular confessions and communions, represented a conversion every bit as deep as the conversion to a belief in the supernatural and the divinity of Jesus Christ which occurred in 1929–31."[130] (Wilson sees the Narnia books as being crucial to the change, although I would again contend that they were only part of the series of sluice-gates which he navigated.) His friends began to be surprised by sides of Lewis which started to emerge in his work—including the Narnia tales themselves—for, as Wilson points out, this softening did not lead to his becoming any more "personal" in his day-to-day conversations.[131] The writing of his autobiography, *Surprised by Joy*, was started in March 1948 but was not sent to the publishers until March 1955, having been partly interrupted by the Narnia Chronicles and *English Literature in the Sixteenth Century excluding Drama*. For the reader, *Surprised by Joy* was not particularly revelatory—in fact it was highly selective, stopping at his conversion and concentrating primarily on his intellectual conversion to Christianity together with the role of *Sehnsucht* in his life. It left out major areas of his life. As his friend Humphrey Harvard told him, it could have been supplemented by another book entitled *Suppressed by Jack*.[132] Significantly, Walter Hooper has an early version of an autobiography—written at about the time of his conversion to theism—which is less personal than the published version.[133] It would seem, however, that this writing process had great significance for Lewis, who told Dom Bede Griffiths in 1956, "The gradual reading of one's own life, seeing a pattern emerge, is a great illumination at our age. And partly, I hope, getting freed from the past as past by apprehending it as structure."[134] Obviously *The Pilgrim's Regress* had not had this cathartic effect, and it would seem that Lewis almost deliberately set about exorcising the past. The writing of *Surprised by Joy* was the turning point in a very long process of

130. Wilson, *C. S. Lewis: A Biography*, 233.
131. Ibid., 235.
132. Hooper, *They Stand Together*, 260.
133. Green and Hooper, *C. S. Lewis: A Biography*, 113.
134. Cited by Sayer, *Jack: C. S. Lewis and His Times*, 198.

shedding his protective layers. But as we shall see in *Till We Have Faces*, Orual's gaining of a very different perspective on her life is a retrospective act that comes after the process of writing, not during.

By the early 1950s Lewis's state of mind, as evidenced in letters, was much improved from the late 1940s. Wilson cites, for example, an extract from Lewis to Sister Penelope:

> I especially need your prayers because I am (like the pilgrim in Bunyan) travelling across "a plain called Ease." Everything without, and many things within, are marvellously well at present. Indeed (I do not know whether to be more ashamed or joyful in confessing it) I realise that until about a month ago I never really believed (tho' I thought I did) in God's forgiveness.[135]

James T. Como sees this as a particularly significant chapter in the life of Lewis; "here begins the rebirth" of his work and creativity.[136] He even connects it, somewhat tangentially with the end of a psychological "delay" that had been triggered by the death of Lewis's mother. As Lewis says in *Prayer: Letters to Malcolm,* forgiving and being forgiven are two names for the same thing.[137]

This sense of forgiveness may have opened him up to a new ability to be vulnerable. In this respect, his relationship with Joy Davidman was crucial. He met her in September 1952—and married her in 1956. The relationship was one that grew from liking to love; which may have been the only way in which the guarded Lewis would have found himself made so vulnerable. There he seems to have found a friendship and intimacy which had profoundly affected and changed him more than all these other "sluicings." Peter Bayley has said that after Lewis's marriage, "Even his voice and laugh seemed quieter. I felt that his sensitive nature had at last come through a carapace of tough masculine clubability."[138] Joy not only nursed him into a more "tender and vulnerable self," as Wilson puts it, but she was significant in the creation of *Till We Have Faces*.[139] She wrote to her former husband that she and Lewis (in March 1955) had "kicked a few ideas around till one came to life. Then we had another

---

135. Wilson, *C. S. Lewis: A Biography*, 234. The letter to Sister Penelope is dated June 1951.
136. Como, *Branches to Heaven*, 193.
137. Lewis, *Prayer: Letters to Malcolm*, 102.
138. Bayley, *C. S. Lewis at the Breakfast Table*, 85.
139. Wilson, *C. S. Lewis: A Biography*, 283.

whiskey each and bounced it back and forth between us. The next day, without further planning, he wrote the first chapter."[140]

What Joy's input was we can only speculate; but there is no doubt that at her death in July 1960 he was devastated. There is a resonance of profound personal truth to the cry in *A Grief Observed*, "Oh God, God, why did you take such trouble to force this creature out of its shell if it is now doomed to crawl back—to be sucked back—into it?"[141] A poem, "As the Ruin Falls," seems to corroborate that this was Lewis's own voice speaking. Presumably and poignantly about the approaching death of Joy, he tells her;

> I cannot crawl one inch outside my proper skin:
> I talk of love—a scholar's parrot may talk Greek—
> But, self-imprisoned, always end where I begin.
>
> Only that now you have taught me (but how late) my lack.
> I see the chasm. And everything you are was making
> My heart into a bridge by which I might get back
> From exile, and grow man. And now the bridge is breaking.
>
> For this I bless you as the ruin falls. The pains
> You give me are more precious than all other gains.[142]

In *A Grief Observed* we find the image that Lewis had used in a significant way over these years—that of a thick skin necessarily shed. But another dimension is added to this in "As the Ruin Falls." There he speaks of his heart, now a bridge out of his former exile, but a bridge that is breaking. And for this he thanks the subject of the poem. He is grateful, he says, that it was his heart that brought him out of exile and enabled him to "grow man"; he even hints that he is grateful for the breaking. The emphasis on the heart in "As the Ruin Falls" is striking. It may be that he felt that the sheer depth of his love for Joy had contributed to his return from exile, to his ability to "grow man" after many years of negating his heart. His outward Stoicism was finally put to rest; his emotions allowed the voice that they had so long been denied. Austin Farrer, a close friend of Lewis's in his final years, comments on his "feeling intellect," a "taking

---

140. Letter from Joy Davidman to Bill Gresham (March 23, 1955) Bodleian Library. Green and Hooper say there was much of Joy in the character of Orual, including her own spiritual journey to Christianity and the sense of being a woman in a man's world (*C. S. Lewis: A Biography*, 263).

141. Lewis, *Grief Observed*, 17.

142. Lewis, "As the Ruin Falls," *Poems*, 124. We have no date for this poem.

of the world into his heart."¹⁴³ Lewis had not so long before completed *Reflections on the Psalms* (1957), and it may be that he was using the word "heart" in the Old Testament sense, incorporating emotions and cognition. In the Hebraic world, the two are integrated; indeed the word is used to indicate every aspect of the "self"; intellect, emotion, will. In *Reflections on the Psalms* Lewis even uses the word in this way; "what gentle heart can leave the topic . . . ?"¹⁴⁴ And so too in the poem; it is only through the heart that he can become a man. That is not to say that he stopped speculating about the relationship between intellect and emotion. Even at the end of *A Grief Observed* he is pondering the question, although he recognizes the ultimate futility of this; "Didn't people dispute once whether the final vision of God was more an act of intelligence or of love? That is probably another of the nonsense questions."¹⁴⁵ He accepts the shattering of his false ideas about God, having recognized that his grief functioned iconoclastically. And in so doing he embraces his emotions in a way that he had not done since his childhood. Lewis embraced orthopathy, although for him, orthopathy was no simple balance of heart and mind. His heart became the bridge between the private core of his being and the external—or objective—world.

Till We Have Faces is the physical outworking of the changes that took place in Lewis. Having allowed the bridge to form, his ability to empathize was given life and his creative ability enhanced. It is a book that is unlike any other that he wrote. Schakel comments:

> Orual is the only character whom Lewis seems to know deeply and to develop fully. It is as if his unwillingness to pay attention to his own personality for so many years prevented him from being able to get into the personalities of his characters in a detailed and convincing way. The prolonged attention to his own consciousness in *Surprised by Joy* enabled him to portray the consciousness of at least one character fully. Not surprisingly, that character is very much like himself.¹⁴⁶

Orual, like Lewis, chooses not to pay attention to herself. But, like Lewis, she finds that this deliberate inattention has been a malignant practice in many ways, for it has crippled her ability to pay attention to those around her. It is noteworthy that *Till We Have Faces* ends with Orual's unveiling and subsequent death. Lewis does not try to portray what the unveiled

---

143. Farrer, "In His Image," *C. S. Lewis at the Breakfast Table*, 242–43.
144. Lewis, *Reflections on the Psalms*, 76.
145. Lewis, *Grief Observed*, 64.
146. Schakel, *Reason and Imagination in C. S. Lewis*, 161.

Orual would look like. He does not try to fix her in any way—that, after all, has been her problem. Nor are we able to speak conclusively of a Lewis without a persona. He himself continued to speak as if he had retained a persona. In *Prayer: Letters to Malcolm* he likens our material surroundings to a stage set in which one acts:

> And you may well say "act." For what I call "myself" (for all practical, everyday purposes) is also a dramatic construction; memories, glimpses in the shaving-glass, and snatches of the very fallible activity called "introspection," are the principal ingredients. Normally I call this construction "me," and the stage set "the real world". . . The dramatic person could not tread the stage unless he concealed a real person: unless the real and unknown I existed, I would not even make mistakes about the imagined me.[147]

Is it possible that Lewis simply adopted another persona? Did he still feel that there was some necessary level of concealment? That it is not possible to lose the construction that is "myself"? What he seems to have concluded is that there is a sense in which we always remain a construction, a mixture of memories, glimpses, and acts. This does not necessarily interfere with the "real I." Paul Tournier, the psychiatrist, concurs; "We are, then, pursuing a chimera in attempting to grasp the essence of our person, completely divested of all adornments and disguises with which life has clothed it. One thing that would have to be got rid of would be memory, which is a fundamental property of life; that would mean getting rid of life itself."[148] To try to reveal the person is to find that one is determined by a deeper mechanism—and so on, until we reach the unconscious forces that, according to Tournier, are no longer personal at all.[149] (Lewis may well have pointed out that the unconscious forces are no less personal.) Tournier uses the word "personage" in exactly the same sense as we have used the word "persona"; for him the personage is acceptable so long as it is an expression of the unique aspects of oneself and is not simply a response to the expectations of others. "It seems that we must resign ourselves to this indissoluble connection between the person and its personage—or rather, between the person and its personages. For we are not only one personage throughout our lives; we are innumerable personages."[150] As Walter Brueggeman points out, the Old (and New) Testament writers seem to exhibit evidence of conversations among the

---

147. Lewis, *Prayer: Letters to Malcolm*, 78.
148. Tournier, *Meaning of Persons*, 66.
149. Ibid., 67.
150. Ibid., 69.

"many selves" of the self.[151] What is important, Tournier concludes, is the bringing of the personage into harmony with oneself. Rather than any cold intellectual analysis, this becomes a dynamic movement of life, a constant adjustment, but, he concludes, in this world any full concord between personage and person remains a utopian ideal.[152]

> This tension that always exists between the person and the personage is one of the conditions of our life, and we must accept it. It is part of the nature of man—indeed it is what makes him a man.[153]

Lewis—like Tournier and like the Old Testament writers—seems to accept this state of affairs at the end of his life. He has no need to find a fixed self. Was that not what he tried to do as an introspective teenager? He had long ago accepted the concept of Heraclitean flux. There may well be a "real I"—and he clearly thinks so—but it cannot be circumscribed. For the most part we live with a phantasmal sense of self—just as we live with a phantasmal sense of God; "the bright blur" as he calls God in *Prayer: Letters to Malcolm*.[154] But it is a very different sense of phantasm to that we find in Beckett, as we shall see in the next chapter. For Lewis, both God and the self are—in one sense—far beyond our grasp. Facades there may be, but there are depths too. The "dramatic construction" has a real, offstage life; "unless the real and unknown I existed, I would not even make mistakes about the imagined me . . . The objects around me, and my idea of 'me,' will deceive if taken at their face value. But they are momentous if taken as the end-products of divine activities."[155] It is a dynamic sense of the self tied to a dynamic sense of God, both continually engaged. It is an open-ended self, wherein the very incompleteness brings it into relation with God. It sounds very like Augustine, as Rowan Williams suggests in his comments on self-knowledge in *De trinitate*: "God cannot be sought without the seeker seeking and finding, wanting and holding to, the creaturely incompleteness, the exigency and expectancy, that *eros* represents. Before we can rightly want God, we must know and want our wanting nature."[156] Lewis early came to know and want his wanting nature; in later years he came to reflect upon his creaturely incompleteness and how the self is a dynamic entity, ungraspable, yet neglected only

---

151. Brueggemann, "'Othering' with Grace and Courage," 12–13.
152. Tournier, *Meaning of Persons*, 79–80.
153. Ibid., 80.
154. Lewis, *Prayer: Letters to Malcolm*, 75.
155. Ibid., 77.
156. Williams, "Paradoxes of Self-Knowledge in the *De trinitate*," 133.

at one's own peril. In this chapter we have seen how this played out in the shape of his life and in his literature, and how he learnt keen lessons through lived experience. But how is it that his thought came to sound so very like Augustine's theology? Let us turn first of all to the influences that shaped Lewis's thought on the self—and the relation to God which he believed to be so intrinsic to that self. Only then shall we be ready to read his *magnum opus* on the self, *Till We Have Faces*.

CHAPTER 5

I: A Sacred Name

Lewis—Theology and Self

Quellenforschung: Lewis's Influences and Theology

ANY QUELLENFORSCHUNG (OR SOURCEHUNTING) in the works of Lewis is as eclectic and challenging as it is in the works of Beckett. Lewis forgot nothing and incorporated ideas without naming sources (with the exception of his specifically academic works). The Bible, Plato, Aristotle, Augustine, Athanasius, Boethius, Old Norse sagas, Bernard of Clairvaux, Nicholas of Cusa, Dante, Spenser, Milton, Malory, Shakespeare, Coleridge, Bishop Berkeley, Jonathan Swift, William James, Rudolph Otto, George MacDonald, William Morris, Jung, Charles Williams, J. R. R. Tolkien, Owen Barfield—to name even these is to do a disservice to others. However, the exploration of sources sheds considerable light and is particularly valuable in aiding the understanding of a mythopoeic piece such as *Till We Have Faces*. I have selected five of the influences that appear to have made most impact upon the mature Lewis's ideas of the self and God. In doing so, we shall gain a sense of his "theology" or the emphases that are peculiar to him, and shall more fully understand his ideas when we meet them in *Till We Have Faces*. But before his influences, let us look at his basic theology and anthropology, or his idea of God and humanity.

Three-Personal God

Believing himself to hold to ancient and orthodox doctrines, Lewis set out only to restate them for his contemporaries. His adult belief had developed via theism, and the impersonal Absolute. In *Surprised by Joy*, he comments that the advantage of this was clear; "There was nothing to fear; better still, nothing to obey."[1] But in 1931 he embraced a triune God, one who personally engaged him from the outset, by initiating the process which led to his conversion. Even at the point when he felt most compelled, he still felt that there was freedom of choice; "I felt myself being, there and then, given a free choice. I could open the door or keep it shut; I could unbuckle the armour or keep it on. I chose to open, to unbuckle, to loosen the rein."[2] And having done so, he found a corresponding movement. God became personal:

> As the dry bones shook and came together in that dreadful valley of Ezekiel's, so now a philosophical theorem, cerebrally entertained, began to stir and heave and throw off its gravecloths, and stood upright and became a living presence. I was to be allowed to play at philosophy no longer . . . My Adversary waived the point. It sank into utter unimportance. He would not argue about it. He only said, "I am the Lord"; "I am that I am"; "I am."[3]

In his own life he had encountered a presence that interacted with him. But ultimately that presence was entirely Other, even (at this point) adversarial, for he demanded total surrender, that he should no longer call his soul his own.[4]

> In the Trinity term of 1929 I gave in, and admitted that God was God, and knelt and prayed: perhaps, that night, the most dejected and reluctant convert in all England. I did not then see what is now the most shining and obvious thing; the Divine humility which will accept a convert even on such terms.[5]

The subjective God of beauty and truth that he had wanted to believe in had become an objective God with personality. Right to the end of Lewis's life, this God remained personal, a God who made demands upon his attention and the way in which he lived his life. In 1960 he wrote to a correspondent:

> We have A. The Scriptural representation of God—a God not only of love but of στοργη "whose bowels are moved" with compassion and who can fall into a "fury." B. A philosophical concept of the absolute Being to which (one can hardly say 'to whom') all these human characteristics are inapplicable.

1. Lewis, *Surprised by Joy*, 163.
2. Ibid., 174.
3. Ibid., 176–77.
4. Ibid., 177.
5. Ibid., 178.

> We have a tendency to regard B as the literal truth and A either as poetical decoration or as a concession to the "primitive" mind of the ancient Jews.
>
> We are right in thinking that A cannot be literally true. But no more can B. B is an abstract construction of our own minds. It represents to us an abstraction, a mere concept, what must in reality be the most concrete of all facts. B can make no claim to be a revelation; we have made it. A does make this claim . . . We can get no further than this in knowledge *about* (*savoir*) God; but we are vouchsafed some knowledge by acquaintance (*connaître*) of Him, in our devotional and sacramental life. This, if it clothes itself in words and images at all, always borrows them from the A view. But these are not the real point, are they? It is as the moment of personal contact fades that they press on the mind, we cry "Father" without attending to all those implications which would become mythological the further we pursued them. As Buber might say God is most fully real to us as *Thou*, less so as *He*, least so as *It*. We must worship the *Thou*, not the *He* in our minds which is just as much an image (therefore a possible *idol*), as a figure of wood or stone.[6]

This God that created the concrete, individual, determinate things (lovers, sandwiches, pineapples and kangaroos) is himself concrete and individual, not a featureless generality, and although mystics may emphasize the unspeakable aspects of his being (more of which later), it is not because of any degree of vagueness but because he is, rather, too definite for the unavoidable vagueness of language.[7] For Lewis, God is *super*personal; all that humans are and much more besides. As he explained in *Mere Christianity*, God is in one sense beyond personality, because personality and body are what is left of positive being when it is diluted into temporal or finite forms. To speak of personality for God is to be limited to anthropomorphisms—and both anthropomorphisms and abstractions about God were equally concessions to human weakness in conceiving of God. Lewis's use of the word "personality" seems to be close to what contemporary theologians would term "personhood," in accordance with the OED's primary definition, "the quality, character or fact of being a person as distinct from being a thing," plus the second definition "that quality or assemblage of qualities which makes a person what he is, as distinct from other persons." As Tolkien put it, in "On Fairy Stories,"

---

6. Lewis, letter to Gracia Fay Bouwman (July 19, 1960) *Letters*, Vol. III, 1173–74.
7. Lewis, *Miracles*, ch. 11.

personality can only be derived from a person.[8] In that sense God is the origin of all personality. "There are no real personalities anywhere else."[9]

On the Divine level, Lewis believed, these personalities are combined—God is not one simple being.[10] Lewis's God is specifically Trinitarian; "Three-personal" is the phrase he uses in *Mere Christianity*. He puts it simply, as befits the broadcast format, but the concepts are profoundly important ones:

> In Christianity God is not a static thing—not even a person—but a dynamic, pulsating activity, a life, almost a kind of drama. Almost, if you will not think me irreverent, a kind of dance. The union between the Father and the Son is such a live concrete thing that this union is also a Person . . . What grows out of the joint life of the Father and Son is a real Person, is in fact the third of the three Persons who are God.[11]

And into that Three-personal life humans are drawn. Humans are taken into this three personal life, their biological life (or *bios)*, is replaced by a spiritual life, or *Zoe*:

> An ordinary simple Christian kneels down to say his prayers. He is trying to get in touch with God. But if he is a Christian he knows that what is prompting him to pray is also God: God, so to speak, inside him. But he also knows that all his real knowledge of God comes through Christ, the Man who was God—that Christ is standing beside him, helping him to pray, praying for him. You see what is happening. God is the thing to which he is praying—the goal he is trying to reach. God is also the thing inside him which is pushing him on—the motive power. God is also the road or bridge along which he is being pushed to that goal. So that the whole threefold life of the three-personal Being is actually going on in that ordinary little bedroom where an ordinary man is saying his prayers. The man is being caught up into the higher kinds of life—what I called *Zoe* or spiritual life: he is being pulled into God, by God, while still remaining himself.[12]

Although clearly Trinitarian in passages such those above, it may be the fiercely personal idea of God which led to a lack of emphasis upon the Holy Spirit in his writings, although it is probably most fair to say that he

8. J. R. R. Tolkien, "On Fairy-Stories," 24.
9. Lewis, *Mere Christianity*, 226.
10. Ibid., 162.
11. Ibid., 175.
12. Lewis, *Mere Christianity*, 163.

uses "God" as synonymous with the Holy Spirit, and his strong sense of God as immanent as well as transcendent is evident in the concept that God is the "motive power" in human prayer. In the same way, Christ as God is central to his beliefs; at the time of conversion, Jesus as the "dying god" gave meaning to other dying gods from mythology, because, as God's Son, his death gave rise to new life. Aslan in the *Narnia Chronicles*, reverberates with parallel imagery to the biblical images and doctrines about Christ, not solely in his death and resurrection in *The Lion, the Witch and the Wardrobe*, but as the Creator of Narnia (*The Magician's Nephew*), and as its final Judge (*The Last Battle*). However, the emphasis in Lewis's writings was upon Christ as Creator and Sustainer. God the Son seems to be less prominent in his thought, and his ambiguity towards specific theories of the significance of Christ's death (particularly the atonement) are evident in *Mere Christianity*; for him, a person can accept what Christ has done, without knowing how it works.[13] However, he wholeheartedly embraced the incarnation as God's way of gathering humanity into himself:

> This is the whole of Christianity. There is nothing else . . . the Church exists for nothing else but to draw men into Christ, to make them little Christs . . . God became Man for no other purpose. It says in the Bible that the whole universe was made for Christ and that everything is to be gathered together into Him. I do not suppose that any of us can understand how this will happen as regards the whole universe . . . What we have been told is how we men can be drawn into Christ . . . It is the only thing we are made for.[14]

To this we shall return. It is enough for now to note the engaging dynamism of Lewis's image of God; for him the personalness of onto-theology was the basis for anthropology, but the relation of humanity to this three-personed God was fundamentally one of response.

Human freedom is constituted by responsiveness ("that responsive love proper to creatures").[15] In *Surprised by Joy* Lewis speaks of God's compulsion as his liberation.[16] "The words *compelle intrare*, compel them to come in, have been so abused by wicked men that we shudder at them; but, properly understood, they plumb the depth of Divine mercy. The hardness of God is kinder than the softness of men, and His compulsion

13. Ibid., 53–59.
14. Ibid., 199–200.
15. The citation is from *Problem of Pain*, 43.
16. Lewis, *Surprised by Joy*, 178.

is our liberation."¹⁷ The response that is most free is that which is the least arbitrary, and that which appears to spring from the greatest inner depth. "Yet, for us rational creatures, to be created means 'to be made agents'. We have nothing that we have not received; but part of what we have received is the power of being something more than receptacles. We exercise it, no doubt, briefly by our sins."¹⁸ To refuse to receive is to turn self-ward.¹⁹ For Lewis, "agency" involves reacting towards the bestowal of God. To receive from God, or to obey, (which for Lewis is essentially the same) is the road to freedom.²⁰ Right-relatedness to God is integral to the person's well-being. "To be God—to be like God and to share his goodness in creaturely response—to be miserable—these are the only three alternatives."²¹

The Oracles of God: Scripture

Lewis aimed at teaching that which reflected Biblical teaching. He believed that "it is Christ himself, not the Bible, who is the true word of God. The Bible, read in the right spirit and with the guidance of good teachers, will bring us to Him."²² Thus, the written word is the avenue for encountering the living Word and he gave the Bible the place of highest authority in his life. For example, in *The Four Loves* he spoke of Paul having "a higher authority with us than St Augustine."²³ That there were complexities in the Bible he freely admitted. *Reflections on the Psalms* sheds some light on his thinking at roughly the same time that he wrote *Till We Have Faces*. The Bible, he said:

> . . . carries "the Word of God"; and we, (under grace, with attention to tradition and to interpreters wiser than ourselves, and with the use of such intelligence and learning as we may have) receive that word from it not by using it as an encyclopedia or an encyclical but by steeping ourselves in its tone or temper and so learning its over-all message.
>
> To a human mind this working up (in a sense imperfectly), this sublimation (incomplete) of human material, seems, no doubt, an untidy and leaky vehicle. We might have expected, we may think

---

17. Ibid., 178
18. Lewis, *Prayer: Letters to Malcolm*, 47–48.
19. Lewis deals with this in *Problem of Pain*, ch. 5.
20. Lewis, "Membership," 125.
21. Lewis, *Problem of Pain*, 43.
22. Lewis, letter to Mrs Johnson (November 8, 1952) *Letters*, Vol. III, 246.
23. Lewis, *Four Loves*, 138.

we should have preferred, an unrefracted light giving us ultimate truth in systematic form—something we could have tabulated and memorised and relied on like the multiplication table.[24]

But, he concludes, the Bible refuses such systematizing:

> Thus on three levels, in appropriate degrees, we meet the same refusal of what we might have thought best for us—in the Word Himself, in the Apostle to the Gentiles, in Scripture as a whole. Since this is what God has done, this, we must conclude, was best. It may be indispensable that our Lord's teaching, by that elusiveness (to our systematising intellect), should demand a response from the whole man, should make it so clear that there is no question of learning a subject but of steeping ourselves in a Personality, acquiring a new outlook and temper, breathing a new atmosphere, suffering Him, in His own way, to rebuild in us the defaced image of Himself.[25]

Here are all sorts of resonances. Reading the Bible should call forth a response from the whole person—not just the rational. Humans are made in the image of God, but they need to steep themselves in the Bible in order to rebuild the image that has been tarnished or defaced. In this way they are steeped in a Personality; and the defaced image of Himself shall be rebuilt in them; they shall gain faces as a result of reflecting the face of God. 2 Corinthians 3:18—the single most resonant biblical verse for *Till We Have Faces*—portrays humans as mirroring God, person to person, face to face. "And we, who with unveiled faces all reflect the Lord's glory, are being transformed into his likeness with ever increasing glory, which comes from the Lord, who is the Spirit." It is the divine face that shines; humans shine insomuch as they reflect the glory of the Lord. Just as human personality is derivative of divine personality, so human glory is derivative of God's glory. It is a view of humanity that emphasizes the *imago dei*, and which encompasses both the tarnished and the glorified. It may be that here Lewis is reflecting his reading of John Calvin, who drew out the idea of the *imago* as being like a mirror.[26] Humans are the brightest mirrors in which God's glory can be seen.

This reflected glory however, is only gained through a relinquishing. Self exists to be abdicated and, by that abdication, becomes the more truly self. This oft-used phrase in Lewis's mid-life work, is very much in the

---

24. Lewis, *Reflections on the Psalms*, 94.
25. Ibid., 95–96.
26. Grenz, *Social God and the Relational Self*, 165. We know Lewis had read something of Calvin from references he made in *English Literature in the Sixteenth Century Excluding Drama*.

spirit of the paradoxical saying of Christ in Luke: "If anyone would come after me, he must deny himself and take up his cross daily and follow me. For whoever wants to save his life will lose it, but whoever loses his life for me will save it. What good is it for a man to gain the whole world, and yet lose or forfeit his very self?"[27] The self cannot be grasped—to lose it is to find it; Christ's sacrifice is a model for the Christian. For Lewis the fundamental law of the universe is the renunciation of the self; "He who loses his life will save it." Images from the New Testament are strung together here; "This is the ultimate law—the seed dies to live, the bread must be cast upon the waters, he that loses his soul shall save it."[28] As we shall see, the death and the casting and the losing cannot be separated from the living and the saving; "the life of the seed, the finding of the bread, the recovery of the soul, are as real as the preliminary sacrifice."[29] Relinquishing does not mean eradication. Rather, the old self is taken off in order to put on the new self "which is being renewed in knowledge in the image of its creator." (Colossians 9:9–10) Here Lewis uses the Pauline idea of the old self (he called this the *bios,*) and the new self (the *Zoe*).[30] The Pauline emphasis is upon renewal and regeneration as a consequence of relinquishment. This emphasis is antithetical to Hampson's desire that humans take control, because God as Other is in opposition to them. There is little evidence of paradox in her thought. Yet, paradox, this holding of bipolarities, was particularly strong in many of the works Lewis wrote in the 1940s; in 1948, in a letter to Barfield, for example, he used the lens of the "coincidence of opposites" or *coincidentia oppositorum*, a phrase by fifteenth century Nicholas of Cusa.[31] This dialectical nature of Lewis's thought has been called the "dance of contraries," by Colin Manlove (although I will argue that his mature work shows him moving beyond this particular emphasis). It is worth noting the biblical influences on his sense of the self and—as we orient ourselves towards the next section—the resonances with Augustine of Hippo:

> Away with thee, away with thee, I say, from thyself. Thou dost hinder thyself. If thou buildest thine own self, thou dost build a ruin. Remain not in thyself, transcend thyself also; put thyself in Him who made thee.[32]

27. Luke 9:24 (NIV). A similar saying is found in John 12:25.
28. Lewis, *Problem of Pain*, 119.
29. Ibid., 121.
30. Lewis, *Mere Christianity*, 159.
31. Lewis, letter to Barfield (August 19,1948[?]) *Letters*, Vol. II, 871.
32. Augustine *Sermons on Selected Lessons of the New Testament* 169.9.

Augustine and Plato: Classic Mentors

Augustine and Plato are here grouped together for two reasons. Probably the most significant of the ancient mentors for Lewis, their thoughts weave together in ways that would lead to repetition if they were dealt with separately. But Lewis distinguished between their ideas; and he held both up against the light of his biblical understanding. When Lewis criticizes Augustine in *The Four Loves* for having a desire to avoid suffering the loss of a friend he is criticizing him for not being in accordance with the Bible. It is a hangover from "the high-minded Pagan philosophies in which he grew up. It is closer to Stoic 'apathy' or neo-Platonic mysticism than to charity."[33] Like Lewis, (and Beckett too) Augustine found in the pages of the Bible a rather unattractive path to the "Wisdom" that he so desired. The texts contained within were not cultivated and polished as his training in rhetoric would have led him to expect of a great book. But by the time he wrote *Confessions,* he was extolling the profundity of the Scriptures. They remained disconcerting, but their very opacity became their beauty, yielding a constant challenge to the intellect, and truths that were all the more valuable because they did not lie so close to the surface; "because while all can read it with ease, it also has a deeper meaning in which its great secrets are locked away. Its plain language and simple style makes it accessible to everyone, and yet it absorbs the attention of the learned."[34] The scriptures had become, for him, the countenance of God, the means by which he could come as close as is possible, before the *eschaton,* to seeing God face to face.[35] Whereas Beckett makes ironic reference to this image, Augustine comes to see the Bible as the earthly means by which we can glimpse the divine self-revelation. For Lewis the reading of scripture helps us to become mirrors "filled with the image of a face that is not ours."[36] The similarity between Augustine's and Lewis's view of the Bible points up resonances that go far beyond a shared view of scripture. Of the many who influenced Lewis's Christian thought, it would seem that Augustine was the most potent. Lewis said that his "glad debts" to Augustine were "incalculable."[37] Gilbert Meilaender says that Lewis's views are best described, quite simply, as Augustinian.[38]

---

33. Lewis, *Four Loves,* 138.
34. Augustine *Confessions* 6.5.
35. Augustine *Sermon* 22.7. Cited by Brown, *Augustine of Hippo,* 262.
36. Lewis, "Christianity and Literature," 8.
37. Lewis, *Four Loves,* 137.
38. Meilaender, *Taste for the Other,* 235.

Both men were trying to elucidate the Bible. For both, Scripture is still the highest authority, and one to which humans must submit. This emphasis gives them what sounds at times remarkably like a single voice against many of the issues that bedeviled Beckett's ability to believe. Their ambivalent attitudes towards Platonism may explain this in part. Both men worked out their Christian beliefs both in contradistinction and incorporation of Idealism, which weaves through the thought of both men. At times Platonic strands were drawn into the fabric, at times they were decisively rejected. Both men were emphatic that the *Logos* had become flesh—and here they fundamentally distinguished themselves from Platonism. Eugene TeSelle comments that Augustine "attacked the Platonists with increasing intensity, for their pride in attempting to bypass incarnation and grace and faith, which are indispensable to true progress."[39] Augustine said that it was *because* he read the books of the Platonists, that he was able to affirm the Christian doctrines as he did, for he came to perceive their teaching as lacking in flesh and blood and all that pertained to them; human fault, frailty, forgiveness.[40]

Yet, Lewis, like Augustine, owed an allegiance to Platonic ideas. His sense of longing was what he traced in the thinking of so many of those friends and writers whom he found so appealing. Thus Plato's allegory of the cave in *Republic* is, for Lewis, a helpful portrayal; this life is just the shadows thrown by the fire, conveying a limited image of the "Really Real" on the back of the cave. For him, in one sense, this earth was the shadowlands, and heaven, the source of all our desires, full of "the intolerable light of utter actuality."[41] Even his children's stories are an outworking of this stance, as can be seen so explicitly in *The Last Battle*. Narnia, as the children experience it, is only a shadow of the real Narnia that is to come. ("It's all in Plato, all in Plato. Bless me! What do they teach them at these schools?"[42]) But Lewis, as he told E. M. W. Tillyard, *based* nothing on Plato.[43] He made significant distinctions; not least that his God is the personal God that is the source of all, unlike Plato's Ideal. But he incorporated the light that Plato had shed into his own vision of the world. In *The Great Divorce*, Hell is a pale and grey city compared with the brightly luminous city of heaven. Lewis uses the figure of George MacDonald to convey the fact that, "Heaven is reality itself. All that is

39. TeSelle, "Augustine," 22.
40. Augustine *Confessions* 7.20.
41. Lewis, *Problem of Pain*, 123.
42. Lewis, *Last Battle*, 154.
43. Lewis, "Open Letter to Dr Tillyard," 155.

fully real is Heavenly . . . The choice of every lost soul can be expressed in the words 'Better to reign in Hell than serve in Heaven.' There is always something they insist on keeping, even at the price of misery. There is always something they prefer to joy—that is, to reality."[44] This choice is starkly outlined in *The Problem of Pain*:

> The characteristic of lost souls is "their rejection of everything that is not simply themselves." Our imaginary egoist has tried to turn everything he meets into a province or appendage of the self. The taste for the *other*, that is, the very capacity for enjoying good, is quenched in him except in so far as his body still draws him into contact with an outer world. Death removes this last contact. He has his wish—to live wholly in the self and to make the best of what he finds there. And what he finds there is Hell.[45]

We are reminded of Augustine's words, ". . . to abandon God and to exist in oneself, that is to please oneself, is not immediately to lose all being; but it is to come nearer to nothingness."[46] Charles Taylor in *Sources of the Self*, comments that for Augustine, "The ultimate sin is to close oneself, but one's reasons for doing so can be of the highest. In a sense, the person who is closed is in a vicious circle from which it is hard to escape. We are closed to grace, because we close ourselves to the world in which it circulates, and we do that out of loathing for ourselves and for this world. But paradoxically, the more noble and sensitive and morally insightful one is, the more one is liable to feel this loathing."[47] It cannot fail to put one in mind of Beckett.

But Augustine and Lewis would still maintain that this closing of oneself is, in theological terms, pride, and it is pride which separates from God. Lewis summarizes Augustine thus, that pride is the "movement whereby a creature (that is an essentially dependant being whose principle of existence lies not in itself but in another) tries to set up on its own, to exist for itself."[48] He continues; "From the moment a creature becomes aware of God as God and of itself as self, the terrible alternative of choosing God or self is opened to it . . . it is the fall in every individual life, and in each day of each individual life, the basic sin behind all particular sins."[49] As Lewis firmly believed; "the highest good of a

---

44. Lewis, *Great Divorce*, 55.
45. Lewis, *Problem of Pain*, 98.
46. Augustine, *City of God* 14.13 (Dyson, 609).
47. C. Taylor, *Sources of the Self*, 451.
48. Lewis, *Problem of Pain*, 59.
49. Ibid., 59–60.

creature must be creaturely—that is, derivative or reflective—good."[50] And he goes on to cite Augustine; "In other words, as St Augustine makes plain (*De Civ. Dei,* 12, cap. I), pride does not only go before a fall but it is a fall—a fall of the creature's attention from what is better, to what is worse, itself."[51] As Alistair McFadyen puts it, "Far from assuring human integrity and autonomy, pride leads to a disintegration and collapse of human being by unplugging it from the energizing source of its life and integrity."[52] Lewis's fiction portrayed this time and again; pride had, after all, been his "besetting sin." Autonomy—*contra* Hampson—is not the best response to harmful self-obeisance. Rather, it is faith. McFadyen interprets Augustine, in saying, "In faith, one internalizes the dynamics of a God who is radically and genuinely for us . . . In faith, one commits personal energy in consensual response to the dynamic in which God is for us, and finds oneself simultaneously filled with joy in God and oneself and others."[53] Whereas pride closes one in (*incurvatus en se*), faith opens out (*excurvatus ad se*) towards joy in God, oneself and others.

Another distinction between the stance of Augustine and Lewis and that of Beckett and the Manichees and Neoplatonists is the attitude towards the ascent to the divine. The Augustine/Lewis view would be that to try to do so is mistaken; but God can descend to the human.[54] In *Prayer: Letters to Malcolm,* Lewis speaks of the "descent" of God to the person, rather than the Ascent of the soul.[55] As Bernard McGinn puts it, "For Plotinus, the soul, however fallen, always remains capable of lifting itself up to the vision of God because it is of divine origin; for Augustine, the soul is a fallen creature, bound by both original and individual sin, and hence any such elevation is always a result of God's action in us . . . Where the Bishop decisively parts company with the pagan philosopher is in his insistence that he could not really gain the strength necessary to enjoy God until he had accepted the Incarnate Christ as the mediator between God and humanity."[56] Christ as God incarnate is an entirely crucial aspect of a God who takes the initiative, who reaches out, beyond himself, to become enfeebled before being elevated. For Beckett, the kenosis of Christ was an end in itself. For Augustine, such a self-emptying is only a means to an

50. Lewis, "Christianity and Literature," 8–9.
51. Ibid., 9.
52. McFadyen, *Bound to Sin,* 218.
53. Ibid., 214.
54. For Lewis on this, see his chapter on "The Grand Miracle," 113–38.
55. Lewis, *Prayer: Letters to Malcolm,* 18–19.
56. McGinn, *Foundations of Mysticism,* 233–34.

end. For Lewis, the kenotic impulse is the law of the universe; as in Christ, so it should be in humans.[57] For Augustine, this sense of dependence upon God was integrally bound to a sense of grace. Unlike the necessary ascent required to reach Plotinus' One, God in grace reaches down towards people. As Andrew Louth puts it, "Augustine's emphasis on grace and on God's own activity towards the soul vastly transcends Plotinus' notion of the soul's dependence on the One."[58] Grace is the antithesis of pride. It is grace that enables the rupture whereby dependence upon God and others is acknowledged. It is not just dependence, but a synergistic combination of trust and grace, as Louth goes on to point out; "Grace becomes more than our dependence on God (an idea we can find in various forms in Platonism and neo-Platonism): rather, to speak of grace is to speak of God's self-emptying and His coming down to us. Grace means God's humility and the awakening of our response in humility."[59] As trust and grace meet, there is a disclosure of the self, which would otherwise be blocked. To quote Rowan Williams; ". . . the self that is present to itself and others without violence or anxiety, the self that might possibly be called a soul, exists in the expectation of *grace*."[60] Lewis characteristically puts it this way; grace, he says, "offers us delight in our dependence . . . For all the time this illusion to which nature clings as her last treasure, this pretence that we have anything of our own or could for one hour retain by our own strength any goodness that God may pour into us, has kept us from being happy. We have been like bathers who want to keep their feet—or one foot—or one toe—on the bottom, when to lose that foothold would be to surrender themselves to a glorious tumble in the surf."[61]

Which leads to yet another area, in which Lewis and Augustine have a rejoinder for Beckett. It is the issue of the will. Robert Houston Smith has pointed out that Lewis adopted and adapted Plato's tripartite self; the rational soul, typified by the mind (which included both *ratio* or logical reasoning, and *intellectus* or understanding in its widest sense); the willful or spiritual element, represented by the chest; and the sensate or appetitive element, exemplified by the stomach and reproductive organs.[62] For Lewis, the complete person had their passions obedient to the will and their will

---

57. Lewis, "Grand Miracle," *Miracles*, 117.

58. Louth, *Origins of the Christian Mystical Tradition*, 144.

59. Ibid., 145–46.

60. R. Williams, *Lost Icons*, 175.

61. Lewis, *The Four Loves*, 146.

62. Smith, *Patches of Godlight*, 169. Smith cites several examples from the *Narnia Chronicles* and *The Great Divorce* as evidence of this.

offered to God. His emphasis upon the will involved—unsurprisingly—the paradoxical. Our will is so intertwined with the will of God that it is only in surrendering it that we shall find it; "Human will becomes truly creative and truly our own when it is wholly God's, and this is one of the many senses in which he that loses his soul shall find it."[63] The purification of the will leads to the enlightenment of the intelligence.[64] For Augustine also, understanding is possible only if the mind desires understanding. As Henry Chadwick puts it, "In Augustine's ethics and psychology the will was a central concept and theme. Its operations are indeed hard to account for; but without the will's decision or ascent to direct attention to a given matter, one can neither perceive with any understanding, nor acquire scientific knowledge, nor come to faith."[65] Indeed, for Augustine, misuse of the will is wickedness; "And when I asked myself what wickedness was, I saw that it was not a substance but perversion of the will when it turns aside from you, O God, who are the supreme substance, and veers towards things of the lowest order, being bowelled alive and becoming inflated with desire for things outside itself."[66] Beckett would no doubt have appreciated the imagery but not Augustine's conclusions; his essentially Schopenauerian approach led, as we have seen, to his negation of the will. Consequently, he negated both his own agency, and that of the God whom he relegated to the realm of Manichaean heavens. We have already seen Beckett's use of the "strait of two wills" image; Augustine shows himself to be aware in Book VIII of *Confessions* of the strange duplicity of the will which seemed to dog Beckett's every step. "I can't go on. I'll go on" resonates with "it was I who willed to take this course and again it was I who willed not to take it" (VII, 10). For Augustine, *akrasia*, or weakness of the will, is when we act against our insight and are therefore prevented from becoming fuller and purer.

Ultimately, for Augustine and Lewis, the Platonists—and Beckett—place too much on the role of the person. The will is primarily important in recognizing the insights given by God, through dependence, faith and grace. But for Lewis, this is Christ's presence within—just as it had been for Augustine. It is not just that all knowing is a form of recognition, of *anamnesis* (which is, Denys Turner points out, a residual but revisionary Platonism) but that, for them both, discovery of God's recognition, was

---

63. Lewis, *Problem of Pain*, 81.
64. Lewis, letter to Dom Bede Griffiths (January 30,1954) *Letters*, Vol. III, 422.
65. Chadwick, *Augustine*, 64.
66. Augustine *Confessions* 7.16.

to recognize his own life in God.[67] And it is here that Augustine most distinctively "baptizes" Plato. Charles Taylor summarizes it thus:

> At its root, constituting this implicit understanding, is the master within, the source of the light which lights every man coming into the world, God. And so, at the very end of its search for itself, if it goes to the very end the soul finds God. The experience of being illumined from another source, of receiving the standards of our reason from beyond ourselves, which the proof of God's existence already brought to light, is seen to be very much an experience of inwardness. That is, it is in this paradigmatically first-person activity, where I strive to make myself more present to myself, to realize to the full the potential which resides in the fact that the knower and known are one, that I come most tellingly and convincingly to the awareness that God stands above me . . . Indeed he is closer to me than I am myself, while being infinitely above me; he is "interior intimo meo et superior summo meo."[68]

For Augustine and the later Lewis, it is perception of the intimate role of God which can begin to give rise to selfhood. "Let me know you, for you are the God who knows me, let me recognize you as you have recognized me."[69] Self-recognition necessarily comes *after* the recognition of God, as the basis of the self. "What I do know of myself I know because You shed your light on me; and what I do not know of myself I shall not know until 'my darkness shall become as noonday' in the vision of your face."[70] Augustine's belief that God actively sought him out was an integral aspect of his belief that God is the initiator. God shed his light, and Augustine was able to perceive—or to recognize himself. It is in this sense that both men believe "By going inward, I am drawn upward."[71] His conviction was emphatically that God was the initiator, one to whom he had to respond; it was God who "cried aloud to me . . . broke my barrier of deafness . . . shone upon me . . . shed [his] fragrance about me."[72] Both men felt that God had compelled them, although they had plenty to say about human engagement—or lack of it—with God. As we have seen, the desire for recognition seemed to underlie Beckett's search. Rowan Williams sees this desire as common to all people—to a greater or

---

67. Turner, *Darkness of God*, 58–60, 66.
68. C. Taylor, *Sources of the Self*, 135–36.
69. Augustine *Confessions* 10.1.
70. Ibid., 10.5.
71. Or as Lewis puts it in the *Narnia Chronicles*, "Further in and further up."
72. Augustine *Confessions* 10.27.

lesser degree perhaps. "To be seen: perhaps this is the foundation of any apprehension of the moral self—not, please God, in the sense of being under the all-seeing eye of a judging scrutiny, but the recognition of a life lived beyond a self-referential framework of what *I* choose or understand. This feels like loss and danger. But equally it entails that the resources for my future don't have to be found in or generated by my choice or by my understanding."[73] Unlike Beckett, Augustine responds to a sense that God has recognized him; self-knowledge, for Augustine, must *start* from this sense of being recognized.

Care needs to be taken here—and Lewis was particularly aware of this when he eventually aligned himself with his thought. Augustine has been accused of opening up a kind of introspection, which led to the modern individualistic and autonomous self. Colin Gunton, for example, argues that Augustine's emphasis upon the mind "encourages the suggestion that knowledge of God is to be found primarily in the mind" and that he calls attention away from the material, "almost, if not explicitly . . . saying that if we know ourselves correctly, we know God in the same act."[74] But this is to miss the complexity of Augustine's thought. I would want to align myself with those who argue that this is far from the case.[75] Augustine never lost sight of the inadequacies and the deceptiveness of the human mind; "The powers of my inner self are veiled in darkness which I must deplore."[76] For Augustine, just as the self who is seeking God has to return to the self, so too, in the "journey not of feet" towards God, there is a stage where the self, must put itself away. Not only is the self not trustworthy, but it is also inadequate. Augustine and Lewis were both emphatic about this.

The Spiritual Master: George MacDonald

"I fancy that I have never written a book in which I did not quote from him," Lewis said of George MacDonald.[77] He said that MacDonald had baptized his imagination at the age of eighteen; and later, after Lewis

---

73. R. Williams, *Lost Icons*, 175.

74. Gunton, "Augustine, the Trinity, and the Theological Crisis of the West," 51.

75. The number who argue against this is growing rapidly: Ellen Charry, Lewis Ayres, Michel Barnes, John Millbank, Rowan Williams, and Mark McIntosh are just a few who would call for a more careful reading of Augustine, with regard to the way in which this subject (in connection with his emphasis of the unity of God [contra Arius]) has been interpreted.

76. Augustine *Confessions* 10.32.

77. Lewis, *George MacDonald*, 33.

himself came to believe, he tried to emulate MacDonald. Catherine Durie points out that the lasting influence of MacDonald upon Lewis would seem to be "devotional" although his first discovery of *Phantastes* in 1916, "carried him across a frontier" from his previous engagement with Romanticism, to a kind of holy Romanticism, which drew everything up into the bright shadow that was Holiness.[78] Lewis had been drawn to Romantic literature at an early age, primarily because it was there, alongside inanimate nature, that he was able to evoke *Sehnsucht*. In a 1947 poem, "The Romantics," (later re-titled "The Prudent Jailor"), Lewis argued that the Romantics dream of the world beyond the prison bars, and that others merely diminish such concepts by giving them a label, such as "Romance." As he pointed out in the third preface to *The Pilgrim's Regress*, it was a very particular definition of Romanticism that he tried to defend there. Romanticism, he said, is "spilled religion," the trail of which, if followed, may lead to taste the cup itself. His concept of myth and fantasy was tied up with this; but his taste in Romanticism always revolved around the fascination with the mysterious and the yearning for that which lay beyond the material, not as escapism but for increased understanding.[79]

Lewis's perceptions of God and the self were probably highly influenced by MacDonald's sermons in particular. Of *Unspoken Sermons* he said, "My own debt to this book is almost as great as one man can owe to another."[80] The inexorability of God was certainly one theme that Lewis perceived in MacDonald. ". . . Love loves unto purity . . . Escape is hopeless. For Love is inexorable. Our God is a consuming fire."[81] In his preface to *George MacDonald: An Anthology*, Lewis suggested that "Inexorable Love" could stand as a title for the whole collection. He particularly appreciated MacDonald's "Christ-like union of tenderness and severity," despite the fact that he emphasized the father heart of God in a way Lewis did not.[82] MacDonald had much to say about the connectedness of God and the self, as Lewis noted. (The anthology selections on the self make up almost a sixth of the book.) For MacDonald, God bestows

---

78. Lewis discusses the impact of his first reading of MacDonald in both *Surprised by Joy* and the preface to *George MacDonald: An Anthology*. Catherine Durie writes about the influence of MacDonald on Lewis in "George MacDonald and C. S. Lewis," 163–85.

79. Kerry Dearborn's interpretation of MacDonald's Romanticism demonstrates that there is a clear resonance with that of Lewis. Kerry Dearborn, *Baptized Imagination*, 28f.

80. Lewis, Preface to *George MacDonald*, 30.

81. Ibid., 39.

82. Ibid., 31

identity, but humans must respond by becoming. Identity is not given at birth—like the dancers in *Lilith* who are close to gaining faces, but only through a steady process of truthfulness. MacDonald's sermon "The White Stone" in *Unspoken Sermons*, is an expansion of this idea, that only God can bestow a name—and it is only bestowed upon those who return to their source, God himself:

> The true name is one which expresses the character, the nature, the being, the *meaning* of the person, who bears it. It is the man's own symbol, his soul's picture, in a word, the sign which belongs to him and to no one else. Who can give a man this, his own name? God alone. For no one but God sees what the man is, or even, seeing what he is, could express in a name-word the sum and harmony of what he sees. To whom is this name given? To him that overcometh. When is it given? When he has overcome . . . We shall not look long before we find that the mystic symbol has for its centre of significance the fact of the personal individual relation of every man to his God . . . To him who offers unto this God of the living his own self of sacrifice, to him that overcometh, him who has brought his individual life back to its source, who knows that he is *one* of God's children, *this* one of the Father's making, he giveth the white stone.[83]

Of MacDonald's emphasis upon God as closely connected to human consciousness, Lewis seems to have drunk deeply. In "Self-Denial" MacDonald wrote:

> It is God feeds us, warms us, quenches our thirst. The will of God feeds us, must be to us all in all; to our whole nature the life of the father must be the joy of the child; we must know our very understanding his—then we live and feed on him every hour in the closest, veriest way: to know these things in the depth of our knowing, is to deny ourselves, and take God instead. To try after them is to begin the denial, to follow him who has never sought his own . . . Self, I have not to consult you but Him whose idea is the soul of you . . . You may be my consciousness but you are not my being . . . For God is more to me than my consciousness of myself. He is my life; you are only so much of it as my poor half-made being can grasp—as much of it as I can know at once.[84]

Here we find many ideas that Lewis embraced; that our selves cannot be separated from God; and that God, not the self, is to be the object of

---

83. MacDonald, "New Name," 67–78, 71–73.
84. MacDonald, "Self-Denial," 216–17.

our focus. In *A Dish of Orts,* for example, MacDonald wrote; "It is God [who] sits in the chamber . . . the candle of our consciousness goes out into the darkness, and sends forth from thence wonderful gifts into the light of that understanding which is his candle."[85] The distinction between consciousness and being is also already familiar to us. Lewis said of MacDonald that, "he is quite as aware as the moderns that the conscious self, the thing revealed by introspection, is a superficies."[86] In "A Sketch of Individual Development" we find another similarity, this time to Lewis's connection between the conscience and consciousness. At what he calls the third birth of the human being, or the third stage in development, the person "not only knows, not only knows that he knows, but knows he knows that he knows—knows that he is self-conscious—that he has a conscience."[87] Obedience is thus integrally connected with the self; to obey the conscience is to progress: "the whole secret of progress is the doing of the thing we know. There is no other way of progress in the spiritual life; no other way of progress in the understanding of that life: only as we do, can we know."[88] Lewis was particularly struck by the message to Anodos in *Phantastes,* "do something worth doing." It was a message Lewis reiterated again and again, having met it frequently in MacDonald's writings. Trust and act; nobleness of thought is insufficient without nobleness of deed. For both men, the conscience must be listened to, and acted upon, but not given the pre-eminent place. MacDonald, in reacting against a certain kind of Calvinistic self-scrutiny, may be the one who gave rise to the term that Lewis gave to his early introspective habit—"disease." Rather, MacDonald taught the need for confidence in God:

> To lose ourselves in the salvation of God's heart! To be no longer any care to ourselves, but know God taking divinest care of us, his own! To be and feel just a resting-place for the divine love—a branch of the tree of life for the dove to alight upon and fold its wings! To be an open air of love, a thoroughfare for the thoughts of God and all holy creatures![89]

It is the opposite of stoic resignation; as Lewis points out in the preface to the anthology, MacDonald was "deeply appreciative of all really beautiful

---

85. MacDonald, "Sketch of Individual Development," para 47.

86. Lewis, Preface to *George MacDonald,* 32.

87. MacDonald, "Sketch of Individual Development," *A Dish of Orts.*

88. MacDonald, "Truth In Jesus," *Unspoken Sermons,* Series II, 403.

89. Ibid., 375.

and delicious things that money can buy, and no less deeply content to do without them."[90]

For it may have been MacDonald, no less than A. K. Hamilton Jenkin, who taught Lewis the pleasures of particularity, the joy of the quiddity of a thing. From MacDonald he learnt it through the transformation caused by the bright shadow of holiness that emanated from *Phantastes*. The Joy that he experienced when reading that text, made the real world brighter. Until this point the visitations of Joy had left the real world a desert.[91] That God is concrete gives greater specificity to all that exists on earth. Christians "must not conceive spiritual joy and worth as things that need to be rescued or tenderly protected from time and place and matter and the senses. Their God is the God of corn and oil and wine. He is the glad creator. He has become Himself incarnate."[92] Christianity does not reject matter. *Miracles* mercilessly challenges the Gnostic vision; "The Incarnation reconciles the ancient Gnostic dualism between spirit and matter, nature and transcendence. The concrete, not the amorphous, is most real."[93] Matter—apples and dancing and swimming on a warm day—is the avenue for much pleasure. Angelic minds may discern the tree-ness of a tree, but humans have senses which enable them to feel and distinguish.[94] But the "tether and tang of the particular," like the love of humans for each other is part of the cost of being made in the image of God. Involvement in the natural world is costly.[95] This is the antithesis of Beckett's withdrawal and repudiation of the world that serves to empty it of meaning and pleasure. Introspection cannot bear the weight of the world.

The People Who Speak One's Own Language: Contemporaries[96]

Lewis was also open to the influences of his contemporaries—to whom we now turn. J. R. R. Tolkien's role in his conversion and in the formation of Lewis's thinking on myth as the expression of eternal truth has been well charted. More pertinent to this project are Owen Barfield and

---

90. Lewis, Preface to *George MacDonald*, 25.
91. Lewis, *Surprised by Joy*, 140.
92. Lewis, *Miracles*, 172.
93. Werge, "Sanctifying the Literal," 77.
94. See Lewis's poem "On Being Human," for an articulation of this (*Poems*, 48–49).
95. See Meilaender's comments on this in his chapter "The Tether and Tang of the Particular," in *The Taste for the Other*.
96. Lewis expressed a desire to have such friends in a letter to A. K. H. Jenkin (cited by Carpenter in *Inklings*, 22).

Charles Williams. Owen Barfield, (whose influence upon Lewis we have touched upon already), played a significant role in shaping Lewis's thinking in his 20s. Lewis said he was the anti-self, the friend who shares your interests but comes to all the wrong conclusions. In *Surprised by Joy*, Lewis acknowledged the impact of Barfield on two areas of his thought; firstly, on destroying his "chronological snobbery," and secondly, in forcing him to accept the idea that the whole universe was "mental," "and our logic was participation in a cosmic *Logos*."[97] Lionel Adey has been the most thorough expositor of Barfield's and Lewis's "Great War" but—as already suggested—Barfield's ideas may have impacted Lewis more than either man recognized. Barfield contends in his *Poetic Diction* that the earliest use of language had not distinguished between the literal and the metaphorical, but had used words in a more "mythological" fashion. For Barfield, consciousness is not so much the thought of individual humans, as the "cosmos" or world about him—his thinking was heavily influenced by Rudolf Steiner's evolution of consciousness. Adey puts Barfield's position this way:

> Barfield contended that, by inducing a "change of consciousness," poetic language caused readers to grow not only in the power of perceiving resemblances but also in knowledge and wisdom. By restoring a lost unity between the perceiver and the perceived, its metaphors enabled them to know (*connaître*) rather than merely know about (*savoir*) things in nature. Primal man, whose unity with nature was inferable from words such as the Greek *pneuma*, signifying wind without, breath within, and spirit above or beneath, experienced the world as no less alive than himself, hence his figurative or "poetic" language.[98]

Lewis accepted Barfield's linguistic argument, an acceptance which not only prepared him for an ability to accept Tolkien's argument that Christianity was true myth, but affected his understanding of language, for it gave him a very high view of word as inseparably connected with that which it is expressing. However, Lewis was unwilling—throughout the Great War at any rate—to accept the unity of the perceiver with that which is perceived. But it may be that he did receive from Barfield a sense that the split between object and subject was a pathological element of recent Western culture. For example, the distinction between *connaître* and *savoir* is one that we have already heard Lewis expound:

---

97. Lewis, *Surprised by Joy*, 160–61.
98. Adey, *Writer, Dreamer and Mentor*, 31.

We can get no further than this in knowledge *about* (*savoir*) God; but we are vouchsafed some knowledge by acquaintance (*connaître*) of Him, in our devotional and sacramental life.[99]

In *Saving the Appearances*, Barfield wrote of "participation" as the link with the Spirit through nature, a participation which was originally flawed and inadequate, but which would, in the course of evolution, come to fruition when humans would experience participation with this Spirit.[100] Although Lewis argued against Barfield's particular idea of the ultimate conscious participation in God, it seems remarkably like the ideas he expounds towards the end of his career. For, as we shall see in the next chapter, Lewis seems at times to come very close to the Christian concept of participation. Unlike Barfield, however, Lewis's participation is not one that is the product of human progress but of God's action.

If Barfield helped shape Lewis's thoughts on language and epistemology, Charles Williams was probably the one who most influenced his thoughts on the nature of God, and who most encouraged the esoteric in his thought. "Lewis always said that he owed everything to Charles Williams," wrote Eric Routley.[101] It may be that Barfield's and William's (and Tolkien's) influences could be said to be of a different ilk *because* he knew them; it was a participatory knowledge, gained through acquaintance (*connaître*), and therefore all the more profound. There is no small irony in this—in view of the specific impact that each man had upon him. William's impact was more to do with a way of perceiving the teachings of Christianity, a bestowing of depth upon an understanding that Lewis already had. For example, it was, in all likelihood, Williams who helped Lewis to overcome the polarities that his mind found within paradox and to hold such polarities as one.[102] Rather than either/or, Williams thought in terms of both/and. The aphorism most associated with him was, "This also is Thou; neither is this Thou"; a saying to which Lewis makes reference three times in *Prayer: Letters to Malcolm*. It was a way of seeing that brought the supernatural and the natural into a constant state of involvement. *Till We Have Faces* is, in this respect, the novel of Lewis's that is most infused with this sense that "it is and it is not."[103] As Lewis said in his article, "The Novels of Charles Williams," ". . . I am convinced

99. Lewis, letter to Gracia Fay Bouwman (July 19, 1960) *Letters*, Vol. III, 1173.
100. Thorson, "Barfield's Evolution of Consciousness," 9–35.
101. Routley, "A Prophet," 33.
102. Brian Horne suggests this in "Peculiar Debt," 88.
103. Lewis, *Till We Have Faces*, 203. (Hereafter abbreviated to *TWHF* in the footnotes.)

that both the content and the quality of his experience differed from mine and differed in ways which oblige me to say that he saw further, and that he knew what I do not know. His writing, so to speak, brings me where I have never gone on my own sail or steam; and yet that strange place is so attached to realms we do know that I cannot believe it is mere dreamland."[104]

This can be seen in the doctrines that Williams emphasized. The concept of exchange, based upon "Bear ye one another's burdens" (Galatians 6:2) was, for Williams, a literal taking of another's concern. Christ's death as substitution was the supreme example of exchange, but the divine and human natures can enjoy mutual exchange. There is no confusion of the divine and the human, however; rather, they co-inhere. "The doctrine of the Christian Church has declared that the mystery of the Christian religion is a doctrine of co-inherence and substitution. The Divine Word co-inheres in God the father (as the Father in Him and the Spirit in Both), but also he has substituted His Manhood for ours in the secrets of the Incarnation and Atonement. The principle of the Passion is that he gave his life 'for'—that is, instead of and on behalf of—ours. In that sense he lives in us and we in Him, He and we co-inhere. 'I live; yet not I but Christ liveth in me' said St. Paul, and defined the web of universal power towards substitution."[105] Lewis did not adopt the terminology of Williams to any great extent, but it seems to me that his already existing emphasis—the need to turn to the other, to reach beyond the self, was greatly enriched by dialogue with Williams.[106] (In perhaps the same way, Lewis absorbed Kierkegaard through Williams; although Lewis claimed to dislike his style, I find, with James Como, that Lewis is much more Kierkegaardian than he was willing to admit.[107])

Williams contributed to Lewis's sense that God is beyond human reason, that he is not circumscribable. In the 1930's Lewis had picked up on Rudolph Otto's idea of the *Numinous*, God as wholly Other—an emphasis that he retained in *Till We Have Faces*.[108] Williams took this further, and like Barfield, compounded Lewis's sense that knowledge was not

---

104. Lewis, "Novels of Charles Williams," 52.

105. C. Williams, *Image of the City*, 152.

106. Certain aspects of William's thought—for example, the reconciling of good and evil, and his fear of immortality—remain entirely absent from the thought of Lewis.

107. C. Williams was responsible for the publishing of Kierkegaard while he worked at the Oxford University Press. So it is possible that Lewis received the ideas of Kierkegaard through Williams; Lewis was emphatic in his letters that he had read very little of Kierkegaard's work directly.

108. See, for example, the first chapter of *The Problem of Pain*.

conveyed by propositions. Focusing on images as purveyors of knowledge, Williams primary image was that of romantic love and Lewis's was *Sehnsucht*. This Affirmative way stressed the importance of images; in Williams, this vision blended with his critical work in his great study of Dante, *The Figure of Beatrice*. There, Beatrice was the way in which Dante *knew* God. Dante's *Divine Comedy*, he felt, was a description of the great act of knowledge, "in which Dante himself is the Knower, and God is the Known and Beatrice is the Knowing."[109] There seems to be something of Beatrice in Psyche, for she too is an image "of nobility, of virtue, of the Redeemed Life, and in some sense of Almighty God himself," just as Beatrice is.[110] Equally, propositions cannot adequately convey that God is "a dreadful goodness"; "holy wisdom is not clear and thin like water, but thick and dark like blood."[111] In *Till We Have Faces*, Orual learns something of the connectedness of holiness and horror just as Stanhope in Williams' *Descent into Hell* teaches Pauline of a God of terror and love.

Finally, with regard to contemporaries of Lewis, François Mauriac's *Vipers' Tangle* (published in English in 1951) is the slow untangling of a life lived in retrospect, intermingled with a journey from self-delusion to some measure of self-understanding.[112] Like *Till We Have Faces*, it is an account of someone who has deluded himself with respect to the truth, and with respect to those around him. And like *Till We Have Faces*, it is written in the form of an accusation that consists of two parts, with the second part revealing a slowly maturing understanding that the world is not as it has been perceived in self-enclosure, and an evolution in perception is gradually revealed. Again, like *Till We Have Faces*, it is a perception which is not complete by the end of the novel, but decidedly works in tandem with a growing perception of a transcendent "Someone." Further, in conjunction with this, the protagonist, Louis, shifts from a rather suspicious approach to his family, to one based more on a wisdom that stems from love.

This shift in understanding is crucial to a correct grasp of the double knowledge, for this emphasis upon wisdom rather than knowledge is central to a correct sense of the self. It was a distinction that Lewis no doubt found in Augustine, particularly in Book XII of *De trinitate*. Andrew Louth tells us, "The distinction is that between knowledge which is concerned with the external world perceived through the sense, knowledge therefore

---

109. C. Williams, "Recollection of the Way," 76.
110. C. Williams, *Figure of Beatrice*, 8.
111. Lewis, *TWHF*, 38.
112. Many thanks to Kirstin Jeffrey Johnson for drawing my attention to this.

concerned with action in the world (*scientia*), and that knowledge, or wisdom, which is concerned with eternal reality and contemplation of it (*sapientia*)."[113] *Scientia* is the consequence of the Fall; prior to the Fall the mode of knowing was *sapientia*. This *scientia/sapientia* distinction appears to be very close to the Lewis/Barfield distinction *savoir/connaître*, although Augustine's *sapientia* seems to carry with it somewhat more of the idea of contemplation than is clear in the writing of Barfield.[114] In the writings of Lewis, frequent reference is made to the need for *connaître* knowledge because all else is illuminated by such wisdom; "the human mind in the act of knowing is illuminated by Divine reason."[115] Lewis put it this way in *The Four Loves*:

> The humblest of us, in a state of Grace, can have some "knowledge-by-acquaintance" (*connaître*), some "tasting," of Love Himself; but man even at his highest sanctity and intelligence has no direct "knowledge about" (*savoir*) the ultimate Being—only analogies.[116]

For both Lewis and Augustine, the Incarnation made such knowledge available to us. This is what integrates the whole mass of our knowledge; "We believe that the sun is in the sky at midday in summer not because we can clearly see the sun (in fact we cannot) but because we can see everything else."[117] It strikes a chord with Mark McIntosh's statement; "Truthful discourse about God would thus seem to require a particular way of knowing and stating things, namely a knowing that does not point at something (for which there is literally no-thing at which to point) but participates in the mystery of the reality it desires to know."[118] As McIntosh continues, for some mystical traditions, "knowledge or wisdom is never a merely noetic factor but involves a new way of living, a practical or (to use the old term) 'habitual' kind of knowledge that is acquired through one's manner of life and sensed perhaps more intuitively than propositionally."[119]

> For the ancient world the process of *noesis* or (to use our thinner word) "knowing" is far more intuitive, and less "private" in that it is not so much "I" who am knowing but that "the known" has drawn me into an encounter with itself. In the formative environ-

113. Louth, *Origins of the Christian Mystical Tradition*, 153.
114. Ibid., 153.
115. Lewis, *Miracles*, 22.
116. Lewis, *Four Loves*, 143.
117. Lewis, *Miracles*, 115.
118. McIntosh, *Mystical Theology*, 27.
119. Ibid., 29.

> ment of Christian mysticism, knowing reality is associated more with intimacy, even the desire, that runs between knower and known . . . and less with our modern conception of a scientific analysis of manipulable objects by the knower. Indeed for St. Paul it is clear that the most complete form of knowledge would not finally be our own act at all, but an event in which I yield myself to God. And God, in this view, turns out to be not the known object but the ultimate Knower in the whole process: "Now I know in part, then I shall know fully even as I have been fully known" (1 Cor 13:12).[120]

The writer of Gal 4:9 underlines the fact that God is the ultimate Knower; "But now that you know God, or rather are known by God . . ." Rowan Williams states that for the mind to acquire this *sapientia* is to see itself sustained by this action of God; "We come to 'image' God by grasping that our reality exists solely within his activity of imparting wisdom and justice . . . The image of God in us might be said to entail a movement into our own createdness, because that is a movement into God's own life as turned outwards."[121] Lewis too reflects this emphasis; "the initiative lies on His side."[122] All knowledge, whether of God, or of self, is dependent upon God—and true self-knowledge recognizes this dependence upon God and acts accordingly. "The instrument through which you see God is your whole self."[123] This is the double knowledge that Lewis most explicitly portrays in *Till We Have Faces*. As Orual says after the gods have buffeted her in a dream, "I lived and knew myself"—and it is to this engagement between living and knowing that we now turn.[124]

I Lived and Knew Myself: Lewis and the Self

Till We Have Faces is a reworking of the myth of Cupid and Psyche, as told by Apuleius, but given a new depth as a consequence of long cogitation by Lewis. As he indicated in his preface to the British edition, "This re-interpretation of an old story has lived in the author's mind, thickening and hardening with the years, ever since he was an undergraduate. That way, he could be said to have worked at it most of his life."[125] He goes on to outline some of the themes; "Recently, what seemed to be the

---

120. McIntosh, *Mystical Theology*, 70.
121. R. Williams, "*Sapientia* and the Trinity," 321.
122. Lewis, *Mere Christianity*, 164.
123. Ibid., 164–65.
124. Lewis, *TWHF*, 215.
125. Lewis, *TWHF*, x.

right form presented itself and themes suddenly interlocked: the straight tale of barbarism, the mind of an ugly woman, dark idolatry and pale enlightenment at war with each other and with vision, and the havoc which a vocation, or even a faith, works on human life." That these are to be found in Lewis's version of the myth is undeniable, but the statement is far from conveying the sum total of this highly suggestive book. When asked about it by Clyde S. Kilby, Lewis's comments upon it pointed in a different direction, this time primarily towards distorted natural human love, possessive and resentful of a family member embracing religion. Psyche "is an instance of the *anima naturaliter christiana* . . . in some ways like Christ because every good man or woman is like Christ." He went on to say, "But of course my interest is primarily in Orual." She is, Lewis says, "an instance, a 'case' of human affection in its natural condition, true, tender, suffering, but in the long run tyranically possessive and ready to turn to hatred when the beloved ceases to be its possession."[126]

Both statements—the preface and the remarks to Kilby, are particularly interesting because both point towards a single aspect of a many faceted book. Lewis had prefaced his remarks to Kilby by commenting, "An author doesn't necessarily understand the meaning of his own story better than anyone else," but it is hard not to conclude that Lewis knew more of "the meaning" than he felt able to say. For one thing, there is probably much of Janie Moore in Orual, because she was the person in Lewis's life who had been, to the very end, probably most jealous of his conversion to Christianity.[127] I am not alone in feeling that Lewis's interpretation is very far from giving the whole picture. James T. Como states that Lewis was wrong "in saying that it is about a woman corrupted by possessive love. That may be what he intended, but he produced very much more . . . and addresses a question that nearly monopolizes the contemporary mind: What is personhood and what are we to make of it?"[128] Manlove summarizes the novel by saying that Lewis deals in this book with "the native evasiveness of the soul."[129] Chad Walsh has commented that "the central psychological theme, though not clear until almost the end of the book, is the quest for self-knowledge."[130] In a letter to one correspondent

---

126. Lewis, letter to Clyde S. Kilby (February 10, 1957) *Letters*, Vol. 3, 830–31.

127. See for example, a letter to Sister Penelope (January 31, 1946) *Letters*, Vol. II, 702. He also makes reference to her possessiveness in unpublished work e.g., May 28, 1948, Bodleian Library.

128. Como, *Branches to Heaven*, 184.

129. Manlove, *C. S. Lewis: His Literary Achievement*, 203.

130. Walsh, *The Literary Legacy Of C. S. Lewis*, 163.

Lewis gave an explanation that seems to come much closer to the heart of the matter than any other of his comments. In explaining the title of *Till We Have Faces* he said: "The idea was that a human being must become real . . . must be speaking with its own voice (not one of its borrowed voices), expressing its actual desires (not what it imagines that it desires), being for good or ill itself, not any mask, veil, or *persona*."[131] His concern in the book is not so much to depict the face of God, but rather, to show how a human can become faceless. Lewis himself, having recently shed his something of an unhelpful persona, wrote a novel that reverberates with the changes and the process of changing; but given the intensely personal nature of the themes explored, it is hardly surprising that he refrains from stating more about this aspect. In one sense there is irony here—that the unveiling of Lewis remained so tacit—or so veiled—that few have seen the personal nature of this book. But the power of the book lies in it *not* being straight autobiography, but myth. Of this Lewis was aware. But, as he himself acknowledged, it may be that he could not yet be fully aware of the full import of that myth; "Into an allegory a man can put only what he already knows: in a myth he puts what he does not yet know and could not come to know in any other way."[132]

Self Deception: Its Face Was Unknown to Me[133]

Chad Walsh's reference to the central psychological theme of "the quest for self-knowledge" is more accurately re-stated by Peter J. Schakel when he speaks of Orual's *gaining* of self-knowledge as the central theme of the book.[134] For self-knowledge is not sought by Orual. On the contrary, her life has been a long process of evasion until, at the end of her life, her defenses are overcome and she is forced to consider the consequences of her actions. Lack of self-knowledge has been a predominant characteristic of life at the palace. It could be said of her father, as of Lear, "he hath ever but slenderly known himself."[135] His death was without affective recognition, just as he gave no affective recognition in life. It was he who first had Orual veiled—to conceal her ugliness. When she takes to wearing the veil

---

131. Lewis, letter to Dorothea Conybeare, in *Letters to a Sister from Rose Macaulay*, 261.

132. Lewis, letter to Father Peter Milward, September, 22, 1956, *Letters*, Vol. III, 789–90.

133. Lewis, *TWHF*, 230. Orual here does not recognize that the face is actually her own.

134. Schakel, *Reason and Imagination in C. S. Lewis*, 52.

135. Shakespeare, *King Lear*, Act I, Scene I.

on a constant basis, Orual declares it to be a sort of treaty made with her ugliness, only retrospectively realizing that it is, as Schakel puts it, a way of covering her "inner ugliness."[136] The veil becomes a multistable image that suggests, not just this, but the veiled goddess of the ancient mystery cults of Isis and Venus and the Neo-Platonic idea that great truths should be veiled.[137] It also conveys ambivalence in Orual's relationship to others, including those closest to her. But it reverberates in particular with the deliberate refusal of accurate perception that Orual dons when she puts on her veil. She refuses to see what is really there, choosing instead to see the facts as they suit her own ends.

Orual's self-deceptions start small but they are many, and they grow in audacity.[138] For example, when she refuses Psyche's suggestion that the god will help her to see properly: "I don't want it. I hate it. Hate it, hate it, hate it."[139] Then, having destroyed Psyche's marriage to the god of the Mountain, she glimpses the palace of the god (just as Psyche described it), but by rationalizing it—in order to avoid facing her own jealousy and spite—she dispenses with it. And later, when in rebuke the god himself appears to her, proving that he is neither villain nor Shadow Brute, she still contrives to manipulate the truth:

> Though my body crouched where I could almost have touched his feet, his eyes seemed to send me from him to an endless distance. He rejected, denied, answered, and (worst of all) he knew, all I had thought, done or been. A Greek verse says that even the gods cannot change the past. But is it true? He made it to be as if, from the beginning, I had known that Pyche's lover was a god, and as if all my questionings of Bardia, questionings of the Fox, all the rummage and business of it, had been trumped up foolery, dust blown in my own eyes by myself.[140]

His declaration, culminating in a "riddle," as Orual calls it ("You, woman, shall know yourself and your work. You also shall be Psyche"), or aporia, passes almost without comment.[141] Back at the palace, she avoids too the probing questions of the Fox. In time she persuades herself that the gods do not actually exist. As Doris Myers has suggested, she chooses to ignore the evidence; "Her choice is not based on the claims of rational-

---

136. Schakel, *Reason and Imagination in C. S. Lewis*, 56.
137. Lewis, *Spenser's Images of Life*, 43.
138. For delineation of these, see Myers, *C. S. Lewis in Context*, 207–9.
139. Lewis, *TWHF*, 92.
140. Ibid., 129–30.
141. Ibid., 130.

ity, or science, versus the claims of faith; it is a choice contaminated by self-centeredness and the desire for control."[142] Colin Manlove sums it up, "Orual's persuasion of Psyche to disobey the god is not just *like*, it is a version of the temptation and fall of man."[143] Jealousy, anger, shame, fear—words often repeated in the novel—combine to make a veiled existence more attractive, or apparently easier, than an exposed existence. The donning of the veil symbolizes the defenses that she uses and is integral to Orual's embarkation upon a complex trajectory of self-deception. For Augustine—and the resonances in *Till We Have Faces* are undoubtedly intentional—the Fall was really, as Rowan Williams puts it, "a fall from the experienced harmony of self with self and self with God."[144]

Over time, the defenses thicken. Her self-deception has become part of her, as the veil has become part of her also. The outer, external Orual begins to become a separate entity, and it is the one that she chooses to nurture. Upon the death of her father, Orual takes the decision that she shall be Queen—and that in doing so, she shall let Orual die. "If Orual could vanish altogether into the Queen, the gods would almost be cheated."[145] Over a period of many years she recreates herself; ". . . the Queen of Glome had more and more part in me and Orual had less and less. I locked her up or laid her asleep as best as I could somewhere deep down inside me; she lay curled there. It was like being with child, but reversed; the thing I carried in me grew slowly smaller and less alive."[146] To the best of her ability she grasps her new role, warring and ruling and making use of the fear that the veil instills in ambassadors and subjects alike. In order to be the Queen, she must drive all the woman out of herself, as she puts it. More significantly, and of this she seems unaware, she is trying to drive the humanity out.

Orual's self-deception has ramifications that damage herself, her retinue, and her kingdom. For the malignant consequences go far beyond "mere" damage to her own humanity. It extends to those who serve her loyally and lovingly. She becomes inured to the outworking of her actions; if she is Queen and hence depersonalized, so she depersonalizes others, and their loved ones in their turn. The Fox, having opted to stay in Glome for her sake, dies largely neglected by her. Bardia dies, worn out in her service. Her love for them has degenerated until it becomes a kind

142. Myers, *C. S. Lewis in Context*, 209.
143. Manlove, *C. S. Lewis: His Literary Achievement*, 211.
144. R. Williams, *Wound of Knowledge*, 72.
145. Lewis, *TWHF*, 152.
146. Ibid., 170.

of hatred. As Lewis argues in "Two Ways with the Self" there are two kinds of self-hatred. Orual exhibits the development that he observed in the kind that hates selves as such:

> It begins by accepting the special value of the particular self called *me*; then, wounded in its pride to find that such a darling object should be so disappointing, it seeks revenge, first upon that self, then on all. Deeply egoistic, but now with an inverted egoism, it uses the revealing argument, "I don't spare myself"—with the implication "then *a fortiori* I need not spare others."[147]

It is a long time before Orual can recognize that in this long phase of her life she is a devourer of men, "the swollen spider, squat at its centre, gorged with men's stolen lives."[148] Her face has become the face of Ungit, the devouring goddess—but she has not noticed. This devouring of others, objectifying and manipulating, can be traced back from a failure in self-love. Just as she has been unable to love herself, so too Orual is unable to extend full—and freeing—love to those around her. Her sin is *cupiditas*, or excessive, and possessive loving, which punishes what it cannot possess. It is love, but it is love distorted, and as Bardia's wife, Ansit, points out to her, such loving is a form of devouring. Lewis's language insists that Orual's self-deception is cannibalistic in its consequences.[149] "Gorged with other men's lives; women's too. Bardia's; mine; the Fox's; your sister's; both your sisters'."[150] Later, once Ansit's accusations have contributed to the long slow process back to unveiling, Orual is able to admit that "a love can grow to nine-tenths hatred and still call itself love."[151]

Such distorted love is intimately connected to a failure in self-knowledge as Rowan Williams points out in his comments on Augustine's anthropology:

> So when we say that someone lacks self-knowledge, we don't mean that she lacks information, or even that she is not given to thinking about herself . . . Lack of self-knowledge is a failure in spiritual and moral *habit*, a deficiency in the skills of living according to nature. It is inseparable from failure in love, in the sense that the mind misconceives its own nature when it loves

---

147. Lewis, "Two Ways with the Self," 120–21.
148. Lewis, *TWHF*, 209.
149. "Devouring" was a word also used by Jung.
150. Ibid., 200.
151. Ibid., 201.

(and so identifies with) objects that do not correspond to its most true and fundamental aspirations . . . Augustine holds together the moral skills of truthful, un-self-regarding love with the capacity for authentic self-awareness.[152]

"Lack of self-knowledge is a failure in spiritual and moral *habit*," as well as a failure in love. Orual's self-knowledge has been distorted by a long orientation away from the truth, just as her original love for Psyche is distorted into the self-regarding *cupiditas*, and the effect is that she is blinded to the consequences of her actions. As Williams later says, with reference to *De trinitate* X, viii, "When [the mind] loves something other than its own loving action (towards God and neighbor), when it is so attached to particular objects and their remembered images that it can no longer distinguish itself, its fundamental orientation to love, from the succession of transient impressions, it fails in self-knowledge."[153] This succinct interpretation by Augustine is an apt summation of the failure in love and concomitant failure of self-knowledge that is played out by Orual. One of the characteristics of the novel is that the characters are both highly particularized—and highly representative; and Orual is a character both particular and representative in her treatment of herself. In *The Problem of Pain* Lewis wrote, "I do not think it is our fault that we cannot tell the real truth about ourselves; the persistent, life-long, inner murmur of spite, jealousy, prurience, greed and self-complacence, simply will not go into words."[154] Orual's self-deception is part of the human condition, and the telling of it is similar to that of the Hebrew *mashal*, as John Sykes has pointed out.[155] In other words, her story of self-deception is intended to aid the reader in a reading of their own life, jolting them into recognition, just as David was jolted by Nathan.

Self-Negation: Die Before You Die

The penultimate stage before Orual's facade is torn asunder is a frenzy of activity, an avoidance of the truth that threatens to rupture through the facade:

> I did and I did and I did—and what does it matter what I did? I cared for all these things only as a man cares for a hunt or a game, which fills the mind and seems of some moment while it

---

152. R. Williams, "Paradoxes of Self-Knowledge in the *De trinitate*," 129.
153. Ibid., 129.
154. Lewis, *Problem of Pain*, 48.
155. Sykes, "*Till We Have Faces* and the Broken-Hearted Reader."

> lasts, but then the beast's killed or the king's mated, and now who cares? It was so with me almost every evening of my life; one little stairway led me from feast or council, all the bustle and skill and glory of queenship, to my own chamber, to be alone with myself; that is, with a nothingness.[156]

Orual as Queen has embraced the Stoic's outlook, with carefully controlled emotions and emphasis upon the material and the rational. We see it when she says that she locked a door in her mind in order to avoid thinking of Psyche and courting madness. She learned to fence, to ride horseback, about "the physical parts of philosophy, about the seminal fire, and how the soul rises from blood . . . about plants and animals and the positions, soils, airs, and government of cities. I wanted hard things now, and to pile up knowledge."[157] The autonomous, self-sufficient life, or *oikeiosis* of Stoicism has already been seen in the figure of the Fox, a philosophy that he later seems to regret, denouncing his "trim sentences" and "prattle of maxims."[158] But Orual has imbibed deeply of his philosophy, as Schakel has spelt out. It suits her to accept only that which can be proven, to fall back on rationalism, for then she need not deal with that which falls outside that rubric.

Lewis spoke from experience when he showed that the self that forgets itself is not on any safer ground than his or her antithetical self, the radically reflexive self that we observed in Beckett's *Three Novels*. Louis Dupré even goes so far as to speak of it as "an even more serious threat to selfhood"; "routine work drudgingly performed, conventional ideas unquestioningly accepted, objective ideas never interiorized gradually erode the very possibility of growth and development . . . If despair means lack of possibility, as Kierkegaard wrote, then the spiritually obtuse live in despair, though they may not know it."[159] And we do glimpse despair in Orual, whether recognized or not, in the ongoing sense of life-seen-through-a-veil, in her sense that all her activity is unimportant. "I did and did and did—and what does it matter what I did?" (Here we glimpse the despair of which Kierkegaard spoke.) Materially she does much to improve the lives of her subjects; fair, diligent, efficient, even kind. But inside she has shrunk so much, that she is a "nothingness." Ultimately all

---

156. Lewis, *TWHF*, 178–79.
157. Ibid., 138.
158. See Schakel, *Reason and Imagination in C. S. Lewis*, 80.
159. Dupré, *Transcendent Selfhood*, 43.

wrong approaches diminish the self. Orual's adult life, this "little death," as Nathan Comfort Starr calls it, is a kind of living death.[160]

But it is not death. Death does not come in this way. Orual will not disappear into the Queen. Lewis makes it clear to the reader that she is an unreliable narrator, one who sets up syllogistic explanations, ignoring or misinterpreting the small but myriad indications that she is falsifying her conscious understanding of her world. Plagued by sounds and sights that reverberate from her unconscious right through to her consciousness, the Queen cannot conquer Orual. Multiple images convey this; images of burial, locking, damming, chaining, gagging, even murder. The most constant one, the weeping sound which so constantly haunts the queen as a reminder of Psyche, may literally be the sound of chains in the well, but it is also, in a sense, the remnant of Orual, hidden, but not silenced.

> I later discovered that there was no part of the palace from which the swinging of those chains could not be heard; at night, I mean, when the silence grows deep. It is a thing no-one would have found out who was not always afraid of hearing one sound; and at the same time (that was Orual, Orual refusing to die) terribly afraid of not hearing it if for once—if possibly, at last, after ten thousand mockeries—it should be real, if Psyche had come back. But I knew this was foolishness.[161]

The use of parentheses here (and elsewhere) is representative of the parenthetical way of Orual the Queen with the old Orual—walled off, buried alive, but still—somehow—present. Having physically walled off the well, Orual is still not free. Her unconscious surfaces in wakeful dreams, when she occasionally senses that she has gagged with stone both herself and Psyche. Try as she does, she is unable to stifle Orual, nor forget the wrong that she has done. Order her consciousness as she will, she cannot silence her unconscious.

For Lewis, the recognition of the surface—"the 'I' as I perceive myself"—involves the recognition of facade as facade.[162] It is not that that the "I" is a necessarily a lie, but that the depths also need to be recognized, mysterious though they may be. And for Lewis, only divine aid can help in this, and he demonstrates this in *Till We Have Faces*. Eventually, exhausted and worn out from her attempt to control and protect her self-image, Orual attempts suicide, but the gods intervene. In the exchange that takes place, Orual's lack of true self-knowledge is starkly

---

160. Starr, "Till We Have Faces," 42.
161. Lewis, *TWHF*, 172.
162. Lewis, *Prayer: Letters to Malcolm*, 76.

evident. In order for her to reach full recognition, she is told that it is necessary for her to "Die before you die. There is no chance after."[163] Well tutored in Greek reasoning, Orual concludes that this necessary death is an extension of her behavior to date, another manifestation of stoicism, a death of passions and desires and vain opinions. Thinking it to be the Socratic "skill and practice of death" she attempts stoic detachment. But this is not the death that Orual has been told to seek. "I would set out boldly each morning to be just and calm and wise in all my thoughts and acts; but before they had finished dressing me I would find that I was back (and knew not how long I had been back) in some old rage, resentment, gnawing fantasy, or sullen bitterness."[164] She cannot fall back on her own virtue and she cannot die. Why do the gods not help? They leave her, she says, for some days, to chew the strange bread they have given her. In time she comes to recognize her own condition. "It was as if I were dead already, but not as the god, or Socrates, bade me die."[165] How can she die before she dies?[166] And what of the first proclamation, "You, woman, shall know yourself and your work. You also shall be Psyche."? Although rejecting the exact form of the Socratic death, Lewis is here embracing the aporetic *method* of the Socratic dialogues (that is, the raising of puzzles without solutions). Like Aristotle, (and unlike Beckett) he believed in the value of the resolution of aporiae as an important source of understanding. It is only retrospectively that Orual is able to embrace the resolution and realizes that the divine Surgeons were at work, to bring out Orual, phoenix-like, from the dying embers.

The Final Unmasking: Self-Knowledge

George MacDonald wrote in "The Final Unmasking" from his *Unspoken Sermons*: "The only terrible, or at least the supremely terrible revelation is that of a man to himself."[167] Lewis, by drawing upon MacDonald's sense of the terror of the revelation of the self, and influences such as the Jungian concept of individuation, combining them with his own experiences, manages to convey a consciousness forced to face that which it has

---

163. Lewis, *TWHF*, 212.

164. Ibid., 213–14.

165. Ibid., 216.

166. It is quite possible that Lewis was influenced to use this wording by his reading of Henry Vaughan's poem, "Regeneration," which concludes "Let me dye before my death." The observation is made by Price in "Seventeenth Century," 150–51.

167. MacDonald, "Final Unmasking," 239.

tried to bury.[168] For Orual, gaining self-knowledge is a "terrible" process of deconstruction as, layer by layer, falsehood and deceptions are stripped away. This image of stripping recurs frequently in Lewis's writings of the early 1950s as Stephen Medcalf has pointed out.[169] In the images which Medcalf considers, the stripping is usually painful—like the loss of layers of skin, for example—and it heralds a transformation in what lay beneath; what Medcalf does not mention is the way in which this stripping occurs in *Till We Have Faces*—probably the most graphic and certainly the most thorough account of them all.

The changes in Orual are wrought by a relentless dialectic of external mirrorings, partially conscious rememberings and divine showings. The first, the external mirrorings, are those in which people reflect her behavior to herself; home-truths from Ansit and Tarin; and a *mashal*— the truth told in myth form—from the priest of Essur. These begin the process, alerting her to her jealousy and the distorted love that has motivated her. And so she is forced to self-scrutiny, turning to the internal world of her memories to try to defend herself. "All day, and often all night too, I was recalling every passage of the true story, dragging up terrors, humiliations, struggles, and anguish that I had not thought of for years, letting Orual wake and speak, digging her almost out of a grave, out of the walled well."[170] Her writing, intended to justify herself before the gods, functions on another level. It becomes a form of confession, a journey of interiority, a spiritual exploration that profoundly changes her. It too functions as a mirror. "In the individual life," said Lewis "as psychologists have taught us, it is not the remembered but the forgotten past that enslaves us."[171] As Orual reflects in Part II of *Till We Have Faces* upon the completed account that constitutes Part I:

> Since I cannot mend the book, I must add to it. To leave it as it was would be to die perjured; I know so much more than I did about the woman who wrote it. What began the change was the very writing itself . . . The past which I wrote down was not the past that I thought I had (all these years) been remembering. I

---

168. Jungian individuation has been described as: "The process leading to a more conscious awareness of one's specific individuality, including a recognition of both one's strengths and one's limitations. Jung describes this process as emerging in middle and later adulthood, first with the recognition of one's neuroses and shortcomings. It continues as an awakening to one's own divided nature (conscious and unconscious) and the ultimate acceptance of that nature" (Ulanov, "Jung and Religion," 317).

169. Medcalf, "Language and Self-Consciousness."

170. Lewis, *TWHF*, 186.

171. Lewis, "De Descriptione Temporum," 12.

> did not, even when I had finished the book, see clearly many things that I see now. The change which the writing wrought in me (and of which I did not write) was only a beginning; only to prepare me for the god's surgery. They used my own pen to probe my wound.[172]

Orual finds that her task becomes a sorting of memories, a sifting of pretexts and motives, neglected as they were in the course of Orual's life, but awaiting scrutiny now, a task that in her dreams becomes a sorting of a huge and hopeless pile of seeds; "sifting and sorting, separating motive from motive and both from pretext."[173] The emphasis is that which we find in Augustine, both in the *Confessions* and *De trinitate*. The Augustinian exploration of memory places equal emphasis on the vastness of capacity, and yet the centrality of it to one's self. "The power of the memory is great, O Lord. It is awe-inspiring in its profound and incalculable complexity. Yet it is my mind: it is my self."[174] Rowan Williams also emphasizes the importance of the role of memory in the *Confessions*; "Identity is ultimately in the hand of God; but this does not mean that it is a non-temporal thing. It is to be found, and in some sense *made*, by the infinitely painstaking attention to the contingent strangeness of remembered experience in conscious reference to God."[175]

There are aids to this making of identity in conscious reference to God, Lewis believed. Writing, reading holy writ and prayer. The latter two may have been given little place in *Till We Have Faces*, because of the difficulty of the pre-Christian context but he speaks of them elsewhere. Prayer—to which we shall return later—is a recurring theme. In *Surprised by Joy* his adult practice of prayer was "the beginning of extroversion," for it brought him out of himself.[176] Moreover, prayer was an intersection between God and humans, a hinge of the relationship. So too with the bible. "To read it is to . . . rebuild in us the defaced image of Himself."[177] Scripture is a means of transformation, in another subject-object embrace. Not only do we see the face of God for now—as Augustine believed—but it is a mirror in which we can see "the reflection of our own silly faces," Lewis said.[178] This image is in accordance with

---

172. Lewis, *TWHF*, 191.
173. Ibid., 193.
174. Augustine *Confessions* 10.17 (Pine-Coffin, 223).
175. R. Williams, *Wound of Knowledge*, 71.
176. Lewis, *Surprised by Joy*, 181.
177. Lewis, *Reflections on the Psalms*, 95–96.
178. Ibid., 102.

James 1:22–24 "Anyone who listens to the word but does not do what it says is like a man who looks at his face in a mirror and, after looking at himself, goes away and immediately forgets what he looks like." Anthony Thiselton makes the same point that scripture not only shapes identities but *transforms* them; "the transforming purpose of scripture entails a hermeneutics of the self."[179] Kierkegaard dwells on this; " . . . so shalt thou, if only thou wilt continue for some time to read God's word thus (and this is the first requisite), thou shalt read fear and trembling into thy soul, so that by God's help thou shalt succeed in becoming a man, a personality . . . Thou shalt, if thou wilt read God's Word in this way, thou shalt (even though it prove terrible to thee—but remember that this is the condition of salvation)—thou shalt succeed in the thing required, in beholding thyself in the mirror . . . For if to thee God's word is only an objective something, then there is no mirror . . . for to look in a mirror surely implies a personality, an ego . . ."[180] A mirror, MacDonald argued in "The Mirrors of the Lord" takes into itself. It doesn't simply reflect.[181] Lewis cited MacDonald's sermon in the anthology; "opening the door to Him, holding up our mirror to Him; then He comes in, not by our thought only, not in our idea only, but He comes Himself and of His own will—comes in as we could not take Him, but as He can come."[182] So humans too, shall be "bright stainless mirrors reflecting back to God his own boundless power and delight and goodness."[183] It is a two way process, where face recognizes face.[184] (And the loss is surely suggestive of Beckett's abyss.) Using the language of Martin Buber, Lewis put it this way in *Prayer: Letters to Malcolm*:

> We are always completely, and therefore equally, known to God. That is our destiny whether we like it or not. But though this knowledge never varies, the quality of our being known can . . . Ordinarily, to be known by God is to be, for this purpose, in the category of things. We are, like earthworms, cabbages and nebulae, objects of divine knowledge. But when we (a) become

---

179. Thiselton, *Interpreting God and the Postmodern Self*, 66.

180. Kierkegaard, *For Self-Examination Proposed to this Age*, 67–68. It is highly possible that Lewis became familiar with this through Charles Williams, who was living in Oxford at this point.

181. MacDonald, "Mirrors of the Lord," *Unspoken Sermons*, Series III, 48.

182. Lewis, *George MacDonald*, 114.

183. Lewis, *Mere Christianity*, 206.

184. Houston (*Mentored Life*, 132) refers to Jean-Luc Marion's likening of Scripture to a face that resists attempts to master it; a face is to be recognised instead, through personal knowledge.

> aware of the fact—the present fact, not the generalisation—and (b) assent with our will to be so known, then we treat ourselves, in relation to God, not as things but as persons. We have unveiled. Not that any veil could have baffled his sight. The change is in us. The passive changes to the active. Instead of merely being known, we show, we tell, we offer ourselves to view . . . By unveiling . . . we assume the high rank of persons before Him. And He, descending becomes a Person to us . . . The Person in Him—he is more than a person—meets those who can welcome or at least face it. He speaks as "I" when we truly call him "Thou."[185]

The emphasis upon the assenting to be so known is crucial—we assent to be known and therefore we assent to know God and to know ourselves. Unveiling—paradoxically—allows us to know God and to know ourselves reflected in Him. But for Orual, in pre-Christian Glome, writing is the primary means of transformation; "the change which the writing wrought in me . . . was only a beginning; only to prepare me for the god's surgery. They used my own pen to probe my wound."[186] It is an "examination of conscience," a Puritan concern, with which Lewis would have been particularly familiar, considering he labored over sixteenth century literature for almost twenty years before publishing *English Literature in the Sixteenth Century excluding Drama* in 1954. There, he challenges the fictive nineteenth century view of Puritanism, and emphasizes the more truly Puritan "farewell to the self with its good resolutions" which was based upon a buoyant humility; "all the initiative has been on God's side; all has been free, unbounded grace. And all shall continue to be free, unbounded grace."[187] Given the similarity of emphasis which we find between Lewis's and the Puritan's sense of written self-examination—both journal and autobiography—it is quite possible that his view stems at least in part from them. Lewis may have drawn—for example—from Walter Hilton, to whom he refers in *Surprised by Joy*, or from William Perkins, to whom he refers in *English Literature in the Sixteenth Century excluding Drama*.[188] Both men emphasized the examination of conscience, although to what extent Lewis would have been in agreement with their emphasis is a question that I cannot resolve here.[189] The motive

---

185. Lewis, *Prayer*, 18–19.

186. Lewis, *TWHF*, 191.

187. Lewis, *English Literature in the Sixteenth Century excluding Drama*, 32–33.

188. Jeffrey, "Proving the Spirit of Christ," 152–60.

189. James Houston comments that Perkins is much less Trinitarian on these matters than Calvin, and ultimately was instrumental in heading, along with others such as Richard Baxter, towards an introspective approach which emphasised the knowledge of

behind Puritan autobiographies was often both didactic and autodidactic, as Owen Watkins argues, ". . . the autobiographer had in addition involved his present self in the task of looking at his past self; he tried to re-create his experiences so as to convey both the impact they had on him at the time and their meaning in the light of subsequent experience and knowledge."[190] It may be that Lewis himself found this to be particularly true in the early 1950s. He comments in *Surprised by Joy*, that for some self-examination begins at conversion, and for others it ends; for him it had ended, or so he obviously believed at the time of writing.[191] But having written *Surprised by Joy* more or less immediately prior to *Till We Have Faces* he had found himself drawn back to a self-examination that he had forsworn; the re-creation of his experiences was heavily autodidactic, whether or not this had been his intention. Like Augustine, Lewis is not claiming absolute objectivity for the memory—we note that Part I of the novel is a biased account by Orual—but for Lewis, like some orthodox Puritans, self-exploration is both temporal, and set in constant dialectic with God as revealed through scripture. As Rowan Williams puts it:

> Truthful self-knowledge thus entails a constantly self-critical autobiographical project, striving to construct the narrative least unfaithful to the divine perspective. It will, of course, never *be* the divine perspective, because what God *sees*, I *learn* (and constantly, with every new action, must unlearn).[192]

The right reading of one's life is one that can only be done with divine aid. Part II is a critique that shifts, erratically, but inevitably towards the divine perspective. Behind Orual's recovery of the truth is the intervention of the gods. Orual herself comments; "the gods kept me to my two labours, the day's and the night's."[193] For her dreams have the quality of visions, which she attributes to the gods, saying: "they so drenched me with seeings that I cannot well discern dream from waking nor tell which is the truer."[194] In one, she is forced by her father to dig through layers of clay and rock until she sees herself in the mirror that she used to dread—only to see that she has the face of Ungit. It is at this point that the begin-

---

self as primary. In doing so they contributed to the modern loss of the double knowledge. "Double Knowledge," 19–20.

190. Watkins, *Puritan Experience*, 237.
191. Lewis, *Surprised by Joy*, 181.
192. R. Williams, "'Know Thyself': What Kind of an Injunction?" 211–27.
193. Lewis, *TWHF*, 194.
194. Ibid., 209.

ning of *anagnorisis*, or recognition in Aristotle's sense, is finally reached by Orual; she can no longer deny "the ruinous face was mine." She has reached, at last, the crucial recognition of her own nature, that she has devoured men's lives. "This vision anyway allowed no denial. Without question it was true."[195] But she clings to a final remnant of succor—that her love for Psyche was genuine. It is for this reason that the gods have not finished yet with her. "The mirrors of the Lord" shall continue to reflect the unflinching truth. By the end of the next vision, a scene of trial, her complaint is demolished. Forcibly unveiled and naked, the old crone with her Ungit face makes her accusations before the crowds. She hears her own voice babbling and realizes what poisonous words she is uttering but it is not until the gods in their turn present her with scenes of her treatment of Psyche that she finally comes to full recognition of the truth. At last there is no deceit in her. As she can now say to Psyche; "Never again will I call you mine; but all there is of me shall be yours. Alas, you know now what it is worth. I never wished you well, never had one selfless thought of you. I was a craver."[196] It has been a long, painful process to bring Orual to this point of honesty and repentance. It is the fulfillment of the god's declaration, made so many years before on the mountainside, "You, woman, shall know yourself and your work. You also shall be Psyche."[197]

Brightface: More Truly Self

Till We Have Faces is a profound statement of the fact that the conditions for true self-knowledge are consonant with the conditions for true selfhood or personhood.[198] Indeed, self-hood and personhood seem to have little distinction in Lewis's work; and "personality" seems to carry the same weight. Personality— "the quality or fact of being a person as distinct from a thing"—recurs throughout his work.[199] He was using it in an older sense, now almost replaced by "personhood."[200] In a sermon

---

195. Ibid., 209.

196. Ibid., 232.

197. Ibid., 130.

198. At the same time, Lewis was hesitant to draw conclusions from the fact that the twentieth century had emphasized subjectivity to such an extent—an "apotheosis of subjectivity." He wondered if Christianity had played into the situation through "Augustine and hundreds of devotional books," but he said that this was a difficult issue and he only offered "guesses." Letter to John Beversluis (April 12, 1962) *Letters*, Vol. III, 1332–33.

199. *Oxford English Dictionary*, Vol. xi, 2nd ed., 1989.

200. For example, W. R. Inge writing in the 1890's used "personality" as a synonym for the self.

entitled "Membership," Lewis stated, "Personality is not a datum from which we start. The individualism in which we all begin is only a parody or shadow of it. True personality lies ahead—how far ahead, for most of us, I dare not say."[201] The notion that personality is locked up inside us, waiting to be expanded or expressed, is Pelagian, and defeats itself.[202] Kierkegaard shared the same view and one that has been translated by the same word—"by God's help, thou shalt succeed in becoming a man, a personality."[203] Both men believed that personality was not something which humans are born with. "And the key to it does not lie in ourselves. It will not be attained by development from within outwards. It will come to us when we occupy those places in the structure of the eternal cosmos for which we were designed or invented."[204] One *becomes* a self, but unlike Existentialist thought, it is not through mere existence, but through an overcoming, through a life constantly given back to God. As Lewis put it in a letter, "I become my own only when I gave myself to Another."[205] This is a constant state of consciousness and effort. For Lewis, personality grows through encounter, desire, obedience, humility, faith, love, and discipline. "Some tendencies in each natural man may have to be simply rejected. Our Lord speaks of eyes being plucked out and hands lopped off—a frankly Procrustean method of adaptation."[206]

To refuse this apparently Procrustean method, is to refuse personhood. In *That Hideous Strength*, Mark Studdock approaches the moment when he would "begin to be a person." Until that point he has been a blank canvas, a puppet in the hand of others.[207] Indeed, he has been in danger of losing any sense of personal identity at all in his identification with the Belbury group. In contrast, Jane, Mark's wife, not only learns this lesson, but foreshadows for us what Orual shall experience. "She had come into a world, or into a Person, or into the presence of a Person. Something expectant, patient, inexorable met her with no veil or protection between . . . the little idea of herself that she had hitherto called me dropped and vanished . . . The name *me* was the name of a being whose

---

201. Lewis, "Membership," 129.

202. Ibid., 131.

203. Kierkegaard, *For Self-Examination*, 67. It was published by OUP in 1941, a year before *Mere Christianity* was published.

204. Lewis, "Membership," 129.

205. Lewis, letter to Mrs Johnson (July 17, 1953) *Letters*, Vol. 3, 348.

206. Lewis, "Membership," *Weight of Glory*, 130.

207. Lewis, *That Hideous Strength*, 575.

existence she had never suspected, a being which did not fully exist but which was demanded."²⁰⁸ It is a lesson that Orual learns late in life.

Certain conditions, for Lewis, were essential to then enable occupancy of those places for which we were designed. Firstly, it is the love of God that enables self-knowledge and selfhood. Self-recognition for Orual, as for Augustine, necessarily comes after the recognition bestowed by the divine. "What I do know of myself I know because You shed your light on me; and what I do not know of myself I shall not know until 'my darkness shall become as noonday' in the vision of your face."²⁰⁹ Augustine is unequivocal on this: "Let me know you, for you are the God who knows me, let me recognize you as you have recognized me."²¹⁰ Recognition necessitates particularity—which love bestows. As MacDonald put it: "For no-one but God sees what the man is . . . He is to God a peculiar being, made after his own fashion and that of no-one else."²¹¹ In *The Problem of Pain*, Lewis adds; "Be sure that the ins and outs of your individuality are no mystery to Him; and one day they will no longer be a mystery to you." Heaven is not for humanity in the abstract. Rather it is for concrete particularity. "Why else were individuals created, but that God, loving all infinitely, should love each differently? And this difference, so far from impairing, floods with meaning the love of all blessed creatures for one another, the communion of saints."²¹² The distinctiveness of each soul is built into the universe, but it is incumbent upon a person to *become* the name that is reserved for him by God.

Secondly, both interiority and exteriority are essential to health. Lewis's recognition of his own inwardness was a crucial part of his mature development, although he remained aware of the dangers. For the mature Lewis, reflexivity is not necessarily evil. As Charles Taylor puts it, "on the contrary, we show most clearly the presence of God in our fullest self-presence. Evil is when this reflexivity is closed in upon itself. Healing comes when it is broken open, not in order to be abandoned, but in order to acknowledge its dependence upon God."²¹³ God is "the ground of our being" the *Ursprung* upon which both subject and object are based.²¹⁴ In

---

208. Ibid., 683.

209. Augustine *Confessions* 10.5.

210. Ibid., 10.1.

211. Lewis, *George MacDonald*, 45–46. The extracts are taken from MacDonald's sermon, "The New Name."

212. Lewis, *Problem of Pain*, 119.

213. C. Taylor, *Sources of the Self*, 139.

214. Lewis did not use "*Ursprung*" but it is the word used by Alois Haas to convey

Prayer: Letters to Malcolm Lewis says, "To be discontinuous from God as I am discontinuous from you would be annihilation."[215] This is not the same as Pantheism—where God is all—rather, he is "all in all," who gives himself through Creation. There is an "ontological continuity between Creator and creature which is, so to speak, 'given' by the relation between them." Lewis would brook no self-creation. He aligned himself with the idea that human nature is "given, discoverable and discovered."[216] God "is always both within us and over against us."[217] The inner turn can be construed as a disease, as Lewis did for so many years, or it can be read—as Mark McIntosh does—as the attempt to create a space in a fragmented world, for the speaking, hearing and searching of God. Beckett's radical reflexivity, albeit more Gnostic than Plotinian, is the inverse; interiority without anchor, a limitless introspection which has neither external referent, nor the desire for one. Overemphasis upon subjectivity is wrong—but so too is total emphasis upon objectivity.

Thirdly, this givenness is tied in with Lewis's concept of desire, wherein Joy or sweet desire, leads ultimately to God—because it comes from God. For both Lewis and Augustine, emphasis upon the dialectic of desire was central to their conversion and thought. In *Till We Have Faces*, Psyche is aware of her longings, and the origin of them, but Orual's way of desire is distorted by other, though lesser, desires, and she is slow to recognize what Lewis perceives to be the source of her desire. It is in this respect that Psyche is "brightface" when on the mountain, for she has found that which she has always consciously longed for.

Consequently (and fourthly), self-recognition is an ongoing process of seeking and desiring aright, in constant dialectic with divine revelation. Self-knowledge is not instantaneous, despite moments of *anagnorisis*. *De trinitate* is a particularly rich reflection upon this whole issue. The process is ongoing and paradoxical; "So [the mind] is in virtue precisely of itself seeking that it can be more aware of itself than not. While it seeks to know, it knows itself as seeking, it knows itself as not knowing."[218] Self-knowledge does not consist of a mere self-awareness for that would throw the knower back into a static understanding. "I lived and knew myself,"

---

the very close connectedness which lies at the root of all phenomena. See "Christliche Aspekte Des 'Gnothi Seauton' Selbsterkenntnis und Mystik," 71–96.

215. Lewis, *Prayer: Letters to Malcolm*, 66–67.
216. Lewis, *English Literature in the Sixteenth Century Excluding Drama*, 380.
217. Lewis, *Prayer: Letters to Malcolm*, 66.
218. Augustine *De trinitate* 10.3.5.

Orual declares after the vision of the golden rams.[219] But it is noteworthy that she subsequently finds out more—much more. It is dangerous to say—as Doris Myers has said—that Orual comes to complete self-knowledge, if this is to imply completeness of cognition.[220] Better to say that she is brought to a place where the conditions for self-knowledge and full selfhood become possible in an ongoing process, a process which is only possible because she has come to recognize the role of the divine in her life. Speaking of Augustine's thought in *De trinitate* Williams says:

> If the mind knows itself, what it knows is the activity of seeking and discovering, not a static object . . . the paradox he presses upon us is that a mind intrinsically incomplete, desirous and mobile . . . can be rightly and intelligibly said to know itself completely. Self-knowledge is being defined, not as cognition of a spiritual substance, but as awareness of the conditions of finitude and the ability to live and act within them. Hence the further point in X, v that to know oneself is to live reflectively according to one's nature, to live in one's proper place in the universe: as a creature (below God), but a reasoning creature (above the animals).[221]

Williams also points out that Augustine "insists with painful intensity on the need to conquer illusion, to see the self as it is in its poverty, confusion and conditionedness, and then to *embrace* that reality and act accordingly."[222] Living reflectively requires a constant orientation towards truthfulness and transparency with self and others.[223] By the time he wrote *Prayer: Letters to Malcolm*, Lewis had come to the realization that this orientation is always necessary, if not always possible; "The prayer preceding all prayers is, 'May it be the real I who speaks. May it be the real Thou that I speak to.'"[224]

Finally, such transparency is the necessary precursor to full personhood because of the supreme value that Lewis finally places on the relationship with the *other*. In the final scenes, Orual's *anagnorisis* is ultimately only because of encounter, both human and divine. "I know now, Lord," she says at the end of the book, "why you utter no answer. You are

---

219. Lewis, *TWHF*, 215.

220. Myers, *C. S. Lewis in Context*, 212.

221. R. Williams, "Paradoxes of Self-Knowledge in *De trinitate*," 129.

222. R. Williams, *Wound of Knowledge*, 116. Williams makes this comment primarily in the context of speaking about Bernard of Clairvaux, with whom Lewis was familiar.

223. MacDonald's text for "The Final Unmasking" was "For there is nothing covered, that shall not be revealed; and hid that shall not be known." Matt 10:26; Luke 12:2.

224. Lewis, *Prayer: Letters to Malcolm*, 79.

yourself the answer." Her change is rooted, through and through, in the clarion call of relationship. The effort of the will has merely created a persona: whereas true encounter leads to personhood. It is not to be found in community, or in faculties such as reason or the memory or will, but is located in honest responses to other "persons," and primarily the personal God. Without transparency, without face-to-face meeting, there can be no relationship. Lewis would agree with Beckett; isolated self-analysis is impossible. Orual eventually realizes this; "I saw well why the gods do not speak to us openly, nor let us answer. Till that word can be dug out of us, why should they hear the babble that we think we mean? How can the gods meet us face to face till we have faces?"[225] It is, once again, the dialectical movement, whereby God and humans work together.

> Instead of merely being known, we show, we tell, we offer ourselves to view . . . By unveiling . . . we assume the high rank of persons before Him. And He, descending becomes a Person to us . . . The Person in Him—he is more than a person—meets those who can welcome or at least face it. He speaks as "I" when we truly call him "Thou."[226]

This is closer to the Eastern idea of synergism than the Western sense of God's radical grace, an area where Lewis perhaps differed in emphasis from Augustine. "For it is not a question of merits but of a co-operation, of a synergy of the two wills, divine and human, a harmony in which grace bears more and more fruit, and is appropriated," is how Vladimir Lossky puts it.[227]

It is to this high view of human personhood, to which we now turn. This face to face meeting of the human person and the divine Person is glimpsed in Orual. Her moment of recognition ("Never again will I call you mine; but all there is of me shall be yours.") is succeeded by a deep sense of plenitude. "Joy silenced me. And I thought I had now come to the highest and to the utmost fullness of being which the human soul can contain."[228] It is an unequivocal statement of a belief that self-transcendence, rather than self-autonomy, leads to a higher state of being on earth and in the *eschaton*.

---

225. Lewis, *TWHF*, 223.
226. Lewis, *Prayer: Letters to Malcolm*, 18–19.
227. Lossky, *Mystical Theology of the Eastern Church*, 198.
228. Lewis, *TWHF*, 232.

CHAPTER 6

Men and Gods Flow In and Out and Mingle

Lewis—Mystical Theology

Lewis's attitude towards mysticism is relatively rarely explored, treading as he did, if not the precipices (as he commented in *Prayer: Letters to Malcolm*), but land relatively seldom charted in narrative form.[1] He wrote, in his Preface to *George MacDonald: An Anthology*, of "the real universe, the divine, magical, terrifying and ecstatic reality in which we all live."[2] His inclusion of the magical and the ecstatic in the "real" suggests the reason why readers of *Till We Have Faces* (including many critics), find its perspective mystifying, for they may be attempting to read it through a lens of materialism, or disenchantment, as Max Weber has put it. It is only when the lens is changed, to allow for the divine, magical and ecstatic, that the novel becomes intelligible. Ultimately, Orual's experience of self-transcendence can only be read through such a lens, as I intend to explore in this chapter. To begin with, however, let us enquire into preliminaries—is Lewis's thinking and theology "mystical" or tied in with any tradition of mysticism?

Old Western Man: Lewis and Mysticism

With regard to what has become viewed as "Christian mysticism," Lewis's thought was nuanced. Whilst he accepted many elements of mysticism he qualified them in a number of ways; from his first reading of William James' *The Varieties of Religious Experience,* he recognized that for some there was a "ready made orthodoxy" in such writings that operated as distinct from the Bible rather than in conjunction with it. Robert Houston Smith is one of the few who has explored the way in which traditional

---

1. Lewis, *Prayer: Letters to Malcolm*, 60.
2. Lewis, Preface to *George MacDonald*, 35.

forms of "mysticism" can be seen in Lewis's work—notably Lucy's encounter with Aslan in *Prince Caspian*, (which Smith calls "Christ-mysticism in its full medieval splendor"), and other incidents where he perceives mystical ascent in the Narnia tales and the planetary romances.[3] (Ransom he sees as becoming a hierophant.) But Smith is aware of what he sees as an ambivalence in Lewis's attitude towards mysticism, pointing out that Lewis's background was not conducive to mysticism with his "most unmystical Protestant background" and his love of reasoned argument.[4] But are these the factors which caused Lewis some ambivalence towards mysticism? For ambivalent he certainly was.

Firstly, Lewis clearly rejected the kind of mystic experience that contemporary writers such as Beckett seemed to be drawn to, which he perceived as "a kind of spurious mysticism among anti-Christian writers."[5] As an adult he was aware of the problems of seeking power through the mind or the supernatural. He wrote in *Surprised by Joy*, "as a schoolboy, I had destroyed my religious life by a vicious subjectivism which made 'realisations' the aim of prayer; turning away from God to seek states of mind, and trying to produce those states of mind by 'maistry.'"[6] He comments, "If only someone had read to me old Walter Hilton's warning that we must never in prayer strive to extort 'by maistry' what God does not give!"[7] In fact, he makes it very clear in his autobiography, that he was not only very aware of the dangers, but that he felt himself to be prone to a particularly strong desire for the preternatural—which he equates (in this context) to the Occult.[8] His inclination was towards an inappropriate desire for spiritual things, which, like all other appetites, he believed, should be "cross-fodder" and could only be made part of our bliss once raised from the dead.[9] It was for such reasons that he avoided engaging in the "mystic way"; "You may wonder that my intense desire to peep behind the scenes has not led me to attempt the mystic way. But would it not be the worst of all possible motives? The saint may win 'a mortal glimpse of death's immortal rose,' but it is a by-product. He took ship simply in humble and selfless love."[10]

3. Smith, *Patches of Godlight*, 135f.
4. Ibid., 154.
5. Lewis, letter to Dom Bede Griffiths (April 24, 1936) *Letters*, Vol. II, 189.
6. Lewis, *Surprised by Joy*, 130.
7. Ibid., 46.
8. Ibid., 45.
9. Lewis, *Prayer: Letters to Malcolm*, 63.
10. Ibid., 63.

Secondly, Lewis perceived mysticism as primarily defined by negative theology. This comes across in a number of points in his work. "If a mystic means one who follows the negative way by rejecting images, then (Charles Williams) was, consciously and deliberately the very reverse."[11] He clarified this definition somewhat in *Miracles*, distinguishing between the "positive and concrete intuition of God" which pertains to the great prophets and saints, and the intellectualizing of the subsequent erudite thinkers, who, in trying to apprehend the statements of the sages, distort them. The sages, in seeing the plenitude of God, have pronounced that he transcends human limitations; the interpreters "take over those negatives (infinite, immaterial, impassible, immutable, etc.) and use them unchecked by any positive intuition."[12] "Even that negative knowledge which seems to us so Enlightened is only a relic left over from the positive knowledge of better men—only the pattern which that heavenly wave left on the sand when it retreated."[13] For him, much that constituted the study of mysticism was merely the shadow of a more positive knowledge of God. He was, nonetheless, very far from claiming that there was no unknowability to God (and we shall see a little more of this later). On the contrary, his "road right out of the self" led him, he tells us in *Surprised by Joy* to "the naked Other, imageless (though our imagination salutes it with a hundred images), unknown, undefined, desired."[14] But like Charles Williams, Lewis chose the Affirmative way in his work.

Behind this choice for the cataphatic approach lay a caution about the negative emphasis that he associated with mysticism. His reading in the radical apophaticism of Plotinus, Pseudo-Dionysius and Nicholas of Cusa may have lain behind this.[15] He may also—like Beckett—have been influenced by Dean Inge (whose *Personal Religion and the Life of Devotion* we know him to have read in June 1931).[16] Inge's suspicion of the *via negativa* we have already noted; his somewhat scathing description includes the following:

> Since God is the Infinite, and the Infinite is the antithesis of the finite, every attribute which can be affirmed of a finite being may be safely denied of God. Hence God can only be *described* by

11. Lewis, "Novels of Charles Williams," in *Of This and Other Worlds*, 52.
12. Lewis, *Miracles*, 92–94.
13. Ibid., 94.
14. Lewis, *Surprised by Joy*, 172.
15. His familiarity with Plotinus and Pseudo-Dionysius is evident in *The Discarded Image*. For his familiarity with Nicholas of Cusa see *Spenser's Images of Life*, 15.
16. Lewis, *They Stand Together*, 416.

negatives; He can only be *discovered* by stripping off all the qualities and attributes which veil Him; He can only be *reached* by divesting ourselves of all the distinctions of personality, and sinking or rising into our "uncreated nothingness"; and He can only be *imitated* by aiming at an abstract spirituality, the passionless "apathy" of an universal which is nothing in particular.[17]

Lewis may also have picked up a certain antipathy for negative theology from his contemporary at Oxford, K. E. Kirk, whose 1928 Bampton Lectures were published in 1931 as *The Vision of God*. Whatever the original source of Lewis's concerns, they translated into a rejection of the apophatic tendencies of contemporary mysticism, for he was quick to see that the *via negativa* when cut loose from the *via positiva*, estranges more than it reconciles. It seems quite possible that he would have shared with Daniel Bulzan the concern that radical apophaticism "contains in rudiment an anti-ontological impulse, at least as far as the created order is concerned."[18] Lewis put it this way; "We feel, if we do not say, that the vision of God will come not to fulfill but to destroy our nature; this bleak fantasy often underlies our very use of such words as 'holy' or 'pure' or 'spiritual.'"[19] The Beatific Vision could be a crushing concept for mere mortals—as Beckett would attest. "We must not allow this to happen if we can possibly prevent it. We must believe—and therefore in some degree imagine—that every negation will only be the reverse side of a fulfilling. And we must mean by that the fulfilling, precisely, of our humanity, not our transformation into angels nor our absorption into Deity. To move from the notion of an abstract and negative deity is to find a God "opaque by the very fullness of His blinding actuality."[20] The actuality of God giving actuality to humans was the recurring point that he strove to convey throughout his entire corpus.

Despite this concern about radical apophaticism, Lewis did not entirely reject the insights of mystics or sages. On the contrary, he resonated with the themes and insights which he found in them; even prior to his conversion he had left behind a narrow concept of the natural world, and embraced a belief in the supernatural, that is, "something which invades, or is added to, the great interlocked event in space and time, instead of merely arising from it."[21] As Robert Houston Smith says, "as soon as one

17. Inge, *Christian Mysticism*, 111.
18. Bulzan, "Apophaticism, Postmodernism and Language," 283.
19. Lewis, "Transposition," 84.
20. Lewis, *Miracles*, 97–99.
21. Ibid., 179.

postulates a ground of being that lies beyond all human grasp and yet is that which is most to be desired, one is already involved in mysticism."[22] Lewis would no doubt have preferred to distinguish between "religion with a real supernaturalism and salvationism on the one hand and the watered-down and modernist versions on the other."[23] Lewis's most significant influences were those who believed in a realm beyond the material, those who shared his sense that the world is a "thin place."[24] Plato, Augustine, Dante, George Herbert, George MacDonald, Rudolf Otto, von Hügel, Jung; these were the thinkers that Lewis found most stimulating. And his friends—Barfield, Tolkien, Charles Williams, Hugo Dyson—were amongst those who rejected Kantian strictures, proposing that the visible material world was only one very small aspect of the whole. For Lewis, the true sages have something to teach us: "I do not at all regard mystical experience as an illusion. I think it always shows that there is a way to go, before death, out of what may be called 'this world'"[25] But he felt that the nature of the mystic journey was vital. Not all mysticism was equal:

> The lawfulness, safety, and utility of the mystical voyage depends not at all on its being mystical—that is, on its being a departure—but on the motives, skill, and constancy of the voyager, and on the grace of God. The true religion gives value to its own mysticism; mysticism does not invalidate the religion in which it happens to occur.
>
> I shouldn't be at all disturbed if it could be shown that a diabolical mysticism, or drugs, produced experiences indistinguishable (by introspection) from those of the great Christian mystics. Departures are all alike; it is the landfall that crowns the voyage. The saint, by being a saint, proves that his mysticism (if he was a mystic: not all saints are) led him aright; the fact that he has practised mysticism could never prove his sanctity.[26]

So in *That Hideous Strength*, the mysterious figure of Withers exhibits a detachment which could be construed as a manifestation of that "diabolical mysticism" to which Lewis refers, whereas the Dimbles and Ransom

---

22. Smith, *Patches of Godlight*, 154.

23. Lewis, letter to Sister Penelope (November 8, 1939) *Letters*, Vol. II, 285.

24. Interestingly, this is the phrase used by Kallistos Ware when he argues that Lewis has a similar approach to that of the Orthodox Church. "God of the Fathers: C. S. Lewis and Eastern Christianity," 53–69.

25. Lewis, *Prayer: Letters to Malcolm*, 62.

26. Ibid., 63. The use of the word "departure" here would seem to be a direct reference to the first chapter—"The Point of Departure"—in Evelyn Underhill's *Mysticism*.

are portrayed as figures ultimately transfigured with laughter, love, creativity and peace, as a result of their receptivity to divine presence.

In many ways Lewis's thinking retrieves, or reaches towards retrieval of some aspects of ancient and early medieval ways of thought. He pointed out in *The Discarded Image* that the Medieval Model of the universe with which he is concerned there has been superceded, and he is not arguing for a return to it. Indeed, he says that the pagan elements embedded in that model "involved a conception of God, and of man's place in the universe, which, if not in logical contradiction to Christianity, were subtly out of harmony with it."[27] But his conclusion is suggestive:

> . . . there is a two-way traffic; the Model is also influenced by the prevailing temper of mind . . . We can no longer dismiss the change of Models as a simple progress from error to truth. No Model is a catalogue of ultimate realities, and none is a mere fantasy . . . But nature gives most of her evidence in answer to the questions we ask her. Here as in the courts, the character of the evidence depends on the shape of the examination, and a good cross-examination can do wonders . . . It determines how much of the total truth will appear and what pattern it will suggest.[28]

Nature gives most of her answers to the questions we ask her. The old models are not entirely full of error—a lesson learned from Barfield many years before—and it may be that the losses are significant. At the very least, there is value in allowing them to interrogate our own world-view—as Lewis suggested in his inaugural speech at Cambridge. "To study the past does indeed liberate us from the idols of our own market-place."[29] And he continued, "I myself belong far more to the Old Western order than to yours . . . I read as a native texts that you might read as foreigners . . . It is my settled conviction that in order to read Old Western Literature aright you must suspend most of the responses and unlearn most of the habits you have acquired in reading modern literature." The statement may equally have applied to the spiritual outlook as well—as hinted at in "idols of our own market-place." It may be that Lewis, with his mind steeped in a pre-modern understanding of the universe, may be able to help us recover that perspective in a way that few others can do. Not—as Lewis would be the first to say—in order to imitate it, but in order to evaluate the losses that we have incurred and to rediscover what is of value of a pattern lost and inexplicable to Beckett and many of his

27. Lewis, *Discarded Image*, 19.
28. Ibid., 222–23.
29. Lewis, "De Descriptione Temporum," *Selected Literary Essays*, 12.

contemporaries. If the loss of God inevitably leads to the loss of human significance, how else can this perspective be retrieved except through a shift in understanding or ways of seeing?

And yet, just as Lewis said, "I base nothing on Plato," so too in the end, he *based* nothing on the medieval worldview. His basis lay elsewhere. Lewis believed firmly that a personal relation to Christ is the only way to knowledge of the divine realities. They *cannot* be known otherwise and even then they remain partial, like a dim reflection in a mirror. The biblical stance on knowledge—the underlying text, by which he judged all else—is utterly implicit in all of his work. It is hardly surprising then that his definition of knowledge should be so in line with Paul's sense of gnosis—which is starkly different to Beckett's Gnosticism. McGinn comments; "Is Pauline gnosis a mystical knowledge? Insofar as gnosis is a hidden knowledge of divine realities that involves a personal relation to Christ, it certainly can be read in this way."[30] When in 1 Cor 13:12 Paul wrote, "Now I know in part, then I shall know fully, even as I am fully known," he is using Gnostic language but depriving it of full Gnostic meaning, by adding on "as I am fully known."[31] It was a God-centered gnosis that prioritized God's initiative, faith and love, rather than the gnosticism with which Beckett familiarized himself, (whereby self-knowledge and personal salvation are primary), or the Greek emphasis upon speculative and rational knowledge. "Herein is love, not that we loved God but that He loved us (I John 4:10)," Lewis wrote in *The Four Loves*.[32] And here we come to the heart of the matter. "We must not begin with mysticism, with the creature's love for God, or with the wonderful forestates of the fruition of God vouchsafed to some in their earthly life. We begin at the real beginning, with love as the Divine energy. This primal love is Gift-love."[33] In beginning with God as the giver, the one who bestows love, Lewis embraces not so much mysticism—which he perceived as the creature's love for God—but a way of thinking which prioritizes God's love for his creatures. In starting here, his thought takes on the hue of what can only be called mystical theology, very far removed from the rationalism which starts from the human understanding.

Ultimately, and this point is not always taken into account by critics of his work, Lewis's perspective shifted towards an emphasis upon the mystical rather than the rational. Robert Houston Smith finally settles for

---

30. McGinn, *Foundations of Mysticism*, 73.
31. Bultmann, *Gnosis*, 43–44.
32. Lewis, *The Four Loves*, 144.
33. Ibid., 144.

Lewis as a "Christian pietist" who in his theological treatises does away with philosophical inquiry and romanticism, and in a "naive and simplistic way" speaks of a simple meeting of man and God.[34] To speak so of Lewis's theology is to reveal—ironically—a lack of understanding of the way in which Lewis's ideas were metamorphosing. In a letter to Griffiths in 1936 Lewis had commented that he saw no real conflict between the rational or the mystical but for him—unlike others—the bridge to faith had been the rational.[35] But this was to change in the decades to come. Peter Schakel has spelt out that this emphasis upon the rational became less and less prominent in his work, becoming, by *Till We Have Faces*, decidedly secondary. But more than that, his very definition of reason inevitably changed as his understanding of knowledge also changed; for him, reason was no longer the power of making deductions, but was closer to recognition. The babbling of Orual as she accuses the gods is reason misused, as is the reasoning of the people at Belbury. In contrast, Ransom's understanding is spiritually received understanding. But, as he went on to spell out in *The Discarded Image*, reason only narrowed to this usage in Samuel Johnson's era. Before the eighteenth century, "reason" was the organ of morality, just as "heart" had not always had merely emotional associations, but a strong sense of the mind, or reason, was integral to it.[36] For Boethius the separating of *ratio* from *intellectus* would have been considered impossible, but Lewis concludes that this separation is very much characteristic of "reason" in his day.[37] Mark McIntosh summarizes the change in this way:

> . . . For the ancient world the process of *noesis* or (to use our much thinner word) "knowing" is far more intuitive, and less "private" in that it is not so much "I" who am knowing but that "the known" has drawn me into an encounter with itself. In the formative environment of Christian mysticism, knowing reality is associated more with the intimacy, even the desire, that runs between knower and known . . . and less with our modern conception of a scientific analysis of manipulable objects by the knower.[38]

Angelic *intelligentia*, Lewis explained in *The Discarded Image*, is where truth is simply "seen," unlike the highest which humans can achieve—

---

34. Smith, *Patches of Godlight*, 163.
35. Lewis, letter to Bede Griffiths (April 24, 1936) *Letters*, Vol. II, 189.
36. Lewis, *Discarded Image*, 156–61.
37. Ibid., 156–61.
38. McIntosh, *Mystical Theology*, 70.

momentary flashes of *intellectus*, or *obumbrata intelligentia*, clouded intelligence. Orual and Mark Studdock try to function without the help of *intelligentia*, and are thrown onto using *ratio*, where nothing is seen and everything has to be proved. It is consistent with this that *Till We Have Faces* portrays a society where—for the most part—"Holy wisdom is not clear and thin like water, but thick and dark like blood."[39] McIntosh continues:

> Indeed for St. Paul it is clear that the most complete form of knowledge would not finally be our own act at all, but an event in which I yield myself to God. And God, in this view, turns out to be not the known object but the ultimate Knower in the whole process: "Now we see but a poor reflection; then we shall see face to face. Now I know in part, then I shall know fully even as I have been fully known" (1 Cor 13:12).[40]

Here we reach the heart of the matter. "Perhaps," Lewis wrote, "it seems rather crude to describe glory as the fact of being 'noticed' by God. But this is almost the language of the New Testament. St. Paul promises to those who love God not, as we should expect, that they will know Him, but that they will be known by Him" (1 Cor 8:3).

Lewis's own way of knowing or seeing became more and more like those whom he called the "sages." His reading of Augustine, Bernard of Clairvaux, Walter Hilton, Julian of Norwich enabled him to absorb their perspective. Of particular relevance to this project, it is interesting to note that all the above were all strong on the necessity of God-given self-knowledge for spiritual knowledge; fifteenth century *florilegia* (devotional manuals) cited extensively from these and other mystics. (The same theme was central to *Piers Plowman*, another of the texts with which Lewis was familiar.)[41] But there were others whose influence we simply cannot trace with any certainty although they may, for all we know, have had a major influence upon his life and thought. Jacob Boehme, Lewis said, had given him the biggest shaking up since he had read *Phantastes*; he spoke as one who has seen and is trying to describe the mystery of creation.[42] And there are many others too, whom we can trace only through brief comments made in various texts, particularly his academic texts, where he traces the influence of one writer upon another. Gregory

---

39. Lewis, *TWHF*, 38.
40. McIntosh, *Mystical Theology*, 70.
41. Houston, "Double Knowledge," 315.
42. Lewis, letter to Arthur Greeves (January 5, 1930) *Letters*, Vol I, 859.

Nazianzus, Francis de Sales . . . it would be impossible to know where to begin or end. Even where there are resonances, certainty is evasive, but there is little doubt that his way of thinking became more and more colored by the perspectives of those in the Christian tradition who *saw* and *knew* life from a perspective that is so colored by the "divine reality" that it can only appear to us now as "mystical." Whether or not this change in perspective was accompanied by "mystical" experiences we cannot know, although a careful reading of *Surprised by Joy* and *A Grief Observed* suggests that he did experience something akin to those.[43]

Dorothy Soelle in *The Silent Cry: Mysticism and Resistance* considers two of Lewis's accounts in *Surprised by Joy* as mystical experiences, belied somewhat by his tone. The first is his "memory of a memory"—his first sensation of desire in the garden as a child. The second is his conversion account on the top of the bus. Here, she says:

> What happens for a brief moment is liberation of the ordered boredom of the commonplace for mystery. Every cover, form, role, and frigidity that normally kept the I under control falls away. The I is free. The lobster's armour breaks into pieces, the snowman melts, and the true self emerges in a fleeting moment, leaving behind the "longing for longing." Freedom and necessity become one; choosing the way and being chosen are the same and the experience gathers itself in the sentence "I am what I do."[44]

Lewis himself did not speak openly on the subject.[45] In any case, we are here most concerned, not with his experiences, but with his shift in perception. Like Psyche, Lewis came to inhabit the god's castle. Orual, as she is at the outset, is more representative of Beckett; in their hands the robes become rags, wine becomes water, the palace disappears into the mist. Similarly, in *The Last Battle* (1956), the Dwarves cannot experience the paradisal world all around them and Aslan says, "Their prison is only in their minds, yet they are in that prison; and so afraid of being taken in that they cannot be taken out."[46] The dwarves have chosen cunning instead of belief, and it has affected their understanding. The alternative way of seeing is inherently visionary; the paradisal world that has been invisible becomes visible. Orual, unlike the dwarves, learns the way of

---

43. For example, *Grief Observed* speaks of a "chuckle in the darkness" and a sense of the presence of "H".

44. Soelle, *Silent Cry*, 22–25.

45. The concluding paragraphs of *The Four Loves* suggest something of his caution. "Perhaps I have only imagined the tasting." (159)

46. Lewis, *Last Battle*, 135.

"seeings"—to the extent that she fears her body will not be able to stand many more of them. The visionary world coinheres with the material world. (It is this very shift in perspective that makes *Till We Have Faces* difficult reading for those who cannot recognize the shift.)

Lewis's "sight" or insight in other areas shifted qualitatively too. His vision became much more unified. By *Perelandra* (1943), Lewis no longer seems to speak of a dialectic; he simply holds apparently opposing positions together. Such a vision can only be understood from a perspective of an underlying unity, the *natura unialis*—the ultimate unity that underlies all being. J. A. Picton emphasizes the centrality of this sense of unity in mysticism, which, "consists in the spiritual realization of a grander and boundless unity, that humbles all self-assertion by dissolving it in a wider glory. It does not follow that the sense of individuality is necessarily weakened . . . Hence the paradox of mysticism."[47] In Lewis's lecture notes on Spenser, for example, he makes reference to the absolute unity that Nicholas of Cusa perceived.[48]

> Who can understand the infinite unity that infinitely transcends and precedes all distinction—which, without being a composite, embraces all in its absolute unity—in which there is neither diversity nor difference and where man does not differ from lion nor heaven from earth?[49]

At the end of *Perelandra* and the Great Dance, the voices of the eldils speak out a vision in which one man's voice cannot easily be distinguished from another's, and even Ransom could not tell what he had contributed to the telling.

> The edge of each nature borders on that whereof it contains no shadow or similitude. Of many points one line; of many lines one shape; of many shapes one solid body; of many sense and thoughts one person; or three persons, Himself . . . Yet the circle is not less round than the sphere, and the sphere is the home and fatherland of circles. Infinite multitudes of circles lie enclosed in every sphere, and if they spoke they would say, For us were spheres created. Let no mouth open to gainsay them. Blessed be He![50]

There are echoes here of Dante's three Trinitarian spheres which he sees at the conclusion of *Paradise*:

47. Cited by Inge, *Christian Mysticism*, 32.
48. Lewis, *Spenser's Images of Life*, 15.
49. Nicholas of Cusa, *De Docta Ignorantia*, i, 24, 54.
50. Lewis, *Perelandra*, 341.

> In that abyss
> Of radiance, clear and lofty, seem'd, methought,
> Three orbs of triple hue, clipt in one bound:
> And from another, one reflected seem'd,
> As rainbow is from rainbow: and the third
> Seem'd fire, breathed equally from both . . .
> . . . O eternal light!
> Sole in thyself that dwell'st: and of thyself
> Sole understood, past, present, or to come;
> Thou smiledst, on that circling, which in thee
> Seem'd as reflected splendour, whil I mused
> For I therein, methought, in its own hue
> Beheld our image painted.[51]

At the heart of the "three orbs of triple hue" lies the human form. Here we have a radical interpenetration of the human and divine, a coinhering, which does not destroy the distinctness. They co-exist and intermingle, retaining their specificity, yet existing in the other at a profound level. It was a doctrine articulated by the Church Fathers and as always with Lewis, it is possible, even probable, that he was familiar with this concept—also known as *perichoresis*—in one of the early Greek fathers (perhaps on this occasion Gregory of Nazianzus). Certainly he knew it as the doctrine of coinherence as articulated by Charles Williams. Paul Fiddes speaks of *perichoresis*—or participation—as "the permeation of each person by the other"—a coinhering without confusion.[52] Lewis himself never used these terms, but the principle glimmers through his writings. The image of the dance, Fiddes points out, has been used historically as a metaphor for the participation of all created beings in God. It is perhaps this sense of unity that is the single factor which underpins the mystical nature of *Till We Have Faces*. Thus Lewis can speak of both the "holiness and horror of divine things," and Orual is both Psyche and Ungit. "Like all these sacred matters, it is and it is not," Orual tells us.

Not that Lewis or the Christian mystics ever claimed completeness of vision for this life. The phrase *per speculum et inenigmate* from 1 Cor 13:12 is found approximately ninety times in the writing of Augustine; "Now we see but *a poor reflection*; then we shall see face to face."[53] Translations abound; "a poor reflection," "through a glass darkly," "by obscure similitude," "in an enigma," in a mystery—or a riddle, as Orual would remind

---

51. Dante Alighieri, *Paradise*, Canto XXXIII, 107–21.
52. Fiddes, *Participating in God*, 71.
53. See Fleteren, "Mysticism in the Confessiones," 309–35.

us. Complete clarity of vision—or *intellectus*—is not attainable in this life, but for Lewis *per speculum et inenigmate* allows glimpses which cannot be achieved in the veiled world of thin rationalism.

The Inconsolable Secret: The Role of Longing[54]

It is a dynamism of human and God, revelation and mystery, self and other which constitutes Lewis's mystical theology. We have already observed Lewis's strong sense that humanity was characterized by a sense of longing. This sense of longing was what he traced in the thinking of so many of those friends and writers whom he found so appealing. Thus Plato's allegory of the cave in *Republic* is, for Lewis, a helpful portrayal; this life is just the shadows thrown by the fire, conveying a limited image of the 'Really Real' on the back of the cave. For him, in one sense, this earth was the shadowlands, and heaven, the source of all our desires, full of "the intolerable light of utter actuality."[55] In this respect, Lewis demonstrated himself to be Platonic; even his children's stories are an outworking of this stance, as can be seen so explicitly in *The Last Battle*. Narnia, as the children experience it, is only a shadow of the real Narnia that is to come. Likewise, Orual may learn to go "bareface" in this life—with all the honesty and idiosyncracy which that may entail—but it is only after death that she too, like Psyche, could become "brightface."

In the hearts of all people, Lewis believed, God has given an indication that the earthly existence is limited and finite. While Christ is the supreme once-and-for-all revelation from the Real, Lewis believed that God has never left himself without a witness.[56] For him this witness could be evidenced in a variety of ways, including the Natural law, whereby morality is evidently inherent in all of us, and could even be seen in ancient pagan myths.[57] So too with what Lewis took to be the universal experience of *Sehnsucht*. Psyche, in *Till We Have Faces,* experiences the longing; "It was when I was happiest that I longed most . . . colour and the smell, and looking across at the Grey Mountain in the distance . . . And because it was so beautiful, it set me longing, always longing . . . The sweetest thing in all my life has been the longing . . . to find the

---

54. The "inconsolable secret" is the phrase used by Lewis in the sermon "Weight of Glory," 28.

55. Lewis, *Problem of Pain*, 123.

56. Romans 1:20.

57. Hence, even Plato's vision of the man who is bound and scourged and impaled (*Republic* II, 361) is a foreshadowing of Christ's death.

place where all the beauty has come from . . . Do you think it all meant nothing, all the longing?"[58]

But it is not just Plato who articulated the importance of desire. Once again Lewis can be seen to be reflecting the biblical picture, which gives full support to the thesis that the longing for God is the true object of all human desires. In the Old Testament the psalmist identifies this sense of longing. Psalm 143:7 is only one example; "Answer me quickly, O Lord; my spirit faints with longing. Do not hide your face from me or I will be like those who go down into the pit." In Hebrews 11 the writer speaks of those pre-Christ who have, like Psyche, lived according to belief in their longings; ". . . they admitted that they were aliens and strangers on earth. People who say such things show that they are looking for a country of their own. If they had been thinking of the country they had left, they would have had the opportunity to return. Instead they were longing for a better country, a heavenly one." And the words of Paul to the Athenians, "It is he who gives to all men life and breath and all things . . . He created them to seek God, with the hope that they might grope after Him in the shadows of their ignorance, and find Him."[59]

Of the theologians who articulate this within the Christian framework, Augustine is perhaps the one who voices it most prominently: "Thou hast created us for Thyself, and our hearts are restless until they rest in Thee" (*Confessions* I, 1). Life, for Augustine, is a journey made on the feet of desire.[60] Like Lewis, Augustine's guiding principle in what Andrew Louth calls his mystical theology, is the longing to return, so evident in the twenty-seventh chapter of Book X of Augustine's *Confessions*:[61]

> I have learnt to love you late, beauty at once so ancient and so new! I have learnt to love you late! You were within me, and I was in the world outside myself, and disfigured as I was, I fell upon the lovely things of your creation . . . You called me; you cried aloud to me; you broke my barrier of deafness. You shone upon me, your radiance enveloped me, you put my blindness to flight. You shed your fragrance about me; I drew breath, and now I gasp for your sweet odour.[62]

For both Lewis and Augustine, "the soul returns to God—not in a moment of ecstasy, but in a long process of renewal which will never end

---

58. Lewis, *TWHF*, 74–76.
59. Acts 17:24–28, William Barclay's translation.
60. See McGinn on this point, *Foundations of Mysticism*, 261.
61. Louth, *Origins of the Christian Mystical Tradition*, 133–34.
62. Augustine *Confessions* 10.27.

in this life, following a way that has been disclosed by the light of the doctrine of the Trinity."[63] Like Lewis, there are shades of baptized Neo-Platonism in Augustine; both felt that that longing was, in effect a way of seeing God *per speculum et inenigmate*.[64]

For both men, the role of desire prevented complacency and stagnation—the "thing you long for summons you away from the self."[65] This is in marked contrast to Beckett's insatiability of yearning; *Three Novels* maintains to the end its Dante-esque feel of figures interminably chasing the whirling standard in the vestibule of Hell.[66] Thomas Cousineau speaks of the narrator of *The Unnamable* exploring "desire and its impasses."[67] Augustine, Lewis, and Beckett would probably find much to agree upon here. But there is a stark difference. Beckett's search is that of a questing man who has retained his emotional acuity—especially with regard to desire—but who finds the possibility of rest elusive, incredible. Lewis and Augustine, in contrast, have identified thirst as the consequence of being made for a communion that is only partially found in this life; "I tasted you, and now I hunger and thirst for you." Humans are resident aliens, *peregrini*, propelled by yearning, perpetually disquieted. For Augustine this disquietude is not primarily the product of evil and suffering. It is not so much disruption as rupture, a bursting forth of the soul in response to God; "You called me; you cried aloud to me; you broke my barrier of deafness." Augustine's concept points towards an abundance that is not the "lack" of Lacan, some gaping emptiness or negation (as Sartre and certain existentialists held). Richard Kearney puts a very different slant on this concept; "This desire of God is no mere deficiency or privation but its own reward—positivity, excess, gift, grace. 'Those who seek the Lord *lack* no good thing' (Psalm 34). Why? Because such desire, according to Augustine is an affirmative "yes" to the summons of a superabundant,

---

63. Louth, *Origins of the Christian Mystical Tradition*, 158.

64. In Augustine's work we do find that longing is explicitly stated to be the working of the Holy Spirit in the hearts of people, something which is perhaps more implicit in Lewis. The way in which Augustine's Neo-Platonism was "baptized" (or otherwise) has been treated by many; I choose to accept Louth's emphasis, supported as he is by others, including Bernard McGinn in *Foundations of Mysticism*.

65. Lewis, *Problem of Pain*, 119.

66. Various articles delineate the substantial influence of Augustine upon Dante including John Took's "Dante, Augustine and the Drama of Salvation," 73–92. Took outlines the Augustinian/Dantean contrast of "merely attenuated humanity" and a more full existence, accessed—as it were—through grace towards a fuller dimension of being and awareness.

67. Cousineau, *After the Final No*, 111.

impassioned God—'Here I am. Come. Yes, I will. Yes, I will. Yes.'"[68] So it was for Lewis; the emphasis is upon desire as constructive, rather than constrictive—an *epektasis*, or desire that will not find fulfillment. Desire is a response to the desire of God, that is, God's desiring calls forth desire. For desire is from God, and leads us back to God.

As such, desire is crucial to the sense of the self. Rowan Williams comments, "The self becomes adult and truthful in being faced with the incurable character of its desire: the world is such that no thing will bestow on the self a rounded and finished identity."[69] It may even be that desire is not sated in heaven. The desire must remain, for it preserves the particularity of individual identities.[70] For Dante, as we have seen, desire would never end, always remaining in tension with fulfillment; just as beatitude in the last canto of *Paradise* remains dynamic—and in doing so, preserves individual identities, rather than negating them.[71] Lino Pertile, in an article which suggests that the *Divine Comedy* cannot be understood outside the tradition of mystical writings, comments; ". . . the preservation of desire in the blessed allows [Dante] to portray them as individual characters, for without the psychological differences of individual desires all identities would necessarily merge and be lost—which means, theologically speaking, that just as eternity does not negate historical time, the achievement of beatitude does not entail the end of individual identities, but their fullest and freest realization.'[72] Lewis seems to concur with this when he speaks of each person's desires as the "secret signature of each soul"; the very differences in desires, he speculates, may mean that "each of the redeemed shall forever know and praise some aspect of the Divine beauty better than any other creature can. Why else were individuals created, but that God, loving all infinitely, should love each differently? . . . For doubtless the continually successful, yet never complete, attempt by each soul to communicate its unique vision to all others (and that by means whereof earthly art and philosophy are but clumsy imitations) is also among the ends for which the individual was created."[73]

68. Kearney, "Desire of God," 114.

69. R. Williams, *Lost Icons*, 153.

70. Following Lacan, interindividualism also emphasises desire as giving rise to the self (Houston, *Mentored Life*, 79).

71. As Lino Pertile points out in "A Desire of Paradise and a Paradise of Desire," Dante may have found this theme in Augustine, Gregory the Great or William of St. Thierry, but it is Bernard of Clairvaux who is the contemplative that leads Dante to his final encounter with the Deity (*Paradise* 32.1).

72. Ibid., 156.

73. Lewis, *Problem of Pain*, 117–19.

The Mystical Death Which Is the Secret of Life

We have already seen that, for Lewis, the self exists to be abdicated and, by that abdication, becomes the more truly self. "Whatever the schemes of classification, whatever the labels used for the different stages, the first step in the Mystic Way is the purgation of the self." So says F. C. Happold.[74] Although Lewis seemed to pay little attention to any such schemes or classifications, he too believed that this was the very first step, as we have seen. "Death of the self" as an image, was perhaps used most emphatically when he first converted—for example, in his letters to Greeves of 18 August 1930. He may have picked this up from MacDonald, for many of the extracts in *George MacDonald: An Anthology* are about ruthless self-denial; "the self is given to us that we may sacrifice it" is just one isolated example.[75] But Lewis's language once again is especially reflective of the language of the New Testament. And the image of stripping, of putting off, so dominant in *Till We Have Faces,* is particularly frequent in both Old and New Testaments.[76] In *The Problem of Pain* he observed that the supreme mystical death was the Crucifixion; "For in self-giving, if anywhere, we touch a rhythm not only of all creation but of all being. For the Eternal Word also gives Himself in sacrifice; and that not only on Calvary. For when He was crucified he 'did that in the wild weather of His outlying provinces which he had done in glory and gladness.'"[77] Christ conformed to the "rhythm not only of all creation but of all being."[78] "From before the foundation of the world He surrenders begotten Deity back to begetting Deity in obedience . . . From the highest to the lowest, self exists to be abdicated and, by that abdication, becomes the more truly self, to be thereupon yet more abdicated, and so forever."[79] For Lewis, there was no alternative; "What is outside the system of self-giving is not earth, nor nature, nor 'ordinary life,' but simply hell . . . That fierce imprisonment in the self is but the obverse of the self-giving which is absolute reality."[80]

74. Happold, *Mysticism*, 58.

75. Lewis, *George MacDonald*, 104.

76. For more on this, see Grenz, *Social God and the Relational Self,* 251f.

77. Lewis, *Problem of Pain*, 121. (The citation is from MacDonald, *Unspoken Sermons*, 3.)

78. Ibid., 121. At no point does Lewis stray towards the use of the term "kenosis" in order to explain his emphasis, although MacDonald does speak of Christ emptying himself. Here, as elsewhere, (the Trinity, sacraments) Lewis avoids getting entangled in theological terminology.

79. Ibid., 121.

80. Ibid., 122.

This surrender allows the self no prerogatives, real or imaginary. "Two Ways with the Self," teases out some of the practicalities of this:

> On the one hand it is God's creature, an occasion of love and rejoicing; now indeed, hateful in condition, but to be pitied and healed. On the other hand, it is that one self of all others which is called *I* and *me*, and which on that ground puts forward an irrational claim to preference. This claim is to be not only hated, but simply killed; "never," as George MacDonald says, "to be allowed a moment's respite from eternal death." The Christian must wage endless war against the clamour of the *ego* as *ego*: but he loves and approves selves as such, though not their sins. The very self-love which he has to reject is to him a specimen of how he ought to feel to all selves; and he may hope that when he has truly learned (which will hardly be in this life) to love his neighbour as himself, he may then be able to love himself as his neighbour: that is, with charity instead of partiality . . . We must die daily: but it is better to love the self than to love nothing, and to pity the self than to pity no-one.[81]

The citations could be multiplied; the concept appears time and time again in Lewis's work, right up until the late works. *I* and *me* can have no claim to preference, because, as he wrote in a letter to a correspondent in 1956, "almost the main work of life is to *come out* of our selves, out of the little, dark prison we are all born in."[82] So too Orual needs this different perspective on her "claim to preference" before she can see what damage her demands have made on Psyche—and the prison that she herself has inhabited. The point of full *anagnorisis* is when she can "flee her self," and put it fully at another's disposal. Manlove puts it well:

> Her whole story is an attempt to justify and fix herself, and a struggle to define the indefinite character of life. It is only when she gives herself away that she gains it: and the self she gains is no fixed thing but has many faces, not excluding Psyche and Ungit. At that point the self is another kind of "nothing," not an empty void on its own, but a thing without boundaries, merged in the nature of others.[83]

A close reading of Lewis's work will call for some nuancing of this. He portrays no eradication of the person. Rather, it is a dynamic process, which allows for a dialectic of renunciation and fulfillment, as Gilbert

---

81. Lewis, "Two Ways with the Self," 120–21.
82. Lewis, letter to Keith Masson, (June 3, 1956), *Letters*, Vol. III, 759.
83. Manlove, *C. S. Lewis: His Literary Achievement*, 212.

Meilaender points out.[84] The two are always tied together in his writing. Even in his 1930 letter to Greeves he speaks of "the dying process" as the beginning of new life. Clearly, he preached a relinquishing of the self; on this he, like MacDonald, was utterly emphatic. But we have already seen that he did not see relinquishing as commensurate with eradication. He seemed to be fully aware that emphasis upon the self's ability to regulate the will throws the self back upon itself, unable to move beyond itself. MacDonald had warned against a wrong kind of self-denial:

> Doing the thing God does not require of him, he puts himself in the place of God, becoming not a law but a law-giver to himself, one who commands, not one who obeys. This diseased satisfaction which some minds feel in laying burdens on themselves, is pampering, little as they may suspect it, of the most dangerous appetite of that self which they think they are mortifying.[85]

"The wrong asceticism torments the self; the right kind kills the selfness" is how Lewis put it in "Two Ways with the Self" (1940).[86] And in "The Weight of Glory" (1941), he wrote, "The New Testament has lots to say about self-denial, but not about self-denial as an end in itself."[87] Rather it is about self-denial for the sake of the other, and even, in a paradoxical way—for the sake of the self, for only a fool thinks that desire can ever be satisfied. In 1947 in *Miracles* he was speaking of "that mystical death which is the secret of life."[88] Emphatically he argued that in vegetable, animal and human life, there must be descent into seed, into womb, before new life can arise. And he added, "So it is in our moral and emotional life. The first innocent and spontaneous desires have to submit to the deathlike process of control or total denial: but from that there is reascent to fully formed character in which the strength of the new material all operates but in a new way. Death and Rebirth—go down to go up—it is a key principle. Through this bottleneck, this belittlement, the highroad nearly always lies."[89] And when he used the image of stripping in the 1950s, semi-violent as the image may be, he, like the biblical writers, tended to couple it with reference to the new garments, which must be put on. Stanley J. Grenz, in his study of the *Imago Dei*,

---

84. See the chapter entitled "The Revelry of Insatiable Love" in Meilander, *Taste for the Other*.
85. MacDonald, "Self Denial," 366.
86. Lewis, "Two Ways with the Self," 120–21.
87. Lewis, "Weight of Glory," 25.
88. Lewis, *Miracles*, 137.
89. Ibid., 117–18.

lists the many Old and New Testament references to this concept.[90] For example, "... you have taken off your old self with its practices, and have put on the new self, which is being renewed in knowledge in the image of its creator." (Col 3:9–10). From the perspective of a psychiatrist, Paul Tournier describes the concept in this way:

> So, with its characteristic realism, the biblical revelation turns us from the utopian dream of a life exempt from all appearance and all protection. For the efforts we were vainly making to isolate our person completely from our personage it substitutes a quite different idea: that of accepting the clothing which God himself gives us, of choosing our personage—the personage God wills us to have.[91]

Orual is slow to learn this dialectic of renunciation and fulfillment. For most of her life she retains the personage which she has chosen to adopt; a disguise. In contrast Psyche allows herself to be dressed by the gods in "the most beautiful things."[92] She has an instinctive sense of the right way with the self, not that which torments the self, but that which having recognized the "self," "kills the selfness" for the sake of others. She risks death by going amongst the fever-ridden people of Glome, on the off-chance that she may have healing hands; "Psyche went on, walking slowly and gravely, like a child going to say a lesson, right in among the foulness. She touched and she touched . . . For hours she touched. The air was stifling even for us who stood in the shadow of the porch."[93] She perceives life as full of small deaths, which she embraces willingly. Her examples—"To leave your home . . . to lose one's maidenhead—to bear a child—they are all deaths'—show no unnecessary abnegation of the self, rather, they involve an attitude to the self which allows new life to arise out of the action. Here is the biblical concept of being conformed to Christ's likeness. Psyche represents the pure Christian soul in *Till We Have Faces*; in life she was an *anima naturaliter christiana* (natural Christian soul) as Lewis told Clyde Kilby in a letter on February 10, 1957.[94] He also commented that she is like Christ—in the way that every good man or woman is like Christ. Her death as ransom for the people of Glome, is an act of self-transcendence, and it is *primarily*—although far

90. Grenz, *Social God and the Relational Self*, 251f.

91. Tournier, *Meaning of Persons*, 73. The original title in French is *Le Personnage et la Personnne*.

92. Lewis, *TWHF*, 85.

93. Ibid., 25.

94. Lewis, letter to Clyde S. Kilby (February 10, 1957) *Letters*, Vol. III, 830.

from exclusively—in this way that Orual shall come to resemble Psyche. It is in this way that she must die before she dies. Orual's gesture towards Psyche is the same gesture which Psyche, so long ago, had made to abandon herself to the gods. This self-abandonment is true *ekstasis*, not for and through one's own self, nor for an arbitrary asceticism, but for and through another. Eventually, "pierced through with arrows of joy and terror," Orual finally declares herself as being unmade, as no-one.[95] Psyche too is no-one, yet, "I loved her as I would once have thought it impossible to love; would have died any death for her."[96] The choice could have been made long before; Orual could have negated her own desire to possess Psyche back on the mountainside. It appeared to be a stark choice—Psyche's desire—or Orual's. But it is not only for the sake of the other; it is for the sake of the self. To have granted Psyche freedom, would also have left Orual free. Released from the prison, the self that transcends its boundaries is gloriously free. *Till We Have Faces* only offers glimpses of the "fullness of being" which Orual feels before she dies, freed and forgiven. But in Psyche we see what awaits her; sacrifice brings her only to the point where she is "a thousand times more her very self than she had been before the Offering."[97]

Lewis's emphasis came to rest upon the transcendence of the self perhaps to avoid connotations of erasure or annihilation. In his approach we see a reversal of the journey of Christendom—for he journeyed back towards a perspective that the Western Church had lost. Rowan Williams's view is that "Western Catholicism by 1300 was rapidly losing the means to express theologically the basic principle of its life, the *ekstasis*, emptying, displacement of self in response to the self-emptying love of God, the communion of God and humanity by the presence of each in the other."[98] In making this journey, Lewis again puts himself in the company of those we now call Christian mystics. Louis Dupré points out that mystics perceive humans as self-transcending beings, not because of what they do but because of what they are in their very nature.[99] Dupré's comments about them ring true of Lewis's perspective:

> . . . the ultimate message of the mystic about the nature of selfhood is that the self is essentially more than a mere self, that transcendence belongs to its nature as much as the act through

95. So too Jane is "unmade" when she meets Ransom in *That Hideous Strength*.
96. Lewis, *TWHF*, 233.
97. Ibid., 232.
98. R. Williams, *Wound of Knowledge*, 138–39.
99. Dupré, *The Deeper Life*, 24.

which it is immanent to itself, and that a total failure on the mind's part to realize this transcendence reduces the self to less than itself.[100]

Lewis put it in lay person's terms in *Mere Christianity*, "It is only the Christians who have any idea of how human souls can be taken into the life of God and yet remain themselves—in fact, be very much more themselves than they were before."[101] And prior to that: "The more we get what we now call 'ourselves' out of the way and let Him take us over, the more truly ourselves we become . . . I am not, in my natural state, nearly so much of a person as I like to believe: most of what I call 'me' can be very easily explained. It is when I turn to Christ, when I give myself up to His Personality, that I first begin to have a real personality of my own . . . Look for yourself, and you will find in the long run only hatred, loneliness, despair, rage, ruin, and decay. But look for Christ and you will find Him, and with Him everything else thrown in."[102] Even in the last book published in his lifetime, *An Experiment in Criticism*, Lewis continued to emphasize this sense of self-transcendence. In great literature he concluded, "as in worship, in love, in moral action, and in knowing, I transcend myself; and am never more myself than when I do."[103]

The importance of this can be demonstrated in *Till We Have Faces* where the need for self-transcendence is given flesh, for a full understanding of the book can only be managed by those who transcend their worldview. Lewis had "Greeks" in mind as the readers of *Till We Have Faces*. In other words, he perceived that those who read his book would be predominantly rationalist in their approach. God, (or the gods), in the mind of such readers, will be perceived as a rational being. The house of Ungit is one aspect of Lewis's attempt to smash the constraints of rationalism and to enable his readers to transcend the dominant modern view. Peter Schakel has put it this way—"a major purpose of *Till We Have Faces* is to convey a fuller, more adequate awareness of the divine nature than that of the rationalists."[104] It is the Priest who voices the argument against "Greek" wisdom:

> They demand to see such things clearly, as if the gods were no more than letters written in a book. I, King, have dealt with the gods for three generations of men, and I know that they dazzle

100. Dupré, "Mystical Experience of the Self," 462.
101. Lewis, *Mere Christianity*, 161.
102. Ibid., 225–27.
103. Lewis, *Experiment in Criticism*, 144.
104. Schakel, *Reason and Imagination in C. S. Lewis*, 21.

> our eyes and flow in and out of one another like eddies on a river, and nothing that is said clearly can be said truly about them. Holy places are dark places . . . Holy wisdom is not clear and thin like water, but thick and dark like blood.[105]

Schakel speaks of Ungit as a "numinous" god, who has about her a sense of the holy, who gives rise to 'the horror of holiness'. The concept of sacrifice is explained by the Priest in such a way as to be illogical, even repugnant, to human understanding. True wisdom is not scientific. Such "scientific" understanding, Schakel says, must "die," must be "sacrificed" and in the place of a pale and thin belief, a dark and thick one must grow. So too the nature of knowledge or *scientia* is necessarily incomplete, and must needs be supplemented or transcended. It is here that faith is given room; *sapientia* is the fruit of faith.

Faith is all-important for this self-transcendence. In the Endnotes of his own *Book of Common Prayer*, Lewis wrote of trust in Christ as a crucial attitude to the self. In note form he wrote: "Salvation not without works because only those who have tried can realise their insolvency and really get into 2nd attitude [ie trust wholly to Christ]. Salvation by faith because until you realize the uselessness of works you are not the new self in the new way."[106] "Trusting wholly in Christ," the self must continually respond to that which is beyond itself, requiring trust in order to remain constantly open to a dynamic knowing and relating. Just as understanding becomes enriched by its openness which does not seek enclosure nor completion, so too, the self is enriched by open-ended dynamism. Just as God cannot be circumscribed, neither can any human self. In *A Grief Observed*, Lewis wrote:

> My idea of God is not a divine idea. It has to be shattered time after time. He shatters it Himself. He is the great iconoclast. Could we not almost say that this shattering is one of the marks of His presence? . . . All reality is iconoclastic. The earthly beloved, even in this life, incessantly triumphs over your mere idea of her.[107]

Rowan Williams points out that for both Augustine and Bernard of Clairvaux, "the inaccessibility of the divine perspective is paradoxically liberating: there is always a resource for the renewal or conversion or enlargement of myself independent of what may happen to be my resources

---

105. Lewis, *TWHF*, 37–38.

106. Punctuation Lewis's. The original is at the Wade Center, Wheaton College. A facsimile of the endnotes is kept at the Bodleian Library.

107. Lewis, *Grief Observed*, 56.

at any given moment."¹⁰⁸ The self is enlarged by faith and unknowing. Denys Turner speaks of John of the Cross when he writes of faith, but his comment is entirely appropriate to this outlook—which held a perspective of "not-knowing" as a vital element of the Christian journey:

> Faith, the darkness of unknowing, is the conviction—but also the practice of the Christian life as organized in terms of that conviction—that "our deepest centre is in God." It is the conviction that our deepest centre, the most intimate source from which our actions flow, our freedom to love, is in us but not of us, is not "ours" to possess, but only ours to be possessed by. And so faith "decentres" us, for it disintegrates the experiential structures of selfhood on which, in experience, we centre ourselves, and at the same time draws us into the divine love where we are "recentred" upon a ground beyond any possibility of experience. There is, at the centre of our selfhood, a ground which is unknowable, even to us.¹⁰⁹

Augustine was intensely aware of this unknowability too; "I cannot understand all that I am. This means then that the mind is too narrow to contain itself entirely," he says in *Confessions* 10.8. But for Augustine and Lewis, unlike Beckett, this unknowability is grounded in hope and in trust—and progress. This necessity of constant progress, (as McGinn points out), is one of the most typical notes of Augustine's spiritual teaching.¹¹⁰ God is found through faith and yet ever sought by hope in this life.¹¹¹ Hope is, in contrast, "in short supply in Beckett's work," as Pilling puts it, with particular reference to Moran's perspective, "That would keep hope alive, would it not, hellish hope."¹¹² For Beckett, hope is misleading and disillusionment can be the only consequence. In the *Three Novels*, the narrators speak of desisting from speaking—the self-transcendence which questioning entails is replaced by solipsistic self-enclosure. ("It's not a question of hypotheses, it's a question of going on."¹¹³) For Lewis, questioning, hope and faith are essential parts of the dynamic progress that pulls us, irresistibly, beyond renunciation towards self-transcendence, and towards the self that is re-centered upon the Other. Where once he had felt a closed door between himself and God, he finds his perspective has changed:

108. R. Williams, "'Know Thyself': What Kind of an Injunction?" 223.
109. Turner, *Darkness of God*, 251.
110. McGinn, *Foundations of Mysticism*, 261.
111. Ibid., 258.
112. Pilling, *Samuel Beckett*, 133.
113. Beckett, *Three Novels*, 404.

> When I lay these questions before God I get no answer. But a rather special sort of "No answer." It is not the locked door. It is more like a silent, certainly not uncompassionate, gaze. As though He shook His head not in refusal but waiving the question. Like, "Peace, child; you don't understand."[114]

For Beckett the door is closed; for Lewis there came to be no closed door, but a Person, irreducibly Other, waiving the question.[115] Orual says, "I know now, Lord, why you utter no answer. You are yourself the answer. Before your face questions die away. What other answer would suffice?"[116]

Only Words, Words: Language

Orual's realization about the inadequacy of words could be perceived as being indicative of a somewhat apophatic approach to language. After asking, "What other answer would suffice?" Orual continues, "Only words, words; to be led out to battle against other words."[117] "Lightly men talk about saying what they mean."[118] Unlike Beckett's narrator, who says, "I'm in words, made of words, others' words," language is here portrayed as manifestly inadequate. Elsewhere Lewis spoke of a preference for wordless prayer. "For me words are in any case secondary. They are only an anchor. Or, shall I say, they are the movements of a conductor's baton: not the music."[119] But to say that Lewis's view of language is entirely apophatic would be a misrepresentation. God, he felt, could be addressed without words—but only when one was operating out of a position of mental and spiritual strength. As the devil in *The Screwtape Letters* points out, the prayer that consists of composing one's spirit to love, "bears a superficial resemblance to the prayer of silence as practised by those who are very far advanced in the Enemy's service."[120] Words as a means of addressing God are limited by circumstances, particularly the "heart" of the speaker. For truth must lie at the heart of all genuine linguistic enterprise. This, not "the babble that we think we mean" is what God listens to—the speech

---

114. Lewis, *Grief Observed*, 58.

115. See the final pages of *The Unnamable* for many references to the closed door, through which the narrator wants to go in the hope of silence and solitude.

116. Lewis, *TWHF*, 234.

117. Ibid., 234.

118. Ibid., 223.

119. Lewis, *Prayer: Letters to Malcolm*, 9.

120. Lewis, *Screwtape Letters*, 25.

which lies at the center of the soul. Because for Lewis, the speaker or writer communicates, he does not express. Communication lies at the center of speech—unlike the manifesto to which Beckett agreed that the writer expresses; he does not communicate. To express is to be trapped in a subjective outlook that offers neither self-knowledge nor engagement.[121] This applies to all kinds of language. Even poetry is not merely an expression but a saying that points towards an object, of which the expression is only a response.[122] Auricular confession, in contrast, leads to gain in self-knowledge; "most of us have never really faced the truth about ourselves until we uttered them aloud in plain words," he wrote in a letter in 1953.[123] The uttering of the truth is ultimately liberating.

Also in contrast to Beckett, Lewis neither denigrates language nor elevates it. Rather than desiring to dissolve the materiality of language, Lewis revels in it. Like Ransom, to find himself at "the white-hot furnace of essential speech" would have been a "heavenly pleasure" for Lewis.[124] In fact, *The Cosmic Trilogy* conveys his concern about the scientific abstractions, journalistic distractions and other abuses of language that he perceived about him. In *That Hideous Strength* language reaches a nadir of confusion at the banquet at Belbury; words no longer *mean*. The aphasia that strikes (or as Withers says, "aspasia which gleams to have selected our redeemed inspector") is the curse of Babel. The very title of the book is taken from a medieval commentary on Genesis and Babel.[125] The leaders of Belbury, in their ambition, have continually distorted truth. When Merlin cries out "*Qui Verbum Dei contempserunt, eis auferetur etiam verbum hominis*," (They that have despised the word of God, from them shall the word of man also be taken away), the confusion is such that most seem to be unable to hear him.[126] The nature of the curse is in keeping with the abuse of language that preceded it.

This emphasis upon clear communication does not negate the mystery of the divine—as we have seen—but is a preference for the *via affirmativa* or cataphatic way—the way of finding God in all things.

---

121. In "Christianity and Literature" Lewis argued that a "Christian" critical theory "would be opposed to the theory of genius as, perhaps, generally understood; and above all it would be opposed to the idea that literature is self-expression." Lewis, "Christianity and Literature," 9.

122. Lewis, "Language of Religion," *Christian Reflections*, 171.

123. Lewis, letter to Mary van Deusen (April 6, 1953) *Letters*, Vol. III, 320.

124. Lewis, *That Hideous Strength*, 687.

125. "The Shadow of that Hyddeous strength/ Sax myle and more it is of length," Sir David Lindsay, *Ane Dialog*. (This is the frontispiece to *That Hideous Strength*.)

126. Lewis, *That Hideous Strength*, 718.

Dorothy Sayers suggests that this kind of mystical theology, which accepts images as valid, appeals most to the artist and poet; "all those to whom the rejection of images would be the rejection of their very means to intellectual and emotional experience."[127] Whilst the exclusivity of her approach—which includes primarily Dante, Thomas Traherne, Charles Williams and William Blake—gives rise to questions, Lewis would seem to belong predominantly to such an affirmative category. Verna E. F. Harrison points out the Eastern Orthodox belief that cataphatic insights lead not only to further cataphatic insights but to a greater awareness of the apophatic.[128] The two grow in tandem. (Indeed, that is the view of Charles Williams too. Both ways, the way of Affirmation and the way of Negation co-inhere.) Although Lewis was probably familiar with this insight as expounded by Gregory of Nyssa, his articulation of it in Orual rings most profoundly of a lived understanding.

Lewis's emphasis may have been shaped by context; Doris T. Myers has contextualized Lewis's view of language, demonstrating that what she refers to as his high view, was articulated against a post-war concern that language deceives.[129] Myers points out that C. K. Ogden and I. A. Richards in *The Meaning of Meaning* (1923) were refuting the idea that words always correspond to reality and that there is a necessary connection between "symbol" and "referent." Lewis, on the other hand embraced a high evaluation of language, that the word is closely connected with the thing it designates. His thinking in the mid-1920s was greatly influenced by Barfield, who was engaged in writing *Poetic Diction*. "Much of the thought which he afterwards put into *Poetic Diction* had already become mine before that important little book appeared."[130] Myers sums it up:

> Barfield's position may be stated in this way: in order to know something, a person must recognize it, and to recognize it, he must be able to relate it to other things. Such relationships are concepts, and concepts must be expressed as resemblances and analogies—metaphors. Since Barfield defines knowledge as "the ability to recognize significant resemblances and analogies," it follows that our knowledge of the universe depends on metaphor. And since human intelligence is a participation in a cosmic Intelligence, the knowledge that human beings gain through metaphor corresponds with the way the universe really is.[131]

127. Sayers, *Introductory Papers on Dante*, 122.
128. Harrison, "Relationship between Apophatic and Kataphatic Theology," 318–32.
129. Myers, *C. S. Lewis in Context*.
130. Lewis, *Surprised by Joy*, 155.
131. Myers, *C. S. Lewis in Context*, 8.

Ultimately, Lewis differed from Barfield in many of his conclusions but in this area they were agreed. Language is incurably metaphorical. In *Miracles* Lewis summarized Barfield's idea that the distinction between metaphorical and literal meanings is a relatively recent distinction:

> . . . words did not start by referring merely to physical objects and then get extended by metaphor to refer to the emotions, mental states and the like. On the contrary, what we now call the "literal and metaphorical" meanings have both been disengaged by analysis from an ancient unity of meaning which was neither or both.[132]

Lewis mentions this "ancient unity of meaning" in *Reflections on the Psalms*, *Miracles*, *The Discarded Image*, *Preface to Paradise Lost*, and the essay "Bluspels and Flalansferes." When "Logical Positivism" took centre stage, under the articulation of A. J. Ayer, Lewis's reply remained consistent. Rather than agreeing that only language that is verifiable is not meaningless, or non-sense, he stressed the opposite; "We might even formulate a rule: the meaning in any given composition is in inverse ratio to the author's belief in his own literalness."[133] His stance against positivism is particularly clear in *The Abolition of Man*.

This emphasis upon metaphor was central to his belief about God and humans, as he articulated in *Miracles*:

> For me the Christian doctrines which are "metaphorical"—or which have become metaphorical with the increase of abstract thought—mean something which is just as "supernatural" or shocking after we have removed the ancient imagery as it was before. They mean that in addition to the physical or psycho-physical universe known to the sciences, there exists an uncreated and unconditioned reality which causes the universe to be.[134]

The original metaphors, he concludes—along with Barfield—in "Bluspels and Flalansferes" are archetypes. But, unlike Barfield, he concludes that imagination is not the organ of truth, but of meaning. "I am a rationalist. For me reason is the natural organ of truth; but imagination is the organ of meaning. Imagination, producing new metaphors or revivifying old, is not the cause of truth, but its condition."[135] Metaphor—and consequently myth—point towards spiritual reality. William Gray

---

132. Lewis, *Miracles*, 80–81.
133. Lewis, "Bluspels and Flalansferes," 262.
134. Lewis, *Miracles*, 82.
135. Lewis, "Bluspels and Flalansferes," 265.

suggests that Lewis had an almost sacramental understanding of good reading:[136]

> (T)he first reading of some literary work is often . . . an experience so momentous that only experiences of love, religion or bereavement can furnish a standard of comparison. Their whole consciousness is changed. They have become what they were not before.[137]

Just as Anodos was changed through the story of Cosmos in *Phantastes*, so Lewis also changed through reading *Phantastes*. Here, perhaps—or perhaps not—drawing on the Platonic tradition that the real can only appear to the human mind through images, Lewis saw such images as not only necessary but good. As Thomas Werge puts it:

> While reason and logic may approximate the paradox of the Incarnation, only faith and imagination can directly apprehend its salvific mystery and be moved by the dramatic images from which that mystery cannot be separated . . . for Lewis the events of the Incarnation, Crucifixion and Resurrection—as well as the images of ordinary, limited, and earthly experience—manifest a coalescing of the concrete and the spiritual. Life is concretely sacramental rather than a gnostic dream.[138]

There is real contract between word and world, as Rowan Williams puts it. "If there is no presence in words, there is no presence in speakers."[139] There can be little doubt that the characters of *That Hideous Strength* reflect this, although Lewis does not specifically theorize on this topic.

Certainly, Lewis was logocentric in perceiving a metaphysics of presence (although not logocentric in the Derridean sense, privileging the written word over the spoken). David Lyle Jeffrey would prefer to speak of being Logos-centered, for it is not the idolizing of the word as an end in itself; philology, he argues, is but a love of words transcended by a higher love.[140] Actually, Lewis seldom uses the word *Logos*; here too there would seem to be an obvious gap. We know that he affirmed the concept of Christ as Word—as we have already seen—but he did not elaborate, and one wonders if he chose to stay clear of an area that had been delineated by Owen Barfield in a way with which Lewis could not agree.[141] His

---

136. Gray, "Spirituality and the Pleasure of the Text," 244.
137. Lewis, *Experiment in Criticism*, 3.
138. Werge, "Sanctifying the Literal: Images and Incarnation in *Miracles*," 84.
139. R. Williams, *Lost Icons*, 176.
140. Jeffrey, *People of the Book*, 9–10, 17.
141. For Barfield in *Saving the Appearances*, the *Logos* was the "faint awareness of

most emphatic use of *Logos* is to refer to the spoken word—as opposed to *Poiema* (the written word) in *An Experiment in Criticism*.[142] And it is in this context that we reach the heart of the matter. Each, Lewis said, enables us in our search for enlargement of our being. They are iconic; they open us to what is beyond ourselves:

> We want to see with other eyes, to imagine with other imaginations, to feel with other hearts, as well as with our own . . . In love, in virtue, in the pursuit of knowledge, and in the reception of the arts, we are doing this. Obviously this process can be described as either an enlargement or as a temporary annihilation of the self. But that is an old paradox; "he that loseth his life shall save it."[143]

Just as the literary enables us to transcend the limits of ourselves, so too it maintains our particularity:

> Literary experience heals the wound, without undermining the privilege, of individuality. There are mass emotions which heal the wound; but they destroy the privilege. In them our separate selves are pooled and sink back into sub-individuality. But in reading great literature I become a thousand men and yet remain myself. Like the night sky in the Greek poem, I see with a myriad eyes, but it is still I who see. Here, as in worship, in love, in moral action, and in knowing, I transcend myself; and am never more myself than when I do.[144]

This theme had been a constant in his life, from his early letters, through *The Personal Heresy*, right up to his final writings. It is highly significant that Orual's book is to be sent to Greece for people to read, for there they may share in her enlargement. It was not to remain in Glome, but it was to go to those who would most understand, and therefore benefit from the reversal of understanding. Language and literature not only call us towards self-transcendence, but in the articulation of our new understanding, we enable the enlargement of others. It is not to be kept to oneself; for we are members of one another.

---

creative activity alike in nature and man" which remained after the decline of original participation.

142. Lewis, *Experiment in Criticism*, 132–41.
143. Ibid., 137–38.
144. Ibid., 140–41.

Men, and Gods, Flow in and out and Mingle: Coinherence and Transposition[145]

Of Lewis's opposition to individualism (although he used the word "individual" with approbation) we have already formed a picture. Thus, in writing of "our first parents" who fell into sin, Lewis says: "They wanted, as we say, to 'call their souls their own'. But that means to live a lie, for our souls are not, in fact, our own."[146] Orual wished to "call her soul her own," but in attempting to do so, she damaged others and herself, for her soul was not, in fact, her own. The sheer interconnectedness of her soul with the souls of others is made clear to her. Lewis had come to identify the damaging effects of not just Stoicism, but the many other ways in which the person is isolated and objectified. It is very much in keeping with the rejection of individualism which took root in Augustine as he grew older; ". . . Augustine's thought in his fifties began to be dominated by the notion that the roots of sin lie in the self's retreat into a privacy which is deprivation; the self is deprived of community . . . The radical flaw in human nature is now transcribed in terms of a retreat into a closed-off self . . . 'Private,' one's 'own,' are now repeatedly opposed by Augustine to the 'shared,' the 'common,' the 'public.' Ultimate pride is total isolation: *l'enfer, c'est les autres*."[147] As we have already seen, for Lewis, lost souls are characterized by a "rejection of everything that is not simply themselves." In *Surprised by Joy* he cites MacDonald, "The one principle of Hell is—'I am my own.'"[148] And in *The Screwtape Letters* he speaks of "the ruthless, sleepless, unsmiling concentration upon self which is the mark of Hell."[149]

Here Lewis stands close to Personalism, with his emphasis upon the value of persons. The theistic idealism of many Personalist writers appealed to Lewis and particularly the kind of dialogical Personalism demonstrated by such as Martin Buber. "Something has stepped between our existence and God to shut off the light from heaven . . . (and) that something is in fact *ourselves*, our own bloated selfhood," sounds like something Lewis would write, but is in fact written by Buber.[150] But, just as Lewis responded to Existentialist desires for fulfillment, and yet set

---

145. Lewis, *TWHF*, 231
146. Lewis, *Problem of Pain*, 63–64.
147. Markus, *Conversion and Disenchantment in Augustine's Spiritual Career*, 32–33.
148. Lewis, *Surprised by Joy*, 165.
149. Lewis, *Screwtape Letters*, ix.
150. Buber, cited in Torrance, *God and Rationality*, 29.

himself against them by his refusal of the idea of self-creation, so too with Personalism.[151] (In fact, he opposed all such labels because he felt that it became much easier to dismiss a person's thought once they had been labeled with an "ism.") It is possible that Buber particularly appealed to Lewis because of his doctoral studies based on Nicholas of Cusa and Jacob Boehme—for whilst Lewis was reacting against depersonalization in modern society, he was not satisfied to speak of community as if it were the opposite of individualism.

Lewis's image of community has been dealt with in some detail in Gilbert Meilaender's *The Taste for the Other: The Social and Ethical Thought of C. S. Lewis*. "We are members of one another," is how Lewis puts it in the sermon entitled "Membership." In that sermon he proposed a consideration of the differences between the secular collective and the mystical body that is the Church. Meilaender summarizes the central premise of Lewis's theological works as follows; "All human beings are made for life in community with God (and, thereby, with one another)."[152] He opposed there and elsewhere what he called "the collective"—huge impersonal organizations—and the growing indifference to persons which he perceived in them.[153] For he believed that "the one really adequate instrument for learning about God is the whole Christian community, waiting for Him together."[154] Lewis's statement in "Membership" indicates how the Church actually encourages personhood:[155]

> There is, in forms too subtle for official embodiment, a continual interchange of complementary ministrations. We are all constantly teaching and learning, forgiving and being forgiven, representing Christ to man when we intercede, and man to Christ when others intercede for us. The sacrifice of selfish privacy which is daily demanded of us is daily repaid a hundredfold in the true growth of personality which the life of the Body encourages. Those who are members of one another become as diverse as the hand and the ear. That is why worldlings are so monotonously alike compared with the almost fantastic variety of saints.

---

151. In a letter written in 1961, Lewis spoke of Buber as an Existentialist, alongside Gabriel Marcel, but that the movement was a mood, not a philosophy. Letter to Mary Van Deusen (February 13, 1961) *Letters*, Vol. III, 1238.

152. Meilaender, *Taste for the Other*, 2.

153. See, for example, "Reply to Professor Haldane," 108.

154. Lewis, *Mere Christianity*, 165.

155. Lewis, "Membership," 119–43.

> Obedience is the road to freedom, humility the road to pleasure, unity the road to personality.[156]

Unity is the road to personality, but collectivism and individualism—and one begets the other—are depersonalizing; it is only in the Body that the person receives value, and is encouraged towards true growth in personality.

As Meilaender points out, Lewis uses various images to convey the way of relations in the "mystical body." For example, in the Great Dance scene that closes *Perelandra*, the figures engage in intertwining indulation which forms the pattern of the dance. In each image, harmony—even revelry—is achieved through constant self-giving and self-surrender. The greatest danger lies in the grasping, a point which Lewis makes in each image. Perhaps the most pertinent is the image of the game with the golden apple of selfhood.[157] In this, the apple becomes an apple of discord among the false gods, as they scramble to hold to it; but the game, when played by the rules, involves the passing of the apple as swiftly as possible. To cling to it is death. "But when it flies to and fro among the players too swift for eye to follow, and the great master Himself leads the revelry, giving Himself eternally to His creatures in the generation, and back to Himself in the sacrifice, of the Word, then indeed the eternal dance 'makes heaven drowsy with the harmony.'"

Constant self-giving is only possible where love exists. *Till We Have Faces* can be read as an exploration of different kinds of love; Lewis went on to publish *The Four Loves* shortly after. Doris T. Myers in *Bareface: A Guide to C. S. Lewis's Last Novel* points out the way in which the novel incorporates the various loves.[158] Although Lewis delineated four specific kinds of love, he also referred to need-love and gift-love. Gift-love can be seen in a pale way when the Fox tells Orual that he shall not press her to hear her secret, for "friends must be free," but it is more forcibly depicted in the concluding scenes, when Orual and Psyche in turn give of themselves to each other. It is gift-love akin to charity, which enables the self-transcendence or *ekstasis* that overcomes the boundaries of self, and in relatedness, leads towards true communion.[159] Orual has, unwittingly, borne much of the anguish for Psyche, and although Psyche achieves the tasks which were set as her punishment, Orual has carried out the

---

156. Ibid., 125.

157. Lewis, *Problem of Pain*, 122.

158. Myers, *Bareface: A Guide to C.S. Lewis's Last Novel*.

159. This idea is articulated in the contemporary debate by Zizioulas in "Human Capacity and Incapacity," 401–4.

same tasks of sifting, sorting, gathering, fetching, but in psychological terms.[160] In effect, they exchange aspects of the consequences of Orual's actions.[161] When Orual accepts Psyche's gift, "youth seemed to come into my breast" and she too, unwittingly, is transformed in the likeness of Psyche, as she subsequently realizes. But Psyche too is ontologically constituted through another; "it was not, not now, she that really counted. Or if she counted (and oh, gloriously she did) it was for another's sake."[162] At the conclusion of the novel, Orual is Psyche; "both Psyches, both beautiful (if that mattered now) beyond all imagining, yet not exactly the same."[163] Underlying it all is love—Psyche's love for Orual; Orual's love for Psyche ("I loved her as I would once have thought it impossible to love"); the god's love for Psyche—and surely the god is Christ himself. Need-love has been replaced by Gift-love. Man can ascend to heaven only because of Christ; "only those into which Love Himself has entered will ascend to Love himself."[164] For both Augustine and Lewis, the way of self-knowledge, is (as the priest of Ungit would say) "in a mystery," the way of love: love of God, neighbor, and self. "Neither let that further question disturb us, how much of love we ought to spend upon our brother, and how much upon God: incomparably more upon God than upon ourselves, but upon our brother as much as upon ourselves; and we love ourselves so much the more, the more we love God."[165]

As the Fox puts it, "We're all limbs and part of one Whole. Hence, of each other. Men, and gods, flow in and out and mingle."[166] Here we find Charles William's doctrines of coinherence and exchange. Just as self-transcendence was foundational to life for Lewis, so for Williams, exchange was the root principle: ". . . we ought to be 'members one of another,'" he wrote in 1941, "*membra*, limbs, not members of the same society. Christians are not members of a club; they are 'members' of the Church."[167] He goes on to say, "Compacts can be made for the taking over of the suffering of troubles, and worries, and distresses, as simply

---

160. See Shakel, *Reason and Imagination in C. S. Lewis*, 69–72.

161. For detail on this see Christopher in "Archetypal Patterns in *Till We Have Faces*," 193–212.

162. Lewis, *TWHF*, 233.

163. Ibid., 233.

164. Lewis, *The Four Loves*, 155.

165. Augustine *De trinitate* 8.8 (219–20).

166. Lewis, *TWHF*, 228.

167. C. Williams, "Way of Exchange," 151. This particular essay was published as a pamphlet in 1941.

and as effectually as an assent is given to the carrying of a parcel. A man can cease to worry about *x* because his friend has agreed to be worried by *x*. No doubt this is only a part of casting all our burdens on the Lord; the point is that it may well be a part of it."[168] In *Arthurian Torso* Lewis wrote; "We can and should 'bear one another's burdens' in a sense much more nearly literal than is usually dreamed of. Any two souls can ('under the Omnipotence') make an agreement to do so: the one can offer to take another's shame or anxiety or grief and the burden will actually be transferred."[169] Transference does not just occur between humans. God too, in the sacrifice of the Word, took on human burdens.

So too with coinherence. It is only by this doctrine that the "mingling" of the characters in *Till We Have Faces* can be understood. It helps us to understand how Psyche and Orual can not only take each other's burdens but can seem to substitute for each other at the novel's conclusion. Here we see the profound sense of connectedness, the mingling of "men and gods," the way in which all is a part of the whole. Nothing can be isolated; all is connected at root. The sacramental rites of the Church are just one aspect of this. For Augustine, all progress to God can only take place in the context of the Church as the mystical body of Christ. McGinn points out that Augustine's vision at Ostia, for example, was a shared experience with Monica, and that, for him, communion with the community of the church was what made possible the brief experiences of God that might be enjoyed in this life.[170] Peter Brown comments that Augustine never claimed to understand how the physical rites of the church actually impacted people, but he credited them with a validity that was both objective and permanent.[171] Certainly, Augustine was frustrated by the Manichean rejection of such; "in their ignorance of the sacraments that heal us they raved against the very remedy that would have cured them of their madness."[172] This sacramental emphasis may well have been heavily influenced by the very early experience, whereby he had heard a voice declare to him; "I am the food of full-grown men. Grow and you shall feed on me. But you shall not change me into your

---

168. Ibid., 151–52. In his own life Lewis believed it highly probable that he had taken the burden of some of Joy's cancer pains in his own legs. See Coghill, "Approach to English" 63.

169. C. S. Lewis, *Arthurian Torso*, 123.

170. McGinn, *Foundations of Mysticism*, 234 and 243.

171. Brown, *Augustine of Hippo*, 222.

172. Augustine *Confessions* 9.4.

own substance, as you do with the food of your body. Instead you shall be changed into me . . . *I am the God who IS.*"[173]

Lewis did not disagree with Augustine's view of the Eucharist although it was not a doctrine that he felt to be personally nourishing.[174] (Even baptism is a mere hint at the end of the *Till We Have Faces*.[175]) His attitiude to the Eucharist is as follows:

> I find no difficulty in believing that the veil between the worlds, nowhere else (for me) so opaque to the intellect, is nowhere else so thin and permeable to divine operation. Here a hand from the hidden country touches not only my soul but my body. Here the prig, the don, the modern, in me have no privilege over the savage or the child. Here is big medicine and strong magic. *Favete linguis*.[176]

But his emphasis instead tended to be upon the continuity between the natural and the supernatural—the sacramental nature of the world. And humans partake of God in myriad ways:

> At present, if we are reborn in Christ, the spirit in us lives directly on God; but the mind, and still more, the body receives life from Him at a thousand removes—through our ancestors, through our food, through the elements.[177]

Lewis displays more of the same belief in his poem "On a Theme from Nicholas of Cusa"—the soul changes by "some far subtler chemistry" when she feeds on good or truth, which are her "savoury food."[178] In a real sense the divine is drawn into the earthly substance. The term Lewis used was "Transposition"; "You can put it whichever way you please. You can say that by Transposition our humanity, senses and all, can be made the vehicle of beatitude. Or you can say that the heavenly bounties by Transposition are embodied during this life in our temporal experience. But the second way is better . . . If flesh and blood cannot inherit the kingdom, that is not because they are too solid, too gross, too distinct, too 'illustrious with being.' They are too flimsy, too transitory, too

---

173. Ibid 7.10.
174. See Lewis's comments in *Prayer: Letters to Malcolm*, 98–100.
175. "Two figures, reflections, their feet to Psyche's feet and mine, stood head downward in the water." *TWHF*, 233. This image is, I think, suggestive of baptism.
176. Lewis, *Prayer: Letters to Malcolm*, 98–100.
177. Lewis, "Weight of Glory," 38.
178. Lewis, "On a Theme from Nicholas of Cusa," *Poems*, 84.

phantasmal."[179] This transvaluation of the material world was for him, suggestive of the Incarnation. With reference to the credal idea that the Incarnation worked "not by conversion of the Godhead into flesh, but by taking of the Manhood into God," he suggested that manhood *could* be drawn into Deity.[180] "And it seems to me that there is a real analogy between this and what I have called Transposition: that humanity, still remaining itself, is not merely counted as, but veritably drawn into, Deity."[181] Paul Fiddes has argued that the first movement allows for a greater sense of human participation in the life of God but Lewis, despite his concept of Transposition, refrains from explicit use of a terminology of participation apart from one comment in *The Problem of Pain*.[182] There he speaks of the call of God to humans as being to a creaturely participation in the Divine attributes.[183] Once again he shies away from using the theological term. It may be that he wished to avoid confusion with Barfield's use of the term. Certainly, Barfield has commented that he does not think Lewis would have been easy with having attributed to him the concept of participation in the life of the Trinity; that in his theological utterances he tended to emphasize the chasm between Creator and creature. (The idea of participation, Barfield says, may have transpired if he and Lewis had been able to continue their "conversation"; but after Lewis's conversion the "Great War" between them was effectively ended by Lewis.) But the two are not exclusive; to speak of participation in God, does not negate the distinction between creature and Creator, unless one is trying to approach it within a rationalistic framework. Lewis seems to have wanted to retain the full sense of the freedom of the Godhead, whilst still allowing for the fullest possible human engagement in that Godhead, in accordance with John 17:22–23, where Jesus prays: "And the glory which You gave Me I have given them, that they may be one just as We are one: I in them, and You in Me; that they may be made perfect in one . . . ." A human, Lewis said, can become a supernatural being by being "born again; that is, 'if it surrenders itself back to God in Christ, it will then have a life which is absolutely supernatural, which is not created at all but begotten, for the creature is then sharing the begotten life of the Second Person of the Trinity."[184]

179. Lewis, "Transposition," 86.
180. Ibid., 87.
181. Ibid.
182. Fiddes, *Participating in God*.
183. Lewis, *Problem of Pain*, 43.
184. Lewis, *Miracles*, 180.

In *Mere Christianity*, as always, a deceptive simplicity almost undermines a further dimension to the concept:

> The whole dance, or drama, or pattern of this three-Personal life is to be played out in each one of us: or (putting it the other way round) each one of us has got to enter that pattern, take his place in that dance. There is no other way to the happiness for which we were made . . . Once a man is united to God, how could he not live forever? Once a man is separated from God, what can he do but wither and die?[185]

In one way, Lewis seems to be coming close to articulating a full doctrine of divinization or deification—the *theosis* of the Greek fathers. Stressing that humans are partakers of the divine nature (2 Peter 1:4), the fathers emphasized that humans share in the transforming life and glory of God. "Christ became man that we might be god," declared Athanasius in *The Incarnation of the Word of God*.[186] (It is worth noting that Lewis was reading Athanasius at around the same time as he was putting together the broadcasts talks that became *Mere Christianity* in the early 40's.[187]) Kallistos Ware states that in *theosis*, humans participate in the energies of God, but not his essence; "Although 'oned' with the divine, man still remains man; he is not swallowed up or annihilated, but between him and God there continues always to exist an 'I—Thou' relationship of person to person."[188] Humans always remain creaturely in contrast with God's uncreated status. The initiative in *theosis* lies with God; humans become by grace what God is by nature. But *theosis* is the process whereby humans become what God intended them to be.

This resonates somewhat with the emphasis of Lewis, as Kallistos Ware testifies.[189] Such resonances between Lewis and the traditions of the Eastern Church could be as a result of his own wide reading in the early Church fathers, but there may have been a level of personal impact in the late 1940s and early 50s when Lewis attended a discussion group that took place in the home of Nicholas Zernov.[190] The influence of Zernov

---

185. Lewis, *Mere Christianity*, 176.

186. Athanasius *Incarnation of the Word of God* 4.20. Augustine made a very similar statement: "The Son of God was made a partaker of immortality so that mortal man might partake of divinity." Homily on Psalm 52:6, See McGinn, *Foundations of Mysticism*, 251.

187. Lewis wrote the Introduction to Athanasius' *The Incarnation of the Word of God*. Sister Penelope's version, however, does not emphasise human deification.

188. Ware, *Orthodox Way*, 28.

189. Ware, "God of the Fathers," 53–69.

190. Zernov lectured in Eastern Orthodox culture at Oxford, 1943–1966. Lewis attended regular Saturday evening meetings at his house along with others such as Hugo

is hard to quantify because Lewis paid no public tribute to him, but he could well have been a further influence upon Lewis's move towards more "mystical theology." As Vladimir Lossky points out, the Eastern tradition has never made a sharp distinction between mysticism and theology; mysticism is "the perfecting and crown of all theology."[191] This is very much in keeping with the direction of Lewis's thought. Lewis is careful, however, to make distinctions; for him, "gods" were not the plural of "God." As he points out in *Reflections on the Psalms*, even gods have beginnings, unlike God's timeless self-existence.[192] In a letter written in 1959, he comments "it is certainly scriptural to say that 'to as many as believed He gave power to become the sons of God' and the statement 'God became man that men might become gods' is Patristic."[193] Nonetheless it is interesting that Lewis chooses to focus on the term "god," rather than on sonship, and the weight which he puts onto the term "gods" is very close to, if not the same as, the concept of *theosis*. For example, in *Mere Christianity* Lewis expresses confidence in the idea that humans could become "gods":

> He said (in the Bible) that we were "gods" and He is going to make good his words. If we let Him—for we can prevent Him, if we choose—He will make the feeblest and filthiest of us into a god or goddess, a dazzling, radiant, immortal creature, pulsating all through with such energy and joy and wisdom and love as we cannot now imagine . . .[194]

In "The Weight of Glory" he writes more of this hidden potential:

> It is a serious thing to live in a society of possible gods and goddesses, to remember that the dullest and most uninteresting person you can talk to may one day be a creature which, if you saw it now, you would strongly be tempted to worship, or else a horror and a corruption such as you now meet, if at all, only in a nightmare . . . There are no ordinary people. You have never talked to a mere mortal.[195]

In *That Hideous Strength*, Ransom resembles Christ in many of his aspects and the Dimbles are transfigured; "a sort of brightness flowed from them

---

Dyson, Austin Farrer, Eric Mascall, Anthony Bloom, James Houston amongst others. See James Houston, "Reminiscences of the Oxford Lewis," 129–43.

191. Lossky, "Theology and Mysticism in the Tradition of the Eastern Church," 169.

192. Lewis, *Reflections on the Psalms*, 71.

193. Lewis, letter to Clyde Kilby (January 20, 1959) *Letters*, Vol. III, 1013–14.

194. Lewis, *Mere Christianity*, 206.

195. Lewis, "Weight of Glory," 39.

that dazzled (Jane), as if the god and goddess in them burned through their bodies."[196] They dance with a heroic energy and their mental abilities overflow with a "dazzling prodigality."[197]

In *Till We Have Faces*, Psyche is apotheosized. The people of Glome perceive Psyche as a goddess, and even the rational Fox says of her, "Terribly does she resemble an undying spirit."[198] Paradoxically, Psyche may have these traits of divinity before she dies, but, long after her death, Orual realizes that she is more real than when she was alive; a thousand times more her very self than she had been before the offering. So much so that Orual declares, "I had never seen a real woman before."[199] Here humanity reaches its greatest fulfillment in divine fullness. And Orual says of herself, "I thought I had come to the highest, and to the utmost fullness of being which the human soul can contain."[200]

It may be that Lewis had in mind the Greek word for fullness, *plērōma*, (rather than the Gnostic sense of the dwelling place of the spirit), in much the same way that Paul used the word in Ephesians, when he prayed that the church in Ephesus may be "filled to the measure of all the fullness of God."[201] But this fullness is only found through the setting aside of the self. Kallistos Ware uses the language of his tradition to put it this way—"*kenosis* is *plerosis*."[202] The image of the human fulfilled by God was articulated by Gregory of Nyssa:

> For the participation in the divine good is such that it makes anyone into whom it enters greater and more receptive. As it is taken up it increases the power and magnitude of the recipient, so that the person who is nourished always grows and never ceases from growth. Since the fountain of all good things flows unfailingly, the nature of the participants who use all the influx to add to their own magnitude (because nothing of what is received is superfluous or useless) becomes both at the same time more capable of attracting the better and more able to contain it. Each

---

196. Lewis, *That Hideous Strength*, 688. The year that this book was published was the year that Charles Williams died—and possibly at the height of Williams' influence on Lewis. Williams' belief in the idea of exchange functioned at this level—because of Christ's archetypal substitution, humans become 'ingodded' by the Triune life. This term is also used by the Eastern Church. See, for example, *The Orthodox Way*, 167.

197. Lewis, *That Hideous Strength*, 686 & 692.

198. Lewis, *TWHF*, 25–26.

199. Ibid., 232.

200. Ibid.

201. Ephesians 3:19

202. Ware, *The Orthodox Way*, 109.

adds to the other: the one who is nourished gains greater power from the abundance of good things, and the nourishing supply rises in flood to match the increase of the one who is growing.[203]

It is this that we observe in Orual, Ransom and the Dimbles—receptivity, growth, and ultimately the utter abundance that is apotheosis.

Equally, Lewis could be said to have aligned himself with the Eastern tradition on the question of union with God—an issue that is closely aligned with *theosis*. Lewis was careful to avoid any suggestion of Neo-Platonic absorption into Deity.[204] He tackles the question in the last chapter of *The Problem of Pain*, and it is in the form of a resounding denial. In Christianity there is no place for such outdated ideas as Union, which, for Lewis, amounts to a form of Pantheism:

> For union exists only between distincts; and perhaps, from this point of view, we catch a momentary glimpse of the meaning of all things. Pantheism is a creed not so much false as hopelessly behind the times. Once, before creation, it would have been true to say that everything was God. But God created: He caused things to be other than Himself that, being distinct, they might learn to love Him, and achieve union instead of mere sameness. Thus he also cast his bread upon the waters. Even within the creation we might say that inanimate matter, which has no will, is one with God in a sense in which men are not. But it is not God's purpose that we should go back into that old identity (as, perhaps, some Pagan mystics would have us do) but that we should go on to the maximum distinctness there to be reunited with him in a higher fashion.[205]

Union is an "old identity" which diminishes "maximum distinctness" whereas union with God allows for distinctiveness. The argument was the same one used by the early Fathers of the Church (such as Gregory of Nyssa), which declared that *creatio ex nihilo* leaves a gulf between the created and the uncreated. The following statement by Kallistos Ware seems entirely evocative of the ending of *Till We Have Faces*.

> He who participates in God's energies is therefore meeting God himself face to face, through a direct and personal union of love, in so far as a created being is capable of this . . . It means that we affirm concerning God, in the most literal and emphatic way, "His life is mine," while at the same time repudiating pantheism.

203. Gregory of Nyssa, *St Gregory of Nyssa: On the Soul and the Resurrection*, 87.
204. See for example, "Transposition," 84.
205. Lewis, *Problem of Pain*, 120.

We assert God's nearness, while at the same time proclaiming his otherness.[206]

The Weight of Glory: God as the Ground of Reality

Lewis, in *Prayer: Letters to Malcolm*, emphatically affirmed God's nearness and his otherness:

> All creatures, from the angel to the atom, are other than God; with an otherness to which there is no parallel: incommensurable. The very word "to be" cannot be applied to Him and to them in exactly the same sense. But also, no creature is other than He is in the same way in which it is other than all the rest. He is in it as they can never be in each other. In each of them he is the ground and continual supply of its reality.[207]

And he continues, "Therefore of each creature we can say, "This also is Thou: neither is this Thou." In this, the last section, I shall try to draw together some strands in Lewis's perception of God as the ground and continual supply of reality and how this results in a concept of self that is radically dynamic. For God is not *parallel* to us, Lewis says, rather he undergirds us:

> But he is the ground of our being. He is always both within us and over against us. Our reality is so much from His reality as He, moment by moment, projects into us. The deeper the level within ourselves from which our prayer, or any other act, wells up, the more it is His, but not at all the less ours. Rather, most ours, when most His . . . To be discontinuous from God as I am discontinuous from you would be annihilation.[208]

We cannot know what source may have lent itself to Lewis's use of the vocabulary of "grounding." It is possible that it was his reading of Jacob Boehme in 1930 that led to his adoption of "ground," as an anglicization of Boehme's *ungrund*, unground or primordial Abyss, (and reminiscent of Alois Haas's *Ursprung*). But a more immediate link—and these were the ones which often seem to have had most impact on Lewis—may have been the thought of Austin Farrer, who became a close friend in the 1950's. Farrer had chosen to perceive God as the underlying cause of his thinking, because he could no longer conceive—as the Personalists

---

206. Ware, *Orthodox Way*, 169.
207. Lewis, *Prayer: Letters to Malcolm*, 70.
208. Ibid., 66–67.

did—of God as being face to face with him.[209] There is, Lewis says, an ontological continuity between Creator and creature:

> We must no doubt, distinguish the ontological continuity between Creator and creature which is, so to speak, "given" by the relation between them, from the union of wills which, under Grace, is reached by a life of sanctity.[210]

It is an ontological continuity bestowed through relation—and reached through the union of wills. Bernard McGinn points out in *The Foundations of Mysticism* that he has shifted towards the vocabulary of "grounding" rather than union. This is because such language encourages the perception that the mystical is always an element in a religious tradition, rather than a "peculiar moment." And secondly, it discourages the perception that the mystical must equate to the idea of union rather than a life-long spiritual journey.[211] McGinn suggests that we focus on speaking of mystical *consciousness*, rather than experience, for the mystical writers usually insist that their mode of access to God is radically different to that found in ordinary consciousness. This then allows us to pay greater attention to a mystical writer's "mind-fullness," which exceeds what is usually referred to as thought, and which McIntosh calls supra-conceptual consciousness.[212]

This immanent view of God as the ground of our being is very like Augustine's sense—"You were within me, and I was in the world outside myself." (*Confessions* X 27). Augustine's *memoria* covers the conscious and unconscious—what is for him the whole mind; (in contrast to *mens* which was only the conscious mind) and God deigns to dwell in it.[213] Also specifically resonant with Augustine is the idea that God watches and recognizes us: "Let me know you, for you are the God who knows me, let me recognize you as you have recognized me."[214] The mind does not contain God, but it touches him—it strains beyond itself to God, as Andrew Louth puts it. Beckett expressed a fundamental desire to be recognized; Lewis and Augustine believed that recognition came from the God who was within; the voice from the depth of oneself that is finally to be "trusted, obeyed, feared and desired more than all other things."[215]

---

209. Farrer, *Glass of Vision*, 7–9. Lewis did not seem to be hampered in the same way—as we see from his use of imagery in *TWHF*.

210. Lewis, *Prayer: Letters to Malcolm*, 67.

211. McGinn, *Foundations of Mysticism*, xix.

212. McIntosh, *Mystical Theology*, 31–32.

213. See Louth, *Origins of the Christian Mystical Tradition*, 142–43.

214. Augustine *Confessions* 10.1.

215. Lewis, "Seeing Eye," 216.

There are several specific points which are related to this, but upon which we can only touch. To leave them unsaid would be to leave loose quite a number of strands which seem to flow seamlessly together in the thought of Lewis. They co-inhere, as it were. Firstly, as God is present in this ontological continuity, we, as creatures, can only choose to grow in both the knowledge and the love. This "mindful-ness" of God is the kind of knowledge that Lewis came to believe in, *connaître* knowledge inextricably tied up with love. For Paul, gnosis is ultimately inferior to love (1 Cor 13:8). But the two are rightly connected; "The man who loves God is known by God" (1 Cor 8:3). As Bernard of Clairvaux said "*amor ipse notitia est*"—love itself is a form of knowing. Lewis put it this way in *A Grief Observed*:

> To see in some measure, like God. His love and His knowledge are not distinct from one another, nor from Him. We could almost say He sees because He loves, and therefore loves although He sees.[216]

And, one could add, loves because he sees. If knowledge is understood as participatory, then love must accompany it. And knowledge becomes love because that which is known is loved. As McIntosh says,

> . . . in mystical contemplation it is not the mystic who knows and loves, but rather the mystic is *known* and *loved* by God. All is grace, and therefore nothing is happening in the intellect or the will except what God is doing; and in God, knowing and loving are aspects of the one Trinitarian act of existence.[217]

At the highest level of knowing and loving, the intellect and will are progressively available to God. In *A Grief Observed* Lewis connects intellect and will in the same way; "Intelligence in action is will *par excellence*."[218] Human beings, said Dante, are the creatures who have intelligence and love.[219] McIntosh reminds us that it is—"in a mystery," as Orual would say—a single activity, which yet allows for distinction:

> For Augustine as for Aquinas, the divine agency is the fount of very real and distinct human agency, indeed the more God is consciously present to Augustine the more really present Augustine comes to be to himself. Together, the divine and human agencies work a single activity—knowing and loving—but this does not mean the inevitable absorption of either agent in the other;

---

216. Lewis, *Grief Observed*, 61.
217. McIntosh, *Mystical Theology*, 71.
218. Lewis, *Grief Observed*, 63.
219. Dante Alighieri, *Paradise*, Canto I. 116.

for divine agency is rather the very foundation of the creaturely participant.[220]

The summation of this connectedness between love and knowledge is found in Eph 3:16–19 where love supersedes knowledge as that which leads to utter fullness of being:

> Out of his infinite glory, may he give you the power through his Spirit for your hidden self to grow strong, so that Christ may live in your hearts through faith, and then, planted in love and built on love, you will with all the saints have the strength to grasp the breadth and the length, the height and the depth; until, knowing the love of Christ, which is beyond all knowledge (*gnōseōs*), you are filled with the utter fullness of God (*plērōma tou theou*).[221]

At this point the whole question of the self threatens to slip away from our concerns, not because it has been obliterated, but because the sense of the *plērōma tou theou* makes tawdry any individual concerns. It even begins to seem like an unimportant concern, a very decided grasping of the wrong end of the stick. Rowan Williams, in "The Paradoxes of Self-Knowledge in *De trinitate*" suggests something of the attitude which should be cultivated:

> The saint's mind images God because its attitude to its own life has become indistinguishable from its commitment to the eternal good; when it looks at itself, it sees the active presence of unreserved charity. Its action is transparent to its divine source . . . The paradoxes of self-knowledge—loving before we know, yet needing to know before we love, knowing completely that we have no complete knowledge—are meant to reinforce this upon us, to show us the impossibility of stating any theory of the self as a determinate object. We are to know and love ourselves as questing, as seeking to love with something of God's freedom (in the sense of a love not glued to specific objects of satisfaction) and seeking so to grasp this as our nature and destiny that we grow in the skills of loving relation and away from *cupiditas*, the possessive immobilizing of what is loved.[222]

Loving, knowing ourselves as questing, commitment to the eternal good. These are the limitations upon us, regardless of our "ontological continuity" with the all-loving, all-knowing One. Humility is essential. Lewis's

---

220. McIntosh, *Mystical Theology*, 222.
221. See McGinn, *Foundations of Mysticism*, 73.
222. R. Williams, "Paradoxes of Self-Knowledge in *De trinitate*," 131.

position as indicated in "Christianity and Literature" is that the Christian attitude to the self must be Augustine's; it is "a narrow house too narrow for Thee to enter—oh make it wide. It is in ruins—oh rebuild it."[223]

Secondly, prayer, which we have already seen to be the intersection between God and humans, the hinge (or "metaphysical joint" as Austin Farrer calls it) of the relationship, becomes increasingly clearly the way in which we can know God. As Farrer put it, "We know on our knees."[224] In *Prayer: Letters to Malcolm*, Lewis posits how encounter in prayer potentially—and he does not say always—allows for the subject-object embrace. No longer was he concerned to draw up a clear boundary between subjectivity and objectivity.

> The attempt is not to escape from space and time and from my creaturely situation as a subject facing objects. It is more modest: to reawake the awareness of that situation. If that can be done, there is no need to go anywhere else. This situation itself, is, at every moment, a possible theophany. Here is the Holy Ground. The Bush is burning now . . . [225]

"Here is the actual meeting of God's activity and man's," Lewis writes. This evokes change. "The most blessed result of prayer would be to rise thinking, 'But I never knew before. I never dreamed . . .'"[226] The two come together, and true knowledge and love are present:

> Here is the actual meeting of God's activity and man's—not some imaginary meeting that might occur if I were an angel or if God incarnate entered the room. There is here no question of a God "up there" or "out there"; rather the present operation of God "in there," as the ground of the matter that surrounds me, and God embracing and uniting both in the daily miracle of finite consciousness.[227]

For Lewis, in the meeting that is prayer the person is most actualized, and God most intimately involved; ". . . in prayer this real I struggles to speak, for once, from his real being"[228] The prayer preceding all prayers should be, "May it be the real I who speaks. May it be the real Thou that I speak

---

223. Lewis, "Christianity and Literature," 11. He contrasts such an attitude with that of Rousseau; *au moins je suis autre*.

224. Essay title in Austin Farrer, *Celebration of Faith*, 45.

225. Lewis, *Prayer: Letters to Malcolm*, 78.

226. Ibid., 76–79.

227. Ibid., 76.

228. Ibid., 78.

to."[229] Once again we are reminded of the necessity of transcending the self, not in order to negate it, but to allow the embrace that can only take place when the human self has true knowledge of itself before God. Lewis does not here speak of self-emptying. He is concentrating on conveying the other side of the paradox; through prayer, when we meet with God, we are most ourselves. Interestingly, in response to Daphne Hampson's critique of kenoticism as self-abnegation, Sarah Coakley uses prayer to demonstrate that it is not so. In contemplative prayer, she says, we make space for God to be God. It is a practice which is transformative, she says, "empowering in a mysterious 'Christic' sense . . . 'Have this mind in you,' wrote Paul, 'which was also in Christ Jesus.'"[230] Lewis puts it this way, where there is prayer at all, there is a union of wills, however feeble.[231] Here there is true mirroring, or to use a parallel but inverse image, here there is no "clawing towards a countenance" such as Beckett speaks of.

Towards the end of *Till We Have Faces* the King—in a vision—forces Orual to dig "far below any dens that foxes can dig." It is hard work, through raw earth, clinging clay and living rock. Finally, she comes to what she has dreaded—the mirror. In the mirror, Orual sees that she has assumed the face of Ungit. It is perhaps one of the most muti-faceted images in the novel. She has become Ungit. Her soul is ugly. It is a point of crisis for Orual. That the Ungit image shifts and changes is not our present concern; what is pertinent here is the way in which Lewis takes Orual into the bowels of the earth, deep *within*, before her image is revealed to her. And the face that she sees is not just her own reflection, but a face that she still insists on calling Holy. She has come face to face with the truth—a truth which has lain deeply buried—and from that point she chooses to go unveiled. This is the true turning point in the novel, the moment of repentance, of *metanoia*. We are reminded of Lewis's comment in *Prayer: Letters to Malcolm*—when we assent with our will to be known, we have unveiled; "Instead of merely being known, we show, we tell, we offer ourselves to view . . . By unveiling . . . we assume the high rank of persons before Him. And He, descending, becomes a Person to us."[232] Prayer then, is an unveiling, first and foremost. Here we assent

229. Ibid., 79.

230. Coakley, "*Kenosis* and Subversion," 108.

231. Lewis, *Prayer: Letters to Malcolm*, 67.

232. Ibid., 18–19. It may be worth noting that Lewis was aware of the inadequacy of the image. "This talk of 'meeting' is, no doubt, anthropomorphic; as if God and I could be face to face, like two fellow-creatures, when in reality He is above me and within me and below me and all about me. That is why it must be balanced by all manner of metaphysical and theological abstractions. But never, here or anywhere else, let us think that

to be known—and here we know. "God is in some measure to a man as that man is to God."[233] For humans cannot truly meet God face to face in this life; like Augustine, Lewis believed that the *visio dei* was only truly fulfilled in the *eschaton*.

Thirdly and finally, we reach that which shall be the fulfillment of the human self, which Lewis simply called glory. Here we see the zenith, the fullest realization of the concepts of co-inherence and exchange. In "The Weight of Glory" he cited Augustine's statement that the rapture of the saved soul will "flow over" into the glorified body, for the body was made for the Lord.[234] Here is no disembodied dualism.[235] And here too God as the ground of our ontology seems relevant to his thought. It is from this that our current desire springs:

> Apparently, then, our lifelong nostalgia, our longing to be reunited with something in the universe from which we now feel cut off, to be on the inside of some door which we have always seen from the outside, is no mere neurotic fancy but the truest index of our real situation. And to be at last summoned inside would be both glory and honour beyond all our merits and also the healing of that old ache.[236]

There, Lewis says, God will either know us—or will say he never knew us. "In some sense, as dark to the intellect as it is unendurable to the feelings, we can be both banished from the presence of Him who is present everywhere and erased from the knowledge of him who knows all. We can be left utterly and absolutely *outside*—repelled, exiled, estranged, finally and

---

while anthropomorphic images are a concession to our weakness, the abstractions are the literal truth. Both are equally concessions; each singly misleading, and the two together mutually corrective. Unless you sit to it very lightly, continually murmuring 'Not thus, not thus, neither is this Thou,' the abstraction is fatal. It will make the life of lives inanimate and the love of loves impersonal" (19).

233. Ibid.

234. Lewis, "Weight of Glory," 38.

235. His concept of the resurrection of the body did not condone that "old picture of the soul reassuming the corpse." The speculations he offered about the resurrection of the body in *Prayer: Letters to Malcolm* included; "We are not, in this doctrine, concerned with matter as such at all: with waves and atoms and all that. What the soul cries out for is the resurrection of the senses . . . At present we tend to think of the soul as somehow 'inside' the body. But the glorified body of the resurrection as I conceive it—the sensuous life raised from its death—will be inside the soul. As God is not in space but space is in God." He concludes his speculations with "Guesses, of course, only guesses. If they are not true, something better will be. For we know that we shall be made like Him, for we shall see Him as He is." (118).

236. Lewis, "Weight of Glory," 36.

unspeakably ignored."[237] Once again we are reminded of Beckett's narrators. But for Lewis, those who unveil to God, and are known of him, "the spirit in us lives directly on God." "When we see the face of God we shall know that we have always known it. He has been a party to, has made, sustained and moved moment by moment within, all our earthly experiences of innocent love."[238] And the promise of Glory beckons forth. It is a fact worth dwelling on—not so much because of one's own ease, but because of our neighbor.

> All day long we are, in some degree, helping each other to one or other of these destinations. It is in the light of these overwhelming possibilities, it is with the awe and the circumspection proper to them, that we should conduct all our dealings with one another, all friendships, all loves, all play, all politics. There are no ordinary people.[239]

In the meantime, we live in the shadowlands. Lewis, like his masters, Augustine and MacDonald, shies away from any sense that the double knowledge is ever fully realized before the *eschaton*. There is never a sense before that in which one can say "This is I." Identity, in this life, will always have its unfinalizability. Rowan Williams highlights the fact that for Augustine, "total" self-knowledge is precisely the knowledge of the self as incomplete, as seeking.[240]

> The mystery of the depths of the self directs us beyond the world of clear and orderly sense experience but is itself only a stage on the road to the greater mystery of God . . . Once having glimpsed this vastness and heard the distant sounds of the "holiday of heaven" . . . the spirit must live by hope, knowing as clearly as ever it will that nothing else can substitute for that vision and its delights.[241]

It may be that the very mystery of the depths of the self, direct us, as Williams says, beyond the world of clear and orderly sense experience. The self, for Lewis, remains necessarily blurred—phantasmic—in this world. The final paragraphs of *Till We Have Faces*, demonstrate, even in Orual's last hours, the intermingling of the realization of the divine perspective, and a residual vein of self-ignorance ("It's strange he should weep; and my women too. What have I ever done to please them?"). Her

237. Ibid., 36.
238. Lewis, *Four Loves*, 158.
239. Lewis, "Weight of Glory," 39.
240. R. Williams, "'Know Thyself': What Kind of an Injunction?," 221.
241. R. Williams, *Wound of Knowledge*, 79–80.

text ends with the words "I might" but the sentence was left incomplete at her death. Therein lies so much that Lewis believed was part of the human life; incompletion, desire, the sense of possibility—and progress. As he wrote in *Prayer: Letters to Malcolm*:

> I sometimes pray not for self-knowledge in general but for just so much self-knowledge at the moment as I can bear and use at the moment; the little daily dose.
>
> Have we any reason to suppose that total self-knowledge, if it were given us, would be for our good? Children and fools, we are told, should never look at half-done work; and we are not yet, I trust, even half-done.[242]

But underneath, sustaining all, is God. Once again, Augustine resonates—as befits their shared interest in the *eschaton*. McGinn points our attention to Augustine's emphasis upon the continuing peregrination of the soul through the power of love as found in later passages such as *De trinitate* 4.17:

> He, then, who is day by day renewed by making progress in the knowledge of God, and in righteousness and true holiness, transfers his love from things temporal to things eternal, from things visible to things intelligible, from things carnal to things spiritual; and diligently perseveres in bridling and lessening his desire for the former, and in binding himself by love to the latter . . . For the likeness of God will then be perfected in this image, when the sight of God shall be perfected. And of this the Apostle Paul speaks; "Now we see through a glass, in an enigma, but then face to face." And again, "But we with open face, beholding as in a glass the glory of the Lord, are changed into the same image, from glory to glory, even as by the Spirit of the Lord."[243]

Unlike Beckett, Augustine and Lewis believed that the beatific vision could not be boring.[244] For just as desire shall not end, neither shall creativity—and neither shall self-transcendence. Lewis believed that especially in the *eschaton*, unity-in-diversity will continue to be achieved by a rhythm of ongoing self-giving. ". . . each soul, we suppose, will be eternally engaged in giving away to all the rest that which it receives . . . Its union with God

---

242. Lewis, *Prayer: Letters to Malcolm*, 32.

243. McGinn, *Foundations of Western Mysticism*, 261.

244. Amongst Beckett's theological questions, he wonders, "Might not the beatific vision become a source of all boredom, in the long run?" *Three Novels*, 167.

is, almost by definition, a continual self-abandonment—an opening, an unveiling, a surrender, of itself."[245]

Kallistos Ware has pointed out how completely Lewis was in line with the Eastern idea of *epektasis,* an eternal life "of infinite progress and unending advance. The perfection and blessedness of Heaven are not static but dynamic, not fixed but inexhaustibly creative."[246]

> St Gregory of Nyssa believed that even in heaven perfection is growth. In a fine paradox he says that the essence of perfection consists precisely in never becoming perfect, but in always reaching forward to some higher perfection that lies beyond . . . The soul possesses God, and yet still seeks him; her joy is full, and yet grows always more intense. God grows ever nearer to us, yet he still remains the Other; we behold him face to face, yet we continue to advance further and further into the divine mystery. Although strangers no longer, we do not cease to be pilgrims. We go "forward from glory to glory" (2 Cor 3:18), and then to a glory that is greater still. Never, in all eternity, shall we reach a point where we have accomplished all that there is to do, or discovered all that there is to know.[247]

Even in heaven perfection is growth. And, Lewis says, when God gives each person the stone with his name on it, their revealed identity remains a secret between God and the person. Ware joins in, taking his cue from the same passage in Revelations; "In God's kingdom each is one with all the others, yet each is distinctively himself, bearing the same delineaments as he had in this life, yet with these characteristics healed, renewed and glorified."[248] It is in an eschatalogical sense that Psyche is a thousand times more her very self. "To enter heaven is to become more human than you ever succeeded in being in earth."[249] It shall no longer be *per speculum et inenigmate.* "Now we see but a poor reflection; then we shall see face to face. Now I know in part, then I shall know fully even as I am fully known" (1 Cor 13:12).

---

245. Lewis, *Problem of Pain,* 121.
246. Ware, "God of the Fathers," 68.
247. Ware, *The Orthodox Way,* 185.
248. Ibid., 184.
249. Lewis, *Problem of Pain,* 100.

Conclusion

And so we reach the end of the project. It has been a study in literature that has tested and challenged the widely held tenet in recent theology, that the self is most fulfilled when functioning as an autonomous entity, independent of God. The project calls into question the logic behind this emphasis, and suggests that the outworking of this demonstrates significant mental, emotional, spiritual and even physical consequences that look remarkably antithetical to the outworking of the self that recognizes its connectedness to God and others.

Certainly, Samuel Beckett and C. S. Lewis could hardly have led us in more different directions. The first, in which Beckett is our guide, is suggestive of the direction to which the self points if it is left to its own devices. It seems that the greater the distance from a particular sense of a personal God, the more the sense of self becomes diminished, disintegrated and isolated. Imprisoned in itself, such a self has no true countenance, although it may don a multiplicity of faces or identities. The material seems to flatly contradict the idea that the self can be as autonomous as Daphne Hampson desires. The second direction—and here Lewis is the guide—is an outworking of the stance which reaches beyond itself to God and suggests that God and the self cannot be separated; the stronger the ties to the particular and personal God, the greater one's own sense of being a particular self. Only with a connection to God can the open and engaged self flourish, for the self appears to be less diminished, less spectral, when it is tied to the plenitude of God. It seems that the fullness of God leads to the fullness of humanity, *contra* Hampson's fears. Where Orual had once described herself, (at her lowest point), as "a gap," she later comes to attain what she can only describe as the highest and utmost fullness of being. Ultimately, this study seems to point towards the essentially paradoxical nature of the self; the self is essentially more than a mere self. As Louis Dupré put it, "transcendence belongs to its nature as much as the act through which it is immanent to itself."[1] Failure

---

1. Dupré, *Transcendent Selfhood*, 104.

to realize this, reduces the self to less than itself. As Teresa of Avila said, "we do ourselves a great disservice."

That is not to go so far as to say that either of the two outworkings can be held up as a generic model that represents an approach to the self in any pure form. As we have seen, each writer's life journey had its own particular twists and turns. Both men had their own shadows to live with and their own temperament with which to work. I have tried to explore how these may have influenced their beliefs and emphases, and in doing so, to suggest the intricate interplay of the given and the chosen. But the basic primary orientation of a person—towards God or towards self—seems to have crucial consequences, of which the two writers could be said to be broadly representative. I cannot claim to have extrapolated all that could be extrapolated from the two writers on the underlying "subjects"—self and God. It is no small source of frustration that there are many aspects of selfhood which have not been adequately addressed—areas which were of particular interest to both authors. The imagination and the emotions; the will, and its connection with desire; place, so prominent in Beckett's search; embodiment (and clothing—both men make many references to clothing); memory; all could have been more satisfactorily explored. Neither space nor time have allowed for these explorations. Perhaps most interesting of all, would have been further consideration of the Augustinian sense of the mind, or *memoria*—consciousness and unconsciousness—which strains "beyond itself to touch God." Although in *Studies in Words* Lewis wrote about the history of the word *synteresis*—the spark of the divine in humans—and its complicated relations with related words such as conscience, sadly, he articulated little by way of theological speculation—other than that which we have already considered—about the meeting of God and the self.

In an attempt at summation, let us return briefly to our two models of the self. It is the self that is less than a self that we observe in Beckett's trilogy. We are taken into a place of self-enclosed inwardness, stasis, fear and frustration.[2] Beckett's narrators conjure a host of unspecified people who exist in limbo—hungry, thirsty, seeking, restless, placeless, nameless, faceless. "To and fro in shadow, from outer shadow to inner shadow. To and fro, between unattainable self and unattainable non-self." Despite their self-focus, the narrators frequently protest their inability to have any sense of self. And as Bernard suggested, the God-less search for the self becomes obsessive and all-consuming. The extreme of this position

---

2. These are the adjectives that are most expressive, I think, of the end of Beckett's trilogy.

evidences itself in a stark refusal of the good. In *Proust* Beckett wrote of the "smug will to live" and "our pernicious and incurable optimism," an attitude which heralds his choice to focus self-ward, rather than Other-ward.[3] It reminds us that inevitably there must be a flipside to Teresa's words—"if we turn from self towards God, our understanding and our will become nobler and readier to embrace all that is good"—for if we turn from God to self, we shall be less able to embrace that which is good. In the end the disengaged self seems to have neither the will nor the understanding to embrace the good; and in that inability it becomes increasingly immobile, fixed by its own choices.

It is hardly incidental that the narrator of *The Unnamable* has no name.[4] This namelessness is suggestive, at best perhaps, of the Jewish apophatic tradition, but, given the context, it is much more profoundly indicative of one who lacks the very elements which are integral to even a basic sense of identity—a name, a place, relationship. S. E. Gontarski points out that Beckett did not create anything that approximates a literary character after the trilogy—"save for an unnamed (even unnamable) narrator."[5] "I who am far, who can't move, can't be found . . . here is no name for me," says the narrator of *The Unnamable*. Hampson speaks of the scandal of particularity, and she seeks to make a virtue out of her refusal, but to reject the idea that God may act in the particulars, and to reject uniqueness, as she does, is to undermine the very self which has such prominence in her writings. It is, as it were, to bestow a namelessness upon all humans, for if there is no such thing as uniqueness, then why is there any need for names? Likewise there can be no recognition, based as it is upon particulars. Beckett regularly returns to the image of a person that cannot find recognition in the face, or eyes, of another. As the narrator in *Molloy* says, "People pass too, hard to distinguish from yourself."[6] There is finally no recognition of God, others, or self.

The second model suggests that in focusing beyond the self, the self finds recognition, joy, beauty, even glory.[7] The acknowledgement of a divine Object and participation in that divine Other enables the self to be dynamic and engaged. As Lewis discovered, the self that is not self-focused, but is Other-focused, can afford to pay attention to itself, and

3. *Proust*, 15.
4. Unless the Unnamable is the name, but that is a much debated critical issue.
5. Gontarski, Introduction to *Samuel Beckett: The Complete Short Prose*, xxv.
6. Beckett, *Three Novels*, 9.
7. This is the vocabulary most expressive of the final pages of *Till We Have Faces*. It is worth noting that Lewis defined glory as "appreciation by God" ("Weight of Glory," 33).

in doing so, can grow. It is an attentiveness that is not obsessive, for this self has already been attested and recognized—by God and by other self-transcending selves—and can return to transcend itself without fear. It is a double movement of self-fulfillment and self-renunciation. The two are mutually tied, emptiness and fullness, dread and beauty, inextricably and mysteriously bound together. But the final emphasis is upon the sense of abundance, even overflow, which *plērōma* implies.

The self that is thus enriched and overflowing must needs remain receptive and open. The healthy self must make progress and change; it is not optional. Orual's refusal to hear the truth as presented to her by Psyche sets her off on long years of functional living, trapped in a rigid persona, rather than the flexible interchange of person and personage. Completion is not something to be sought, for the self is not finalizable; indeed participation in the divine good makes anyone into whom it enters greater and more receptive, growing in power and magnitude, as Gregory of Nyssa points out. In this way, true self-knowledge shall be acquired—through prayerful engaging, not through introspective analysis. Erroneous self-understanding in Orual is accompanied by the concomitant error in her understanding of the divine; the two are connected at root. It reflects what Bernard of Clairvaux pointed out for us;

> Thus the knowledge of thyself will be a step to the knowledge of God: He will become visible in His image, which is renewed in thee; whilst thou, beholding with confidence as in a glass the glory of the Lord, art changed into the same image from glory to glory, even as by the Spirit of the Lord (2 Cor 3:18).[8]

The self that beholds the glory of God, becomes more like God.

This reciprocal nature of the self, however, does not wipe out the particulars of the self. Rather, it enhances them. Unlike the characters in Beckett's *Three Novels*, the characters in *Till We Have Faces*—Orual, Redival, the Fox, Psyche—are richly diverse. The distinction between Orual and Psyche may appear to be blurred when they both become God-filled, but it is not eradicated. It is a mutual indwelling—the mingling of men and gods—but not a dilution of particularity. The paradoxes of the self entail not only a transcendent God who is most vitally present in particulars, but a personal God whose presence calls out our particular personalities. Knowledge of God works only to heighten the tether and tang of the particular. Hampson rejects a particular and personal God for fear that such a one should constrict her self and disallow her particular-

---

8. Bernard of Clairvaux, *Cantica Cantorum*, 237.

ity, but this is based on a false logic. Lewis presents us with a coincidence of contradictories that resonates with the words of Christ; "For whoever wants to save his life will lose it, but whoever loses his life for me will save it. What good is it to gain the whole world, and yet lose or forfeit his very self?"[9]

Psyche understands this instinctively. In her, love and knowledge are combined. She knows, despite her fear, that her death is a door out of a little dark room, that she must self-transcend, both for her own sake, and for the people of Glome. And so it is after her death, that she is a thousand times more her very self. The name Psyche, translated as "soul" in philosophical terms, in *Till We Have Faces* is resonant with the New Testament usage, which conveys the sense of "life" or "true self," and is much more in line with the Hebrew sense of the word.[10] It is a name that suggests wholeness—or fullness—of being in body, mind, and spirit.[11] In "The New Name," MacDonald wrote that each person receives their name, face to face from God:

> And what an end lies before us! To have a consciousness of our own ideal being flashed into us from the thought of God! Surely for this may well give way all our paltry self-consciousness, our self-admirations and self-worships! Surely to know what He thinks about us will pale out of our souls all our thought about ourselves! And we may well hold them loosely now, and be ready to let them go.[12]

To receive one's true name is to come home. To adopt the words of McIntosh, it is "a homecoming to the divinely-beloved self, beyond the false selves projected onto the soul by prevalent ideologies."[13] To receive one's name is to receive a gift, for it shall, at last, express the true meaning of the person. "Who can give a man this, his own name? God alone.

---

9. Luke 9:24 NIV. A similar saying is found in Matthew and John.

10. N. T. Wright suggests something of the fullness of the word *psyche* as used in a New Testament context: "Some, including many Jews, believed that to be complete, humans needed bodies as well as inner selves. Others, including many influenced by the philosophy of Plato (fourth century B.C.), believed that the important part of a human was the 'soul' (Gr: *psyche*), which at death would be happily freed from its bodily prison. Confusingly for us, the same word psyche is often used in the New Testament within a Jewish framework where it clearly means 'life' or 'true self,' without implying a body/soul dualism that devalues the body." Wright, *John for Everyone: Part 2*, 179.

11. Ironically, the Fox says to Orual, ". . . after all these years, you have never even begun to understand what the word *soul* means."

12. MacDonald, "New Name," 75–76.

13. McIntosh, *Mystical Theology*, 206.

For no-one but God sees what the man is . . ."[14] God alone then, can truly know us, but equally, we must become the name that he has reserved for us.

The first step is to assent to be so known—as Lewis put it in *Letters to Malcolm*—we need to unveil. Prayer was, for him, the primary means of unveiling. Prayer as we are, rather than prayer as we think it should be. "Instead of merely being known, we show, we tell, we offer ourselves to view."[15] We shall "know on our knees," for the self that prays is the self that knows itself. This is the road to the knowing, the receiving of the name, the acquiring of a face, rather than Beckett's desperate "clawing towards a countenance." This is the double knowledge. For how can God meet us face to face until we have faces?

---

14. MacDonald, "New Name," 71.
15. Lewis, *Prayer: Letters to Malcolm*, 18.

Bibliography

Abrams, M. H. *A Glossary of Literary Terms*. Fort Worth, TX: HarcourtBrace, 1999.
Ackerley, Chris. "Samuel Beckett and Thomas à Kempis: The Roots of Quietism." In *Beckett and Religion*, edited by Marius Buning, Matthijs Engelberts, and Onno Kosters, 81–92. Atlanta: Rodopi, 2000.
Adey, Lionel. *C. S. Lewis's "Great War" with Owen Barfield*. English Literary Studies 14. Victoria, BC: University of Victoria, 1978.
———. *Writer, Dreamer and Mentor*. Grand Rapids: Eerdmans, 1998.
Albright, Daniel. *Representation and the Imagination: Beckett, Kafka, Nabokov, & Schoenberg*. Chicago: University of Chicago Press, 1981.
Alighieri, Dante. *The Vision of Dante Alighieri*. Translated by Rev. Henry Francis Cary, MA. London: Bell, 1901.
Alvarez, A. *Samuel Beckett*. London: Fontana, 1973.
Amiran, Eyal. *Wandering and Home: Beckett's Metaphysical Narrative*. University Park: Pennsylvania State University Press, 1993.
Anzieu, Didier. "Beckett and the Psychoanalyst." *Journal of Beckett Studies* 3.2 (1993) 23–34.
Arikha, Avigdor. "Waiting for the Author of 'Waiting for Godot.'" *Mexico City News* (20 January 1987).
Athanasopoulou-Kypriou, Spyridoula. "Samuel Beckett Beyond the Problem of God." *Literature and Theology* 14 (2000) 34–51.
Augustine. *The City of God Against the Pagans*. Translated by R. W. Dyson. Cambridge: Cambridge University Press, 1998.
———. *Confessions*. Translated by R. S. Pine-Coffin. Middlesex: Penguin, 1961.
———. *De trinitate*. Edited by Marcus Dodds. Edinburgh: T. & T. Clark, 1873.
———. *Sermons on Selected Lessons of the New Testament*. Oxford: John Henry Parker, 1845.
Bair, Deirdre. *Samuel Beckett*. London: Cape, 1978.
Baker, Phil. *Beckett and the Mythology of Psychoanalysis*. London: MacMillan, 1997.
Baldwin, Hélène L. *Samuel Beckett's Real Silence*. University Park: Pennsylvania State University Press, 1981.
Barfield, Owen. *Light on C. S. Lewis*. Edited by Jocelyn Gibb. London: Geoffrey Bles, 1965.
———. "Lewis and/or Barfield." In *Owen Barfield on C. S. Lewis*, edited by G. B. Tennyson, 104–19. Middletown, CT: Wesleyan University Press, 1989.
———. *Saving the Appearances: A Study in Idolatry*. New York: Harcourt, Brace & World, 1957.
Barge, Laura, "Beckett's Metaphysics and Christian Thought: A Comparison." *Christian Scholars Review* 20 (1990) 33–44.

———. "Beckett's Questing Hero: Mystic or Pseudomystic?" *Cithara: Essays in the Judeo-Christian Tradition* 24.2 (1985) 49–58.
———. *God, the Quest, the Hero: Thematic Studies in Beckett's Fiction*. North Carolina Series in the Romance Languages and Literature 230. Chapel Hill: University of North Carolina Press, 1988.
Barnard, G. C. *Samuel Beckett: A New Approach*. London, Dent & Sons, 1970.
Barth, Karl. *The Theology of John Calvin*. Translated by Geoffrey W. Bromiley. Grand Rapids: Eerdmans, 1995.
Bauman, Zygmunt. *Postmodern Ethics*. Oxford: Blackwell, 1993.
Beckett, Samuel. *Beckett's Dream Notebook*. Reading: Beckett International Foundation, 1999.
———. *The Complete Short Prose*. New York: Grove, 1997.
———. *Disjecta: Miscellaneous Writings and a Dramatic Fragment*. London: Calder, 1983.
———. *Dream of Fair to Middling Women*. London: Calder, 1993.
———. *The Letters of Samuel Beckett, vol. 1: 1929–1940*. Cambridge: Cambridge University Press, 2009.
———. *Three Novels: Molloy, Malone Dies, The Unnamable*. New York: Grove, 1958.
Beckett, Samuel, and George Duthuit. *Proust: Three Dialogues*. London: Calder & Boyars, 1965.
Ben-Zvi, Linda. "Samuel Beckett, Fritz Mauthner, and the Limits of Language." *PMLA* 95 (1980) 183–200.
Berger, Peter, Brigitte Berger, and Hansfried Kellner. *The Homeless Mind: Modernization and Consciousness*. New York: Vintage, 1974.
Bernard of Clairvaux. *Cantica Cantorum: 86 Sermons on the Song of Solomon*. Translated by S. J. Eales. London: Paternoster, 1895.
Boyle, Mary. *Schizophrenia: A Scientific Delusion*. London: Routledge, 1970.
Brown, Peter. *Augustine of Hippo*. London: Faber & Faber, 1967.
Brueggemann, Walter. "'Othering' with Grace and Courage." In *The Covenanted Self: Explorations in Law and Covenant*, edited by Patrick D. Miller, 1–17. Minneapolis: Fortress, 1999.
Bryden, Mary. "No Stars without Stripes: Beckett and Dante." *The Romantic Review* 87.4 (1996) 541–56.
———. *Samuel Beckett and the Idea of God*. London: MacMillan, 1998.
Bultmann, Rudolph. *Gnosis: Bible Key Words from Gerhard Kittel's Theologisches Worterbuch Zum Neuen Testament*. London: Adam & Charles Black, 1952.
Bulzan, Daniel. "Apophaticism, Postmodernism and Language: Two Similar Cases of Theological Imbalance." *Scottish Journal of Theology* 50.3 (1997) 261–87.
Buning, Marius. "The 'Via Negativa' and its first stirrings in *Eleutheria*." In *Beckett and Religion*, edited by Marius Buning, Matthijs Engelberts, and Onno Kosters, 43–54. Atlanta: Rodopi, 2000.
Butler, Lance St. John. *Samuel Beckett and the Meaning of Being: A Study in Ontological Parable*. London: MacMillan, 1984.
Calder, John. *The Philosophy of Samuel Beckett*. London: Calder, 2001.
Calvin, John. *Institutes for Christian Religion*. Chapter 1, Section 2. Online: http://www.reformed.org/books/institutes/bk1ch01.html.
Capps, Donald. *The Depleted Self: Sin in a Narcissistic Age*. Minneapolis: Fortress, 1993.
Caputo, John D. *The Prayers and Tears of Jacques Derrida*. Indianapolis: Indiana University Press, 1997.

Carlson, Thomas A. "The Poverty and Poetry of Indiscretion: Negative Theology and Negative Anthropology in Contemporary and Historical Perspective." *Christianity and Literature* 47.2 (1998) 167–93.
Carnell, Corbin Scott. *Bright Shadow of Reality: Spiritual Longing in C. S. Lewis*. Grand Rapids: Eerdmans, 1999.
Carpenter, Humphrey. *The Inklings*. UK: HarperCollins, 1997.
Cary, Philip. *Augustine's Invention of the Inner Self: The Legacy of a Christian Platonist*. Oxford: Oxford University Press, 2000.
Chadwick, Henry. *Augustine*. Oxford: Oxford University Press, 1986.
Chadwick, Owen. *The Reformation*. Harmondsworth, UK: Penguin, 1977.
Christopher, Joe R. "Archetypal Patterns in *Till We Have Faces*." In *The Longing for a Form*, edited by Peter J. Schakel, 193–212. Kent, OH: Kent State University Press, 1977.
Coakley, Sarah. "*Kenosis* and Subversion: On the Repression of 'Vulnerability' in Christian Feminist Writing." In *Swallowing a Fishbone?*, edited by Daphne Hampson, 82–111. UK: SPCK, 1996.
Coe, Richard. *Beckett,* London: Oliver & Boyd, 1964.
Coghill, Nevill. "The Approach to English." In *Light on C. S. Lewis,* edited by Jocelyn Gibb, 51–66. London: Geoffrey Bles, 1965.
Como, James T. *Branches to Heaven: The Geniuses of C. S. Lewis*. Texas: Spence, 1998.
———. *C. S. Lewis at the Breakfast Table*. Florida: Harcourt Brace Jovanovich, 1992.
Connor, Steven. "Beckett and Bion." A paper given at the "Beckett and London Conference," Goldsmiths College, 1997. Online: http://www.bbk.ac.uk/eh/eng/eng/skc/beckbion.
———. "Beckett's Low Church." A lecture given at the "Beyond Belief Symposium," English Institute, Harvard University, 28 September 2007. Online: http://www.bbk.ac.uk/english/skc/lowchurch/lowchurch.pdf.
———. "How He Was: Samuel Beckett's Lives." Review of *Damned to Fame: The Life of Samuel Beckett* by James Knowlson (London: Bloomsbury, 1996) and *Samuel Beckett: The Last Modernist* by Anthony Cronin (London: Harper Collins, 1996). First published in *Bullán: An Irish Studies Journal* 4.1 (1998) 121–26.
Cousineau, Thomas. *After the Final No: Samuel Beckett's Trilogy*. Newark: University of Delaware Press, 1999.
Coward, Harold, and Toby Foshay. *Derrida and Negative Theology*. New York: State University of New York Press, 1992.
Cronin, Anthony. *Samuel Beckett: The Last Modernist*. London: Flamingo, 1997.
Davies, Gaius. *Genius, Grief and Grace: A Doctor Looks at Suffering and Success*. UK: Christian Focus, 2001.
Davies, Paul. *The Ideal Real: Beckett's Fiction and Imagination*. Toronto: Associated University Press, 1994.
Davison, Gerald C., and John M. Neale. *Abnormal Psychology*. New York: Wiley, 2001.
Dearborn, Kerry. *Baptized Imagination: The Theology of George MacDonald*. London: Ashgate, 2006.
Derrida, Jaques. *Acts of Literature*. Edited by Derek Attridge, London: Routledge, 1992.
Diagnostic and Statistical Manual of Mental Disorders: DSM-III-R. 3rd ed. Washington, DC: American Psychiatric Association, 1987.
Downing, David. *The Most Reluctant Convert: C. S. Lewis's Journey to Faith*. Downer's Grove, IL: InterVarsity, 2002.

Driver, Tom. "Columbia University Forum." Summer 1961. In *Samuel Beckett: The Critical Heritage,* edited by Raymond Federer and Lawrence Graver, 21–25, London: Routledge & Kegan Paul, 1979.

Duckworth, Colin. *Angels of Darkness: Dramatic Effect in Samuel Beckett with Special Reference to Eugene Ionesco.* New York: Barnes & Noble, 1972.

———. "Beckett and the Missing Sharer." *Beckett and Religion* (Samuel Beckett Today/ Aujourd'hui 9) (2000) 133–44.

Dupré, Louis. *The Deeper Life: An Introduction to Christian Mysticism.* New York: Crossroad, 1981.

———. "The Mystical Experience of the Self and Its Philosophical Significance." In *Understanding Mysticism,* edited by Richard Woods, 449–66. London: Athlone, 1981.

———. *Transcendent Selfhood: The Loss and Rediscovery of the Inner Life.* New York: Seabury, 1976.

Durie, Catherine. "George MacDonald and C. S. Lewis." In *The Gold Thread: Essays on George MacDonald,* edited by William Raeper, 163–85. Edinburgh: Edinburgh University Press, 1990.

Eagleton, Terry. *Literary Theory.* Minneapolis: University of Minnesota Press, 1996.

Emery, Clark. *William Blake: The Book of Urizen.* Coral Gables, FL: University of Miami Press, 1966.

Esslin, Martin. "Samuel Beckett: The Search for the Self." *The Theatre of the Absurd.* Harmondsworth: Penguin, 1968.

———. "Towards the Zero of Language." In *Beckett's Later Fiction and Drama,* edited by James Acheson and Kateryna Arthur, 44. London: MacMillan, 1987.

Farrer, Austin. *A Celebration of Faith.* Edited by Leslie Houlden. London: Hodder & Stoughton, 1970.

———. *The Glass of Vision.* Westminster: Dacre, 1948.

———. "In His Image." In *C. S. Lewis at the Breakfast Table and Other Reminiscences,* edited by James T. Como, 242–43. San Diego: Harcourt Brace Jovanovich, 1992.

Ferrante, Joan. "A Poetics of Chaos and Harmony." In *The Cambridge Companion to Dante,* edited by Rachel Jacoff, 153–71. Cambridge: Cambridge University Press, 1993.

Fiddes, Paul S. *Participating in God: A Pastoral Doctrine of the Trinity.* London: Darton Longman & Todd, 2000.

Fletcher, John. *The Novels of Samuel Beckett.* London: Chatto & Windus, 1964.

———. *Samuel Beckett's Art.* London: Chatto & Windus, 1967.

Fleteren, Frederick Van. "Mysticism in the Confessiones—A Controversy Revisited." In *Augustine: Mystic and Mystagogue,* edited by Frederick Van Fleteren, Joseph C. Schnaubelt, and Joseph Reino, 309–36. New York: Peter Lang, 1994.

Freud, Sigmund. *The Origins of Psychoanalysis.* London: Imago, 1954.

Giddens, Anthony. *Modernity and Self-Identity: Self and Society in the Late Modern Age.* Cambridge: Polity, 1991.

Gilchrist, K. James. "2nd Lieutenant Lewis." *Seven: An Anglo-American Literary Review* 17 (2000) 61–77.

Gosse, Edmund. *Jeremy Taylor.* London: MacMillan, 1904.

Graver, Lawrence, and Raymond Federman. *Samuel Beckett: The Critical Heritage.* London: Routledge & Paul, 1979.

Gray, Katherine Martin. "Beckettian Interiority." In *Beckett and Psychoanalysis,* edited by Sjef Houppermans, 95–103. Atlanta: Rodopi, 1996.

Gray, William. "Spirituality and the Pleasure of the Text: C. S. Lewis and the Act of Reading." In *English Literature, Theology, and the Curriculum,* edited by Liam Gearon, 240–48. London: Cassell, 1999.
Green, Roger Lancelyn, and Walter Hooper. *C. S. Lewis: A Biography.* London: Collins, 1974.
Gregory of Nyssa. *St. Gregory of Nyssa: On the Soul and the Resurrection.* Translated by Catherine P. Roth. New York: Crestwood, 1993.
Grenz, Stanley. *The Social God and the Relational Self: A Trinitarian Theology of the Imago Dei.* London: Westminster John Knox, 2001.
Gruen, John. "Samuel Beckett talks about Beckett." *Vogue* (December 1969).
Gunton, Colin. "Augustine, the Trinity and the Theological Crisis of the West." *Scottish Journal of Theology* 43 (1990) 33–58.
Haas, Alois. "Christliche Aspekte Des 'Gnothi Seauton' Selbsterkenntnis und Mystik." *Geistliches Mittelalter* (1984) 71–96.
Hamilton, Alice and Kenneth. *Condemned to Life: The World of Samuel Beckett.* Grand Rapids: Eerdmans, 1976.
Hampson, Daphne. *After Christianity.* London: SCM, 1996.
———. *Christian Contradictions: The Structures of Lutheran and Catholic Thought.* Cambridge: Cambridge University Press, 2001.
———. *Swallowing a Fishbone: Feminist Theologians Debate Christianity.* London: SPCK, 1996.
———. *Theology and Feminism.* Oxford: Blackwell, 1990.
Happold, F. C. *Mysticism: A Study and an Anthology.* London: Penguin, 1963.
Harrison, Verna E. F. "The Relationship between Apophatic and Kataphatic Theology." *Pro Ecclesia* 4.3 (1995) 318–32.
Harvey, Lawrence E. "Samuel Beckett on Life, Art, and Criticism." *Modern Language Notes* 80 (Dec. 1965) 545–62.
———. *Samuel Beckett, Poet and Critic.* Princeton: Princeton University Press, 1970.
Hill, Leslie. *Beckett's Fiction: In Different Words.* Cambridge: Cambridge University Press, 1990.
Hobson, Harold. "Samuel Beckett, Dramatist of the Year." *International Theatre Annual.* London: Calder, 1956.
Hoeller, Stephan A. "What is a Gnostic?" In *The Gnostic Archive,* n.p. Online: http://www.gnosis.org/whatisgnostic.htm.
Homer, Paul L. *C. S. Lewis: The Shape of His Faith and Thought.* New York: Harper & Row, 1976.
Horne, Brian. "A Peculiar Debt: The Influence of Charles Williams on C. S. Lewis." In *A Christian for All Christians: Essays in Honour of C. S. Lewis,* edited by Andrew Walker and James Patrick, 83–97. Washington, DC: Regnery, 1992.
Horney, Karen. *Neurosis and Human Growth: The Struggle Toward Self-Realization.* London: Routledge & Paul, 1951.
———. *Our Inner Conflicts.* New York: Norton, 1945.
———. *Self Analysis.* New York: Norton, 1942.
Hooper, Walter. *They Stand Together: The Letters of C. S. Lewis and Arthur Greeves (1914–1963).* London: Collins, 1979.
Houston, James. "The 'Double Knowledge' as the Way of Wisdom." In *The Way of Wisdom: Essays in Honour of Bruce K. Waltke,* edited by J. I. Packer and Sven Soderlund, 308–26. Grand Rapids: Zondervan, 2000.
———. *The Mentored Life.* Colorado Springs: NavPress, 2002.

———. "Reminiscences of the Oxford Lewis." In *C. S. Lewis: Essays and Memoirs*, edited by David Ordham, 129–43. Nashville: Broadman & Holman, 2000.
Hunt, Celia. "Autobiography and the Psychotherapeutic Process." In *The Self on the Page: Theory and Practice of Creative Writing in Personal Development*, edited by Celia Hunt and Fiona Sampson, 181–97. London: Kingsley, 1998.
Inge, W. R. *Christian Mysticism*. London: Methuen, 1899.
Iser, Wolfgang. "Subjectivity as the Autogenous Cancellation of its Own Manifestations." In *Samuel Beckett's Molloy, Malone Dies, The Unnamable*, edited by Harold Bloom, 71–83. New York: Chelsea, 1988.
Jacobsen, Josephine, and William R. Mueller. *The Testament of Samuel Beckett*. London: Faber & Faber, 1964.
James, William. *The Varieties of Religious Experience*. Middlesex: Penguin, 1982.
Jeffrey, David L. "Proving the Spirit of Christ: Walter Hilton's Acid Test." In *Alive to God: Studies in Spirituality*, edited by J. I. Packer and Loren Wilkinson, 152–60. Illinois: InterVarsity, 1992.
Jeffrey, David Lyle. *People of the Book: Christian Identity and Literary Culture*. Grand Rapids: Eerdmans, 1996.
Juliet, Charles. *Conversations with Samuel Beckett and Bram Van Velde*. Leiden: Academic, 1995.
———. *Rencontre avec Samuel Beckett*. Paris: Fata Morgana, 1986.
Junker, Mary. *Beckett: The Irish Dimension*. Dublin: Wolfhound, 1995.
Katz, Daniel. "'Alone in the Accusative': Beckett's Narcissistic Echoes." In *Beckett and Psychoanalysis*, edited by Sjef Houppermans, 57–71. Atlanta: Rodopi, 1996.
Kaufman, Gershen. *The Psychology of Shame*. London: Springer, 1989.
Kearney, Richard. "Desire of God." In *God, the Gift, and Postmodernism*, edited by John D. Caputo and Michael J. Scanlon, 112–15. Bloomington: Indiana University Press, 1999.
———. *The Irish Mind: Exploring Intellectual Traditions*. Dublin: Wolfhound, 1985.
Kellman, Steven G. *The Self-Begetting Novel*. New York: Columbia University Press, 1980.
Kennedy, Sighle. *Murphy's Bed: A Study of Real Sources and Sur-Real Association in Samuel Beckett's First Novel*. Lewisburg, PA: Bucknell University Press, 1971.
Kenner, Hugh. *A Reader's Guide to Samuel Beckett*. London: Thames & Hudson, 1973.
Kerr, Fergus. *Immortal Longings: Versions of Transcending Humanity*. London: SPCK, 1997.
Kierkegaard, Søren. *For Self-Examination Proposed to this Age*. Translated by Walter Lowrie. Oxford: Oxford University Press, 1941.
———. *Journals and Papers*. Vol. 1. Edited and translated by Howard V. Hong and Edna H. Hong. Bloomington: Indiana University Press, 1967.
———. *The Journals of Soren Kierkegaard*. Edited by Alexander Dru. London: Fontana, 1958.
———. *Sickness Unto Death*. Translated by Alastair Hannay. London: Penguin, 1989.
Kilby, Clyde. "Till We Have Faces: An Interpretation." In *The Longing for a Form: Essays on the Fiction of C. S. Lewis*, edited by Peter J. Schakel, 171–81. Kent, OH: Kent State University Press, 1977.
King, Don W. *C. S. Lewis, Poet: The Legacy of his Poetic Impulse*. Kent, OH: Kent State University Press, 2001.
Knowlson, James. *Damned to Fame: The Life of Samuel Beckett*. London: Bloomsbury, 1996.
Knowlson, James, and Elizabeth Knowlson. *Beckett Remembering, Remembering Beckett: A Centenary Celebration*. London: Bloomsbury, 2006.

Laing, R. D. *The Divided Self: An Existential Study in Sanity and Madness*. London: Tavistock, 1969.
Lasch, Christopher. *The Culture of Narcissism: American Life in an Age of Diminishing Expectations*. New York: Norton, 1979.
Lewis, C. S. *All My Road before Me: The Diary of C. S. Lewis, 1922–1927*. San Diego: Harcourt Brace Jovanovich, 1991.
———. *Arthurian Torso: Containing the Posthumous Fragment of "The Figure of Arthur" by Charles Williams and a Commentary on the Arthurian Poems of Charles Williams by C. S. Lewis*. London: Oxford University Press, 1948.
———. "Bluspels and Flalansferes." In *Selected Literary Essays*, 251–65. Cambridge: Cambridge University Press, 1969.
———. *C. S. Lewis: Letters to Children*. London: Collins, 1985.
———. *Christian Reflections*. London: Fount, 1998.
———. "Christianity and Culture." In *Christian Reflections*, edited by Walter Hooper, 14–45. London: Fount, 1998.
———. "Christianity and Literature." In *Christian Reflections*, edited by Walter Hooper, 1–13. London: Fount, 1998.
———. *The Collected Letters of C. S. Lewis*. Vol. 1: *Family Letters, 1905–1931*. San Francisco: HarperSanFrancisco, 2007.
———. *The Collected Letters of C. S. Lewis*. Vol 2: *Books, Broadcasts, and War, 1931–1949*. San Francisco: HarperSanFrancisco, 2007.
———. *The Collected Letters of C. S. Lewis*. Vol 3: *Narnia Cambridge and Joy 1950–1963*. San Francisco: HarperSanFrancisco, 2007.
———. *The Cosmic Trilogy*. London: Bodley Head, 1989.
———. "De Descriptione Temporum." In *Selected Literary Essays*, 1–14. Cambridge: Cambridge University Press, 1969
———. "The Dethronement of Power." *Time and Tide* 36 (October 22, 1955).
———. *The Discarded Image*. Cambridge: Cambridge University Press, 1964.
———. *English Literature in the Sixteenth Century Excluding Drama*. Oxford: Clarendon, 1954.
———. *An Experiment in Criticism*. Cambridge: Cambridge University Press, 1961.
———. *The Four Loves*. London: Geoffrey Bles, 1960.
———. *George MacDonald: An Anthology*. London: Fount, 1983.
———. *The Grand Miracle*. Edited by Walter Hooper. New York: Ballantine, 1970.
———. *The Great Divorce*. London: Fount, 1997.
———. *A Grief Observed*. London: Faber & Faber, 1961.
———. *A Grief Observed*. London: Faber & Faber, 1966.
———. "The Language of Religion." *Christian Reflections*. Edited by Walter Hooper. London: Fount, 1998.
———. *The Last Battle*. Middlesex: Puffin, 1977.
———. *Letters of C. S. Lewis*. London: Collins, 1988.
———. "Membership," *The Weight of Glory and Other Addresses*. New York: Touchstone, 1996.
———. *Mere Christianity*. New York: Macmillan, 1952.
———. *Miracles*. London: Fount, 1998.
———. *Of This and Other Worlds*. Edited by Walter Hooper. London: Fount, 1982.
———. "On a Theme from Nicholas of Cusa." In *Poems*, edited by Walter Hooper, 70. London: Harper Collins, 1994.
———. "An Open Letter to Dr. Tillyard." In *Essays and Studies of the English Association*, 21:153–68. Oxford: Clarendon, 1936.

———. *Perelandra.* New York: Macmillan, 1990.
———. "The Personal Heresy in Criticism." In *Essays and Studies of the English Association,* 19:7–28. Oxford: Clarendon, 1934.
———. *The Pilgrim's Regress.* Glasgow: Fount, 1986.
———. *Poems.* Edited by Walter Hooper. London: Harper Collins, 1994.
———. "The Poison of Subjectivism." In *Christian Reflections,* edited by Walter Hooper, 72–80. London: Fount, 1998.
———. *Prayer: Letters to Malcolm.* London: Fount, 1974.
———. Preface to D. E. Harding, *Hierarchy of Heaven and Earth: A New Diagram of Man in the Universe.* London: Faber & Faber, 1952.
———. *A Preface to Paradise Lost.* Oxford: Oxford University Press, 1942, 1960.
———. Preface to St. Athanasiaus, *The Incarnation of the Word of God.* Translated by Sister Penelope. London: Geoffrey Bles, 1944.
———. *The Problem of Pain.* London: Fount, 1977.
———. "Psycho-Analysis and Literary Criticism." *Selected Literary Essays.* Cambridge: Cambridge University Press, 1969.
———. *Reflections on the Psalms.* London: Fount, 1982.
———. "A Reply to Professor Haldane." *Of This and Other Worlds.* London: Fount, 1982.
———. *The Screwtape Letters: Letters from a Senior Devil to a Junior Devil.* Fount, 1955.
———. "The Seeing Eye." In *Christian Reflections,* edited by Walter Hooper, 212–23. Fount, 1998.
———. *Selected Literary Essays.* Cambridge: Cambridge University Press, 1969.
———. *Spenser's Images of Life.* Cambridge: Cambridge University Press, 1967.
———. *Studies in Words.* Cambridge: Cambridge University Press, 1960.
———. *Surprised by Joy.* London: Fount, 1955.
———. *That Hideous Strength.* In *The Cosmic Trilogy,* 349–753. London: Bodley Head, 1989.
———. *Till We Have Faces.* London: Fount, 1998.
———. "Transposition." In *The Weight of Glory and Other Addresses,* 72–89. New York: Touchstone, 1996.
———. "Two Ways with the Self." In *The Grand Miracle,* edited by Walter Hooper, 119–21. New York: Ballantine, 1970.
———. "The Weight of Glory." In *The Weight of Glory and Other Addresses,* 25–52. New York: Touchstone, 1996.
Lewis, Warren. *C. S. Lewis, 1898–1963.* Bodleian Library, Oxford. M.S. Facs, d290, D9.vii.80.
Loades, Ann. "C. S. Lewis: Grief Observed, Rationality Abandoned, Faith Regained." *Journal of Literature and Theology* 3 (1989) 107–21.
Long, Joseph. "Divine Intertextuality: Samuel Beckett, *Company, Le Depeupleur.*" *Samuel Beckett Today/Aujourd'hui* 9 (2000) 145–57.
Lossky, Vladimir. *In the Image and Likeness of God.* Edited by John H. Erickson and Thomas E. Bird with an introduction by John Meyendorff. Oxford: Alden, 1975.
———. *The Mystical Theology of the Eastern Church.* New York: St. Vladimir's Seminary, 1998.
———. "Theology and Mysticism in the Tradition of the Eastern Church." In *Understanding Mysticism,* edited by Richard Woods, 169–78. London: Athlone, 1981.
Louth, Andrew. *The Origins of the Christian Mystical Tradition: From Plato to Denys.* Oxford: Clarendon, 1981.
Macaulay, Rose, *Letters to a Sister from Rose Macaulay.* Edited by Constance Babington-Smith. London: Collins, 1964.

MacDonald, George. *A Dish of Orts*. Online: http://www.gutenberg.org/dirs/etext05/8orts10.txt.
———. *Unspoken Sermons, Series I–III*. Eureka: Sunrise, 1989.
Manlove, Colin. *C. S. Lewis: His Literary Achievement*. London: MacMillan, 1987.
Markus, Robert A. *Conversion and Disenchantment in Augustine's Spiritual Career*. Villanova, PA: Villanova University Press, 1989.
Martin, Thomas. *Reading the Classics with C. S. Lewis*. Grand Rapids: Baker Academic, 2000.
May, Gerald G. *Will and Spirit: A Contemplative Psychology*. New York: Harper Collins, 1982.
McFadyen, Alistair. *Bound to Sin*. Cambridge: Cambridge University Press, 2000.
McGinn, Bernard. *The Foundations of Mysticism*. New York: Crossroad, 2002.
McIntosh, Mark A. *Mystical Theology*. Oxford: Blackwell, 1998.
McMillan, Dougal, and Martha Fehsenfeld. *Beckett in the Theatre*. New York: Riverrun, 1988.
Medcalf, Stephen. "Language and Self-Consciousness: The Making and Breaking of C. S. Lewis's Personae." In *Word and Story in C. S. Lewis: Language and Narrative in Theory and Practice*, edited by Peter J. Schakel & Charles A. Huttar, 109–44. Columbia: University of Missouri Press, 1991.
Meilaender, Gilbert. *The Taste for the Other: The Social and Ethical Thought of C. S. Lewis*. Grand Rapids: Eerdmans, 1978.
Miller, Josephine Sutton. *Samuel Beckett: Mystique Raté*. PhD diss., University of South Florida, 1998.
Mills, David. *The Pilgrim's Guide: C. S. Lewis and the Art of Witness*. Grand Rapids: Eerdmans, 1998.
Mooney, Sinead. "'Integrity in a Surplice': Samuel Beckett's (Post-)Protestant Poetics." In *Beckett and Religion*, edited by Marius Buning, Matthijs Engelberts, and Onno Kosters, 223–38. Atlanta: Rodopi, 2000.
Mooney, Sinéad. *Samuel Beckett*. UK: Northcote, 2006.
Murphy, P. J. "Beckett and the Philosophers." In *The Cambridge Companion to Samuel Beckett*, edited by John Pilling, 222–40. Cambridge: Cambridge University Press, 1994.
Myers, Doris T. *Bareface: A Guide to C. S. Lewis's Last Novel*. Columbia: University of Missouri Press, 2004.
———. *C. S. Lewis in Context*. Kent, OH: Kent State University Press, 1994.
Nicholas of Cusa. *De Docta Ignorantia*. Translated by Germain Heron. London: Routledge & Paul, 1954.
Nicholi, Armand M., Jr. *The Question of God: C. S. Lewis and Sigmund Freud Debate God, Love Sex, and the Meaning of Life*. New York: Free Press, 2002.
Nussbaum, Martha C. *Love's Knowledge: Essays on Philosophy and Literature*. Oxford: Oxford University Press, 1990.
O'Hara, J. D. *Samuel Beckett's Hidden Drives: Structural Uses of Depth Psychology*. Gainesville: University of Florida Press, 1997.
Olney, James. "Memory and the Narrative Imperative: St. Augustine and Samuel Beckett." *New Literary History* 24 (1993) 857–80.
Oury, Scott. "'The Thing Itself': C. S. Lewis and the Value of Something Other." In *The Longing for a Form*, edited by Peter J. Schakel, 1–19. Kent, OH: Kent State University Press, 1977.
Pattie, David. *The Complete Critical Guide to Samuel Beckett*. London: Routledge, 2000.

Pertile, Lino. "A Desire of Paradise and a Paradise of Desire: Dante and Mysticism." In *Dante: Contemporary Perspectives*, edited by Amilcare A. Iannucci, 148–66. Toronto: University of Toronto Press, 1997.
Phillips, Adam. *On Flirtation*. London: Faber & Faber, 1994.
Pilling, John. *Beckett Before Godot*. Cambridge University Press, 1997.
———. *Samuel Beckett*. London: Routledge & Paul, 1976.
Porter, H. Abbot. *Beckett Writing Beckett: The Author in the Autograph*. Ithaca, NY: Cornell University Press, 1996.
Price, Michael W. "Seventeenth Century." In *Reading the Classics with C. S. Lewis*, edited by Thomas Martin, 140–60. Grand Rapids: Baker Academic, 2000.
Rabinovitz, Rubin. "Beckett and Psychology." *Journal of Beckett Studies* 11/12 (1989) 65–79.
———. "The Self Contained: Beckett's Fiction in the 1960s." In *Beckett's Later Fiction and Drama*, edited by James Acheson and Kateryna Arthur, 50–64. London: MacMillan, 1987.
Renner, Charlotte. "The Self-Multiplying Narrators of *Molloy, Malone Dies*, and *The Unnamable*." In *Samuel Beckett's Molloy, Malone Dies, The Unnamable*, edited by Harold Bloom, 95–114. New York: Chelsea, 1988.
Rieff, Philip. *The Triumph of the Therapeutic: Uses of Faith after Freud*. London: Chatto & Windus, 1966.
Rolnick, Philip. *Person, Grace, and God*. Grand Rapids: Eerdmans, 2007.
Routley, Erik. "A Prophet." In *C. S. Lewis at the Breakfast Table and Other Reminiscences*, edited by James T. Como, 35. San Diego: Harcourt Brace Jovanovich, 1992.
Rudolph, Kurt. *Gnosis: The Nature and History of Gnosticism*. San Francisco: Harper & Row, 1977.
Ryan, Christopher. "The Theology of Dante." In *The Cambridge Companion to Dante*, edited by Rachel Jacoff. Cambridge: Cambridge University Press, 1993.
Sass, Louis A. *Madness and Modernism: Insanity in the Light of Modern Art, Literature, and Thought*. New York: Basic, 1992.
———. "The Self and Its Vicissitudes in the Psychoanalytic Avante-Garde." In *Constructions of the Self*, edited by George Levine, 17–58. New Jersey: Rutgers University Press, 1992.
Sayers, Dorothy L. *Introductory Papers on Dante*. London: Methuen, 1969.
———. *The Mind of the Maker*. San Francisco: HarperSanFransisco, 1987.
Sayers, George. *Jack: C. S. Lewis and His Times*. London: MacMillan, 1988.
Schakel, Peter J. *Reason and Imagination in C. S. Lewis: A Study of Till We Have Faces*. Grand Rapids: Eerdmans, 1984.
Schopenhauer, Arthur. *The World as Will and Representation*. 2 vols. Translated by E. F. J. Payne. New York: Dover, 1969.
———. *The World as Will and Idea*. 3 vols. Translated by R. B. Haldane and J. Kemp. London: Paul, Trench, & Trübner, 1896.
Schwab, Gabriele. *Subjects without Selves: Transitional Texts in Modern Fiction*. Cambridge: Harvard University Press, 1994.
Seigel, Jerrold. *The Idea of the Self*. Cambridge: Cambridge University Press, 2005.
Sells, Michael A. *Mystical Languages of Unsaying*. Chicago: University of Chicago Press, 1994.
Sharkey, Rodney. "Irish? Au Contraire!: The Search for Identity in the Fictions of Samuel Beckett." *Journal of Beckett Studies* 3.2 (1993) 1–18.
Smith, Robert Houston. *Patches of Godlight: The Pattern of Thought of C. S. Lewis*. Athens: University of Georgia Press, 1981.

Soelle, Dorothy. *The Silent Cry: Mysticism and Resistance.* Minneapolis: Fortress, 2001.
Starr, Nathan Comfort. "Till We Have Faces." In *Religious Dimensions in Literature,* edited by Lee A. Belford, 28–47. New York: Seabury, 1982.
Steiner, George. *Real Presences.* Chicago: University of Chicago Press, 1989.
Sturrock, John. *The Language of Autobiography: Studies in the First Person Singular.* Cambridge: Cambridge University Press, 1993.
Sykes, John. "*Till We Have Faces* and the Broken-Hearted Reader." *Premise* 5.3 (1998) n.p.
Symington, Joan, and Neville Symington. *The Clinical Thinking of Wilfred Bion.* London: Routledge, 1996.
Taylor, Charles. "Inwardness and the Culture of Modernity." In *Philosophical Interventions in the Unfinished Project of the Enlightenment,* edited by Axel Honneth et al., 88–110. Cambridge: MIT Press, 1992.
———. *The Malaise of Modernity.* Concord, Ontario: Anansi, 1991.
———. *Sources of the Self: The Making of the Modern Identity.* Cambridge: Cambridge University Press, 1989.
Taylor, Jeremy. *Holy Dying.* Oxford: Clarendon, 1989.
Taylor, Mark C. *Deconstructing Theology.* Chicago: Scholars, 1982.
Teresa of Avila. *The Interior Castle.* Translated by Kieran Kavanaugh, O.C.D. and Otilio Rodriguez, O.C.D. New Jersey: Paulist, 1979.
TeSelle, Eugene. "Augustine." In *An Introduction to the Medieval Mystics of Europe,* edited by Paul E. Szarmach, 19–35. Albany: State University of New York Press, 1984.
Thiselton, Anthony C. *Interpreting God and the Postmodern Self.* Edinburgh: T. & T. Clark, 1995.
Thorson, Stephen. "Barfield's Evolution of Consciousness: How Much Did Lewis Accept?" *Seven* 15 (1998) 9–35.
Thomas, à Kempis. *The Imitation of Christ.* London: Penguin, 1963.
Tillyard, E. M. W. "The Personal Heresy in Criticism: A Rejoinder." *Essays and Studies* 20 (1935) 7–20.
Tolkien, J. R. R. *Tree and Leaf.* Oxford: Oxford University Press, 1969.
Took, John. "Dante, Augustine and the Drama of Salvation." In *Word and Drama in Dante: Essays on the Divina Commedia,* edited by John C. Barnes and Jennifer Petrie, 73–92. Dublin: Irish Academic, 1993.
Torrance, Thomas F. *God and Rationality.* Oxford: Oxford University Press, 1971.
Tournier, Paul. *The Meaning of Persons.* New York: Harper & Row, 1957.
———. *A Place for You.* New York: Harper & Row, 1968.
transition 21, Paris, 1932. 148–49.
Turner, Denys. *The Darkness of God: Negativity in Christian Mysticism.* Cambridge: Cambridge University Press, 1995.
Ulanov, Anne Belford. "Jung and Religion: The Opposing Self." In *The Cambridge Companion to Jung,* edited by Polly Young-Eisendrath and Terence Dawson, 315–32. Cambridge: Cambridge University Press, 1997.
Underhill, Evelyn. *Mysticism.* Oxford: Oneworld, 1999.
Vaknin, Sam. *Malignant Self Love: Narcissism Revisited.* Narcissus, 1999.
Vitz, Paul C., and Susan M. Felch. *The Self: Beyond the Postmodern Crisis.* Delaware: ISI, 2006.
Wain, John. "C. S. Lewis." *Encounter* 22 (1964) 51–56. Critical Thought Series 1: *C. S. Lewis,* edited by George Watson. Cambridge: Scolar, 1992.
Wakeling, Patrick. "Looking at Beckett—The Man and the Writer." *Irish University Review* 14 (1984) 5–17.

Walling, Jane. "'Dim Whence Unknown': Beckett and the Inner Logos." In *Beckett and Religion*, edited by Marius Buning, Matthijs Engelberts, and Onno Kosters, 105–18. Atlanta: Rodopi, 2000.

Walsh, Chad. *C. S. Lewis: Apostle to the Sceptics*. New York: MacMillan, 1949.

———. *The Literary Legacy of C. S. Lewis*. New York: Harcourt Brace Jovanovich, 1979.

Wapnik, Kenneth. "Mysticism and Schizophrenia." In *Understanding Mysticism*, edited by Richard Woods, 321–37. London: Athlone, 1981.

Ware, Kallistos. "God of the Fathers: C. S. Lewis and Eastern Christianity." In *The Pilgrim's Guide: C. S. Lewis and the Art of Witness*, edited by David Mills, 53–69. Grand Rapids: Eerdmans, 1998.

———. *The Orthodox Way*. New York: St. Vladimir's, 1990.

Watkins, Owen C. *The Puritan Experience*. London: Routledge & Kegan Paul, 1972.

Weber, Max. *The Protestant Ethic and the Spirit of Capitalism*. London: Unwin University Books, 1974.

Werge, Thomas. "Sanctifying the Literal: Images and Incarnation in *Miracles*." In *Word and Story in C. S. Lewis: Language and Narrative in Theory and Practice*, edited by Peter J. Schakel & Charles A. Huttar, 76–85. Columbia: University of Missouri Press, 1991.

Williams, Charles. *The Figure of Beatrice: A Study in Dante*. London: Faber & Faber, 1943.

———. *The Image of the City*. Selected by Anne Ridler. London: Oxford University Press, 1958.

———. "Recollection of the Way." In *Dante: A Collection of Critical Essays*, edited by John Freccero. New Jersey: Prentice-Hall, 1965.

———. "The Way of Exchange." In *The Image of the City*, edited by Anne Ridler. London: Oxford University Press, 1958.

Williams, Rowan. "'Know Thyself': What Kind of an Injunction?" In *Philosophy, Religion, and the Spiritual Life*, edited by Michael McGhee, 211–27. Cambridge: Cambridge University Press, 1992.

———. *Lost Icons*. Edinburgh: T. & T. Clark, 2000.

———. "The Paradoxes of Self-Knowledge in the *De trinitate*." In *Collectanea Augustiniana*, edited by T. J. Bavel, 123–34. Holland: Leuven University Press, 1992.

———. "*Sapientia* and the Trinity: Reflections on the *De trinitate*." In *Collectanea Augustiniana*, edited by T. J. VanBavel, 316–32. Holland: Leuven University Press, 1990.

———. *The Wound of Knowledge*. London: Darton Longman & Todd, 1990.

Wilson, A. N. *C. S. Lewis: A Biography*. London: Flamingo, 1991.

Wolosky, Shira. *Language Mysticism: The Negative Way of Language in Eliot, Beckett and Celan*. Stanford: Stanford University Press, 1995.

Wright, Iain. "What Matter Who's Speaking?: Beckett, the Authorial Subject and Contemporary Critical Theory." In *Comparative Criticism* 5, edited by E. S. Shaffer, 59–86. Cambridge: Cambridge University Press, 1985.

Zizioulas, John. "Human Capacity and Incapacity." *Scottish Journal of Theology* 28 (1975) 401–4.

Index

Ackerley, Chris, 85, 101, 102
Adey, Lionel, 143, 182
Albright, Daniel, 28
Alvarez, A., 50
Amiran, Eyal, 118
Anzieu, Didier, 40, 41
Arikha, Avigdor, 86
Athanasopoulou-Kypriou, Spyridoula, 61
Augustine, 7–8, 9, 21, 34–35, 52, 66, 73–78, 92, 96, 97–98, 100, 101, 113, 140, 160, 161, 162, 167, 169–77, 185–86, 191, 192–93, 198, 201, 202, 204–7, 212, 216, 219, 221–22, 223, 230, 231, 238, 241, 242–43, 245, 250, 251, 253, 255–57

Bair, Deirdre, 30, 44, 54, 71
Baker, Phil, 37
Baldwin, Hélène L., 35, 94, 103–4, 111
Barfield, Owen, 13, 143–44, 152, 153, 154, 162, 169, 181–83, 184, 186, 212, 213, 234–35, 236, 244, 265, 275
Barge, Laura, 15, 31, 32, 59, 63, 86, 89, 95, 109
Barnard, G. C., 44–46, 53, 88
Barth, Karl, 8
Bauman, Zygmunt, 51
Beckett, Samuel
    apophaticism/negative theology, 18, 94, 100–110, 119–22.
    Bible, 34, 72–73
    deconstruction, 28–29, 52, 105–7, 115–23

desire, 26, 28, 32, 33–34, 48, 49, 50, 67, 71, 75, 77, 79–82, 85, 88–90, 91, 93, 95, 97, 99–102, 106–9, 111–12, 118, 121, 250
Gnosticism, 67, 86, 87, 90–95, 99–100, 109
introspection, 29–32, 33, 35, 43–44, 49–52, 56–57, 118–19
influences
    Democritus, 101
    Arnold Guelincx, 101
    John of the Cross, 34, 73, 96, 99, 103, 105, 119
    Manichaeism, 74–76, 92
    Neo-Platonism, 76, 93–94, 117–18, 120
    Plato, 117–18
    Protestantism, 34, 66, 68–73, 94
    Puritanism, 69–70
    Quaker, 70–71
    Schopenhauer, 27, 65, 76, 100–101, 119
    Thomas à Kempis, 53, 83, 94–96, 107–8, 111–12, 118
    Jeremy Taylor, 83
kenosis, 77, 106
knowledge, 30, 34, 41–42, 45, 80–81, 90–94, 96, 102–10, 118
language, 26, 29, 31, 44, 47–48, 51, 57, 71, 95, 97, 102–4, 107, 110–21
longing, 35, 51, 89, 90–91, 100, 116
mysticism, 87–123
narcissism, 54–56, 102
psychoanalysis, 36–42, 55–56, 89

Beckett, Samuel (*continued*)
    psychology, 21–57, 89, 92, 93
    relationships, 42, 45, 49, 51, 67, 105,
        114–20, 125
    schizophrenia/schizoid, 37, 41, 44–
        56, 88, 89, 106, 110, 113–15,
        121
    self abnegation, 85, 105
    self-denial, 83
    self-knowledge, 24, 40–41, 69–70,
        84, 93, 96, 100, 118
    self-negation, 117
    self-perception 33, 69, 115
    self-surrender, 42, 85
    self-transcendence, 89
    surrender, 42, 85
    unknowing, 102, 106–8
Ben-Zvi, Linda, 112, 113
Berger, Peter, 51
Bernard of Clairvaux, 6–7, 162, 206,
    216, 223, 230, 251, 262
Boyle, Mary, 45
Brown, Peter, 75, 242, 170
Brueggemann, Walter, 57, 159, 160
Bryden, Mary, 59, 60–61, 62, 64, 68,
    69, 72, 73–74, 77, 78, 80, 82,
    83, 84, 86, 87, 92, 98, 99 104,
    108, 117
Bultmann, Rudolph, 214
Bulzan, Daniel, 120, 211
Buning, Marius, 70, 103, 104
Butler, Lance St. John, 62

Calder, John, 85–86
Calvin, John, 7, 8, 9, 66, 146, 168, 180,
    200
Capps, Donald, 55–56
Caputo, John D., 106–7, 270
Carlson, Thomas A., 105, 120
Carnell, Corbin Scott, 127–28
Carpenter, Humphrey, 13, 146, 181, 130
Cary, Philip, 8
Chadwick, Henry, 175
Chadwick, Owen, 70
Christopher, Joe R., 241
Coakley, Sarah, 254

Coe, Richard. 44, 70
Coghill, Nevill. 242
Como, James T., 124–25, 156, 143,
    184, 188
Connor, Steven, 38–41, 44, 47–48, 83,
    103, 108
Cousineau, Thomas, 37, 222
Coward, Harold, and Toby Foshay, 107
Cronin, Anthony, 39, 66

Dante Alighieri, 23, 55, 78–82, 111,
    162, 185, 212, 218–19, 222–23,
    234, 251
Davies, Gaius, 135
Davies, Paul, 59
Davison, Gerald C., and John M. Neale,
    45
Dearborn, Kerry, 178
Derrida, Jaques, 45, 56, 105–7, 110
Downing, David, 150
Driver, Tom, 72, 87
Duckworth, Colin, 60, 61
Dupré, Louis, 194, 228–29, 259
Durie, Catherine, 178

Eagleton, Terry, 106
Emery, Clark, 91
Esslin, Martin, 68, 113

Farrer, Austin, 157–58, 246, 249–50, 253
Ferrante, Joan, 79
Fiddes, Paul S., 219, 244
Fletcher, John, 21–22, 24, 27, 44
Fleteren, Frederick Van, 219
Freud, Sigmund, 10, 37, 38, 40, 41, 54,
    55, 72, 147–48

Giddens, Anthony, 49, 55–57, 120
Gilchrist, K. James, 130
Gosse, Edmund, 83
Graver, Lawrence, and Raymond
    Federman, 87
Gray, Katherine Martin, 41
Gray, William, 235–36
Green, Roger Lancelyn, and Walter
    Hooper, 155, 157

Gregory of Nyssa, 234, 248, 258, 262, 247
Grenz, Stanley, 224, 226–27, 168
Gruen, John, 33
Gunton, Colin, 177

Haas, Alois, 204, 249
Hamilton, Alice, and Kenneth, 67, 87, 92
Hampson, Daphne, 2–9, 86, 116, 169, 173, 254, 259, 261, 262
Happold, F. C., 94, 224
Harrison, Verna E. F., 234
Harvey, Lawrence E., 16, 24
Hill, Leslie, 52, 115
Hobson, Harold, 52
Hoeller, Stephan A., 93
Homer, Paul L., 153
Horne, Brian, 183
Horney, Karen, 12, 40–41
Hooper, Walter, 130, 155, 157
Houston, James, 6, 8, 146–47, 199, 200, 216, 223, 246
Hunt, Celia, 12, 40

Inge, W. R., 18, 34, 98–99, 101, 103, 105, 202, 210–11, 218
Iser, Wolfgang, 24, 35–36, 53

Jacobsen, Josephine, and William R. Mueller, 12, 33, 65, 67, 118
James, William, 18, 36, 50, 75, 102, 127, 162, 208
Jeffrey, David L., 200, 236
Juliet, Charles, 52, 61, 71, 104
Junker, Mary, 69, 73

Katz, Daniel, 54–55
Kaufman, Gershen, 127
Kearney, Richard, 73, 222, 223
Kellman, Steven G., 31
Kennedy, Sighle, 101
Kenner, Hugh, 26, 27–28, 44, 68, 69
Kerr, Fergus, 100
Kierkegaard, Søren, 27, 36, 121, 133, 146, 151–52, 184, 194, 199, 203

Kilby, Clyde, 14, 188, 227, 246
King, Don W., 132
Knowlson, James, 22, 30, 34, 37, 38, 39, 42–44, 69 70,71, 73, 76, 77, 78, 81

Laing, R. D., 47, 49, 53, 88.
Lasch, Christopher, 53–54, 55, 57, 120.
Lewis, Warren, 129, 134
Lewis, C. S.
  apophaticism/negative theology, 210–11, 232, 234, 261
  Bible, 162, 166–71, 198, 208, 246
  coinherence, 219, 238, 241–42
  deconstruction, 141, 197
  deification, 245–47
  desire, 127–28, 135, 136, 138, 139, 148–50, 171, 175, 176, 188–87, 189, 196, 203, 205, 209, 210, 215, 217, 220–23, 226, 228, 238, 250, 255, 257, 260
  glory, 128, 168, 194, 216, 218, 224, 244, 245, 252, 255–64
  knowledge, 164, 175, 177, 182–87, 199, 210, 214–16, 227, 230, 234, 237, 251–57, 262–63
    double knowledge, 124, 185, 187, 210, 216, 256, 264
  Gnosticism, 214
  introspection, 136–41, 145, 150–54, 159, 177, 180–81, 205, 212
  influences
    Owen Barfield, 143–44, 152–54, 162, 169, 181–86, 212–13, 234–36, 244
    Dante 162, 185, 212, 218–19, 222
    George MacDonald, 150, 162, 171, 177–81, 196, 199, 204, 206, 208, 212, 224–26, 238, 256, 263–64
    Manichaeism, 131
    Neo-Platonism, 170, 174, 183, 190, 222, 248
    Plato, 162, 170–76, 212, 214, 220–22, 236, 263

Lewis, C. S., influences (*continued*)
  Charles Williams 163, 172, 192–95, 209, 220, 222, 229, 244, 251, 257
  Joy, 127, 135, 139, 148, 150, 152, 181, 205, 207
  kenosis/kenotic, 141, 142, 173–74, 224, 247, 254
  language, 164, 170, 182–83, 232–37
  longing, 127–28, 132, 135, 148, 171, 205, 217, 220–22, 255
  mysticism, 187, 208–23, 224, 246
  persona, 142–47, 153–54, 159, 189, 262
  psychoanalysis, 147–50
  psychology, 147
  self abnegation, 254
  self-knowledge, 144, 148, 152, 160, 177, 188–206, 233, 241, 252, 256–57, 262
  self-surrender, 143, 240
  self-transcendence, 147, 208, 227, 229–31, 237, 240, 241, 257
  Sehnsucht, 127, 139, 148, 155, 178, 185, 220
  subjectivity/objectivity, 139–52, 202, 205, 253
  transposition 238, 243, 244
Loades, Ann, 128–29
Long, Joseph, 59
Lossky, Vladimir, 102–3, 207, 246
Louth, Andrew, 147, 117–18, 185–86, 221–22, 250

Macaulay, Rose, 189
MacDonald, George, 13–14, 81, 150, 161, 171, 177–80, 196, 199, 204, 206, 208, 212, 224–26, 238, 256, 263–64
Manlove, Colin, 188, 191, 225, 169
Markus, Robert A., 66, 238
May, Gerald G., 88, 102
McFadyen, Alistair, 173
McGinn, Bernard, 18, 93–94, 97, 117, 173, 214, 221, 221, 222, 231, 242, 245, 250, 252, 257

McIntosh, Mark A., 103, 177, 186–87, 205, 215–16, 250–52, 263
McMillan, Dougal, and Martha Fehsenfeld, 27
Medcalf, Stephen, 138, 145, 147, 152–54, 197
Meilaender, Gilbert, 170, 181, 226, 239–40
Miller, Josephine Sutton, 95–97
Mooney, Sinead, 39, 68–69, 72
Murphy, P. J., 12, 16, 27, 29
Myers, Doris T., 149, 190–91, 206, 234, 240

Nicholas of Cusa, 162, 169, 210, 218, 239, 243
Nicholi, Armand M., Jr., 148
Nussbaum, Martha C., 51–52, 66, 99–100, 113, 116

O'Hara, J. D., 37, 50, 56
Olney, James, 74
Oury, Scott, 140

Pattie, David, 11, 30–31
Pertile, Lino, 223
Phillips, Adam, 39
Pilling, John, 55, 60, 61, 63, 67, 70, 76, 83, 100, 109, 112, 117, 231
Porter, H. Abbot, 32
Price, Michael W., 196

Rabinovitz, Rubin, 16, 24, 50
Renner, Charlotte, 12, 23
Rieff, Philip, 1
Routley, Erik, 183
Rudolph, Kurt, 91, 93
Ryan, Christopher, 79

Sass, Louis A., 1, 22, 45–50, 53, 56, 57, 88, 106, 109–10, 113–14, 120
Sayers, Dorothy L., 15, 234
Sayers, George, 154
Schakel, Peter J., 132, 144, 152–53, 158, 189–90, 194, 215, 229–30

Schopenhauer, Arthur, 27, 65, 76, 100–101, 119, 130, 175
Schwab, Gabriele, 34, 111, 121
Seigel, Jerrold, 23
Sells, Michael A., 107
Sharkey, Rodney, 68
Smith, Robert Houston, 174, 208–9, 211–12, 214–15
Soelle, Dorothy, 217
Starr, Nathan Comfort, 195
Steiner, George, 17, 109, 121–22, 141, 182
Sturrock, John, 39
Sykes, John, 193
Symington, Joan, and Neville Symington, 38, 47

Taylor, Charles, vi, 7, 17–18, 22, 25, 31, 57, 76, 100–101, 111, 146, 172, 176, 204
Taylor, Jeremy, 83–84
Taylor, Mark C., 105–6
Teresa of Avila, 7–9, 34, 120, 260, 261
TeSelle, Eugene, 171
Thiselton, Anthony C., 199
Thorson, Stephen, 183
Tillyard, E. M. W., 17, 124, 142–43, 171
Tolkien, J. R. R., 13, 152, 153, 162, 164–65, 181–83, 212
Took, John, 222
Torrance, Thomas F., 238
Tournier, Paul, 55–56, 85, 159–60, 227

Turner, Denys, 7, 108–9, 119–20, 175–76, 231

Ulanov, Anne Belford, 197
Underhill, Evelyn, 18, 75–76, 212

Vaknin, Sam, 54

Wain, John, 145
Wakeling, Patrick, 42
Walling, Jane, 64
Walsh, Chad, 145, 188–89
Wapnik, Kenneth, 88
Ware, Kallistos, 212, 245, 247–49, 258
Watkins, Owen C., 70–71, 201
Weber, Max, 71, 208
Werge, Thomas, 181, 236
Williams, Charles, 153, 162, 182–85, 199, 210, 212, 219, 234, 241, 247
Williams, Rowan, 7, 122, 160, 174, 176–77, 187, 191, 192–93, 198, 201, 206, 223, 228, 230–31, 236, 252, 256
Wilson, A. N., 13, 137, 144–45, 147, 152, 154, 155–56
Wolosky, Shira, 24–26, 51, 95, 103, 105, 113, 115, 118–19
Wright, Iain, 24, 28–29, 102, 110–11, 113

Zizioulas, John, 240